Praise for *Suicide Pact*

There is no one more qualified than Judge Andrew Napolitano to serve as our guide through American legal and political history to show how power-hungry politicians have used the magic words "national security'" to break free from the chains of the Constitution and put us in the chains of authoritarianism.

— Former Congressman Ron Paul
(R–Texas)

Former judge, law professor, and author Andrew Napolitano documents how unlimited perpetual wars concentrate unaccountable power in the presidency and proceed to shred constitutional boundaries and due processes, crush public budgets, and expand an American Empire that, like all Empires, will eventually devour itself. Read the gripping details about how our constitutional balance of powers and individual rights are being repealed de facto by the merger of political and economic power that led to President Eisenhower's farewell warning regarding the "military-industrial complex" and its destructive impact on our liberties. Whether you're Left or Right, Napolitano's documented thesis will resonate.

— Ralph Nader, Author of
*Unstoppable: The Emerging Left-
Right Alliance to Dismantle the
Corporate State*

With the judiciousness of a judge (which he once was), the perspective of a historian (which he here proves himself to be), and the passion of an alarmed patriot (which his many viewers on Fox News know him to be), Judge Napolitano calls attention to the foremost constitutional challenge of our day, that of circumscribing executive power.

— George Will, Syndicated
Columnist

Today, our constitutional liberties are under assault, and Judge Napolitano's sharp legal analysis documenting the steady erosion of American freedom should be a wake-up call for Republicans, Democrats, Independents, and Libertarians alike.

— Sen. Ted Cruz (R-Texas)

Our Founders agreed that when there are not enough citizens informed on why they are Americans in this self-governing republic, the Constitution would flounder. And this is why Judge Andrew Napolitano's *Suicide Pact* is so greatly needed and so continually absorbing a public service.

Never before in our history have so many Americans—students and adults—been so unaware of the disappearance of the separation of powers ignored by imperial administrations from Bush-Cheney and now the even more un-American regime of President Obama.

In *Suicide Pact*, Judge Napolitano, as always, brings the Constitution and our individual personal liberties alive—thereby strengthening the active American identities of this and future generations. No matter who is elected president in 2016, this is the book to revive us as Americans.

— Nat Hentoff, Author of *The War on the Bill of Rights and the Gathering Resistance*, *Living The Bill of Rights: How To Be An Authentic American*, and *The First Freedom: The Tumultuous History of Free Speech in America*

Nobody in America today is a stronger and more energetic champion of individual rights, natural freedom, and strictly limited government than Fox News' Judge Andrew Napolitano. *Suicide Pact* is his best work yet. It's a can't-put-it-down history lesson, a page-turning legal argument, and his single-strongest statement ever on just how far America has strayed from its promise of being a government of laws and not of power-hungry men.

Suicide Pact doesn't just dazzle with its historical reach and depress with its unvarnished depiction of executive-branch power grabs; it provides a map for how we can all fight back and move into a future that delivers fully on individual freedom.

Even when I don't agree with him (a rare occurrence!), I learn more from Judge Napolitano than any other legal analyst and writer. If you care about your freedom, your country, and your future, read *Suicide Pact* and pass it along to everyone you know.

— Nick Gillespie, Reason.tv; Reason.com

SUICIDE
PACT

Also by Andrew P. Napolitano

Constitutional Chaos: What Happens When
Government Breaks Its Own Laws

The Constitution in Exile: How the Federal Government Has
Seized Power by Rewriting the Supreme Law of the Land

A Nation of Sheep

Dred Scott's Revenge: A Legal History of Race and Freedom in America

Lies the Government Told You: Myth, Power,
and Deception in American History

It Is Dangerous to Be Right When the Government
Is Wrong: The Case for Personal Freedom

The Freedom Answer Book

Theodore and Woodrow: How Two American
Presidents Destroyed Constitutional Freedom

SUICIDE PACT

The Radical Expansion of Presidential Powers and the Lethal Threat to American Liberty

JUDGE ANDREW P. NAPOLITANO

NELSON
BOOKS

An Imprint of Thomas Nelson

Published in Nashville, Tennessee, by Nelson Books, an imprint of Thomas Nelson. Nelson Books and Thomas Nelson are registered trademarks of HarperCollins Christian Publishing, Inc.

Thomas Nelson, Inc., titles may be purchased in bulk for educational, business, fund-raising, or sales promotional use. For information, please e-mail SpecialMarkets@ThomasNelson.com.

Library of Congress Control Number: 2014950845

ISBN-13: 978-0-7180-2193-1

Printed in the United States of America

14 15 16 17 18 RRD 6 5 4 3 2 1

This book is dedicated to
James Conley Sheil,
born in Newark, New Jersey, on May 25th 1964
and died in Little Falls, New Jersey, on March 19th 2013.
He was the author's
alter ego, constant companion, and patient teacher,
who edited all the author's previous books while on earth
and this present book from Heaven.
Requiescat In Pace.

Government requires make-believe. Make believe that the king is divine, make believe that he can do no wrong or make believe that the voice of the people is the voice of God. Make believe that the people have a voice or make believe that the representatives of the people are the people. Make believe that governors are the servants of the people. Make believe that all men are equal or make believe that they are not.

—Edmund S. Morgan

We must remember that in time of war what is said on the enemy's side of the front is always propaganda, and what is said on our side of the front is truth and righteousness, the cause of humanity, and a crusade for peace. Is it necessary for us at the height of our power to stoop to such self-deceiving nonsense?

—Walter Lippman

Of all the enemies to public liberty war is, perhaps, the most to be dreaded, because it comprises and develops the germ of every other. War is the parent of armies; from these proceed debts and taxes; and armies, and debts, and taxes are the known instruments for bringing the many under the domination of the few. In war, too, the discretionary power of the Executive is extended; its influence in dealing out offices, honors, and emoluments is multiplied; and all the means of seducing the minds, are added to those of subduing the force, of the people. The same malignant aspect in republicanism may be traced in the inequality of fortunes, and the opportunities of fraud, growing out of a state of war, and in the degeneracy of manners and of morals engendered by both. No nation could preserve its freedom in the midst of continual warfare.

—James Madison

Contents

Foreword

Judge Andrew P. Napolitano informs us that our government tells us "noble lies" to soften the blow of our loss of liberty. It's not that we are asked to trade our liberty for security, but that we are programmed through prevarication to believe that our "protectors" only have our best interest at heart.

When James Clapper lies to Congress about spying on Americans, he sees it as a noble lie, done as his patriotic duty for God and country. I tend to believe them that their motives are noble. They actually believe that the priests of the intelligence community must lie to the masses in order to achieve a higher truth—security.

Like de Unamuno's priest, they believe that the truth can and should be massaged because the masses can't handle the truth.

Only problem is, we the people are not asked to choose liberty or security. In fact, we the people are often misled to believe that the only way to protect the homeland is by acquiescing, by placing our freedoms at the feet of our protectors.

Lincoln said any man can stand adversity, but if you want to test a man give him power.

Even Lincoln sometimes failed that test, as Judge Napolitano recounts in Lincoln's suspension of habeas corpus; the test is nonetheless one that challenges liberty lovers everywhere. Can a nation or individual tempted with power resist the allure to grab even more power in times of fear and war?

Indeed, Lincoln's test of a man is also a true test for a nation. To test a nation's belief in freedom, challenge the people with the emotions of fear and vengeance that often accompany war.

As the Judge points out, our history is replete with examples of our nation in time of war succumbing to fear and choosing to restrict the very freedom we ostensibly were fighting for.

If I told you that a country passed laws that imprisoned a pastor for fifteen years for Christian pacifism, you might think I was talking of Iran. If I told you that a woman was imprisoned for ten years for criticizing her government, you might think I was speaking of the gulag in the Soviet Union. If I told you that a salesman was arrested and imprisoned for seven to twenty years for calling wartime regulations a big joke, you would think I was surely exaggerating or even making it up. I'm not. Each horrific injustice occurred in America, the land of the free.

Make no mistake, I believe America to be the greatest, freest nation ever conceived. But that doesn't mean we should let a Pollyanna tint obscure the times in our history when we retreated from liberty instead of manning the barricades.

In *Suicide Pact*, Judge Napolitano describes these miscarriages of justice. From the Alien and Sedition Acts of 1798 to the Espionage Act of 1917 to the Patriot Act of 2001, fear and prejudice clouded our judgment and caused us to choose security over liberty.

Now President Obama says he just wants to "balance" liberty and national security.

Judge Napolitano succinctly answers President Obama. To Napolitano, it isn't possible to balance rights and security because "rights and [national security] are essentially and metaphysically so different that they cannot be balanced against each other."

Rights are inherent and a natural extension of self; national security is a "commodity" that is purchased as a "result of a mixing of an individual's labor and resources." A good may be desired but isn't a right.

You can't have a right to someone else's labor. You can't have a right to a thing or a good because that implies that you somehow have a right to the person's labor that created that good. National security is not a right. It is a good that requires someone's labor, and anyone who thinks you can or should trade liberty (a right) for security (a good) misunderstands the concept of natural rights.

I had this discussion with Senator Bernie Sanders, the Socialist from Vermont. He seemed astonished when I maintained that health care cannot be a right because it would imply that someone has a right to the physician's or nurse's or hospital janitor's labor.

Judge Napolitano doggedly points out that this fundamental misunderstanding of rights has time and time again caused us to relinquish our rights, particularly in time of war.

Even when members of Congress try to correct a problem, they often get it only half correct. The Judge describes the Non-Detention Act of 1971, a belated response to the injustice perpetrated by the internment of Japanese Americans during WWII. As the Judge points out, Congress changed the law but didn't outlaw detention, just shifted the power from the President back to Congress. Detention was still allowed "pursuant to an Act of Congress."

This point still has great significance. In 2011, Congress passed the NDAA (National Defense Authorization Act) and expanded the possibility of indefinite detention of American citizens without trial.

In fact, when I debated Senator McCain on the Senate floor, I was incredulous. I asked, "Does this mean an American citizen could be detained indefinitely and sent to Guantanamo Bay without a jury trial?" McCain replied, "If they're dangerous." Aghast, I shot back, "Sorta begs the question, doesn't it? About who gets to decide who's dangerous and who's not?"

In trying to fix this language, I begrudgingly supported the Feinstein-Lee amendment, even though it still contained the language allowing detention "pursuant to an Act of Congress." In 2013, I fought to alter the language by inserting the words "consistent with the Constitution" to make it clear that detention would require a jury trial.

My understanding was that the language was acceptable to promoters of the amendment, but we never got a chance as Senator Harry Reid killed the filibuster by breaking the rules of the Senate. Previously, it required a two-thirds majority vote to change Senate rules; Harry Reid used the nuclear option to change the rules with only a simple majority.

Caught up in the melee was our effort to kill indefinite detention. Harry Reid quashed all amendments, and we are forced to wait for another day to take up the fight.

Maybe the biggest constitutional question of our day is whether or not a judge's warrant is required for records held by a third party such as a bank or an Internet provider and whether a single warrant can apply to millions of individuals' records.

Edward Snowden revealed that the government was using a single warrant, issued by a secret court, to obtain billions of records from millions of individuals. At least one federal judge has declared this practice unconstitutional.

Judge Napolitano unravels the labyrinthine assault on civil liberties that has taken place as a side effect of the War on Terror. The Judge describes the anomaly that allows a secret court to address these issues, despite the fact that the FISA Court lacks the two sides that typically gather in opposition in a courtroom. As Judge Napolitano puts it, the "lack of adversity corrupts the truth-seeking function of the courts of law."

Senator Ron Wyden and I are attempting to correct this problem by making it easier to establish standing to protest court orders from the intelligence community. Our legislation also would allow communication companies to appeal secret FISA Court rulings to a non-secret federal appeals court and ultimately to the Supreme Court.

The hardest thing for citizens to realize is that we must jealously guard our constitutional liberties, especially in times of war. When fear and vengeance arise, precisely then we must be especially vigilant of our

Bill of Rights. Currently, the majority in Congress give prejudice to security over liberty, a dangerous situation.

Judge Napolitano gets it, and I hope his new book will help the American public to get it; to wake up and mount a defense of our most precious liberties before it's too late.

Sen. Rand Paul (R-KY)

Introduction

In my previous books, I have attempted to demonstrate that because our rights come from our humanity and are integral to each of us, only we can surrender them. Some folks surrender their rights when they violate the rights of others and get caught. Under this theory of natural rights, a bank robber gives up his freedoms by his aberrant behavior. But he doesn't give up your freedoms, or mine, or those of the bank he has just robbed, or even those of the bank's shareholders and depositors, just his own.

No rational society would long permit a justice system to stay in place in which everyone's rights were diminished because the bank robber got caught. He is the bad guy, he chose to gamble his freedom for the loot he took, and he lost the gamble.

But what happens if he does not get caught? Would a rational justice system punish the bank because the robber got away? Before you answer that quickly and obviously, let's look briefly at the nature of human freedom.

When Saint Thomas More was representing himself in his treason trial, he made a brilliant, yet unsuccessful argument to his jury about the nature of freedom. The treason charge against him, and under the dreadful laws at the time, the proven act of treason, was his silence—his refusal to assert affirmatively that his former employer and confidant, King Henry VIII, and not the pope, was the lawful head of the Roman Catholic Church in England.

Thomas had been the lord chancellor under Henry—the sixteenth-century version of today's British prime minister—and Henry needed his consent to help legitimize his break with Rome. Thomas had also been the pope's lawyer in English courts, so having him on Henry's side would have been a great public relations coup for the king.

Thomas knew that his jury was chosen by the king's people and that he'd be convicted. But he also knew that he could strike a blow for fidelity to first principles—here, the Natural Law—if his argument was compelling, yet simple. So he argued that whether the earth was round or flat, an issue of public dispute in that era, the government could not, by act of Parliament or by king's command, change its shape.

He was, of course, appealing not only to the common sense of his jurors but also to their understanding of the laws of nature. And those laws, which established natural abilities and natural limitations—men can sing but they can't fly—restrained even the government. He then argued that silence was a natural right, and thus, he could not be punished for exercising it. If free speech was a natural right, then surely silence was. He lost. He joked with his executioner, who wept as he did his sad duty. More was beheaded. Four hundred years later he was canonized.

But his argument—that there are areas of human behavior in the exercise of which we do not need a permission slip from the government—imposes an affirmative obligation on the part of all governments to abide those rights. And when Thomas Jefferson wrote the Declaration of Independence, he made the same argument against King George III as Saint Thomas had made against George's ancestor, King Henry VIII.

The argument declared that our rights are derived from our Creator, not from the government, and they are inalienable. That argument—which was not original to either Thomas—was adopted by the first U.S. Congress and remains American law today.

None of this should be new to anyone reading this book. And yet, it has largely been ignored by every American government since George Washington. Those governments have all reflected the inevitable growth of the power of government and the shrinkage of personal freedoms.

Not only has American government grown, but within the government, the executive branch of government has grown to dominate the legislative and judicial branches. George Washington believed he could execute soldiers without a trial, and John Adams believed it somehow was constitutional to punish speech that brought his government, or him personally, into disrepute.

Lincoln suspended natural rights, disobeyed lawful orders of the Supreme Court, and arrested newspaper publishers and elected officials who disagreed with him, all while reflecting the profoundly, embarrassingly immoral white supremacist attitudes of his day.

Woodrow Wilson tricked the nation into fighting a useless war and then used the war as an excuse for punishing speech critical of his administration with long jail terms. He seized private property without paying for it and even arrested a rival presidential candidate.

Franklin D. Roosevelt arrested Americans on the basis of their race and put them into concentration camps. He executed first and then sought judicial approval. He even stole millions of dollars in gold from innocent, law-abiding Americans. He no doubt fomented the Japanese attack on Pearl Harbor and then punished innocent military officers for not having caught him.

If you measure unpunished brutality by the number of innocent deaths in the shortest period of time, Harry Truman was the greatest war criminal and mass killer in history for the quarter million Japanese civilians he murdered in a few moments at Hiroshima and Nagasaki, after Japan had effectively surrendered. Then his Department of Justice set about systematically prosecuting people for publicly considering the wisdom—or lack thereof—of communism because the boss needed to look tough.

But (with the exception of Hiroshima and Nagasaki) all this pales in comparison with the constitutional monstrosities that followed the attacks on America on September 11th 2001.

C. S. Lewis once remarked that the greatest trick the Devil has pulled off was to convince us that he does not exist. This book argues that the greatest trick the federal government ever pulled was convincing us that we should voluntarily surrender our liberties, just because the monsters who perpetrated the 9/11 attacks did not get caught beforehand.

It is a central premise of this work that the federal government has never taken seriously the concept of natural rights, all the while paying lip service to that first principle. I argue that the government believes that it—and not the Creator—is the source of human freedom; and it alone can decide when to expand personal freedoms and when to contract them. And it believes that it can restrict freedom by majority vote or judicial ruling or executive fiat.

The first half of this book is a cursory history of presidential law-making and lawbreaking in the years before 9/11. The second half concentrates on the presidencies of George W. Bush and Barack Obama.

It is they who incarcerated without charge or trial, and who claimed the power to do so even after acquittal. It is they who have operated a Devil's Island off the coast of Florida where prisoners were routinely tortured and where they had no hope of a fair hearing, much less eventual freedom. It is they who claimed the power to torture and kill non-combatants, and who did so. President Obama even went so far as to suggest that his summary murder of innocent Americans and foreigners is somehow consistent with constitutional language that forbids it. Each started wars without a declaration of war from Congress. Each signed legislation into law he had no intention of enforcing. Each claimed to derive power to make law and adjudicate its application from some extra-constitutional source he could not name.

And each effectively sought to punish the shareholders and depositors of a bank when the bank's robber got away. They both believed that they could take away rights and create new ones. Surely one could, out of fear and desperation, surrender one's rights to the government in return for a promise of safekeeping. That would be asinine, as it is tantamount to slavery, but it would be lawful.

One is simply without the moral, constitutional, or lawful power to surrender someone else's freedom. Yet that is just what Bush and Obama did: Using fear and loathing, they persuaded innocent Americans and duped Congresses that they had nothing to lose and nothing to hide by surrendering freedom—their own and everyone else's—into the arms of a government that would keep them safe and secure.

The consequence of this surrender is a federal government that acts as if it can regulate any behavior, right any wrong, and tax any event or non-event, all for "national security" reasons. The post-9/11 federal government plainly admits that it takes freedom from us in order to keep us safe.

But who or what will keep our freedoms safe from the government? To address that problem and to understand its scope, the reader is invited to dive in to this book and to do so with a warning: There is no happy ending.

Apologia

When the Bush administration began its aggressive public assault on personal freedoms shortly after 9/11, one of the mantras that its apologists began using was a popularly distorted one-liner from a dissent in a 1949 U.S. Supreme Court decision known as *Terminiello v. Chicago*. The one-liner has been variously articulated but most often is stated, "The Constitution is not a suicide pact."

I am mocking those who misuse this statement by incorporating the most incendiary of its words into the title of this book. I intend the phrase "suicide pact" to mean that a Constitution which permits the government to violate it and the president to do so secretly and with impunity is a suicide pact with the states that formed it and the American people whose freedoms it was intended to secure because it will result in such a loss of liberty that it will bring about the self-immolation of our formerly free society—its suicide, if you will. But those who use it in defense of what this book attacks surely have another meaning in mind.

Here is how the statement that the apologists for big government misuse came about.

On February 7th 1946, Fr. Arthur Terminiello, a Roman Catholic priest who was a fierce opponent of communism and of the Truman administration's treatment of it, gave an incendiary speech in a hall in Chicago, which the sponsors of the speech had rented for that purpose. The sponsors obtained the required permits from the Chicago police.

The speech utterly delighted Fr. Terminiello's supporters and profoundly antagonized his opponents. The opponents numbered about sixteen hundred persons, and the supporters about half that number.

When it became apparent that violence might break out, the Chicago police asked Fr. Terminiello to stop speaking and depart the speech venue. When he disregarded their wishes, they arrested him and charged him with breach of the peace. That charge was defined in Chicago in the late 1940s to mean any behavior that stirs the public to anger or invites dispute or brings about unrest or creates a disturbance. The police did not arrest any of the rioters who broke windows and stormed the stage from which Fr. Terminiello spoke and who obviously came to silence this priest; only the priest who gave the speech was arrested.

Fr. Terminiello was convicted in a trial court, and that conviction was upheld by an Illinois appellate court and eventually by the Illinois Supreme Court. He appealed to the U.S. Supreme Court, which reversed his conviction. In doing so, it moved the direction of First Amendment jurisprudence closer to where it is today: With the exception of "free-speech zone" nonsense, a near absolute protection for public political speech. It did so by invalidating the Chicago ordinance and recognizing that the values protected by the freedom of speech presume that speech will arouse and annoy. Moreover, the speaker cannot be punished because the loudest gaggle in the audience—which came to the speech in order to become annoyed and then silence the speaker—fully got what it expected.

Four justices dissented, among whom was Justice Robert H. Jackson. Justice Jackson had been one of FDR's attorneys general and was Truman's chief prosecutor at the Nuremberg trials. He was also the mentor to a future chief justice, William H. Rehnquist, who was one of his law clerks. Justice Jackson argued that a federal court had no business second-guessing Chicago cops who were trying to prevent a riot.

He regretted that the Court used Fr. Terminiello's hateful speech as an instrument to change First Amendment jurisprudence. His reading of the First Amendment informed him that it does not tolerate violent disruption and does permit punishing or silencing political speech which is likely to lead to violence.

His dissent is powerful but wide of the mark; and no Supreme Court decision has permitted the so-called heckler's veto—which is what happens when an aroused audience succeeds in silencing a speaker it has come to silence by drowning him out or by successfully demanding his arrest.

Now, back to the title of this book. The last line of Justice Jackson's dissent is the line the Bush and eventually the Obama apologists persist in misquoting. Justice Jackson lamented that liberty and order are often adversaries, and he yearned for each to accommodate the other, rather than liberty being in the default position.

Justice Jackson obviously rejected the Natural Law and chided his colleagues in the Court's majority for having upheld it. In the concluding line of his now jurisprudentially disregarded lament, he wrote, "There is a danger that, if the Court does not temper its doctrinaire logic with a little practical wisdom, it will convert the constitutional Bill of Rights into a suicide pact."

There you have it. The final line of a poorly reasoned dissent which in sixty-five years has never become the law, which predicted an outcome that never came to pass, and the proponents of which use to assault the Natural Law *ad nauseam* and to their own frustration, is ultimately toothless.

If Justice Jackson were still with us, my guess is he'd have no difficulty deciding today which is the greater danger to personal freedom: A priest who harangues a crowd that came to be harangued and a Court that permits it, or presidents who write their own laws and start their own wars, who arrest without charge, torture in defiance of law, spy in defiance of the Constitution, and murder in defiance of the ancient and common understanding of right and wrong.

So, I apologize for turning Justice Jackson's statement on its head. The reader can decide whether this was done for petty or for profound reasons, or perhaps as a warning—a warning that we are far more likely to collapse as a society from too little freedom than from too much.

Part 1

THE STRUGGLE FOR NATURAL LIBERTY

1770–1880

1

A Philosophical Primer

War is in fact the true nurse of executive aggrandizement.[*]

—JAMES MADISON

W hich would you choose: To be free or to be secure? State security and personal freedom often run along tense lines with each other, but our Constitution and its philosophical roots clearly bias freedom over safety. In many ways, the first hundred years of American history represented a struggle between various presidential, congressional, and judicial precedents—both good and bad—to arrive at a philosophical and constitutional consistency for ensuring a free, yet secure nation. From the Revolution to the fall of the Federalists, to the Civil War and Reconstruction, America's textual commitment to personal freedom was tested in the exigencies of war. This part explores the philosophical roots of the freedom bias, the constitutional allocation of war-making authority, and the events just described.

---

[*] James Madison, *Writings of James Madison: 1790–1802*, ed. Gaillard Hunt, vol. 6 (New York: G. P. Putnam's Sons, 1906), 174.

Individual Rights, Personal Autonomy, and Self-Ownership

What is the philosophical basis for a constitutional bias in favor of personal freedom? By examining the Enlightenment philosophies that influenced our Founding Fathers and scrutinizing war as a mechanism for enlarging state power, we arrive at a lens through which the legal history of personal liberty in a free society and war waged by the state may be properly construed.

When our Founding Fathers drafted the Constitution—the successor document to the Articles of Confederation—they recognized that the proper role of government is not a nanny or Big Brother but a limited entity designed to protect the people's natural liberties. "The Fathers rather frequently indicated that our rights were founded on the law of nature."[1] Almost uniformly, individuals like Madison, Jefferson, and Washington subscribed to the concept of the Natural Law and the inherent dignity of all persons:[2] A dignity that bears with it the promise of "certain unalienable Rights, . . . among [which] are Life, Liberty, and the Pursuit of Happiness."[3]

This belief in inherent human rights permeated through the drafting of the Constitution. The influence of the Enlightenment philosophers John Locke and Thomas Hobbes upon the Drafters anchored the document in Natural Law and personal liberty, and an eye toward its preservation.[4] In fact, the Drafters enshrined the protection of the rights inherently held by persons prior to any social compact in the Constitution itself, as the Ninth Amendment provides that "[t]he enumeration in the Constitution of certain rights shall not be construed to deny or disparage others retained by the people."[5] The Supreme Court, while eschewing the phrase "natural rights," has been more than willing to find indistinguishable "unenumerated, fundamental rights."[6] The use of the word *retained* all but tips the Framers' hands as to their recognition of the source of rights as being individual humanity.

Underpinning this legal recognition of natural rights is an understanding of liberal philosophy, not liberal in the modern misuse of the word, but in its original meaning. John Locke was considered a *classic* liberal,* espousing philosophies which recognize the inalienable dignity and self-ownership of every human being. Beginning with Saint Thomas Aquinas and Fr. Francisco Suárez, passing through John Locke's *Two Treatises of Civil Government*, proceeding into Thomas Jefferson's Declaration of Independence, and continuing to the modern philosophies of Ludwig von Mises, Friedrich Hayek, Ayn Rand, and Murray Rothbard, a classic liberal or libertarian theory offers a world vision based on the premises of self-ownership, personal autonomy, non-aggression, and the primacy of the individual over the state.

The State of Nature and Natural Rights

Classic liberal philosophy begins in the State of Nature. In Hobbes's *Leviathan*, the world without the government is nasty; however, it was John Locke who advanced a theory of the State of Nature that under-pins our constitutional constructs and provides a valid basis for a limited constitutional government based solely on the consent of the governed. The Lockean State of Nature, or the natural state of mankind, is an anar-chy and exists in any territorial region without a legitimate government. Since our rights come from our humanity in the State of Nature, they pre-exist any legal system, and the depth and reach of a person's rights

---

* Llewellyn H. Rockwell Jr. concisely explained,

    In the 18th and 19th centuries, the term liberalism generally meant a philosophy of public life that affirmed the following principle: societies and all their compo-nent parts need no central management and control because societies generally manage themselves through the voluntary interaction of its members to their mutual benefit. Today we cannot call this philosophy liberalism because the term has been appropriated by the democratic totalitarians. In an attempt to recover this philosophy for our own time, we give it a new name, classical liberalism [or libertarianism].

    Llewellyn H. Rockwell Jr., "An American Classical Liberalism," Ludwig von Mises Institute, 1996, http://mises.org/etexts/classical.asp. Rockwell has been appropriated by the democratic totalitarians. In an attempt to recover this philosophy for our own time, we give it a new name, classical liberalism (or libertarianism).

are absolute. Every person has individual sovereignty, the absolute right to possess and control his person and rights:

> [The State of Nature] is a state of perfect freedom to order their actions, and dispose of their possessions and persons, as they think fit, within the bounds of the law of nature, without asking leave, or depending upon the will of any other man.
>
> A state also of equality, wherein all the power and jurisdiction is reciprocal, no one having more than another; there being nothing more evident, than that creatures of the same species and rank, promiscuously born to all the same advantages of nature, and the use of the same faculties, should also be equal one amongst another without subordination or subjection.[7]

The core concept of Natural Law is the idea of self-ownership and limitless personal liberty. However, "[t]he state of nature has a law of nature to govern it, which obliges every one: and reason, which is that law, teaches all mankind, who will but consult it."[8] Locke leaves his readers with an unsatisfactory anarchy, governed only by a discoverable-through-reason Natural Law and self-help as an enforcement mechanism.* Like Hobbes before him, Locke recognized that life in the State of Nature could be "solitary, poor, nasty, brutish, and short,"[9] affirming that the State of Nature is "full of fears and continual dangers,"[10] as no perceptible mechanism exists for a weaker person to enforce his natural rights against a stronger person infringing upon those rights.[11]

In order to resolve this issue of perfectly equal rights with perfectly

---

* "[M]an in that state have *an uncontroulable liberty to dispose of his person or possessions*, yet he has not liberty to destroy himself, or so much as any creature in his possession, but where some nobler use than its bare preservation calls for it. The state of nature has a law of nature to govern it, which obliges every one: *and reason, which is that law, teaches all mankind, who will but consult it*, that being all equal and independent, no one ought to harm another in his life, health, liberty, or possessions." John Locke, *The Two Treatises of Civil Government*, ed. Thomas Hollis (London: A. Millar et al., 1764), bk. 2, §6, emphasis added, http://oll .libertyfund.org/?option=com_staticxt&staticfile=show.php%3Ftitle=222.

unequal protection, individuals yield some of *their* rights or liberty to a government via a social contract.[12] Such a contract, like our Constitution, states expressly the role, powers, and limitations of the government and is legitimized by the consent of the parties to the contract.[13]

Some theorists, most notably Lysander Spooner, argue that the Constitution does not serve as a valid social compact because no one has expressly consented to it since the 1780s.[14] In his three-part work, *No Treason*, Spooner argued that former Confederate soldiers were not guilty of treason, as none of them had ever agreed to the Constitution, and the North had violated it with the suspension of liberties during the war.[15] Locke, however, distinguished between tacit, or implied, and express consent, arguing that people tacitly consent to being governed by virtue of living and participating in the society, of which the Constitution is the Supreme Law of the Land.[16]

Regardless of to which school of thought one ascribes, the core concept remains unchanged. Because humans are inherently sovereign over themselves qua the principle of self-ownership, only when they consent to give up that sovereignty to the state in order to legitimize the state's exercise of sovereignty over them is the state's power morally legitimate. In essence, whether dealing with Locke or Spooner, personal sovereignty mandates the necessity of personal consent to any form of government for it to be morally legitimate.

Leaving the State of Nature: Consent, Government, and Law

Thus, leaving the State of Nature involves the creation of a limited, principled government.* The primary tenet of government under a lib-

---

* While some libertarians, most famously Murray Rothbard, argue for an anarcho-capitalist approach to government—that is to say there may be no monopoly on state power by consent of the governed, but if states exist then the reach of their monopoly should be systematically minimized. See Murray N. Rothbard, *The Ethics of Liberty* (New York: New York University Press, 1998), 161–273, 193. This book is of the opinion that in early twenty-first-century America a minimal state is necessary. A history of the exercise of state power in its constitutional and rightful role would hardly go anywhere by denying the premises

ertarian scheme is the Non-Aggression Principle, which provides that all violence or threats of violence against a person or his legal property are inherently illegitimate.[17] The Non-Aggression Principle essentially provides that any unconsented to interference with a person or his things—beneficial or harmful—is unlawful.[18] This definition does not include aggression in self-defense.[19]

Under a minimalist conceptualization, a government exists solely to protect the people from "aggression"—force or fraud—or at least to provide a forum for the people to protect themselves from force or fraud.[20] Any other exercise of government power beyond defending against and adjudicating matters of force or fraud—beyond defending natural rights—is illegitimate aggression itself, and thus, an improper assault on natural rights.[21]

Although Locke best articulated the structure of society and state, the modern articulator of the Natural Law itself is Saint Thomas Aquinas. In the *Summa Theologica*, Aquinas wrote that the Natural Law exists above the laws of man and that the validity of the laws of man depends on their compatibility with the Natural Law.[22] Moreover, and more famously, Aquinas reinforced his positive position with a negative bar adapted from Augustine's *lex iniusta non est lex?* philosophy. Aquinas argued that the laws of man which do not comport with the Natural Law in some qualifying sense are laws only in the most narrow and hollow sense, with nominal ontological validity and no deontological force.[23] More simply, in a metaphysical sense, they are only really laws insofar as they are printed and promulgated, but they have no real moral or ethical binding force to impose a duty of obedience.

Accordingly, through Locke and Augustine, there is a complete scheme of natural liberty. All persons are born with absolute and autonomous

---

of any governmental powers at all. That need for a minimal state is a view shared by many mainstream libertarians and objectivists such as John Locke, Ludwig von Mises, Friedrich Hayek, Robert Nozick, and Ayn Rand. Suffice to say that Nozick's argument that a private judicial/defense firm in an anarcho-capitalist state would eventually arise as a monopolist by purely market forces, thus creating a de facto government, is compelling. See Robert Nozick, *Anarchy, State, and Utopia* (Hoboken, NJ: John Wiley & Sons, 2001), 88–148.

moral control over their bodies, over their property, and over their labor,[24] tempered by the limited surrender to the government of their individual rights, for example, *the right to enforce the Natural Law.* That is to say, after leaving the State of Nature, people have an unlimited right to exercise all personal liberties that they have not delegated to the government: "This natural liberty consists properly in a power of acting as one thinks fit, without any restraint or control, *unless by the law of nature* [such action is abrogated]."[25] An abrogation of those rights not in accord with the Law of Nature lacks validity. In order to administer the Natural Law and to prevent force or fraud, a minimal state ought to be formed; and in order to control the state, a constitution, a supreme law of the land, needs to be adopted, enacted, and accepted by all over whom the state can govern.

It is the central purpose of this work to explore the exercise of constitutional war powers by the President of the United States of America in the era after September 11th 2011, through the lens of the Natural Law and the U.S. Constitution, namely, by addressing purportedly lawful presidential encroachment on an individual's enjoyment of self-ownership and natural liberty and constitutional guarantees.

War as an Organ of State Health and Power

No single action—by any branch of the federal government pursuant to any constitutional provision—has had the breadth and afforded deference as an action pursuant to the war power. War is a double-edged sword: It is a jingoist boon and an individual-rights bust.

"War is the health of the state," Randolph Bourne famously proclaimed in his 1918 essay, "The State."[26] Ostensibly, this notion is counterintuitive: How can something which kills innocents as well as combatants, costs an astronomical sum, and has untold destructive potential be the health of the state? In answer, Bourne argued persuasively:

> The moment war is declared, . . . the mass of the people, through some spiritual alchemy, become convinced that they have willed

and executed the deed themselves. They then, with the exception of a few malcontents, proceed to allow themselves to be regimented, coerced, deranged in all the environments of their lives, and turned into a solid manufactory of destruction toward whatever other people may have, in the appointed scheme of things, come within the range of the Government's disapprobation. The citizen throws off his contempt and indifference to Government, identifies himself with its purposes, revives all his military memories and symbols, and the State once more walks, an august presence, through the imaginations of men. Patriotism becomes the dominant feeling, and produces immediately that intense and hopeless confusion between the relations which the individual bears and should bear toward the society of which he is a part.[27]

Bourne's essay is not famous simply for that biting analysis of the psychology of war, but also for its specific discussion of individual liberty subsuming to state power. He gave one of the most comprehensive descriptions of war hysteria to date. Bourne did not limit his analysis to broad feelings, but concretely discussed the state's assault on dissident or unpopular opinions, even specifically reaching an infamous case discussed in chapter 5, *Abrams v. United States*.

. . . Minority opinion, which in times of peace, was only irritating and could not be dealt with by law unless it was conjoined with actual crime, becomes, with the outbreak of war, a case for outlawry. Criticism of the State, objections to war, lukewarm opinions concerning the necessity or the beauty of conscription, are made subject to ferocious penalties, far exceeding in severity those affixed to actual pragmatic crimes. Public opinion, as expressed in the newspapers, and the pulpits and the schools, becomes one solid block.

. . . A white terrorism is carried on by the Government against pacifists, socialists, enemy aliens, and a milder unofficial persecution against all persons or movements that can be imagined as connected with the enemy. War, which should be the health of the State, unifies all the bourgeois elements and the common people, and outlaws the rest.

. . . The punishment for opinion has been far more ferocious and unintermittent than the punishment of pragmatic crime. . . . A public opinion which, almost without protest, accepts as just, adequate, beautiful, deserved, and in fitting harmony with ideals of liberty and freedom of speech, a sentence of twenty years in prison for mere utterances, no matter what they may be, shows itself to be suffering from a kind of social derangement of values, a sort of social neurosis, that deserves analysis and comprehension.[28]

What is gained from Bourne's somewhat-over-the-top rhetoric is an understanding of a nation during war: A galvanized people fearful of dissent and willing to accept suppression of their and others' natural rights to free speech based on the seemingly xenophilic content of a viewpoint alone.

Not to belabor an obvious point, one I have previously made,[29] but individual autonomy suffers *incomparably* during war: The rights to life and liberty are abrogated by the draft or internment camps;[30] the right to free expression is limited whereby the mere distribution of literature the government hates or fears (and condemns as "subversive") can lead to jailing;[31] the right to property and to contract is destroyed by rationing and industry boards designed to control and set prices;[32] most recently, the right to private association and the natural right to privacy have been trounced by the dawning of government programs designed to snatch the identifying information, the geolocation data, and the content of almost every telephone call, and e-mail.[33]

Debunking Myths: Freedom as a Bias Against Security, Not a Balancing Act

Americans have a fundamental disconnect between understanding goods and rights, which has led them to a determination that freedom and security must be balanced. This section focuses on debunking that odious misconception.

Rights, specifically natural rights, are intangible and enforceable personal legal choices that are inalienable and exist *a priori* to any political or economic system, and for the exercise of which one does not need government approval. A good is a commodity or service that is the result of a mixing of an individual's labor and resources, and either others' labor, resources, or both. One is the inherent product of human character and existence that cannot be exchanged or assigned—even via a market—and the other is derivative of one's or another's labor, which is freely transferable and developed for a market. By way of example, the freedom of speech, the freedom of movement, and the freedom of self-defense are intangible and legal rights: One cannot sell or alienate them.[34] Conversely, military contractors responsible for large parts of Joint Special Operations Command (JSOC) and CIA operations all over the globe are private firms that sell goods and security services to the highest bidder. Thus, security and legal services are goods that result from a policeman or a lawyer mixing his or her labor with resources like guns and legal memoranda or, more commonly, like a gym membership or health insurance. Rights come from within us. Goods are purchased by us. Without rights, we lack humanity. With rights, we can accumulate enough wealth to purchase goods.

This brings us to our balancing problem: How can one balance a derivative against an *a priori* right? One cannot. In order to create a social arrangement that validly enacts laws or defines man's relationship to other persons and their property, the underlying premise of self-ownership and natural rights both precedes and acts as precedent to the *lawful* acquisition of any good.[35] As was just demonstrated, security, like that provided by the government, is a good, which cannot be freely exchanged between persons or entities, like states, without first recognizing *a priori* natural rights. Therefore, in considering the good of security and the right of free speech, no balancing act is possible or even conceivable; on the contrary, there is a bias in favor of precedent freedom and natural rights at the expense of consequent goods. Rights and goods are essentially and metaphysically so different that they cannot be balanced against each other.

Complicating this scheme somewhat is a theory of precedence of rights, for example, that the right to life precedes the right to property. The best way to illustrate this is by a hypothetical situation. Imagine that Jean Valjean, the character from *Les Misérables*, has just stolen the bread to feed his starving family. Javert, the ardent police officer, is a perfect example of "legalists in Western literature,"[36] as his moral code comports totally with the legal code. If Javert arrests Valjean for the crime of theft, is Javert right to do so? Some might think that, yes, Valjean violated another's right to property, and he should suffer the penalty. That represents the Javert-legalist perspective. Another perspective is that the right to life of Valjean's family is superior to the ownership right of the person whose bread was stolen, and thus, necessity creates an exception to what would otherwise be a violation of natural rights: "St. Thomas Aquinas, in *Summa Theologiae*, opined that the natural law requires whatever material things a person possesses in superabundance be used to help the poor, and further stated that such goods may be taken by a needy person in a time of imminent danger. John Locke similarly declared that, in the state of nature, the needy have a right to the '[s]urplusage' of their fellows."[37]

This section provided a brief view of the classic liberal utopia: A place where rights do not succumb to goods, where rights are inherent to the human condition, where the only lawful government is that which prevents force or fraud by means of a social compact that respects *a priori* rights, and where all are aware that war—the state's mode of protection against aggressive external force—is an instrument to strengthen the unity of the state at the expense of individual liberty.

2

A Constitutional Overview of the Duty to Defend and the Power to Wage Successful War

There never was a good war or a bad peace.[*]

—Benjamin Franklin

W hen the British colonies won their independence in the American Revolutionary War, the new country entered the world stage in a state of chaotic and competitive uncertainty. Out of that chaos came the Articles of Confederation, an impractical interworking of what appeared to be the first central government between the newly freed and tenuously

---

[*] Benjamin Franklin to Josiah Quincy, September 11, 1783, in *The Friend of Peace*, ed. Noah Worcester (1827), 304.

united thirteen states. As a loose confederation of individually sovereign states, most of the military power remained with the states themselves,[1] thereby leaving the national government unable to defend the new nation. Within six years, it became apparent that the Articles had placed the nation close to chaos.

There were no provisions under the Articles for an executive to enforce the law or for a national court system to interpret the law. There simply existed a toothless legislative body composed of delegates from the thirteen states.[2] While the Articles supported the notion of a Continental Army and provided for a unified nation for dealing with the European powers, it was largely illusory.[3] The states normally would not volunteer their militias unless it served their individual interests.[4] As well, the use of monopolies, cartels, and tariffs isolated the states from one another economically, and that drove up prices and drove down supply. And, of course, the moral, legal, and constitutional problem of slavery was waiting to explode.

Facing threats from domestic sources, including the infamous Shays' Rebellion, and foreign threats from European powers, the central government concluded that change was needed.[5] Thus, there evolved a demand for a stronger federal government, one with a unified central base which could raise and maintain an army, provide for the defense of the nation, and keep commerce among the states regular. That demand led to the drafting and later adoption of the U.S. Constitution in 1789.

The Allocation of War Powers Under the Constitution

When the Framers of the Constitution initially crafted this country's governing document, they intentionally designed the government to operate in a manner that made it difficult to declare war and to utilize extended military force. Realizing the all-too-familiar truisms of war between the countries of Europe made blood spill often over the jealousy of kings,* the Framers were focused on restricting war to only the gravest of national threats of violence. The Founding Fathers were aware that the sole reason for the existence of government was to make sure that our natural rights were preserved and that freedom reigned supreme. It followed then that there was a need for an adequate and reliable military to protect the nation from its foreign enemies. Cognizant of the immense power a national army instills in a central government, the Framers made sure to reserve the power of financing this military machine to the people (through the Congress)[6] and to divvy up the military powers among the different branches of government. Specifically, the power to finance the armies and to declare war was separated from the power of commanding the army, and that was separated from the power of adjudicating individuals as enemies of the state.

Congress

Article I, section 8, of the U.S. Constitution sets forth the proper procedure for the declaration of war and is commonly known as the War Powers Clause. The provision states: "Congress shall have Power To . . . declare War, grant Letters of Marque and Reprisal, and make Rules concerning Captures on Land and Water."[7] In addition, Congress exclusively holds the authority to "raise and support Armies" and to "provide and maintain a Navy."[8] The Constitution is explicit in its requirement that Congress alone is the branch permitted to declare a war on behalf of the United States against another country or group.

Under the Constitution, without a declaration from Congress, the president may not, under any circumstances (unless repelling an

---

* Hamilton discussed this in the *Federalist Papers*. "[Some wars] take their origin entirely in private passions; in the attachments, enmities, interests, hopes, and fears of leading individuals. . . . Men of class . . . assuming the pretext of some public motive, have not scrupled to sacrifice the national tranquillity to personal advantage or personal gratification." See Alexander Hamilton, *Federalist* No. 6, Library of Congress, http://thomas. loc.gov/home/histdox/fed_06.html.

invasion), use military force or wage war against another entity on behalf of the United States. Unfortunately, presidents have not held this view in the modern era. In 230 years, there have been only eleven official declarations of war issued by the U.S. Congress.[9] At this writing, the last explicit declaration of war was issued against Germany in World War II.[10] Constitutionally, this is entirely perplexing as there have been numerous conflicts that most Americans would consider to be wars since World War II, such as the Korean War, the Vietnam War, the Gulf War, the Afghanistan War, the Iraq War, the Libyan War—to cite but a few examples burned, no doubt, into the public's consciousness.

Although lower courts have held some instances of presidential action without congressional authorization unconstitutional,[11] the Supreme Court has never intervened to stop a war that the president has initiated without a declaration of war from Congress. Having little guidance on this from the Court, Congress took matters into its own hands with the War Powers Resolution of 1973,[12] discussed in chapter 9.

Moreover, a congressional declaration of war was explicitly placed into the Constitution as a check on presidential power. The Framers were careful to place this burden on the representatives of the American people in Congress, not in the potential despotic, tyrannical hands of one man: The president. Yet with the modern acquiescence of Congress to the demands of the executive branch in matters of war, we have seen a shift of accountability. Professors Alfred and Steven Blumrosen wrote:

> The declarations of war in the first half of the twentieth century made clear that Congress was taking full responsibility for its decision. Each member was recorded as voting for or against the war and could be judged by their constituents for that act. In contrast, the AUMF [Authorization for Use of Military Force] authorizes the President to make the decision and, thus, absolves Congress of that responsibility and relieves its members of accountability. For more than half a

century, Congress has allowed the President to do the work of taking the nation to war, *instead of following the Constitution.*[13]

Congress should not have the ability to shift the blame of war to the president. Likewise, the president should not be able to usurp a constitutionally mandated prerogative of Congress, even with Congress's consent. The severe implications of war deserve ample time, debate, consideration, and consensus by the federal government. The Framers were right to place this task solely upon the legislative branch. Only in the houses of Congress can the American people be represented in the appropriate deliberation to launch the country into all-out war against another country or some non-state entity. This was not to be a country under the will of a military dictator; rather, it was to be a republic of the people and "the genius of the people must be consulted."[14]

The President

Article II, section 2, of the U.S. Constitution empowers the president as "Commander in Chief of the Army and Navy of the United States."[15] Early presidents, including George Washington, John Adams, Thomas Jefferson, and James Madison, correctly understood the structure of the Constitution and its explicit requirement of congressional authorization for military offensives. "No early President felt free to wage war merely because another nation had declared war on the United States. Each understood that to wage war was to declare it, a power the Constitution granted Congress, and not the President."[16]

Furthermore, those who would argue that both the president and Congress share the ability to wage war on behalf of the United States are incorrect: "To say that the Congress may issue formal declarations of war but that the President may nonetheless start a war at his discretion is to endorse mutually incompatible propositions."[17] More recent presidents have exercised their commander in chief powers to send troops to foreign countries, even in peacetime, without the permission or approval of Congress.[18] The Court, in its infinite wisdom, has only sparingly analyzed the lawfulness of doing so, holding that there are problems in terms of who would have standing to sue.*

Defensive measures, such as repelling an invasion, however, construct a much different scenario for the president. The Supreme Court has held that the president "has no power to initiate or declare war," but if there were an invasion, "the President is not only authorized but bound to resist by force . . . without waiting for any special legislative authority."[19] It was important to the Founders, James Madison in particular, that the president must have the power to repel sudden attacks. Insomuch as the president may repel an invasion or suppress sudden aggression, his authority concludes thus, in the absence of congressional authorization for offensive action. "[T]hose who are to conduct a war *cannot* be proper judges of 'whether a war ought to be commenced, continued, or concluded.'"[20]

Although the president may not unilaterally wage war on another country, organization, or entity without authorization from Congress, the courts have granted the president much leeway in his capacity as commander in chief to deploy troops abroad. The Johnson and Nixon administrations used the power to commit troops without the consent of Congress to a variety of conflicts. For example, in 1964 Congress issued broad war-making authority for the Vietnam conflict to then President Lyndon B. Johnson with the passage of the Gulf of Tonkin Resolution. When Congress repealed the authorization in 1971, several lawsuits were filed to enjoin President Nixon from continuing the war in Vietnam. The courts refused to rule upon the merits of these cases, leaving the president full reign to continue war unilaterally in Southeast Asia.[21] Regrettably, this marks just a small fraction of unconstitutional

---

* During the Yugoslavia conflict, a congressman attempted to sue then President Bill Clinton for not complying with the War Powers Resolution and the provision of war in the Constitution. A district court judge dismissed the suit because of a lack of standing. The Circuit Court of Appeals affirmed the decision. *Campbell v. Clinton*, 203 F.3d 19 (D.C. Cir. 2000); Erwin Chemerinsky, *Constitutional Law: Principles and Policies*, ed. Vicki Been et al., 4th ed. (New York: Aspen Publishers, 2011), 290 n19.

power expansion on the part of the executive branch. Discussed in later sections, several American presidents—some even considered to be American heroes—have openly attacked civil liberties and disregarded the Constitution.

3

NATIONAL SECURITY IN THE REVOLUTIONARY WAR ERA

I only regret that I have but one life to give for my country.[*]

—CAPT. NATHAN HALE

The Continental Congress

When General Washington rode out to accept his command at Cambridge, he was within a few feet of one of the most famous spies in the American Revolution: Dr. Benjamin Church.[1] Church was an agent of the British government prior to the Revolution, as early as 1775.[2] At

---

[*] Captain Nathan Hale, on the occasion of the unfortunate conclusion of his first spying mission for the Continental Congress. "Nathan Hale," www.nycgovparks.org/parks/cityhallpark/monuments/654.

the time his treason was uncovered—through the carelessness of a lady of the night*—he held several prominent posts, including chief physician and director general of the Continental Army, and delegate to the Massachusetts Provincial Congress.[3] Dr. Church was a man with the pedigree of a Founding Father, but to the rebels was a wolf in sheep's clothing.

Rather than being tried by the Continental Congress, he was court-martialed with Gen. George Washington himself as judge.[4] Church was charged with "communicating with the enemy"[5] because no espionage statute existed at the time[6] (that was created in 1917). However, Church survived his conviction and sentence because the Articles of War adopted by the Continental Congress capped the maximum penalty for such communications at thirty-six lashes and a modest fine.[7] As a result, the Continental Congress soon adopted the death penalty for such correspondences with enemy agents, at Washington's request.[8]

I recount this story for three reasons: First, to show how seriously dire the Revolution was. It is unimaginable today that the state of national security would be in such peril that President Obama would have a Chinese spy employed as surgeon general and intimately involved in military decisions. Second, because the attention on spies and intelligence in American history has tended to focus on the Benedict Arnold affair and then skip to the intrigues of the Cold War, many forget the important role that intelligence gathering and spies played in every major American war. Paul Revere, more famous for his ride than as a spy, ran a group of American spies in Boston that provided much valuable intelligence to the folks actually fighting the war.[9] Third, and of paramount importance for our purposes, Church was afforded the process due to an officer of the Continental Army

---

* He entrusted her to get a letter to his accomplices. Casting aside discretion, she attempted to enlist the aid of a patriot client to contact prominent British officials. Eventually, the client decided to contact the local Continentals and turn her over to Washington. John Bakeless, *Turncoats, Traitors, and Heroes* (Cambridge, MA: De Capo Press, 1959), 11–15.

during a war when "the courts" were not merely closed, but ten years away from conception.

Intelligence was so precious in 1775 that the Continental Congress formed three committees to function as a "congressional CIA": The Secret Committee, the Committee of Correspondence, and the Committee on Spies. The aptly named Secret Committee was the first of these, created on September 18th 1775.[10] It was essentially an espionage ring charged with obtaining military intelligence and engaging in covert operations against the British army and navy during the Revolution.[11] Its members engaged in treason against the British government. Among its members was Benjamin Franklin, who served as a spy during the war.[12]

> This Committee was given wide powers and large sums of money to obtain military supplies in secret, and was charged with distributing the supplies and selling gunpowder to privateers chartered by the Continental Congress. The Committee also took over and administered on a uniform basis the secret contracts for arms and gunpowder previously negotiated by certain members of the Congress without the formal sanction of that body. The Committee kept its transactions secret, and destroyed many of its records to assure the confidentiality of its work.
>
> The Secret Committee employed agents overseas, often in cooperation with the Committee of Secret Correspondence. It also gathered intelligence about Tory secret ammunition stores and arranged to steal them. The Secret Committee sent missions to plunder British supplies in the southern colonies. It arranged the purchase of military stores through intermediaries so as to conceal the fact that the Continental Congress was the true purchaser. The Secret Committee used foreign flags to protect its vessels from the British fleet.[13]

Benjamin Franklin didn't serve on just one intelligence committee. During the Revolutionary War, it would be apt to call his activities essential to running the CIA–like Secret Committee, as well as the

State Department–like Committee of Correspondence.[14] Early on, the Founding Fathers changed the Committee of Correspondence to the Committee of Secret Correspondence[15]—apparently they liked to keep something secret by calling it secret, notwithstanding Franklin's famous quip that three people can keep a secret only if two of them are dead!

Keeping with the tendency to hide the real purpose of intelligence work, the resolution to create the committee appointed it "for the sole purpose of corresponding with *our friends in Great Britain* and other parts of the world."[16] The Founding Fathers had a broad vision for their intelligence network: The Committee of Secret Correspondence "employed secret agents abroad, conducted covert operations, devised [and cracked] codes and ciphers, funded propaganda activities, authorized the opening of private mail, acquired foreign publications for use in analysis, established a courier system, and developed a maritime capability apart from that of the Navy."[17] One result of the committee's work was the securing of an alliance with France in 1778 through Ambassador Benjamin Franklin.[18]

John Adams, the president who advocated for and later signed into law the profoundly unconstitutional Alien and Sedition Acts in 1798,[19] was selected to sit on the Committee on Spies.[20] The committee was charged with "consider[ing] what is proper to be done with persons giving intelligence to the enemy, or supplying them with provisions."[21] Thomas Jefferson also sat on the committee.[22] In its final report, the committee concluded by borrowing definitions from English law,[23] punting the issue of how to punish traitors to state legislatures and meanwhile declaring that such persons are "guilty of treason against such colony."[24]

Thus, the foundation was laid for the establishment of a covert foreign intelligence and operations arm of the American government, a tradition of fair judicial process prior to punishing alleged traitors (through the example of Dr. Church), and a body of law which protects accused treasonous actors and respects their rights under definitions borrowed from the English.

The Treason Clause and the First Amendment

In the *Federalist* No. 43, James Madison described the inclusion of a Treason Clause as addressing a "peculiar danger" and a "great judgment."[25] What exactly was this danger?

In the Revolutionary era, the word *traitor* had a broad meaning. To contextualize it with modern examples, the term as used in the 1700s would apply not only to the traditional Benedict Arnold but also to the Pullman strikers in 1894[26] or to domestic terrorists today.[27] Those sorts of criminals, the Timothy McVeighs of the world, were the ones the Founding Fathers wanted to ensure would enjoy "additional procedural protections beyond . . . and preceding what the Fifth Amendment provides."[28] Imagine that today if a labor strike got a bit out of hand, the Justice Department's reaction would be to trounce union members' right to assemble in protest by arresting and charging them with treason—a capital offense! England was none too kind to traitors and did not afford those accused of the crime much protection.[29] Male traitors were hung, drawn, and quartered—a gruesome process involving dismemberment, castration, hanging, and disembowelment[30]—often on scant evidence for the crime of *imagining* the death of the king.

The Founding Fathers believed the harsh treatment of traitors as compared to other criminals resulted from the sentiments of the judge, jury, prosecutor, and lawmaker being distorted by the unique feeling of harm following an attack on the government, as Randolph Bourne described.[31]

The Founders felt compelled to make another advance in codifying the rights of even the most hated criminals: Spies and traitors.[32] Thus, they grafted into the Constitution a restrictive and exclusive definition of the crime of treason and enumerated protections for those within its ambit:

> Treason against the United States, shall consist only in levying War
> against them, or in adhering to their Enemies, giving them Aid and

Comfort. No Person shall be convicted of Treason unless on the Testimony of two Witnesses to the same overt Act, or on Confession in open Court.

The Congress shall have Power to declare the Punishment of Treason, but no Attainder of Treason shall work Corruption of Blood, or Forfeiture except during the Life of the Person attainted.[33]

The Treason Clause reflects the minimum bar of protecting individual liberty against encroachment of the state: It prevents the government from attacking a person's rights under the guise of crime against the state; it does not include an affirmative protection of the right to dissent and to protest in assembly.

In order to prevent the national security interests of the government from encroaching on the political interests of "factions,"[34] through lesser means than the noose or sword, the Founders later included an amendment to the Constitution. The First Amendment enlarged the protections of the Treason Clause's negative bar[35] by pronouncing that minority faction dissenters would be subject to "no [congressional] law . . . abridging the freedom of speech, or of the press; or the right of the people peaceably to assemble, and to petition the Government for a redress of grievances."[36]

Accordingly, between the Treason Clause and the First Amendment, the Founding Fathers rejected seven hundred years of English precedent and ensconced a bias in favor of the freedom to express dissenting opinion, in negative constitutional clothing, at the expense of the national security prerogatives of the government;[37] and they did so in express terminology that recognized the primacy of natural rights.

The Pompton Mutiny and the Whiskey Rebellion

As lofty as the Founders' words sound to us, they were flawed men. Several owned slaves while concurrently espousing ideals of natural rights and individual equality.[38] For our purpose, their most notable flaw was their proclivity toward violating their own laws affording protections to those who "betray" the United States. The best examples of this inclination to "[c]ry 'Havoc,' and let slip the dogs of war"[39] at the expense of individual liberty are the Whiskey Rebellion and the Alien and Sedition Acts of 1798.

However, our forebearers also showed an inclination to strive to be better, and to treat men with respect toward their natural liberties, complying with the Constitution. This section focuses on the Whiskey Rebellion and executing traitors, while the next addresses the abominable 1798 acts.

In 1791, during Washington's first term, western Pennsylvania farmers decided to resist by force the government's collection of an excise tax on whiskey.[40] The Militia Act of 1792 required that a federal judge certify that "combinations too powerful to be suppressed by the ordinary course of judicial proceedings" were preventing the government from enforcing the laws before the president could send out the militia to suppress any insurrection.[41] Supreme Court Justice James Wilson made that certification in a process similar to granting a warrant and effectively, by virtue of that declaration, the farmers were branded as traitors. Washington called up several Pennsylvania militia; it was "the first and only time a sitting American president led troops in the field."[42]

Earlier, when faced with mutineers from the New Jersey Continentals, Washington took a different route. Around ten years before the Whiskey Rebellion, on January 20th 1781, Washington was facing extreme circumstances at Valley Forge and "fear[ed] the total dissolution of the Army." A group of about two hundred New Jersey troops, following the example of their Pennsylvania neighbors who had mutinied earlier and resolved on favorable terms,[43] decided to stop following orders and marched toward Trenton.[44] Washington ordered General Howe to put down the rebellion with force.[45] Two men were executed as ringleaders.[46]

Thus, when George Washington was faced with mutiny under dire circumstances before he was president, he chose to exercise power under the authority of war, unequally ordering executions for two traitorous mutineers and negotiating in good faith with the Pennsylvania mutineers. At stake, of course, in New Jersey in 1781 and Pennsylvania in 1794, was the right to life. Would Washington respond differently to a revolt against authority when he was president, bound by a social compact that contained a Treason Clause?

In 1794 when the Whiskey Rebellion finally ended, facing an overwhelming force of 12,950 militiamen,[47] two men stood convicted of treason. However, this time, the rebellion ended "not with a bang but a whimper":[48] "A few men were arrested and brought back to Philadelphia for [civilian] trial[s in a Pennsylvania state court]; all were acquitted except two, and these were eventually pardoned,"[49] by Washington.[50]

Setting the example for future presidents, Washington permitted the rebels to be tried in, and freed by, state courts, and later exercised his *personal, presidential prerogative* of mercy toward those who brought their grievances against the government, even in the form of violence, by pardoning them.* Washington, despite overseeing many battles, still seemed to have the utmost reverence for due process and an individual's right to life.

The Alien and Sedition Acts of 1798

In the late 1790s, the federal government initiated its first statutory encroachment upon free speech and the First Amendment to the U.S. Constitution: The Alien and Sedition Acts of 1798.

History of the Acts: The XYZ Affair

Of all the foreign events that took place in the 1790s, none was as influential on the new government of the United States as the French Revolution.[51] After the French revolt—during which the king had been executed without trial—every major European power declared war on France in fear that its own respective monarchy would suffer

---

* It is interesting as well in terms of power precedents that Washington, the federal president, pardoned those convicted of state crimes adjudicated by state courts.

challenges to its authority and a similar grisly fate. Under the leadership of President Washington, the United States maintained a strict policy of unity at home and neutrality abroad.[52] In its refusal to support either the British or the French in the aftermath of the French Revolution, the United States incurred the hostility of both countries.[53]

The British navy began seizing American sea vessels, and France began declaring American ships to be pirates. Naturally, these acts of aggression brought the United States and Britain to the brink of war for the second time.[54] President Washington dispatched Chief Justice John Jay to London to negotiate an Anglo-American peace treaty in 1794.[55] France interpreted the treaty with Britain as a cancellation of the long-held alliance between the United States and France, thus fanning the flame between the two countries for years to come.[56]

In 1796, a bitter American presidential election transpired between John Adams and Thomas Jefferson. The two major parties of the time, the Federalists and the Democratic Republicans, were fiercely at odds with each other. Some Americans even darkly predicted "a civil war in which 'we shall divide' into Federalists and [Democratic] Republicans."[57] With a narrow lead of three electoral votes, John Adams and the Federalists defeated Thomas Jefferson and the Democratic Republicans to become the second President of the United States, and Jefferson became the vice president. Soon after his inauguration, Adams requested that Congress establish a provisional army and increase the size of the navy to protect American merchant ships abroad and to defend the nation against attack.[58]

Finally reaching the presidency after two terms as Vice President of the United States, Adams was eager to negotiate an agreement with France. He dispatched a delegation led by Secretary of State John Marshall, who later served as Chief Justice of the United States Supreme Court, to Paris.[59]

When the American emissaries arrived at the French capital, the final French revolutionary government, the Directory, was experiencing a financial crisis, resulting from the post-Revolution conflict and French military losses in Europe. Marshall viewed the French government with intrigue and considered the French both arrogant and decadent.[60]

The American envoys found themselves unable to meet French foreign ministry officials. Instead, Marshall and his colleagues were approached by three French intermediaries who informed Marshall that the French foreign minister would not meet with the Americans unless certain concessions were made: A low-interest loan to France from the United States, an assumption by the United States of all merchant claims against France, and a substantial bribe to the French foreign minister, the Marquis de Talleyrand.[61]

Marshall and the other American envoys were flabbergasted. They were neither prepared nor willing to make such concessions as they were doubtful that they would even be able to see the French foreign minister in the first place.[62]

It was a very good thing that the Americans did not succumb to the demands of the French because the situation quickly changed. With the number of French military victories in Europe increasing, the French changed the terms of the proposed agreement with Marshall. When the American envoys once again rejected the French offer, Talleyrand threatened to invade the United States. Word eventually reached Adams back in Washington, prompting a wave of patriotic fervor to sweep the nation and leading to a call for a formal declaration of war against France.[63]

The Republicans became suspicious of Adams and demanded to see copies of the correspondence between Adams and Marshall. Adams obliged. However, he replaced the names of the French intermediaries and Talleyrand with the letters W, X, Y, and Z.[64] Historians have referred to the events which almost led to the quasi war with France as the XYZ Affair.

As happened many times in American history, Congress was all too willing to have a knee-jerk reaction to the threat of war. To quote Randolph Bourne: "The citizen throws off his contempt and indifference to Government, identifies himself with its purposes, revives all his military memories and symbols, and the State once more walks, an august presence, through the imaginations of men."[65] Congress granted virtually every request made by Adams, including funds for the addition of warships, fortification of the nation's harbors, and the creation of the Department of the Navy.[66]

The relationship between political parties became even more adversarial following the crisis in Europe.[67] Republicans saw the possibility of war with France as "an extension of the American promise of liberty, republicanism, and democracy,"[68] while the Federalists saw it "as a menacing harbinger of disorder, licentiousness, and atheism; . . . a clear and present danger to the established order."[69] To Adams and the Federalists, immediate action was needed to prepare the nation for war, whatever the cost. Despite the unwavering call for a formal declaration of war, Adams adamantly declined to seek one. After dispatching a new set of emissaries to Paris, Adams was eventually able to negotiate peaceful terms between the United States and France with Napoleon, who in November 1799 overthrew the French Directory.[70]

The Three Alien and Sedition Acts

At this critical juncture, the Federalists observed and seized the opportunity to strike a major blow at the Republicans. The Federalist-controlled Congress enacted legislation manufactured to quash both dissenting opinion and their opponents, the Republican Party. They called their new law the Alien and Sedition Acts of 1798.[71] The legislation was composed of four acts: the Alien Enemies Act, the Alien Friends Act, the Sedition Act, and the Naturalization Act.[72]

The Alien Enemies Act[73] provided that, in the case of a declared war, citizens or subjects of an enemy nation residing in the United States could be detained, confined, or deported at the discretion of the president. The thinking behind this was that enemy aliens have an allegiance to a nation with which the United States was at war. Many Americans in the late 1790s held the belief that the nation was facing an internal danger from foreign-born immigrants.[74] Between 1790 and 1800, waves of immigrants came to America from countries like France, Ireland,

and Germany.[75] Moreover, the Federalists viewed these immigrants as a political base for the Republicans.[76] Unbelievably, this Act is still valid law today,[77] and the attitudes that supported it are still prevalent.

The second Alien Act to be made law by Congress was the Alien Friends Act.[78] Seen as an emergency measure that would expire on the final day of Adam's term of office, the Act imbued the president with the power to seize, detain, and deport *any* non-citizen he deemed a danger to the United States. Edward Livingston, a New York Democratic-Republican congressman observed: "[With] no indictments, no jury, no trial, no public procedure, no statement of the accusation, no examination of the witnesses in its support; no counsel for defence: all is darkness, silence, mystery and suspicion."[79]

These two legislative actions themselves were morally outrageous and directly contrary to the Natural Law and the Constitution. Not only did the Alien Friends Act violate the search and seizure provisions of the Fourth Amendment, it disregarded the innate principle that all persons, regardless of citizenship, are presumed innocent and retain personal freedoms until they are provided due process and proven guilty of a crime under the law. The Alien Friends Act placed entirely too much (unconstitutional) power in the hands of the president, ostensibly as a war power. With this power, the president was able to sidestep due process, the right to counsel, and judicial review all at once. Thankfully this law, unlike its companion piece, the Alien Enemies Act, is one for the history books and has expired.

The Sedition Act of 1798[80] went even further in eroding fundamental free speech rights, and the Act became the centerpiece legislation of the Federalist Congress. Throughout the rest of U.S. history, based on this precedent, the national wartime sedition–type acts would repeat as a principal instrument in repressing American liberty. Section 2 of the Act reads, in part, as follows:

> That if any person shall write, print, utter or publish . . . any false, scandalous and malicious writing or writings against the government of the

United States, or either house of the Congress of the United States, or the President of the United States, with intent to defame [them] . . . , or to bring them . . . into contempt or disrepute; or to excite against them . . . the hatred of the good people of the United States, . . . then such person . . . shall be punished by a fine not exceeding two thousand dollars, and by imprisonment not exceeding two years.[81]

Containing a sunset provision, the Act automatically expired at the end of Adams's term.[82] "The ability of the opposition press to attack the Alien and Sedition Acts was chilled by the prospect of prosecution under the Acts themselves."[83] Supporters of the Act justified the legislation as an emergency power that was necessary to save the country in light of the prospect of war.

However, the First Amendment was designed to protect against government abuse such as this. But it is not just the Constitution that directly states "no" such piece of legislation may be enacted, but also the Natural Law. Speech is one of the few abilities that human beings share across all creeds, faiths, races, and ethnicities. By nature, it connects us, it strengthens us, and it empowers us. Speech as affirmation or as dissent should be cherished and respected. No one, not even a government with the consent of all governed, has the right to restrict or alienate an individual's peaceful expression of speech, particularly government that expressly contracts that right in the social compact. Not surprisingly, these "emergency" national security laws proved to be entirely deceptive.

With the downfall of the Federalists nationally, Jefferson and the Democratic Republicans were able to win the presidency and a majority of congressional seats in the election of 1800. Congress repealed the Naturalization Act in 1802, and with the exception of the Alien Enemies Act, the other Acts were allowed to expire.[84] The Federalists' action flew in the face of the fundamental principle of free speech: "If all mankind minus one, were of one opinion, and only one person were of the contrary opinion, mankind would be no more justified in silencing that one person, than he, if he had the power, would be justified in silencing mankind."[*]

How could the same generation, in some instances, the same human beings who wrote, "Congress shall make no law . . . abridging the freedom of speech," enact a law that did just that?

Congressman Matthew Lyon

Imagine being fined an impossible amount of money or being silenced and thrown in jail just for expressing a political opinion. Next, imagine that there is no ability to declare bankruptcy, so you stay in jail until the fine is paid. Then imagine that you are a U.S. congressman, imprisoned under such a scheme for mocking the president. These thoughts are not just figments of imagination; they were reality in 1798.

In the course of the congressional debates on the passage of the Alien and Sedition Acts of 1798, several Republicans became widely recognized and despised by the Federalists.[85] One such Republican was Congressman Matthew Lyon of Vermont. In the October 1st 1798 issue of a magazine that he had established in Vermont, Lyon

---

[*]   John Stuart Mill, *On Liberty* (Boston: Ticknor and Fields, 1863), 35. Mill went on to describe the evils of suppressing that one opinion:

> Were an opinion a personal possession of no value except to the owner; if to be obstructed in the enjoyment of it were simply a private injury, it would make some difference whether the injury was inflicted only on a few persons or on many. But the peculiar evil of silencing the expression of an opinion is, that it is robbing the human race; posterity as well as the existing generation; those who dissent from the opinion, still more than those who hold it. If the opinion is right, they are deprived of the opportunity of exchanging error for truth: if wrong, they lose, what is almost as great a benefit, the clearer perception and livelier impression of truth, produced by its collision with error.
>
>   It is necessary to consider separately these two hypotheses, each of which has a distinct branch of the argument corresponding to it. We can never be sure that the opinion we are endeavoring to stifle is a false opinion; and if we were sure, stifling it would be an evil still.

Ibid., 35–36; see Geoffrey R. Stone, *Perilous Times: Free Speech in Wartime* (New York: W. W. Norton, 2004), 238, discussing the language in the 1940 case *Cantwell v. Connecticut*, which reflects a much more tolerant attitude.

proclaimed: "When the executive puts forth a proposition injurious to my constituents and the Constitution, I am bound by oath . . . to oppose it; if outvoted, it is my duty to acquiesce—I do so; But measures which I opposed [in Congress] as injurious and ruinous to the liberty and interest of this country . . . you cannot expect me to advocate at home."[86]

On October 5th 1798, a federal grand jury indicted Matthew Lyon for sedition.[87] The indictment officially charged Congressman Lyon with "malicious" intent "to bring the President and government of the United States into contempt" and that he had violated the Sedition Act both by accusing the Adams administration of fostering "ridiculous pomp, foolish adulation, and selfish avarice," and by quite thoroughly stating in his magazine that President Adams should go to a "mad house." After an hour of deliberation, the jury returned a guilty verdict. Stunned, Lyon expected a slap on the wrist and a modest fine. Instead, Justice Paterson of the Supreme Court,[88] serving as a circuit justice, imposed a sentence of four months in jail and a fine of one thousand dollars. The court also ordered that Lyon would stay in jail indefinitely past the four months if his fine were to remain unpaid.[89]

This is not the end of this melodramatic tale—what happened next is truly inspiring. Congressman Lyon launched a vigorous congressional reelection campaign. From inside his jail cell he championed his cause of natural rights and free speech with the U.S. Constitution as his platform.[90] Not only did Lyon win a stunning reelection victory, but several thousand Americans signed a petition asking President Adams to pardon him. The States of Virginia and Vermont competed to raise enough funds for the release of Lyon, eventually raising almost double the fine amount.[91]

The will of the American people had made itself known: Censorship and tyranny are not akin to the American way. When Lyon returned to Washington to take his seat in the House, the Federalists attempted to block him. However, they were unsuccessful in their bid, failing to reach a two-thirds majority.

The Kentucky and Virginia Resolutions of 1798; Nullification

Individuals in Congress were not the only ones who saw through the haze of quasi-war patriotism to the unconstitutional nature of the Alien and Sedition Acts. Kentucky and Virginia passed resolutions[92]—said to have been drafted by Thomas Jefferson and James Madison, respectively, and written incognito—which declared that the Alien and Sedition Acts were unconstitutional and unenforceable.[93]

While the Alien and Sedition Acts were the main cause for the authoring of the Kentucky and Virginia resolutions, the larger and more infamous constitutional issue which emerged, and to which we now turn, concerned federalism. More specifically, they turned to the notion that a state had the power to nullify federal law if it deemed the law inconsistent with the Constitution.[94] The resolutions present a visualization of an American governmental structure not as a unitary, all-powerful government but as a "league of sovereign states,"[95] that ceded some of their autonomy and power to the federal government via the Constitution, for the express stated purposes and only the express stated purposes set forth in the Constitution.

The resolutions present the correct interpretation that the Constitution is a contract made not between the people and the federal government but the states and the federal government. "Because the Constitution is a contract, [the resolutions argued], it is to be interpreted according to the 'intent' of the contracting parties."[96] The original intent of the contracting parties, the states, was the strict adherence by the federal government to the plain reading of the Constitution.

The states did not cede their sovereign power only to have the federal government later interpret how much power was actually given; rather, a finite and limited amount of autonomy was transferred. "Strict construction was justified by reference to the 'maxim of political law' that a sovereign can be deprived of any of its powers *only* by its express consent narrowly construed."[97] Out of the states the federal government was created: Original governmental authority not released to the federal government at the time of ratification remains with the states themselves.

Several other states rejected the open-ended claims of Kentucky and Virginia that a state could nullify federal law; however, the resolutions and the Republicans who authored them were "triumphantly vindicated" when, in the election of 1800, the Federalists were thrown out of office and the Republicans gained control of both Congress and the presidency.[98] With the influx of new elected officials, America saw an end to the destructive Alien and Sedition Acts (discussed *supra*). Although Madison later stated that he did not approve of the Nullification Doctrine, the Kentucky and Virginia resolutions were instrumental in South Carolina's decision to nullify federal law in 1832, which is widely seen as a catalyst for the War between the States.[99]

In large part, the doctrine of nullification follows logically from the idea of the consent of the governed. In his book *Nullification: How to Resist Federal Tyranny in the 21st Century*, the historian and economist Thomas E. Woods discussed the transfer of sovereignty from the people to the state governments and from the states to the federal government.[100] Woods effectively pointed out that in the American constitutional democracy, sovereignty ultimately rests with each person as an individual.[101] Thus, when the people formed political combinations as states, they carved out and transferred the ability to exercise sovereignty over those states, but retained ultimate custody of political powers. The states, by act of state legislature or convention, ratified and adopted the Constitution; the people did not do so as individuals. Therefore, when speaking of the Constitution, it is most appropriate to refer to it as an agreement among "we the states," not "we the people": "The states, rather than some [collective] single American people, created the federal Union" and were the parties to that contract.[102]

Nullification then seems to follow very logically: The people have and retain the sovereign power; the people delegate some of that sovereign power for use by the states to prevent domestic force or fraud in accord with state constitutions; the states enter a compact called the

Constitution for mutual protection against foreign force or fraud and to facilitate trade, and they delegate some of those powers to the federal government; the federal government acts in a manner inconsistent with the Constitution under the pretense of preventing force or fraud; the action taken by the federal government is null and void as it did not have the legal power to act in that manner, and the other party to the contract may declare it to be null. Woods also pointed out that the open defiance of federal marijuana laws, the REAL ID Act of 2005, and the federal time zones in several states are modern examples of states exercising nullification power.* The act of joining the Union was a simple act of the legislature of each of the fifty states. There is nothing in the history of those simple legislative acts to suggest that all states must conform to all acts of Congress—even those that are clearly *ultra vires.*** "All of us need to be reminded that the Federal Government did not create the States; the States created the Federal Government."[103] What they gave, they can correct or even take back by a simple legislative action.

---

* States have been regulating and legalizing marijuana in defiance of FDA and congressional edicts as well as passing resolutions nullifying or declaring noncompliance with the REAL ID Act. Thomas E. Woods, *Nullification: How to Resist Federal Tyranny in the 21st Century* (Washington, DC: Regnery Publishing, 2010), 7–9.

** "Beyond the powers."

4

The Civil War and Reconstruction Eras

*No one can believe that, in framing a government intended
to guard still more efficiently the rights and liberties
of the citizen, against executive encroachment and
oppression, they would have conferred on the president
a power which the history of England had proved to be
dangerous and oppressive in the hands of the crown;
and which the people of England had compelled it to
surrender, after a long and obstinate struggle on the
part of the English executive to usurp and retain it.*[*]

—Ex parte Merryman

---

[*] *Ex parte Merryman*, 17 F. Cas. 144, 150 (C.C.D. Md.) (Taney, Circuit Justice).

After the struggle for liberty known as the American Revolution, and the events leading up to the final political battle between the Federalists and Democrat-Republicans in which Thomas Jefferson defeated Aaron Burr and the outgoing Federalists in the presidential election in a House vote, the Era of Good Feelings and the Age of Jackson ensued. However, differences over the powers of the state with respect to the federal government and the stain of the immorality of ongoing slavery brought tensions between the Northern and Southern states of the Union. Despite several compromises, there was war in 1861 and a second struggle for liberty.

Habeas Corpus During the Civil War: *Ex parte Merryman* and Lincoln's Usurpation of Congressional Prerogative

There are some constitutional provisions that embody the quintessence of natural liberty itself. Habeas corpus, which draws its roots from ancient English common law, provides an efficient, fair, and natural safeguard of liberty. By granting a writ, courts can command the production of a confined person before a judge so as to assure the legitimacy of the government's forcible limitation on an individual's freedom. Habeas corpus is an essential ingredient to personal freedom and was expressly embodied in the Constitution, in the Founding Fathers' effort to create a competent, yet controlled government.[1] Long had the Framers endured the oppression of the king without due process and a fair judiciary—something they believed they made sure to provide all Americans when they made the bold step to declare independence.

The Framers invested considerable time debating the wording of the provision to be placed within their founding document. James Madison is reported to have drafted one version, which resembles what would later be the First Amendment: "The Legislature of the United States shall pass no law on the subject of religion; nor touching or abridging the liberty of the press; nor shall the privilege of the writ of Habeas Corpus ever be suspended, except in case of rebellion or invasion."[2] The Framers opted for a far more limited provision, not expressly enumerating a right to the writ of habeas corpus—the Drafters of the Constitution assumed that all persons already possess it by virtue of the Natural Law. Hence the document provides that "the Privilege of the Writ of Habeas Corpus shall not be suspended, unless when in Cases of Rebellion or Invasion, the public Safety may require it."[3] Because the clause is placed in Article I, the Suspension Clause gives Congress alone the power to suspend the privilege of habeas corpus. Strictly speaking in Natural Law and historical analysis, habeas corpus is not a privilege, but an inalienable right. If all mankind but one cannot morally silence the one, it cannot unlawfully incarcerate the one.

During the antebellum period, Congress never invoked its suspension power.[4] Yet on May 28th 1861, the clause came into the full focus of the Chief Justice of the Supreme Court, Roger Brooke Taney. Chief Justice Taney fervently proclaimed that President Abraham Lincoln had *purposely* and *illegally* violated the Constitution by suspending the right to habeas corpus along the military line between Washington, DC and Philadelphia.[5] Taney had issued a writ of habeas corpus for John Merryman to be delivered to the federal courthouse in Baltimore in order to determine the lawfulness of the government's detention of him.[6] Lincoln's response to the chief justice's writ of habeas corpus and what ensued afterward have captivated historians and legal scholars for the last one hundred fifty years.[7]

In 1861, after actual fighting initiated in the War between the States, President Lincoln called on the Northern states to supply an army for the Union. In an effort to reach Washington, troops that had been recruited from the Union states traveled to Washington via the port city of Baltimore, Maryland. This proved to be more precarious than convenient for the Union army. Pro-Confederate mobs ravaged the state roads, blockading the routes leading to the nation's capital. Fearing the loss of Maryland to the Confederacy, the president requested an official legal opinion from his attorney general on suspending habeas corpus. The

Maryland situation became dire, and the president issued an order to Gen. Winfield Scott, then the commander of the Union army, stating that if there was any resistance on the "military line," from Annapolis to Washington, *the officer in command was authorized to suspend habeas corpus* in order to gain control of the road. This order was not made public; rather, it was confined to executive secrecy.[8]

John Merryman, a pro-Confederate state militia lieutenant from Maryland, was accused of involvement in inciting several riots, cutting telegraph wires, and burning several bridges. Merryman was arrested by a federal military official, charged, among lesser offenses, with treason and being a commissioned officer in an organization intending hostility toward the government,[9] and detained indefinitely, without court appearance or any semblance of constitutionally mandated process. Merryman's attorney sought a writ of habeas corpus from the federal court in Baltimore.

When Chief Justice Taney, sitting as a circuit justice in Baltimore, issued a bold and commanding order to General Cadwalader to appear with John Merryman in the Baltimore federal courthouse within twenty-four hours, he could hardly have foreseen the constitutional shouting match that was about to transpire. Sending a colonel in his stead, the general politely refused the chief justice's order, citing President Lincoln's executive order suspending habeas corpus. Enraged, the chief justice replied, declaring the actions of the president illegal.[10] A writ of attachment* was issued for the general as well, and a U.S. Marshal went to enforce the order. The marshal was refused entry to the army base. Taney responded with a long and scathing opinion which he sent to major newspapers and to Lincoln himself.[11] The opinion soon garnered excited responses from across the nation.[12] Lincoln, revealing his antipathy for the Constitution, personal liberty, and the rule of law, rebuked the chief justice and refused

---

* A court order that provides a law enforcement official with the power and direction to seize property that is in the possession of a judgment debtor in order to satisfy the judgment held by the creditor. In this case the body of John Merryman.

to obey the order: "Are all the laws, *but one*, to go unexecuted, and the government itself go to pieces, lest that one be violated?"[13]

Merryman's case represents an egregious expansion of executive power. The judiciary entered into a fight with the executive, attempting to keep true to the Constitution. Lincoln did not believe that Chief Justice Taney's opinion controlled actions taken in pursuance of his role as commander in chief.

Lincoln viewed the suspension of the writ of habeas corpus as a *military* decision and thus immunized from judicial order.[14] From a constitutional perspective, President Lincoln could not be further from correct. As the president, Lincoln had neither right nor authority to suspend the writ. As commander in chief, he had the power to command the armed forces of the United States, but that had no bearing on an enumerated congressional power. "The power to issue the writ is given by law. It requires a law to change a law, and the president cannot make a law."[15] Congress did not authorize the president's actions when the military arrested and detained John Merryman; the president acted on fictional powers that his attorney general, Edward Bates, concocted.

Congress debated the legitimate suspension of the writ for a little more than two years.[16] However, this did not stop the president from issuing numerous proclamations essentially suspending the writ of habeas corpus across the entire nation through vesting his "authority" to do so in his military agents.[17] These illegal presidential proclamations resulted in the arrests of hundreds of individuals. "The arrests were made on suspicion. Prisoners were not told why they were seized. . . . [T]he purpose of the whole process was temporary military detention."[18]

In 1863, the Republican-controlled Congress mustered enough votes to pass an official suspension of the writ. Now this is truly ironic. Representing only two-thirds of the country, the Republican Party—the political force that was able to pass the Thirteenth, Fourteenth, and Fifteenth Amendments through Congress thereby abolishing slavery in the United States—was the same group that suspended one of the most ancient and natural rights possessed by humans.

Lincoln viewed this as validation, the ratification of two years of unconstitutional presidential conduct. Here again, Lincoln was wrong because it is never legal for a president to trample the natural rights of the people or to usurp the constitutional power of Congress. The president derives his executive powers from the Constitution and from no other source. Congress may have been wrong as well since it delegated its delegated powers to the subjective wishes of military officers not because invasion or rebellion required it, but to enable the arrest of troublemakers who had committed no crime.

We now know that Congress would not and did not sanction the president prior to 1863. The author of the suspension legislation, Sen. Jacob Collamer (R-VT), noted that the suspension was necessary to confirm that the president can lawfully exercise the power to "'secure' persons from 'the commission' of acts 'dangerous to the Government' in instances where they could not be charged criminally."[19]

It would seem as though a logical conclusion can be made that Congress was not enacting the suspension for well-thought-out rationale and necessity, but rather out of fear in wartime. Thankfully, there was some restraint on the part of Congress. In the second and third sections of the Act allowing for the suspension of habeas corpus, Congress placed certain limitations,[20] including the notification by cabinet officials of names to federal judges of individuals arrested during the suspension period and anyone under indictment for violating federal law who was entitled to bail before the suspension retained such entitlement.

Moreover, violations of these sections subjected the offending federal officers to a fine and/or imprisonment.[21] The restrictions indicate "Congress viewed suspension as a limited exception—justified by the dramatic nature of the times—to the requirement that the detention of persons within protection be effected through the ordinary criminal process."[22] The term *suspension* connotes that this ability of Congress is a finite power. The clause was never meant to provide federal officials a blank check for arbitrarily arresting and detaining individuals. It was meant as a last resort to be used only in the direst of circumstances. The

Founders possessed the foresight to write the Constitution in this manner, and Congress should adhere to this school of thought.

Presidential Military Commissions: *Ex parte Vallandigham* and *Ex parte Milligan*

The concept of military tribunals and commissions is not a modern one. During the War between the States, Lincoln divided the North into military districts for administrative reasons.[23] Commanding officers were permitted to arrest and detain anyone associated with opposition to the war, clearly unlawful arrests.[24] Concurrently, tribunals were convened to adjudicate individuals who committed crimes in areas where martial law had been declared and where habeas corpus had been suspended. Commissions are the offspring of an old and cruel military justice device, called the drumhead courts, which operated outside the typical court-martial structure.[25] Drumhead courts get their name from the use of a drumhead as a table instead of a judicial bench—the commanding officer sat behind the drumhead and passed summary judgment on his or enemy troops, typically for battlefield offenses committed moments before. American tradition dictated that such courts would not be used against civilians, but Lincoln had made his decision.

In an affair that would become the Supreme Court case *Ex parte Vallandigham*, Congressman Clement Vallandigham of Ohio asserted that President Lincoln had waged war "for the purpose of crushing out liberty and erecting a despotism" and "restrain[ing] the people of their liberties."[26] Gen. Ambrose Burnside had recently issued General Order No. 38 to the citizens of Ohio, a tyrannical repression of free speech that made "declaring sympathies" with the enemy an offense against the military Department of Ohio, punishable by exile to the Confederacy.[27] Lincoln believed that his commander in chief powers somehow included the power to write criminal laws.

General Burnside arrested Congressman Vallandigham on charges of "declaring disloyal . . . opinions" and giving voice to the Rebel Cause.[28]

Not unlike the case of Congressman Matthew Lyon, discussed in chapter 3, Vallandigham's claims were a scathing rant against the incumbent president.[29] Although reports have placed animosity between Lincoln and General Burnside,[30] the president defended his general's actions, proffering that Vallandigham's words were encouraging soldiers to desert the army.* The lower court judge, in denying Vallandigham a writ of habeas corpus, viewed the judicial branch as a "junior partner [in times of war], rather than a critical check on the executive."[31]

When the case reached the Supreme Court, the justices finessed the possibility of a ruling, but ultimately punted the case on standing issues.[32] The Court curiously found that military commissions were not covered by the 1789 Judiciary Act that grants the Court's habeas jurisdiction over inferior courts, nor were they a question of "law or equity within the meaning of [Article III of the Constitution]."[33] As a result of the Supreme Court's reluctance to arrest Lincoln's war machinery, Vallandigham, *a sitting U.S. congressman from Ohio*, was ultimately *shipped to the rebellious South* as punishment for his exercise of the freedom of speech.[34]

Contrarily, the Supreme Court in *Ex parte Milligan* held that the president had no authority to try civilians by military commission in areas where the civilian courts were still available to exercise their legitimate jurisdiction.[35]

Lambdin Milligan was arrested along with four other men for plotting to steal Union army weapons and invading a Union prisoner-of-war camp in Indiana. When their plan was discovered, the five men were taken into custody by military officials and were subsequently tried by a military tribunal. The tribunal returned a guilty verdict, and the men were sentenced to death by hanging. Milligan soon after appealed directly to the Supreme Court, requesting a writ of habeas corpus be issued. Along with issuing the writ, the Supreme Court was

---

* "Must I shoot a simpleminded soldier boy who deserts," Lincoln asked, "while I must not touch a hair of a wily agitator who induced him to desert?" Don E. Fehrenbacher, ed., *Lincoln: Speeches and Writings 1859–1865* (New York: Library of America, 1989), 460.

careful to articulate that during a suspension of the writ of habeas corpus, the government may only detain individuals, not try them in a court established by the president when there are civilian courts still in operation.

It is important to note that five of the justices went even further to expound on the issue. The justices held that even Congress itself did not wield the authority to circumvent the courts. Lincoln's administration rested its entire argument on the basis of a "constitutional necessity defense":[36] That in time of war, the need for national security outweighs and can miraculously trump civil liberties. In a truly ridiculous statement, Lincoln's attorney noted: "The officer executing martial law is at the same time supreme legislator, supreme judge, and supreme executive. As necessity makes his will the law, he only can define and declare it; and whether or not it is infringed, and of the extent of the infraction, he alone can judge."[37] Put in other terms, Lincoln's government proffered that "[a]ntiquated idealism had to give way to pragmatic realism."[38]

The extra-constitutional nature of these proclamations cannot be overstated. The president, through his attorney general,[39] was essentially advocating for dictator-like control of the government. Lincoln would have the Court declare the president a Caesar in times of war instead of having a federal government with checks and balances. Moreover, the Founders never would have approved of such a power grab, even in times of war. James Garfield, co-counsel for Milligan and future president, expounded, "[When] personal rights are merged in the will of the commander in chief, [what you have] is organized despotism. . . . [D]id not the 'first law of the Revolutionary Congress,' which was 'passed September 20th, 1776,' say that 'no officer or soldier should be kept in arrest more than eight days without being furnished with the written charges and specifications against' him?"[40]

In a split decision, the *Milligan* Court sided with liberty rather than security, broadly providing that the "Constitution of the United States is a law for rulers and people, equally in war and in peace, and covers with the shield of its protection all classes of men, at all times, and under all circumstances."[41] Justice David Davis, Lincoln's former law partner, campaign manager, and Supreme Court appointee, wrote for the majority, striking against his former political ally's policies after the exigencies of war no longer existed. Another Lincoln appointee, Chief Justice Salmon P. Chase, who had recently succeeded Chief Justice Taney, authored the concurring/dissenting opinion.

The case was decided after the Civil War ended and Lincoln was dead, and the Court's timing in issuing the ruling led many to believe that the case was irrelevant as it was now moot. Bryant Smith, reviewing a piece on *Milligan* for the *Texas Law Review* in 1930, is quoted as stating: "On neither point is the case of any great importance, partly because of the improbable recurrence of conditions in which the government might be inclined to resort to such power, and partly because if the case had come before the Court while the war was yet still in progress, the decision might very well have been the other way."[42]

Smith's comments have proven inexorably wrong. Seventy years after his erroneous commentary and 135 years after *Milligan*, the Bush and Obama administrations' use of military commissions and the Supreme Court decisions that have followed are, for the most part, far more faithful to Taney in *Merryman* and Davis in *Milligan* than to Lincoln. Lincoln's successors, however, fully embraced and expanded upon his set of executive precedents.

These cases, *Vallandigham* and *Milligan*, represent a battle between the various branches of government. The president is seizing power from the other two branches of the federal government: From Congress in declaring a suspension of the writ of habeas corpus and from the judiciary in creating military commissions when civilian courts were still in operation. The timing of these decisions is also telling. The Court waited until the Civil War ended and Lincoln was dead before it issued the decision in *Ex parte Milligan*, avoiding a wartime battle between the executive and judicial branches.[43] Chief Justice William Rehnquist, writing in a general audience book and not from the bench, noted that peacetime "offers an opportunity for detached reflection on these important questions which are not so calmly discussed in the midst of a war."[44]

Can the president abrogate constitutional protections in the name of necessity in wartime? We see that he has done so only when the other branches of the federal government fail to realize their constitutional obligations. The purpose of the Constitution was to prevent this despotic, king-like behavior on the part of any president, no matter his goal. Necessity can never be a constitutional justification to assume extra-constitutional power—either the government has the constitutional authorization to do something, or it does not.

Ex parte McCardle

After Lincoln's assassination, Congress moved the country toward radical Reconstruction, dividing the South into military districts through the Reconstruction Acts. These districts were governed by the military. President Andrew Johnson had vetoed the legislative measures, but Congress overrode him. There was, however, one case in the Supreme Court pipeline that could overturn the oppressive Reconstruction Acts: Ex parte McCardle.[45]

William McCardle was a Confederate soldier. After the war, he was the editor of a newspaper that published several articles "alleged to be incendiary and libellous [sic]" by the military authorities occupying his district.[46] He "was not in the military service of the United States, but was held in custody by military authority for trial before a military commission" pursuant to the aforementioned Acts of Congress.[47]

Because Congress was afraid that the Court would overturn the Reconstruction Acts, it engaged in a practice called jurisdiction stripping. Congress controls the appellate jurisdiction of the Supreme Court, per Article III of the Constitution: "[T]he supreme Court shall have appellate Jurisdiction, both as to Law and Fact, with such Exceptions, and under such Regulations as the Congress shall make."[48] Thus, in March 1868, while the McCardle case was under consideration, Congress passed an act which took away the Supreme Court's power to hear habeas corpus petition appeals from the inferior courts.

The Supreme Court responded by taking a middle-of-the-road and politically shrewd approach. Writing for the majority, Chief Justice Salmon P. Chase held, "It is quite clear . . . that this court cannot proceed to pronounce judgment in this case, for it has no longer jurisdiction of the appeal."[49] However, it rejected the government's stance that this stripped *all* habeas jurisdiction from the Court: "Counsel . . . supposed, if effect be given to the repealing act in question, that the whole appellate power of the court, in cases of habeas corpus, is denied. But this is an error. The act of 1868 does not except from that jurisdiction any cases but appeals . . . under the act of 1867. It does not affect the jurisdiction which was previously exercised."[50] The Court held that Congress had closed off appeals only by those denied habeas corpus relief, not all appeals. This jurisdiction-stripping issue would become relevant in the Global War on Terror a century and a half later.

The Posse Comitatus Act of 1878

The Posse Comitatus Act (PCA) was enacted in 1878 to prevent the U.S. military from policing the Southern Military Districts after the Civil War.* With the defeat of the Confederacy in 1865, the use of the military as a police force in the South became common practice.[51] Not unlike the British government one hundred years earlier that housed its troops in the homes of American colonists, the federal government quartered troops in the homes still standing in the Southern states during the Reconstruction era. In a heated national election, the presidency was

---

* 18 U.S.C. §1385 (2012). "The phrase 'posse comitatus' is literally translated from Latin as the 'power of the county' and is defined at common law to refer to all those over the age of 15 upon whom a sheriff could call for assistance in preventing any type of civil disorder." United States v. Hartley, 796 F.2d 112, 115 (5th Cir. 1986) (citations omitted). The phrase is a poor translation, and it is supposed to mean "force of the country," as in prohibiting the formation of a posse that is the "force of the country."

determined by Congress in a deal that awarded the office to Rutherford B. Hayes of Ohio. In return for the southern electoral support, congressional Republicans removed the military occupation of the South, officially ending the Reconstruction era.[52]

The PCA regulates and generally proscribes the participation of military personnel in domestic civilian law enforcement on U.S. soil. "The legislative history of the act leaves little doubt that the statute is indeed meant 'to preclude the Army [or now in modern times, the Navy, Marines, and Air Force as well] from assisting local law enforcement officers in carrying out their duties.'"[53] Moreover, "the statute is not an anachronistic relic of an historical period the experience of which is irrelevant to the present. It is not improper to regard it, as it is said to have been regarded in 1878 by the Democrats who sponsored it, as expressing 'the inherited antipathy of the American to the use of troops for civil purposes.'"[54]

In its original form, the Act read:

> From and after the passage of this act it shall not be lawful to employ any part of the Army of the United States, as a posse comitatus, or otherwise, for the purpose of executing the laws, except in such cases and under such circumstances as such employment of said force may be expressly authorized by the Constitution or by act of Congress; and no money appropriated by this act shall be used to pay any of the expenses incurred in the employment of any troops in violation of this section and any person willfully violating the provisions of this section shall be deemed guilty of a misdemeanor and on conviction thereof shall be punished by fine not exceeding ten thousand dollars or imprisonment not exceeding two years or by both such fine and imprisonment.[55]

The PCA "reflects a strong American tradition against the use of military that stretches back before the founding of the nation."[56] The Founders were all too familiar with the routine military involvement of civil affairs under the British monarchy.[57] The Act embodies the principle of a limited role of the military in American life and also the subordination of the military to civilian authority. The federal government is a civilian system, not a military regime; the Constitution provides a framework that allows for the people's elected representatives, not the military, to govern.

To those who would be victimized by the military domestically, the PCA represents the legacy of those who were struggling with liberty. The government could not use its vast and powerful instruments of state warfare against domestic criminals without either a constitutional reason or an accountable Congress. The government could not use the weapons reserved for other powerful and awesome foes against its own people without constitutionally based necessity.

More broadly, it showed a rejection of this military scheme being applied to what are, at their core, law enforcement concerns. Military justice and civilian justice are in many ways different and inapposite, and the application of one to the other threatens recognized liberties. The law has proscribed the government from using the military to stop marijuana smokers and kidnappers, but left it leeway to end open defiance of constitutional and natural order or prevent a foreign state from imposing a similar order.

Part 2

THE NOBLE LIARS

1900–46

5

Turn-of-the-Century America

The Wilson Administration and World War I

War is the health of the State. It automatically sets in motion throughout society those irresistible forces for uniformity, for passionate cooperation with the Government in coercing into obedience the minority groups and individuals which lack the larger herd sense. The machinery of government sets and enforces the drastic penalties; the minorities are either intimidated into silence, or brought slowly around by a subtle process of persuasion which may seem to them really to be converting them.[*]

—Randolph Bourne

* Randolph Bourne, "The State," AntiWar.com, http://www.antiwar.com/bourne.php.

In 1917, the United States was heading into the Great War. President Woodrow Wilson's message to the American people had drastically changed from "[H]e kept us out of the war!" to "Beat back the Hun!"[1] Wilson was itching for and America was inching toward one of the bloodiest, most damaging, morally purposeless state conflicts in world history. In *The Republic*, Plato theorized that members of the Guardian, or ruling class, mirroring the example of the gods, could employ "useful," "noble" lies to trick the masses into following their rule, noting that if certain "falsehoods" were told to the people, it would help by making them "care more for the [state] and each other."[2]

World War I served as a pretext for some of the most significant and unpalatable violations of the Constitution by presidents in the history of the country: It was Wilson's noble lie. Most notably, during the turn of the century and through the end of World War I to the First Red Scare, Congress passed a series of laws that eviscerated the right to political expression and hence personal liberty, stopping just short of actually excising the Bill of Rights from the Constitution. These were the first espionage statutes.[3]

The Advent of State Secrecy Statutes: The Defense Secrets Act of 1911

Prior to 1911, the U.S. government didn't codify many national security laws.[4] This began to change in 1909 when Congress enacted two provisions of law, which made giving intelligence to the enemy treasonable, proscribed the unlawful entry onto military bases, and prohibited the theft of government property or records.[5] These provisions were, in some sense, the first state secret, or espionage, statutes created, but they were of "general applicability,"[6] not specifically applicable to spilling the national-secret beans, so to speak.

In 1911, during the Taft administration, Congress took its "first attempt . . . to protect military information [with comprehensive proscriptions]."[7] The final product that Congress put together was the

Defense Secrets Act of 1911[8] which, despite trying to clear up the opaque 1909 statutes, ended up being a vague, barely workable document, lacking an intent requirement or enumeration of to whom information may not be communicated:

> This inartful language [of the 1911 statute] . . . [was] carried over to the present [Espionage Act of 1917], which present[s] the most difficult problems of interpretation of any of the espionage statutes. The 1911 statute provided a more severe penalty for communication, regardless of intent, of illegally obtained information to a foreign government. . . .
>
> [N]othing in the lackadaisical debates which led to it reflected an awareness that publication of defense information might pose a problem for national security.[9]

Despite Congress's "lackadaisical"[10] approach to national security at the time, it would not make the same mistake in 1917 when it chose to face the German, Austro-Hungarian, and Ottoman armies.

The Espionage Act of 1917

The Espionage Act of 1917[11] was introduced to Congress in June of that year, following Woodrow Wilson's April 2nd 1917 request for a congressional declaration of war and Congress's April 6th acquiescence. Congress, however, was not as obliging when it came to expanding the president's powers; "[h]eated debate [over the Act] stretched over two frenetic sessions. . . . Concern about enemy spying, triggered by American entry into World War I, accounted for some of the increased consideration, but most of the significant debate was not provoked by worry over espionage in the usual sense."[12]

When the bill was first introduced into the House, Congress took major issue with three of Wilson's proposals. First, was the so-called press censorship provision:[13] ". . . [T]he Wilson Administration proposed [either] to censor, or punish after the fact, (exactly which was never resolved) publication of defense information in violation of Presidential regulations. The desirability of such a measure was seen by its adherents to derive from the obvious harm that would befall military interests when untimely publications fell into enemy hands. Proponents of the measure pointed to the Civil War experience when the Union cause had been jeopardized by newspaper retailing of military plans."[14]

Obviously, there was vehement disagreement over this provision. Rep. Edwin Webb (D-NC) argued in committee that "the press should be willing to give up its right to publish what the president 'thinks would be hurtful to the United States and helpful to the enemy,'"[15] adding "'[U.S. citizens are in] one of those situations where we have to trust somebody.'"[16] He was met with substantial opposition, and that provision failed the House by forty votes.[17]

Interestingly, in the Judiciary Committee, Rep. Andrew Volstead (R-MN), the future author of the 1919 act that would criminalize the sale of alcohol in the United States, supported the press provisions.[18] The word *publish* appeared only once in the final form of the bill, proscribing the publication of military information with intent to communicate it to the enemy, which incurs a penalty of up to thirty years in prison and a fine.[19]

Another offensive provision that more focuses on an individual's right to political expression was the "disaffection" provision, which was described as "even more troublesome than the Sedition Act of 1798."[20]

The provision stated that "whoever, when the United States is at war, shall wilfully . . . cause or attempt to cause disaffection in the military or naval forces of the United States . . . shall be punished by . . . imprisonment for not more than twenty years."[21] The inclusion of the incredibly broad term *disaffection*, literally "to alienate the affection or loyalty of . . . to fill with discontent and unrest,"[22] unsurprisingly caused much dismay to many members of Congress. The same Representative Webb who lauded suppression of a free press, for example, defended the natural liberties of U.S. citizens when he argued that it would criminalize writing to a soldier to "'tell him the sad conditions back home.'"[23] In final form, Section 3 of the Act provides:

[1] Whoever, when the United States is at war, shall wilfully make or convey false reports or false statements with intent to interfere with the operation or success of the military or naval forces of the United States or to promote the success of its enemies [2] and whoever when the United States is at war, shall wilfully cause or attempt *to cause insubordination, disloyalty, mutiny, refusal of duty,* in the military or naval forces of the United States, or shall wilfully obstruct the recruiting or enlistment service of the United States, to the injury of the service or of the United States, shall be punished by a fine of not more than $10,000 or imprisonment for not more than twenty years, or both.[24]

The breadth of the disaffection provision, which restricts even private and whispered conversations, was at least abrogated by the Webb Amendment to a more specific class of speech, but still runs sweepingly afoul of the First Amendment's protections. This section provided the basis for criminal prosecutions under the statute for "disloyal utterances" or attempting to interfere with recruitment or enlistment—speech completely protected by the First Amendment's command that "Congress shall make no law . . . *abridging* the freedom of speech,"[25] let alone *criminalizing* it.

A final constitutionally abhorrent provision of the Act was the non-mailability provision.[26] As first introduced, this provision granted the postmaster general—at the time a position traditionally held by a political patronage appointee of the president[27]—the broad power to obstruct the delivery of mail which he believed was treasonous or anarchist in character.[28] The postmaster general would have the power to decide who got what private letter or publication, *at his sole discretion,* due to its "disloyal" content. Congressmen—senators and representatives alike—were displeased with the sweeping legislation, which invaded the political privacy of individuals and stampeded over the right to private association.[29]

Some went as far as to call it "oppressive," a "menace to freedom," and "a far greater evil than the evil which is sought to be prevented."[30] In the end, the language was narrowed to permit the postmaster to carry out this task,[31] but Congress essentially bent to the president's will on the matter. This was not the first time Congress faced a nonmailability statute. In 1835, Congress rejected President Andrew Jackson's attempt to get similar legislation approved.[32]

Despite clear congressional intent to limit Wilson's attempts to rob individuals of their rights under the guise of war necessity, Wilson would later find creative legislative interpretations to assist in his systematic assault on civil liberties.

The Sedition Act of 1918

The Sedition Act of 1918[33] represents one of the most constitutionally repugnant excuses for a law that Congress has ever enacted. With this Act, however, the blame shifts to Congress. When the Wilson Justice Department first proposed what would become the Sedition Act of 1918, it sought to amend the Espionage Act "narrow[ly]"; the "Senate Judiciary Committee, however, took it upon itself to go far beyond [the Justice Department's] recommendations, resulting in [some of] the most repressive legislation in American history."[34]

Montana's Democratic Senators Henry Myers and Thomas Walsh introduced broad amendments to the original proposal modifying the Espionage Act which, when finally enacted, read:

> Whoever, when the United States is at war, shall willfully utter, print, write or publish any disloyal, profane, scurrilous, or abusive language about the form of government of the United States or the Constitution of the United States, or the military or naval forces of the United States, or the flag of the United States, or the uniform of the Army or Navy of the United States into contempt, scorn, contumely, or disrepute, or shall willfully utter, print, write, or publish any language intended to

incite, provoke, or encourage resistance to the United States, or to promote the cause of its enemies, or shall willfully display the flag of any
foreign enemy, or shall willfully by utterance, writing, printing, publication, or language spoken, urge, incite, or advocate any curtailment of
production in this country of any thing or things, product or products,
necessary or essential to the prosecution of the war in which the United
States may be engaged, with intent by such curtailment to cripple or
hinder the United States in the prosecution of war, and whoever shall
willfully advocate, teach, defend, or suggest the doing of any of the acts
or things in this section enumerated, and whoever shall by word or act
support or favor the cause of any country with which the United States
is at war or by word or act oppose the cause of the United States therein,
shall be punished by a fine of not more than $10,000 or the imprison-
ment for not more than twenty years, or both.[35]

The Justice Department and many senators claimed that this
amendment was needed to protect dissenters from crowds who would
riot upon hearing disloyal statements.[36] Think about that for a second:
Instead of protecting the minority's right to put forth speech that may be
offensive to the listener, the government arrested individuals for *speaking* under the guise of "protect[ing]" the speaker from mob violence
by criminalizing the spoken words. This is the sort of warped thinking that results from the wartime herd mentality Bourne decried in his
composition "The State," which is discussed throughout this book, but
was published in 1918.[37]

Some senators fought against the approval of the Sedition Act. Sen.
James K. Vardaman (D-MS) asserted that this Act represented "a lack of
confidence in the intelligence and patriotism of the American people."[38]
Opponents of the 1918 Act compared it to the Sedition Act of 1798; one
opponent, Sen. James A. Reed (D-MO), argued that the 1918 Act went
beyond the 1798 Act because it lacked elements of "falsity and malice."[39]
Theodore Roosevelt, a former president at the time, showed an unchar-
acteristic adherence to the constitutional principles he once swore to

uphold but spent his presidency assaulting* and declaimed the 1918 Act as making it "a crime to tell the truth" and labeling those who proposed it as "foolish or traitorous."[40] Characteristically, however, he showed considerable bravado and challenged Wilson, saying he would "give the government the opportunity to test its constitutionality."[41]

Opponents, rallying around Sen. Joseph I. France (R-MD), introduced an amendment, the France Amendment, which would import a canon of construction into the Act: That it not be "construed as limiting the liberty . . . of any individual to publish or speak what is true, with good motives and for justifiable ends."[42] Debate in the Senate became heated, with one senator declaring the Act a "war upon the American people," and another claiming that those who would see the France Amendment become part of the bill "throw a cloak of protection around every spy in this country."[43]

The comparison to a war against the American people is not, however, that inapt. In addition to having the actual army, the president has a veritable army of lawyers in the Department of Justice to assist in carrying out the laws. The France Amendment failed, and the Act passed the Senate 48–26 and the House 293–1.[44] The lone dissenter in the House, Rep. Meyer London of New York, a Socialist Party member, dissented because of the rejection of the France Amendment and the implicit rejection of the right to speak the *truth*.

Between the original 1917 Espionage Act and the 1918 amendments known as the Sedition Act, the freedom of the press, the right to dissent, the right to *speak* "disloyal utterances," the right to political expression, and the freedom from cruel and unusual punishments (such as twenty years in federal custody for publicly or *privately* disagreeing with the president) had been excised from the Constitution and replaced with statutes levying decades-long prison sentences upon those who whispered against Wilson's War. There is no question that these Acts laid the groundwork for an unconstitutional and unprecedented—even by the standards of the

---

* Andrew P. Napolitano, *Theodore and Woodrow: How Two American Presidents Destroyed Constitutional Freedom* (Nashville: Thomas Nelson, 2012).

1798 Acts—expansion of executive power at the expense of personal liberty. Later, the reader will find the deplorable application of these statutes to Wilson's political enemies and to minority, dissenting opinions.

Property and Economic Rights: The Declaration of War, the Overman Act of 1918, and the War Boards

In declaring war, Congress expressly declared that the "President . . . is hereby, authorized and directed to employ the entire . . . military forces of the United States and the resources of the Government to carry on war against the Imperial German Government; . . . *all of the resources of the country are hereby pledged by the Congress of the United States.*"[45] This language is ambiguous as to whether it refers only to the property of the federal government or that of property owners in the entire country, including private property.

This ambiguity, as to whether this is the largest violation of the Fifth Amendment Takings Clause in history or a reallocation of public resources, shows a callous disregard by Congress for the need for restrictive language in respecting property and economic rights of all individuals. While Supreme Court precedent at the time was highly respectful of economic rights, discussed below, Congress and President Wilson showed complete disregard for that jurisprudence. Precise draftsmanship of legislation is especially needed in times of hysteria.

The reach of President Wilson's Justice Department wasn't the only arm of presidential power expanded in 1918. Sen. Lee Overman (D-NC) introduced what he called the Departmental Reorganization Act.[46] The Overman Act permitted the president to take command of the entire federal bureaucracy

> . . . for the national security and defense, for the successful prosecution
> of the war, for the support and maintenance of the Army and Navy,
> for the better utilization of resources and industries. . . . The President
> is hereby authorized to make such redistribution of functions among

executive [and administrative] agencies as he may deem necessary, including any functions, duties, and powers hitherto by law conferred upon any executive department, commission, bureau, agency, office, or officer, in such manner as in his judgment shall seem best fitted to carry out the purposes of this Act.[47]

The Act also gave the president broad discretion in reporting to Congress unilateral executive actions taken in carrying it out.[48] Pursuant to the Overman Act, Wilson created three entities: The National War Labor Board, the War Industries Board, and the Committee on Public Information. Together, these three entities commanded the economy, labor relations, and public information.

Notably, during this period and until 1937, the Supreme Court insisted on robust protection for economic liberties. In *Lochner v. United States* in 1905, the Supreme Court had held that the "general right to make a contract in relation to [a] business is part of the liberty of the individual protected by the Fourteenth Amendment to the Federal Constitution. Under that provision, no State can deprive any person of life, liberty, or property" via legislation or fiat, but only via due process—notice, jury trial, and the right to appeal.[49] Further, the "right to purchase or to sell labor is part of the liberty protected by this amendment."[50]

Thus, when one examines Wilson's iron-fisted control of wages, prices, and production, *infra*, it is important to remember that while these controls may seem anathema and Sovietesque today, these were particularly condemnable in the early twentieth century, when the Constitution was said to protect, as Locke described, the natural right to profit from one's labor. The *Lochner* Court even referenced this point, viewing every law that interferes with economic rights as an "unconstitutional . . . illegal interference with the liberty of the individual in adopting and pursuing such calling as he may choose."[51] Thus, not only did New York's legislation regulating the hours that bakers may work in *Lochner* run squarely into the Fourteenth Amendment, but so also would similar legislation at the federal level collide with its companion provision in the Fifth Amendment, guaranteeing due process of law against encroachment on natural liberty. Further, price and wage regulations are hardly innocuous: They represent the value of a person's labor. As we recall, the right to profit from one's labor in contract comes directly from the right to self-ownership. Removing one's ability to contract his labor or resources alienates that person from his personhood by abrogating his self-ownership rights, be it a hardworking laborer or a risk-taking factory owner.

The National War Labor Board (NWLB), rather than the Supreme Court, was essentially "the court of last resort in all labor disputes for the entire country."[52] In order for the NWLB to be more palatable to the American citizenry, it was proffered to operate as a mediator; "[n]evertheless, in practice it was only necessary to invoke the aid of the President, or that of the other departments or war controls of government, to secure the most drastic powers."[53] The NWLB's membership consisted of five representatives from labor, five from industry, and two public members, one of whom was expected to be pro-business. Initially, they were William Howard Taft, the former president and future chief justice, and the prolabor member, Frank P. Walsh; however, "[m]ore often than not, Taft joined with Walsh and the labor members to override the objections of the industry representatives."[54]

The NWLB's political nature and autocratic style led to several instances of employer *and* employee resistance to rulings:

> In the Smith and Wesson case the refusal of the employer to abide by the board's finding ended by a prompt commandeering of the plant by the government. Similarly, when the Bridgeport strikers refused to obey the board the President ordered them back to work under pain of deprivation of employment through the Federal Employment Bureau. They obeyed.
>
> . . . Before the armistice there had been only two instances of actual refusal to abide by the decision of the board. The drastic settlement of those cases by the President had brought all parties into line.

After the armistice, however, many employers who objected to the board's decrees in their cases asserted that the board was created only for the duration of the war and that the armistice had ended the board and the force of its decisions. They proceeded to defy the board with varying degrees of openness.[55]

In the Smith and Wesson case, the NWLB essentially overrode a 1917 Supreme Court case about the right to contract with employees because it was "contrary to the principles of the National War Labor Board," thereby invalidating employment contracts that required a promise not to join a union—"even if [they] were lawful when made."[56] When the employer refused to abide by the NWLB decision that it never consented to abide by, the president commandeered the plant.[57]

In the Bridgeport case, strikers refused to break up when they learned that they would not be entitled to advantageous employee classifications under the NWLB ruling, which, based on government misrepresentations, they believed they were entitled to. Wilson responded thusly to the strike, "[I]t is my duty to use means [like those used at Smith and Wesson] equally well adapted to the end with lawless and faithless employees."[58] He threatened to bar them from employment in wartime industries and, by virtue of their unemployed status, reenter them into the draft pool—a daunting prospect.[59]

To add a last bit of despotism, the NWLB "required all employers and workers who sought the assistance of the NWLB to renounce strikes and lockouts for the duration of the war."[60] Therefore, the NWLB abrogated not only the freedom of speech and freedom to contract, but also the freedom of association and the right to bargain collectively.

The War Industries Board more directly interfered with economic liberties. Established by the president's National Defense Council in 1917 and working through its own bureaucracy created on May 28th 1917, the board literally existed to "fix prices" in U.S. industries.[61] Even Congress was uncomfortable with the president's exercise of power via the War Industries Board.[62] Previously, the reader saw the observation that the declaration of war passed by Congress may have laid the groundwork for the largest takings of private property for public use without just compensation in American history.[63] This observation is more apt in light of the War Industries Board's activities. The best-documented example of this sort of unconstitutional administrative seizure is the Wool Division Controversy.

The War Industries Board created a subsector called the Wool Division to control the wool industry.[64] The division soon issued regulations stating, "The necessities of the Government at this time are such as to require the use of all existing agencies for concentrating the wool near the centers of consumption. Therefore, *all the wool of the 1918 clip must be distributed through approved dealers in approved centers of distribution.*"[65] In order to comply with this regulation, there was a complicated contracting scheme:

> It was foreseen that the shortage of supply relative to the extraordinary demands of the war would cause the price of wool to rise in 1918 to exorbitant heights and that the Government would be required of necessity to pay such high prices, unless means were devised to prevent this rise. Although the Government could doubtless have appropriated wool for war purposes, the constitutional requirement that it must pay just compensation for what it takes is one which war does not suspend. By the ingenious plan of the Wool Division constitutional and attendant practical difficulties were avoided. In order to obtain a permit to act as an "approved" dealer . . . dealers signed an agreement to comply with the regulations of the Wool Division, the effect of which was to direct all wool to the Government at a price set in advance by the Government and agreed to by the dealer, rather than to direct wool to the Government at a price to be judicially determined.[66]

The constitutionally protected freedom to contract is supposed to be safeguarded by the government from force or fraud, even—especially—from the government. In this era, the freedom to contract was even more strongly reinforced by the *Lochner* line of cases. However, the Wilson administration's War Industries Board set the prices and compelled those engaging in the sale of any wool in the United States to comply with regulations that set the prices. The government itself engaged in both force and fraud through this appropriation scheme.

Defending from a charge equivalent to unjust enrichment after the war in 1929, some dealers claimed that because they were "already wool merchants [in the years preceding the war] . . . [they] had the right to deal in wool unrestrained by the [price-fixing] regulations."[67] Essentially, these defendants were claiming that they had the natural right to sell the product of their labor at the price a willing buyer would voluntarily pay. The Seventh Circuit Court of Appeals rejected that argument:

> Although defendants were wool merchants, they could not have handled wool in 1918 without the consent of the government, because the government had appropriated all wool for its own purposes and had the undoubted right to say by whom, as its agents, wool should be acquired from the growers, or other owners. The War Industries Board, and all of its subdivisions, were merely agents, speaking for the President, and so far as the regulations are involved, they are to be considered as his acts. In addition to his constitutional powers, the President had the broad powers hereinabove shown, vested in him by congressional action. . . .
>
> The defendants commenced and continued to act as government agents in exact accordance with the regulations [by signing the contract to obtain a license], and were paid by and received from the government and the manufacturers, to whom wool was allocated by the government, the prices and the commissions that were not provided for in any other way than in the regulations. Although the defendants were, in a sense, buyers and sellers of wool, yet they were

only such, in 1918, as agents for the government, acting for a commission paid by the government. The government had the right, in those extraordinary times, to protect sellers of wool, by providing that out of all of the transactions the government's agents should not have more than the specified profit, and that whatever those agents gained in addition thereto should be disposed of as the government might decide. We are of opinion that defendants are bound by the contract alleged.[68]

The court here used circular reasoning to justify the unconstitutional and unrightful taking of wool: Because the wool owners had signed contracts to abide by regulations that made them agents of the government, they could not negotiate the price of sale because that was fixed by the other party of the contract—the government—at its sole discretion. In law, such contracts are said to lack mutuality: That is, they are not enforceable by the court because the terms of the contract show that the exchange of goods or services was not bargained for, but on terms essentially dictated by one party.[69] It protects individuals who do not have a fair bargaining position, such as yeoman shepherds against the president of the United States. However, in this instance, the court denied that five-hundred-year-old defense.

Clearly, the actions of the NWLB and the War Industries Board were large violations of economic rights—such as the right to contract and negotiate the value of the product of mixing one's labor and one's property—in disregard for Supreme Court precedent.

Wilson's Domestic War on Americans: The Return of Political Suppression in the United States— Sponsored by the Supreme Court and Congress

If one wanted to find a point before 1917 where anyone in America could be charged with "conspiracy to publish disloyal material intended to . . . cause contempt for the government of the United States" and receive a multiyear prison sentence for it, one needed to look all the way back to the era of the Alien and Sedition Acts.* But President Woodrow Wilson, like President John Adams before him, was not a man who happily endured criticism[70] and not a man who would permit a piece of parchment to stop him from using governmental power to silence political opposition. H. L. Mencken lamented, "Between Wilson and his brigades of [government] informers, spies, volunteers, detectives, perjurers, and complaisant judges . . . the liberty of the citizens has pretty well vanished in America."[71] While many historians have termed World War I as "Wilson's War" in referring to the League of Nations blunder or the unspeakable horrors of trench warfare in a multiyear stalemate,[72] this section focuses on Wilson's other war: His war on dissident and "disloyal" opinion in the United States. Specifically, this section focuses on the use of the congressional acts as a contrivance to carry out the Wilson administration's crackdown on free and *rightful* expression through the war and subsequent Red Scare, and the Supreme Court precedent *upholding* these abuses—despite clear and profound First Amendment impediments—which would not be corrected until *Brandenburg v. Ohio*, generations later and after lives were lost.[73]

Suppression of Unpopular Viewpoints During the War

The First Amendment is essentially a legal shield, protecting the marketplace of ideas from untoward abridgment by government. The Wilson administration's actions during the war are best described as a two-pronged attack on that shield: First, unconstitutionally suppressing competition in the marketplace, and second, unethically, albeit not *per se* unconstitutionally, flooding the marketplace of ideas with fallacious propaganda. Despite the rosy picture taught in government-owned

---

* "For 120 years, from the expiration of the Sedition Act of 1798 until America's entry into World War I, the United States had no federal legislation against seditious expression. The lessons of 1798 had carried the nation through the War of 1812, the Mexican War, the Civil War, and the Spanish-American War." Geoffrey R. Stone, *Perilous Times* (New York: W. W. Norton, 2004), 144–45.

schools of Americans cheerfully going into World War I as a unified nation,* there was significant opposition to the war, and the "hoist the flag and let her fly"[74] picture painted for five generations of school-children was profoundly erroneous.

The Wilson administration's vital need to imbibe the public with "a sense of national purpose [in the public] and [to] dampen criticism" led to "one of the most fiercely [politically] repressive periods in American history."[75] Following along lockstep with Congress and the president, federal judges tended to sanction the actions of vigilante groups and political oppression by "prosecution."[76]

In the 1918 November midterm elections, this need was best demonstrated. President Wilson himself asked the American electorate for a "vote of confidence" in the form of a Democratic majority:[77] In fact, Wilson said directly to the American people that the failure to achieve Democratic majorities would be a "repudiation of my leadership."[78] In response to Wilson's appeal, the American voters gave a majority in both houses to the Republican Party, ousting Wilson's Democratic majorities. Three hundred thousand U.S. citizens dodged the draft in World War I, compared to *at best* 125,000 during the Vietnam War,[79] and accordingly Congress authorized a million men to be drafted over the course of the war.[80] Obviously, Wilson was struggling with controlling public opinion against the war, which would have fueled legal or congressional or popular challenges to the war. Thus, by executive order,[81] Wilson established the Committee on Public Information in 1917 to flood the marketplace of ideas and unleashed the wrath of the Justice Department and U.S. Postal Service to enforce the Espionage and Sedition Acts of 1917 and 1918.

---

* Bill Murray, "Over There," recorded June 28, 1917, romanticized going to war overseas in song form, http://www.firstworldwar.com/audio/overthere.htm. "Over There" was a huge hit, becoming "the anthem for America's war effort." "The American Variety Stage, 1870–1920," Library of Congress, March 12, 1997, http://memory.loc.gov/ammem/vshtml /vssnde.html. "And we won't come back till it's over, over there."

Flooding the Marketplace of Ideas: The Work of the Committee on Public (Mis-)Information

The Wilson administration's campaign to prepare the American people for war began with the 1915 sinking of the *Lusitania*, a few years before the Committee on Public Information (CPI) existed. Wilson needed more than just a lack of opposition to entering war: He needed to galvanize America through a propaganda apparatus. Considering that there was no legitimate threat of invasion to America or direct attack operating as *causus belli*,*[82] the administration had quite a task in front of it. In order to accomplish its ends, under the leadership of George Creel, the CPI orchestrated and perpetuated a propaganda campaign of mass misinformation through disingenuously harping on the *Lusitania* incident as *causus belli*, encouraging intolerance for German culture, and creating a false "myth of unique German savagery that continues to color the thinking of many persons."[83]

Wilson used the *Lusitania* incident as the first strike at the hearts of the American people on the road to war. Popular thought is that the *Lusitania* was sunk because of the unrestricted submarine warfare employed by the indomitable German Imperial Navy: This is, *at best*, a mischaracterization of the event. The RMS** *Lusitania* was a British ship, flying only British colors, carrying—through an active war zone—four million rifle cartridges and more than a thousand cases of shrapnel shells intended for use against the Germans.[84] Further, the German government took out an ad in the *New York Times* advising American passengers booked on British ships going into British waters that German U-boats would be taking shots at them; some doomed *Lusitania* passengers even received telegrams to this effect beforehand.[85]

Moreover, the *Lusitania* was built to be converted into a military vessel if necessary, and thereby, it had twelve deck gun emplacements at the

---

*   "[Just] case for war."

**   Royal Mail Ship.

time of its sinking, albeit without actual guns mounted.[86] Seeing a ship of apparent (and actual) military value, a German U-boat launched a single torpedo at the bow of the *Lusitania*—which purportedly would allow a ship time to evacuate.[87] Unfortunately, the blast from the torpedo reached the tons of explosive materials onboard, causing a second explosion, thus sinking the *Lusitania* and killing more than one thousand passengers onboard, 128 of them Americans, within a few moments.[88]

Secretary of State William Jennings Bryan advised President Wilson that the *Lusitania* was carrying "6,000,000 rounds of ammunition on board, besides explosives,"[89] and that "a ship carrying contraband should not rely on passengers to protect her from attack."[90] Wilson, speaking in Philadelphia on May 10th 1915, urged calm in response to the attack. Later, in one of the most curious flip-flops in history, he retracted his original position because he felt it expressed "no backbone."[91]

Wilson now blamed his initial, reasonable response on his "heart [being] in such a whirl"[92] over courting his second wife. He reversed position and began hard-lining the Germans by insisting on an admission of war crimes with respect to the *Lusitania*.[93] Of course he had been distracted. Why would Wilson miss a chance to step into the war to end all wars?[94] The German letter responding to the incident was published in the *New York Times* on June 8th 1915, raising essentially all the points raised earlier about the *Lusitania*'s military value.[95]

Dismissing the German government's arguments as "trivial," President Wilson's response was to "promptly [order] his cabinet to plan for rearmament."[96] Secretary of State William Jennings Bryan resigned on June 8th 1915 over Wilson's now revealed belligerence, stating, "I cannot join without violating what I deem to be an obligation to my country and the issue involved is of such moment that to remain a member of the Cabinet would be as unfair to you as it would be to the cause which is nearest my heart, namely, the prevention of war."[97]

With the affair stretching until 1916, Wilson still insisted on an express German disavowal of the justness of the attack, despite a German offer for compensation as an "act of grace."[98] In his speech about making the world "safe for democracy" and asking for a declaration of war, President Wilson referenced unrestricted submarine warfare as the *causus belli*.[99] With a pretext paralleled only by the Gulf of Tonkin incident, Wilson needed a propaganda machine to beat the drums of war.

The CPI produced unprecedented amounts of visual propaganda in World War I: "Under [Creel's] direction, the CPI produced a flood of pamphlets, news releases, speeches, newspaper editorials, political cartoons, and even motion pictures."[100] These images ranged from the subtle wink and nod of a femme fatale, encouraging the purchase of liberty bonds, to the incredible and stupendous. The most effective elements of this propaganda were the incredulous atrocity stories:

> German soldiers, the world was gravely informed, amused themselves by cutting off the hands of Belgian babies. Another oft-repeated tale related how German soldiers amputated the breasts of Belgian women out of sheer viciousness. A slightly different variation of this story asserted that the amputation had been carried out by syphilitic Germans who, having ravished the women, wished to warn their countrymen thereby. There were persistent rumors about the crucifixion of Canadian soldiers. Perhaps the most repulsive and widely circulated of these fabrications was that concerning a German corpse factory where the bodies of both Allied and German soldiers killed in battle were allegedly melted down for fats and other products useful to the German war effort.[101]

Despite the fact that American journalists called these stories "groundless," the CPI not only failed to contradict the stories about atrocities being committed against *American troops and women* but also *used them* to perpetuate the myth of the Visigoth Imperial savagery.[102] Of the posters the CPI produced, the most famous images were of a bloodthirsty Hun lying in wait across the Atlantic or a psychotic adaptation of King Kong in an Imperial helmet with a screaming woman under his arm.[103] And where did these stories come from? Either complete fabrication or the tales of wars long since passed.[104]

The committee on public misinformation wasn't concerned with only spreading hate of the German army via lies, but a larger assault on the entire German culture. As one commentator has stated: "This American propaganda led to intolerant behaviors on the home front. Americans were encouraged to reject German culture, and under this encouragement, sauerkraut was renamed liberty cabbage, hamburger was renamed Salisbury steak, [dachshunds] were renamed liberty dogs, German measles were renamed liberty measles, and the City University of New York reduced by one credit every course taught in German. Fourteen states banned the speaking of German in public schools."[105]

In fact, one town in Michigan changed its name from Berlin to Marne—an effort both to shed Germanic nomenclature and to honor those soldiers lost at the Second Battle of the Marne.[106] With respect to movies, films like *Wolves of Kultur* and *Pershing's Crusaders* flooded American theatres. One picture, *To Hell With The Kaiser*, was so popular that Massachusetts riot police were summoned to deal with an angry mob that had been denied admission."[107] One well-attended 1918 film, *The Kaiser, the Beast of Berlin*, was actually a propaganda film about the sinking of the *Lusitania*.[108] Wagner, Bach, Beethoven, and Mozart were strongly discouraged from being played in musicians' public performances![109] Thus, not only was the animus of the American people turned toward the Imperial troops and their reasons for entering war, but toward the entire society of the German people. It was a total culture war.

Although none of what the government did in terms of flooding the marketplace of ideas directly violated the Constitution or any federal statutes, it nevertheless constituted the use of known falsehoods to whip the country into a belligerent, anti-German frenzy, and it had a resounding effect in the marketplace of ideas, with the belligerent attitudes of the government becoming mainstream.[110] The government's arguments were based on indoctrinating Americans with intolerance and ire, not logic or reason.[111] Moreover, as a participant in the marketplace of ideas, the government has unlimited funds and ability to pursue a monopolistic control of the thought market.

The negative consequence of this, in terms of market theory, is readily apparent: The market fails because of government intervention. The object of thought and ideas is to arrive at the truth or at least a verified conclusion. The marketplace of ideas disseminates thought and reason, and when it is polluted by a flood of uncorrectable, government-backed misinformation, it does not achieve its purpose of distilling truth and sifting out misleading information, but turns into a crucible of lies fomented by linguistic chaos. This effect on the market was magnified greatly by the Wilson administration raising impenetrably high barriers to entry (several year-long prison sentences) on anyone who wished to contradict its lies, discussed below. Thus, the CPI, in conjunction with other arms of the Wilson administration, unrightfully monopolized the marketplace of ideas with falsehoods, which, while not strictly prohibited by the First Amendment, is totally inconsistent with its values.

In terms of natural liberty, however, this is a unique perversion of the right to self-ownership. One of the most intimate, personal components of self-ownership is the control over your thoughts and ideas, which ones are private and which ones are public. The universal *human* capability of intelligent communication ensconces a right to communicate freely *all* thoughts and expressions, regardless of content and popularity. The knowing influx of known lies by the government into the free marketplace of ideas, coupled with government suppression of alternative viewpoints, is particularly troublesome because it directly attacks an emanation of the freedom of speech essential to individual autonomy: Reasonable consideration of differing perspectives.

From a social-contract perspective, the analysis is more damning. In a social compact, the power of the government to act in any manner derives from the people's acquiescence *en masse* to the ability of the government to act only as they have agreed to in the compact that it may. Parties to a contract have a duty not to misinform the other party or parties to the contract in a material manner. The people have ceded the power to make war to the government in this compact, but their representatives cannot do so under false pretenses and through falsehoods and remain faithful to the compact—that is fraud of the highest caliber. Wilson's misinformation justifying war with Germany and social conditioning of the people represent an unconscionable violation of the social compact. His precedent of using a noble lie to drum up false justification for war and perverting the social contract would be honored by many future presidents, including FDR in responding to Pearl Harbor and bringing the United States into World War II, Lyndon Baines Johnson in responding to the Gulf of Tonkin incident and bringing the United States into the Vietnam War, and George W. Bush in responding to the 9/11 attack and dragging the United States into the Middle Eastern Wars.

Barriers to Entry: The Justice Department, Voluntary Organizations, the Postmaster General, and the Federal Courts

Enforcing the Law with Voluntary Organizations: Executive Endorsement and Judicial Insulation of Mob Violence

In order to enforce the wildly unpopular draft, the Espionage Act of 1917, and the Sedition Act of 1918, the Justice Department decided to enlist the help of mobs and thugs. In the early 1900s, America was still a nation plagued with lynching and similar violence across the country. Attorney General Thomas Gregory, in "the first month of the war, . . . asked loyal Americans to act as voluntary detectives and to report their suspicions directly to the Department of Justice."[112] Hundreds of thousands of "loyal" Americans signed up to inform on their countrymen in "voluntary associations."[113]

However, these voluntary associations were not just the average neighborhood watch; they were effectually an unconstitutional domestic spying and enforcement arm of the Justice Department: "The activities of these organizations went well beyond the reporting of alleged disloyalty.

With implicit immunity [from the courts and Justice Department], they engaged in wiretaps, breaking and entering, bugging offices, and examining bank accounts and medical records. Vigilantes ransacked the homes of German Americans. . . . Matters had gotten so far out of hand [by the end of the war], however, that such pleas [for sanity and normal process of law] were essentially ignored."[114]

Human natural liberty is the basis for the right to enforce privacy rights via self-defense. The issue is that without government, there is unequal protection of liberties, which is why we leave the State of Nature and create a government in the first place. The government cannot enlist the help of a mob—that it created and riled up—in order to enforce the laws. It encourages lawlessness under the guise of lawful conduct. Moreover, examine the investigatory actions taken by these organizations: Warrantless spying, wiretapping, and breaking into buildings. If the Justice Department did any of these things without a court warrant, it would violate the Fifth Amendment right to due process and the Fourth Amendment right to be free from search and seizure without probable cause. The Justice Department cannot evade these constitutional and natural laws merely by endorsing and enlisting the help of non-governmental mobs of thugs to do the dirty work which it is forbidden to do. Who will protect us from a mob doing the government's dirty work?

The endorsement and implicit immunity from prosecution, discussed in more detail below, were a clear enough link between these groups that they should be construed as arms of the state, reaching into the homes of German Americans:

Attorney-General Gregory used these groups in a series of mass raids designed to round up "slackers"—individuals who failed to register for the draft. . . . The most notorious of these raids occurred in New York City in early September of 1918. For three days, members of the American Protective League "blanketed the city, stationing themselves at subway entrances, patrolling parks and squares, and guarding the ferries and bridges. More than 20,000 hapless men, accosted on the streets, were hauled off to armories or to jail, often at bayonet-point.[115]

Thus, in World War I, the Justice Department employed mob violence and intimidation to substitute for due process and natural liberty, in violation of constitutionally protected rights and the Natural Law.

And what did the vast majority of the federal judiciary, whose judges heard cases brought by the Justice Department, do when faced with civil assault suits and criminal charges levied against mob violence against not-even-accused German sympathizers? Nothing. As Voltaire once said, "It is forbidden to kill; therefore all murderers are punished unless they kill in large numbers and to the sound of trumpets."[116] A report from the National Civil Liberties Bureau found 164 incidents of mob violence related to the war between April 1917 and March 1919 and noted the underreporting of "hundreds of cases."[117] The best illustration of the judicial response to anti-German mob violence is the story of John Meints.

Meints was a German American farmer who was suspected of "being interested in or contributing to a Non-Partisan League newspaper . . . [or being] disloyal because he was not [monetarily] supporting war bond drives."[118] He was kidnapped, dropped outside of town, and told never to return.[119] He reported the incident to the Department of Justice, whose agents "investigated and told him it was safe to go back home."[120] However,

> . . . about a month after he returned to Luverne, [Minnesota,] men forced their way into the house of one of Meints' sons and demanded to see Meints. The men then forcibly removed him from the house and drove to the South Dakota border. According to court records, once they reached the border, masked men "assaulted him, whipped him, threatened to shoot him, besmeared his body with tar and feathers, and told him to cross the line into South Dakota, and that if he ever returned to Minnesota he would be hanged."[121]

Meints, apparently unable to find justice by way of criminal prosecution for his attackers, sued thirty-two of them in federal court for the tort of false imprisonment.

The district court jury acquitted the defendants because it found that Meints was "disloyal." The judge took no steps to overturn the verdict. Eventually, in 1921, after the war ended, the Eighth Circuit Court of Appeals reversed the lower court ruling, but ordered a new trial to be held *in the same court*, rather than direct a verdict.[122] Meints, apparently frustrated, settled the case.[123] Meints, quite obviously, was deprived by the government of his personal liberty to move about because, after entrusting the government with those matters in the social compact, the government betrayed that confidence.

Criminal Prosecutions Under the Acts

More than two-thousand prosecutions were initiated under the Espionage and Sedition Acts between 1917 and 1921.[124] Of the few hundred reported prosecutions in 1919, the National Civil Liberties Bureau calculates that 103 individuals were handed sentences of ten to thirty-five years for disloyal utterances, while barely more than thirty acquittals for either *treason* or espionage were reported.[125] In a true testament to wartime hysterical absurdity, Robert Goldstein, producer of the film *The Spirit of '76*, a patriotic picture about the American Revolution, was convicted under the Sedition Act because the film portrayed a historical massacre of Americans, where "British soldiers bayoneted women and children."[126] The reasoning: It tended to promote insubordination by making an ally look bad *through portraying historically accurate events*.[127] These were not the only oppressive acts taken by the Justice Department and permitted by the judiciary. Walter Matthey was convicted and sentenced to a year in prison under the Espionage Act for *listening to and applauding a speech* which contained "disloyal utterances."[128] A California man was jailed for *laughing* at army drills.[129]

Those were just a few of a litany of malicious, baseless, highly unconstitutional persecutions carried out by the Justice Department and state prosecutors. "In one instance, a traveling [Montana] wine and brandy salesman was sentenced to 7 to 20 years in prison for privately calling wartime food regulations a 'big joke.'"[130] Thirty German American residents of South Dakota decided to petition their governor for reforms in the draft procedure, threatening to vote the other way in the next election.[131] They were answered with charges for obstruction of enlistment services.[132] In front of an entirely female audience (no draftable male soldiers around), Rose Stokes was convicted under the Espionage Act for stating, "I am for the people and the government is for profiteers," receiving a ten-year sentence because she "chill[ed] enthusiasm" for the war.[133] Rev. Charles Waldron distributed a pamphlet advocating conscientious objection under an idea of Christian pacifism; he was sentenced to fifteen years in prison.[134] Religious leaders were the most aggressively pursued disloyal citizens.[135]

In one of the most famous cases in U.S. history, Eugene V. Debs, the nationally recognized leader of the Socialist Party and perennial presidential candidate, was prosecuted under the Act. During the speech for which he was arrested, he joked about the potential for criminal prosecution under the Espionage Act:

I have just returned from a visit over yonder (pointing to the workhouse), where three of our most loyal comrades are paying the penalty for their devotion to the cause of the working class. (Applause.) They have come to realize, as many of us have, that it is extremely dangerous to exercise the constitutional right of free speech in a country fighting to make democracy safe in the world. (Applause.)

I realize that, in speaking to you this afternoon, there are certain limitations placed upon the right of free speech. I must be exceedingly careful, prudent, as to what I say, and even more careful and prudent as to how I say it. (Laughter.) I may not be able to say all I think; (laughter and applause) but I am not going to say anything that I do not think. (Applause.)[136]

Debs, in painful irony, was convicted and sentenced to ten years in prison for giving that speech and "eulogi[zing]" a few other similar cases. Wilson labeled Debs a "traitor to his country" because of his speeches.[137]

The Wilson administration's decision in this matter smacked of political motivation. In the 1912 presidential campaign, Debs received almost a million votes to Wilson's six million.[138] Although Wilson trounced a different Socialist Party candidate in 1916 who received about half the votes that Debs received,[139] Wilson certainly preferred to keep his political opponents behind bars for the time being with the rising anti-war sentiment. When Debs ran again for president in 1920—from a jail cell—he received nearly a million votes.[140] However, Debs's health "was severely undermined" by prison conditions, and after his release in 1921, he spent his "remaining days" trying to recover; he died in 1926.[141]

The United States Will Not Mail Your Ideas: The Postmaster in World War I

The nonmailability provision of the Espionage Act provided the postmaster general, Albert Burleson, with broad discretion to refuse to deliver "disloyal mail." Using this discretion, more than "400 publications were denied mailing privileges at some time or another during or after the war"[142] at the behest (or, more accurately, fiat) of the postmaster general. One publication, the *Freeman's Journal and Catholic Register*, was "suppressed" under the Espionage and Sedition Acts for "reprinting *Thomas Jefferson's* views that Ireland should be an independent republic."[143] The ostensible reason for the suppression was the potential negative impact on our ally, Great Britain, similar to the reasoning articulated in the *Spirit of '76* film prosecution. Another newspaper, *The Public*, was censored because it had the gall to assert that the war should be funded from tax revenue, not liberty bond sales.[144] "[S]cores of other books, magazines, and newspapers" were censored under the Espionage and Sedition Acts.[145] The *New York World* lamented this era as "an intellectual reign of terror in the United States."[146] Many writers and artists fled the country,[147] leaving a lacuna in the American intelligentsia: So much for the marketplace of ideas.

But what sort of process was attendant to these suppressions? Surely there must have been some due process:

> Wilson now and then made suggestions to Burleson . . . but the Postmaster General usually had the last word in censorship matters. On two occasions . . . Wilson did override Burleson's orders of exclusion. More often, though, Burleson simply ignored Wilson's reservations and persisted in his campaign to cleanse the mail of all "disloyal" publications. The responsibility for restraining the postmaster general rested "squarely upon Woodrow Wilson." Wilson realized this, but generally did nothing.[148]

The man responsible for censoring disloyal material that could cause contempt for the government, Albert Burleson, was Wilson's presidential campaign manager.[149] "[M]any publications moderated their editorial content" as a result of Burleson's oppressive mail regime.[150] The Supreme Court and lower federal courts of the time generally upheld convictions of newspaper editors for their hand in disseminating disloyal material.[151]

The repression of publications by the fiat of a patronage appointee with political motivations is repugnant to the Natural Law, as well as to the First Amendment's protection of the freedom of speech and of the press. Persons have a natural right to speak their minds without the fear of severe reproach or reprisal by their elected government or its political lackeys.

Give Us Your Tired, Your Hungry, and Your Loyal: Deportations Under the Alien Act of 1918

As a final despotic gift to the American people from the political branches of the federal government, Congress passed the Alien Act of 1918. (Now, the Alien and Sedition Act of 1918 is, actually, a perfect description.) The Alien Act of 1918[152] provided that aliens who believe in anarchist views—despite whether they are peaceful or not—may be deported upon a warrant signed by the secretary of labor followed by an administrative, not judicial, proceeding.[153] "In 1918 alone, the United

States deported 11,625 individuals under this act."[154] That means during the Wilson administration, 11,625 individuals were deprived of property, the rights to political expression, and the natural liberty to live wherever one may choose.[155]

Law enforcement's preliminary investigations were "conducted in secret," and the "entire process" was done administratively by the Department of Justice absent counsel, jury, or judge.[156] They were tried in front of "inspectors" and Justice Department officials who were charged with "mak[ing] every possible effort to obtain evidence of the alien's membership in one of the proscribed parties."[157] Detainees slated for deportation hearings were sent to Deer Island near Boston. There, they were "held practically *incommunicado*," subjected to deplorable conditions that left them exposed to extreme cold and unsanitary conditions.[158] One detainee committed suicide by jumping out a window, one was committed to a mental health facility, and other detainees were "driven nearly, if not quite, to the verge of insanity."[159]

The Supreme Court Abides

With federal courts all but endorsing mob violence, assaults on natural liberty and sentences abounding throughout the courts to the tune of ten or twenty or thirty years in prison for speech alone, and an out-of-control Justice Department, how would the Supreme Court respond? In a series of decisions handed down during the war and the Red Scare, the Supreme Court—the counter-majoritarian branch *designed* to protect the rights of the minority against the oppression of an overbearing majority—*abided*. Between 1918 and 1921, the Supreme Court handed down opinions in *Schenck v. United States*,[160] *Frohwerk v. United States*,[161] *Debs v. United States*,[162] *Abrams v. United States*,[163] *Schaefer v. United States*,[164] and *Pierce v. United States*,[165] which stamped as legitimate the persecutions under the Espionage and Sedition Acts.

The first of these six cases, *Schenck*, involved the appeal of Charles Schenck and Elizabeth Baer. They were convicted of publishing a pamphlet that called the draft "unlawful."[166] The pamphlet "confined itself to peaceful measures such as a petition for the repeal of the act."[167] The First Amendment provides that "Congress shall make *no* law . . . abridging the freedom of speech, or of the press, or the right of the people peaceably to assemble, and to petition the Government for a redress of grievances."[168] Thus, this case seems as though it would have an obvious result, and one marvels at the fact that this case needed to reach the Supreme Court for adjudication. However, in a truly stunning move, Justice Oliver Wendell Holmes Jr., writing for a unanimous court, upheld the convictions because the speech presented a "clear and present danger" to Congress's successful provisioning of the army for the war.[169] Realizing his folly, Justice Holmes would later reverse course and change his First Amendment jurisprudence on how to apply the "clear and present danger" test, but not until after much damage to life and liberty.[170]

On March 10th 1919, seven days after *Schenck*, the Supreme Court handed down an opinion in *Frohwerk v. United States*. Frohwerk was a copy editor for a Missouri-based paper.[171] Copy editors typically deal with grammar, typeface, and style issues; they do not create content. Some articles he edited were anti-draft articles, none of which he wrote.[172] Nevertheless, he was convicted of violating and conspiring to violate the Espionage Act of 1917 and sentenced to ten years.[173] Justice Holmes, again writing for a unanimous court and citing *Schenck*, upheld the convictions, despite the fact that it "does not appear that there was any special effort to reach men who were subject to the draft."[174]

The same day as *Frohwerk*, the Court decided Debs's fate in *Debs v. United States*. As the Court recounted, the Ohio speech he gave "eulog[ized]" the draft opponents in jail and "expressed opposition to Prussian militarism in a way that naturally might have been thought to be intended to include the mode of proceeding in the United States."[175] Again, writing for a unanimous Court, Holmes upheld the convictions.[176]

Abrams v. United States represents the most important of these four opinions; while *Debs* and *Schenck* may have been popular or interesting, *Abrams* shows why First Amendment jurisprudence was reversed in the next fifty years. The defendants were five Russian intellectuals who wrote a pamphlet largely in Yiddish—distributed by throwing them out tenement windows in New York City—encouraging Marxist policies and deriding Wilson and the war.[177] Abrams rented the rooms in which they worked.[178] The convictions were upheld; however, this time Justice Clarke was writing for a divided Court.[179] Holmes wrote a dissent in which Justice Brandeis joined, arguing,

> But as against dangers peculiar to war . . . the principle of the right to free speech is always the same. It is only the present danger of immediate evil or an intent to bring it about that warrants Congress in setting a limit to the expression of opinion where private rights are not concerned. Congress certainly cannot forbid all effort to change the mind of the country. Now nobody can suppose that the surreptitious publishing of a silly leaflet by an unknown man, without more, would present any immediate danger that its opinions would hinder the success of the government arms or have any appreciable tendency to do so.[180]

Later, this dissent would prove instrumental in the jurisprudence underlying reversing the jurisprudence in these four cases (but not the cases themselves) and in placing First Amendment rights on the path to the constitutional pedestal achieved in *Brandenburg v. Ohio*.

Schaefer v. United States upheld another set of Espionage Act convictions against German newspaper editors.[181] Writing for the majority, Justice McKenna held:

> The indictment is based on the Espionage Act . . . and *its restraints are not excessive nor ambiguous. . . .*
>
> But simple as the law is, perilous to the country as disobedience to it was, offenders developed, and when it was exerted against them [offenders] challenged it to decision as a violation of the right of free speech assured by the Constitution of the United States. . . . That great

ordinance of government and orderly liberty was invoked to justify the activities of anarchy or of the enemies of the United States, and *by a strange perversion of its precepts* it was adduced against itself.[182]

In a similar vein, *Pierce v. United States* upheld the convictions of four Socialists who argued that the war was being perpetrated for profit-making reasons.[183] In both cases, Brandeis and Holmes joined in dissent.

Thus, for anarchists, aliens, pacifists, and Socialists, there was no refuge in the First Amendment or the Court. Be they party leader or pacifist preacher, no one who disagreed with Wilson was safe from prosecution under the Alien and Sedition Acts. With no avenue open for political redress, or even to suggest publicly that policy ought to be changed, these movements (besides the pacifists) grew violent and radical. The suppression of natural rights to the freedom of speech, the freedom of religion (even Christian pacifism), the freedom to seek redress of grievances, and the guarantee of due process of law were enough to radicalize the American political minority.

After the War in Europe Ends, the War Against the Home Front Continues: The First Red Scare, the Palmer Raids, and the Overman Committee

After the war, America entered a socially turbulent and chaotic period. Four million GIs returned from overseas seeking jobs.[184] The work of the National War Labor Board, discussed above, had created tension between labor and management by imposing resolutions which only the exigencies of war could render tenable.[185] With Eugene V. Debs behind bars, the Socialist Party, fueled in part by the systematic oppression of its leadership and in part by the Bolshevik Revolt in Russia, split into radical and moderate factions.[186] The voluntary organizations created during the war showed no signs of abating their work of creating loyalty through vigilantism.[187] Woodrow Wilson, the man who centralized government powers in the United States in the executive, suffered several debilitating strokes during the summer and autumn of 1919.[188] His true personality lost its mask and manifested itself as that of a bitter, delusional man with "warped" judgment.[189] On October 2nd 1919, he suffered a stroke that incapacitated him, leaving the First Lady effectively in charge of his presidency.[190]

As is typical with such a massive societal upheaval and governmental power vacuum, there was chaos. In 1919, there were dozens of labor strikes, bombings of politicians' offices and homes, and incidences of street violence.[191] In the 1919 May Day riots, Socialists parading in the streets of Cleveland, Boston, and New York clashed with police and voluntary associations.[192] In the fall of 1919, Attorney General A. Mitchell Palmer saw an opening to run for president with the power vacuum that Wilson's incapacity had created. (Wilson was physically unable to seek the third term he desired.[193]) Bolstering his résumé for the run, Palmer saw the public outcry for order and fear of Communist revolutionaries and anarchists as an opportunity.

Palmer capitalized. Establishing the General Intelligence Division (GID) within the Justice Department, he endeavored to suppress the "constant spread of a disease of evil thinking."[194] The GID, headed by a young J. Edgar Hoover, amassed the names of more than two hundred thousand individuals suspected of having radical beliefs and fueled the public with misinformation, "fabricat[ing] or exaggerat[ing] charges that Communists and other radicals had instigated violent strikes and race riots."[195] With ringing endorsements from the press—even some that expressly approved crushing civil liberties—and under the authority of the Espionage, Alien, and Sedition Acts, Palmer conducted a series of warrantless raids into the homes of suspected radicals between 1919 and 1920, imprisoning and deporting thousands for thought crimes.[196]

In 1918, the Senate created a special committee to investigate Bolshevik and un-American propaganda. It was called the Overman Committee after its chairman, Sen. Lee Overman, author of the Overman Act.[197] The committee went beyond reporting on propaganda activities.[198] It painted a stark picture of the effect of a Communist revolt in America and recommended suppressing the freedom of speech and the freedom to associate via sedition laws, increasing deportations, and suppressing foreign-language publications.[199]

Palmer's raids and the Overman Committee's proceedings represent some of the many systematic attacks on civil, political, and natural liberties conducted during Wilson's War on America. The rights to private association, to the freedom of press, to the freedom of speech, to be secure in one's home and affects, to be free of warrantless invasion, to shout from the rooftops and to whisper in the parlor, and to *think* what one wishes were brutally suppressed during this time.

The End of Wilson's War on Americans

In 1920, the clamor for the repression of dissent was beginning to fade, and the pendulum began to swing away from totalitarianism toward respect for natural liberties. The first part of the counter-attack on the Wilson administration was a publication authored by, among others, a Harvard Law School professor and future Supreme Court justice, Felix Frankfurter, meticulously documenting the abuses suffered under Palmer's Justice Department.[200] As a result, Palmer was unceremoniously hauled before the House Rules Committee, though he survived that test of his power.[201] His end would come, however, on May Day of 1920, when he and Hoover cried wolf, reporting to the American people of imminent attacks (bombings, assassination, urban violence, etc.) aimed at overthrowing the American government. In the May Day Scare, nothing happened, destroying Palmer's credibility and his sway with the public.[202] He became a laughingstock after that incident and lost his party's nomination for president, dying in 1936.

That summer, in a second wave of liberty, judges began to enjoin the deportation of aliens because of political affiliation or ideology.[203] Congress repealed the Sedition Act on December 13th 1920, but never repealed the Espionage Act of 1917.[204] Wilson—his wife acting in his stead—commuted and reduced the sentences for violations of the Acts before leaving office; however, he refused to pardon Debs or to reduce his sentence.[205] President Harding eventually pardoned Debs, and President Coolidge ordered the release of the remaining political prisoners just before 1924.[206] As a result of the experience of severe political repression in World War I, John Dewey, Crystal Eastman, Roger Baldwin, and Walter Nelles founded the American Civil Liberties Union (ACLU) in 1920 to fight government oppression.[207]

The Supreme Court played its part in this counter-attack too. In the 1923 case *Meyer v. Nebraska*, the Court held that there is a constitutional right to learn German in schools, signaling a late but strong blow against the culture war perpetrated against German Americans.[208] However, the Court was obstinate in its refusal to respect the natural right to free political expression embodied in the First Amendment. The Court would not correct First Amendment jurisprudence until forty-six years later, when *Brandenburg v. Ohio* became the law of the land, establishing more robust protections for speech that have only bolstered it since.

Woodrow Wilson waged a shameless war on the peaceful exercise of the freedom of speech. The effects of that war would be felt for generations after Wilson was dead and his immediate successors respected traditional American values.

6

The World War II Era

The Freedom of Speech and Power Over Property

> *You know I am a juggler, and I never let my right*
> *hand know what my left hand does. . . . I may have*
> *one policy for Europe and one diametrically opposite*
> *for North and South America. I may be entirely*
> *inconsistent, and furthermore I am perfectly willing to*
> *mislead and tell untruths if it will help win the war.*[*]
>
> —FRANKLIN DELANO ROOSEVELT

A review of the wartime behavior of President Woodrow Wilson and President Franklin Delano Roosevelt—who saw themselves as guardians of cohesive societal order—shows that each was involved in the dissemination of substantial falsehoods and each was, accordingly, a "noble" liar. In World War I, this was the lie of the threat to the American way: the "widespread" and "endemic," but fictitious German American

---

[*] Warren F. Kimball, *The Juggler: Franklin Roosevelt as Wartime Statesman* (Princeton, NJ: Princeton University Press, 1991), 7, stated in 1942.

spy network; the sinking of the not-so-innocent RMS *Lusitania*; and the mythos of Hun-like savagery being perpetrated against women and children overseas.[1] In World War II, Roosevelt propagated noble lies about the Axis powers that controlled, focused, and fueled wartime hysteria. This section discusses the deprivation of the freedom of speech and economic liberties, as well as the mass internment of hundreds of thousands of Americans, and Roosevelt's "noble" lies via the familiar, ignoble conventions of wartime autocracy and "national security" edicts.

The Freedom of Speech

In the Depression era, the freedom of speech was undergoing a renaissance. The Court was beginning to give due deference to the natural supremacy of the individual right, rather than to the political convenience of the state. In famous dissents, Justices Holmes and Brandeis were still lobbing brazen attacks at the institutionalization of opinion prosecution. In between the lines of two early miscarriages of justice, the Court laid the framework for a vigorous expansion of individual autonomy in the political realm. One of those miscarriages is *Gitlow v. New York*; the other is *Whitney v. California*.[2]

Gitlow is a 1925 Supreme Court case upholding convictions under a New York law criminalizing "advocacy of criminal anarchy": No doubt the Founding Fathers would have been convicted of this felony, defining criminal anarchy as "the *doctrine* that organized government should be overthrown by force or violence . . . or by any unlawful means."[3] Gitlow and his co-defendants were members of the left-wing branch of the Socialist Party, which advocated overthrow of the government.[4] Their criminal act was printing and distributing a manifesto advocating that viewpoint,[5] as Marx put forth in the *Communist Manifesto*.[6] They printed in Yiddish and in English that the laboring classes ought to bring about "militant and 'revolutionary Socialism,' based on 'the class struggle' and mobilizing the 'power of the proletariat in action,' through mass industrial revolts developing into mass political strikes and 'revolutionary mass action,' for the purpose of conquering and destroying the parliamentary state and establishing in its place, through a 'revoluntionary [sic] dicta-torship of the proletariat,' the system of Communist Socialism."[7]

Notably, this battle was fought by the newly formed ACLU.[8] Holmes and Brandeis were again in dissent.[9] However, the silver lining was the ACLU's first victory: The incorporation of First Amendment protections to state laws.[10] Prior to *Gitlow*, the First Amendment did not apply to state laws; only the individual state's bill of rights could do so.[*] *Gitlow* was the first case where parts of the federal Bill of Rights were selectively incorporated into state constitutions.[11]

In the 1927 case *Whitney v. California*, the defendant was convicted under a state statute for aiding in the establishment of the Communist Party. The defendant had authored and advocated for a party resolution endorsing a ballot-box-only method of proletariat revolution.[12] However, the final party resolution failed to "advocate the use of the ballot to the exclusion of violent and unlawful means of bringing about the desired changes in industrial and political conditions."[13] The defendant—who personally advocated for a ballot-box-only stance and against the advocacy of violence resolution later adopted at the convention in ques-tion—was denied First and Fourteenth Amendments protection, and her conviction upheld.[14] Brandeis and Holmes concurred in this decision as to the Fourteenth Amendment concern, but vehemently and famously did not concur with the Court's First Amendment analysis.[15]

Whitney would not be overruled until the seminal case *Brandenburg v. Ohio* in 1969. After *Whitney*, however, the Court enforced the freedom of speech against oppressive state statutes, even expressing a need for tolerance for dissenting and wrong viewpoints.[16]

---

[*]   See Barron v. Baltimore, 32 U.S. 243 (1833). In the days before the Due Process Clause of the Fourteenth Amendment, guaranteeing that "[n]o state shall make or enforce any law which shall . . . deprive any person of life, liberty, or property, without due process of law," the Court would not apply the federal Bill of Rights to state action. U.S. Const. amend. XIV, §1. *Barron v. Baltimore* was the first case to establish this doctrine in 1833. 32 U.S. 243 (1833). This trend continued for almost ninety years. For example, *United States v. Cruikshank*, 92 U.S. 542 (1875), failing to incorporate selectively the First Amendment.

The Supreme Court was moving toward John Stuart Mill's vision on free speech: "If all mankind minus one, were of one opinion, and only one person were of the contrary opinion, mankind would be no more justified in silencing that one person, than he, if he had the power, would be justified in silencing mankind." When the terror of fascism began to spread across Europe through Hitler, Mussolini, and Franco, however, the Court and other branches of government would fall far short in endeavoring to improve protection for natural liberty in the United States, regressing into permitting unilateral and unlawful persecution of aliens, citizens, and dissidents.

While the Shadows of Nazism and Communism Fell Over Europe

Public perception of the attacks on dissident viewpoints shifted considerably as the Nazi specter rose in Europe. This length of time in the mid-1930s was the fascist "Brown Scare."[17] Congress did not have the same respect for the freedom of political expression as the Supreme Court did in the 1930s. Thus, Congress formed special committees to combat the spread of fascism, which were met with mixed reactions, depending on the year they began their work. The precedent of congressional investigatory committees legally probing advocates of "subversive" ideas paved the way for the FDR administration to abuse civil liberties when war hit.

The Fish Committee

In the first part of the 1930s, congressionally sanctioned attacks on minority political groups were met with opprobrium. "[F]ollowing the publication of the forged anti-Soviet documents by . . . [the NYC police commissioner]," Congress created a committee to investigate Communist activities: The Fish Committee[18]—the first political minority investigation body since the Overman Committee in 1918. Rep. Hamilton Fish III (R-NY) chaired the special committee of the House to investigate anti-Communist activities. His work focused on victimizing members of the Communist Party and the ACLU as a Communist sympathizer organization.[19]

In 1929, one year prior to his appointment as chair of this committee, Fish fell for "an amusing scam . . . that bilked [him] of thousands of dollars in pursuit of a fictitious cache of communist documents and money . . . that was supposed to prove the USSR's control of the Red network."[20] Clearly he was the most qualified man for the job. The committee reported to the House on January 19th 1931,[21] recommending measures reviving World War I institutions such as barring subversive literature from the mail, creating a new spy system, and expediting deportation of subversives.[22] However, due to the strong public sentiment against constitutional abuses of World War I, and Fish's 1929 run-in with communism, "the anticommunist effort suffered the cruelest [sic] fate of all: it became a laughingstock," and the committee's work was largely ignored.[23] Laughable ignorance is a timid phrase to describe the committee's findings. Some legislative attempts were made to harass the ACLU in subsequent years based on the committee's work.[24]

McCormack-Dickstein Committee

After the Nazi Party formed a majority government in the Reichstag and Adolf Hitler became chancellor of Germany in 1933, America got scared of fascist and Nazi activity within its own borders. To address that point, in 1934, the House authorized a special committee to investigate "Nazi propaganda activities and certain other propaganda activities."[25] The committee was nicknamed the McCormack-Dickstein Committee after its chair and vice-chair, Rep. John W. McCormack (D-MA) and Rep. Samuel Dickstein (D-NY).[26] The McCormack-Dickstein Committee was the "forerunner of the [House] Committee on Un-American Activities."[27]

Rep. Lindsay Warren (D-NC), reflecting on the Fish and McCormack committees in 1937, noted that these sorts of investigatory bodies are "generally for the self-glorification and advertisement of those who conduct them."[28] During its existence, the committee had a lackluster career as far as investigating Nazi propaganda and "other" activities. Despite interviewing hundreds of witnesses in several cities,[29] it was referred to

a total of seven times in the 1935 *Congressional Record*:[30] The first three
to buy more time to report and to extend the length of the committee.[31]

The Special Committee on Un-American Activities Authorized to
Investigate Nazi Propaganda and Certain Other Propaganda Activities
expired in 1935 and was not re-commissioned, despite a 1937 attempt
that was defeated in the House by a vote of 184 to 38.[32] Good riddance as
well: It had accumulated 4,300 pages of testimony without any significant
discoveries. Eventually, the committee chair, Rep. John D. McCormack
(D-MA), would undergo a rebirth in individual-rights ideology, becoming Speaker of the House during the 1960s and 1970s and ushering in
a redeeming pro–civil liberties agenda. On the contrary, Dickstein was
posthumously discovered to be a Soviet agent when the USSR's archives
were declassified after the Cold War. However, when the war in Europe
was beginning to grow, the House unsurprisingly felt war hysteria brew-
ing. On May 26th 1938, by a vote of 191 to 41, the House formed the
House Un-American Activities Committee to investigate disloyal subversive ideologues.[33] HUAC, as it came to be known, was quickly nicknamed
the Dies Committee for its chair, Rep. Martin Dies (D-TX).[34]

HUAC/Dies Committee

The House Special Committee on Un-American Activities, or
Dies Committee, was "the direct predecessor of HUAC."[35] As perfectly
described in a 1967 student note, the "[Dies] Committee's performance
during the War years, while occasionally sensational, was on the whole
a lack-luster, one-man operation."[36] Originally, the Dies Committee was
supposed to focus on the activities of one organization in particular, the
German American Bund:

> . . . [T]he Bund was a "militant group of patriotic Americans"
> determined to stand fast against "[r]acial [i]ntermixture" and the
> "liberal-pacifist forces undermining" the traditional values of the
> United States. . . . [Membership stood at] 25,000 members by 1938.
> Most Bund members had been born in Germany and about half were

still German citizens. The Bund published several newspapers . . . [M]uch of the material consisted of propaganda produced by the Nazi Party in Germany. The Bund also established youth camps to inculcate children in Nazi philosophy.

. . . [T]he German government on March 1, 1938, officially cut ties to the Bund on the ground that it was "an unfortunate embarrassment."[37]

Bund members were also required to aver that they were "of Aryan descent, free of Jewish or colored racial ties."[38]

However, "the Dies Committee directed most of its attention not at the Nazis but at Communists."[39] In fact, Dies's intention all along had been to uncover "alleged Communist 'influences' in the New Deal."[40] Thus, the Dies Committee pursued "liberal organizations [and persons] whose activities it tarred as 'Un-American,'" such as Democratic gubernatorial candidates endorsed by the Communist Party; future Supreme Court Justices and Attorneys General Frank Murphy and Robert Jackson; Eleanor Roosevelt; the ACLU; the Boy Scouts; Hollywood; and several ranking members of the Roosevelt administration.[41] Accordingly, the committee's work was billed as "'an orgy . . . of fantastic accusations.'"[42] Despite its nonsense work product and "wildly irresponsible" methods, including publishing the names of government officials with bogus Communist ties, the special committee "remained popular with the public" and was made a permanent committee in 1945, paving the way for Sen. Joseph McCarthy to run a parallel Senate committee during the 1950s Red Scare.[43]

The FBI and Domestic Spying: When Did the Government Start Spying on Americans?

The FBI began as a crime-fighting force, but its practice slowly developed it into the chief spying arm of the federal government. In 1901, a radical anarchist assassinated President McKinley while he was greeting well-wishers after giving a speech in Buffalo, New York. This event became the precipitation for domestic spying in the United States.

"The Department of Justice and the Department of Labor had been keeping records on anarchists for [several] years,"[44] but mere record-keeping was not effective enough to keep the president safe. Theodore Roosevelt, now president after the assassination, did not want to go the way of his predecessors: Lincoln, Garfield, and McKinley. In 1905, he appointed Charles Bonaparte, a fellow progressive, as attorney general.[45] Two years later, the Department of Justice was relying heavily on Secret Service agents to conduct investigations for it.[46]

After Congress enacted legislation prohibiting the president's personal bodyguard from working for his apolitical investigatory agency, Roosevelt, in 1908, secretly approved a "corps of special agents" responsible directly to the attorney general.[47] The group of agents became the Bureau of Investigation in 1909, which was tasked with enforcing the 1910 Mann Act, combating interstate prostitution.[48] During World War I and the Red Scare, "the Bureau acquired responsibility for the Espionage, Selective Service, and Sabotage Acts and assisted the Department of Labor by investigating enemy aliens."[49] The future director of the FBI, J. Edgar Hoover, joined a subsector of the Bureau in 1917, the General Intelligence Division, assisting then Attorney General Palmer in spying on and persecuting political dissidents in the post-war Red Scare.[50] For his troubles, Hoover was made assistant director of the Bureau in 1921.[51]

However, that position turned out to be a stepping-stone, and Hoover became director of the FBI in 1924, staying in that post until 1972.[52] Hoover began his term as director by turning the FBI into a professional crime-fighting force "glor[ified]" by Americans.[53] From the mid-twenties to the mid-thirties, the FBI shifted away from being the brute squad for political persecution. The G-Men "captured the public's imagination" through coverage of the sensational capture stories of gangsters like "Machine Gun" Kelly, John Dillinger, and "Pretty Boy" Floyd.[54] This changed in the midst of the Brown Scare: "Seizing the opportunity Roosevelt presented in 1936 to enable the bureau to return to its earlier ways, Hoover confidentially instructed his agents 'to obtain from all possible sources information concerning subversive activities being conducted in the United States by Communists, Fascists, and representatives' of other subversive organizations, defining 'subversive activities' as including, among other things, 'the distribution of literature . . . opposed to the American way of life.'"[55]

Thus, in 1936, Hoover "revived [in total secrecy] the General Intelligence Division" of World War I, collecting and categorizing the names of thousands of "subversives."[56] The federal government and the FBI would never abandon domestic spying operations again.

Wartime Hysteria Explodes: The Fall of France

To the Allies, the game of world domination became an incipient disaster when France was taken by Germany. In the West, this was thought impossible because "France's army seemed a powerful bulwark against possible Nazi aggression." Churchill once (seriously) commented in 1933 on that point, announcing, "'Thank God for the French Army.'"[57]

After getting taken by surprise and losing large swaths of territory early on in World War I, France constructed a large defensive barrier during the time between the two world wars called the Maginot Line, protecting its German border.[58] In just six weeks, however, the German army had routed the French via Belgium and entered Paris.[59] On June 22nd 1940, France surrendered. "Hitler insisted on signing the document of capitulation in the same railway carriage used when Germany had surrendered in 1918. The humiliation of France was complete."[60] This inconceivable military defeat was attributed to the work of fascist, Nazi, and Communist underground elements in France.[61] To borrow a modern American-youth-inspired colloquialism: In response, America freaked out.

The Alien and Sedition Act of 1940: The Smith Act

While France was losing on its western front in May 1940, FDR wasted no time blaming a "treacherous . . . fifth column," a term that refers to subversive, underground militants within a society, for the failure of the French military, and asking for hundreds of millions of dollars in defense appropriations.[62] In 1940, Congress passed the Alien

Registration Act, or Smith Act after its author, Rep. Howard W. Smith (D-VA).[63] The Smith Act would prove nothing more than the Alien and Sedition Acts of 1940, criminalizing a broad spectrum of constitutionally protected, expressive political behavior in Title I, and expediting deportation proceedings for alien thought criminals.

Title I is the portion of the Act which reinstated the sedition crime of the World War I era. In "practical effect, this was [a] [more restrictive version of the 1918 Sedition Act, akin to a version of an amended] sedition act Attorney General Palmer had failed to persuade Congress to pass in 1920."[64] The act made criminal these acts.

> SECTION 1. . . . [while] inten[ding] to interfere with, impair, or *influence the* loyalty, *morale*, or discipline of the . . . forces of the United States—(1) to advise, counsel, urge, or in any manner *cause . . . disloyalty . . .* by any member of the military . . . ; or, (2) to *distribute any written or printed matter* which advises, counsels, or urges . . . disloyalty . . . by any member of the military . . . of the United States.
>
> SECTION 2. . . . (1) to knowingly . . . advocate . . . or teach the duty, necessity, desirability, or propriety of overthrowing or destroying any government in the United States by force. . . .
>
> (2) . . . to print, publish, *edit*, issue, circulate, sell, distribute, or publicly display any written or printed matter . . . [advocating the same].
>
> (3) to organize or help organize any society, group, or assembly . . . [advocating the same].[65]

Of course, from a historical perspective, no restraint on the ability of a person to give or attempt to give oral advice that may "in any manner cause . . . disloyalty," or to distribute or attempt to distribute any writing that "advises, counsels, or urges . . . disloyalty," such as the one contained in Section 1, would be complete without a potential ten-year prison sentence attached to chill the freedom of speech, which this Act obligingly afforded.[66] The laws in Section 2 also provided for that hefty penalty. Remember that in World War I, the *Freeman's Journal and Catholic Register* was repressed under the 1917 and 1918 Espionage and Sedition Acts for "reprinting Thomas Jefferson's views that Ireland should be an independent republic,"[67] and the Espionage Act was in full force at this time. Imagine the government's likely response if a person had published an essay about the Lockean right to rebel against tyrannical government, and the profound influence of that concept on the Founding Fathers![68]

In amending the original bill to include Title II, Smith revealed his reasoning for writing a universal sedition statute into Title I rather than a limited one against aliens—he was concerned for equality: "We have laws against aliens who advocate the overthrow of the government by force, but . . . there is nothing . . . prevent[ing] a treasonable American citizen from doing so. . . . [T]his amendment makes it unlawful for any person, be he American citizen or alien, to *advocate* the overthrow of the Government . . . by force."[69] This, of course, on its face, chilled and punished pure speech—even ineffective, hypothetical, pedagogical, or innocuous speech.

Titles II and III were the "alien" of the "alien and sedition" Act. Title II permitted the detention and the deportation of aliens "upon warrant of the Attorney General" for violations of Title I[70]—effectively avoiding the inconvenience of due process, better known as a jury trial. Title III required all aliens to "regist[er] and to be fingerprinted" at their local post offices within thirty days or face criminal penalty.[71] That local post offices were used for the fingerprinting made the Act seem less threatening by avoiding having law enforcement officials perform the task in a police station or a detention facility.[72]

A small minority of congressmen fought against the Act. On the floor of the House of Representatives on June 22nd 1940, Republican-turned-Labor-Party-member Rep. Vito Marcantonio (L-NY) gave a vitriolic and vigorous defense of natural rights:

> . . . [T]he test of a democracy lies in the ability of that democracy to maintain its liberties, to preserve those liberties, and to have more

freedom rather than less freedom during the period of crisis. I know that the overwhelming majority of the Members of this body believe to the contrary. . . .

I believe [those Members' position] is the most incongruous proposition I have ever heard. On the one hand you say you want to preserve American liberty and you then attempt to preserve American liberty by destroying American liberty.

. . . You are not protecting democracy by discriminating against the noncitizen by forcing him to be fingerprinted and registered. What difference is there between this procedure and that of Gestapo Germany? What protection are you giving our democracy when you substitute for the traditions and institutions of American freedom the concepts and practices of Hitlerism? . . . You are destroying the very thing you are trying to protect, and that is going to the very roots of American democracy.[73]

Despite this effort, the Act passed the House in a vote of 382 to 4.[74] As one yea vote, Rep. Hatton Sumners (D-TX), keenly observed, "We are coming under the influence of war psychology, or something very closely akin to it."[75]

FDR signed the Act into law, expressly rejecting the notion that it was "an improper encroachment on civil liberties."[76] The legislative branch of the federal government enacted legislation that the now-late A. Mitchell Palmer could only have dreamed of; the FBI was again in the process of dragneting the citizenry and lawful resident aliens, and the Court while picking off particularly odious state laws showed no stomach for challenging FDR on national security law after the court-packing incident, discussed below.[77]

FDR was the self-proclaimed Guardian of security, but *quis custodiet ipsum Custodem?*[*] Luckily for advocates of the freedom of speech, FDR's attorneys general resisted imbuing the public with a noble lie of seditions

---

[*] "Who will guard us from the Guardian?"

and a "fifth column" and watched the Guardian. That is not to say, however, there were not Paschal lambs whose natural rights were sacrificed. Moreover, that is not to say that the proper safeguard for natural rights is beneficent leadership performing consequentialist or utilitarian cost analysis. Rights are not a good, but an inalienable, intangible legal characteristic of being human.

Pelley and the Great Sedition Trial

At the height of the Brown Scare, FDR was under tremendous pressure by the popular Dies Committee to persecute Americans who were perceived as Communist and Nazi sympathizers and seditionists.[78] By 1939, FDR was putting "constant pressure" on his then Attorney General Frank Murphy to indict disloyal elements.[79] Murphy placated FDR by prosecuting some groups, such as anti-Semitic ones and recruiters for the Communists in the Spanish Civil War.[80]

In 1940, FDR appointed Attorney General Frank Murphy to the Supreme Court. His successor, Robert H. Jackson, would also resist this pressure and also be appointed to the Supreme Court in 1941.[81] Jackson's successor, Frank Biddle, would have a tougher time resisting FDR's urgings. In his seminal work on the freedom of speech during war, *Perilous Times: Free Speech in Wartime*, upon which much of the present work relies, the eminent Professor Geoffrey R. Stone focused on two important cases under Biddle's term as attorney general. This work will also address those two cases: the Pelley Trial and the Great Sedition Trial, albeit for different reasons.

The Pelley Trial was the prosecution of the "American Hitler."[82] William D. Pelley was an American social leader, preacher, editorialist, publisher, and Nazi.[83] Before war was declared against Germany, Pelley ran a group called the Silver Shirts, an anti-Semitic group that operated training camps and engaged in recruitment efforts in mock Nazi uniforms.[84] Pelley had been a thorn in Roosevelt's political side since 1938, and FDR sought to prosecute him twice before the Smith Act was even passed.[85] In the wake of Pearl Harbor, FDR had just the political capital and the legislative backing through the Espionage and Smith Acts to do it. Charging Pelley with violations of those Acts for statements he made between December 1941 and February 1942 in his circular, *The Guardian*, FDR's Justice Department secured a conviction that was appealed to the Seventh Circuit.[86]

In chapter 5, the Seventh Circuit was noted to be a vehicle for advantageous government national security litigation in the First World War: It would not disappoint in the Second World War. Pelley's legal defense was saddled from the outset. His lawyers were incompetent, and he was tried in the Seventh Circuit where the precedent was beneficial to the government.[87] In order to convict, the government needed to establish as a matter of fact that Pelley's statements were false. There are two issues with that: First, not all of them were false; second, what about *opinion* statements?

Pelley stated that the American fleet suffered losses in Pearl Harbor that crippled the Pacific fleet and that our foreign policy before the war had caused Japan's attack. Today, that statement is known to be indisputably true. The Seventh Circuit's opinion, in discussing the element of falsity on appeal, said Pelley's argument "hardly needs consideration" and continued, "[O]ne who broadcasts falsely, as verities, misstatements of the country's continued failure in battle, asserts that it is destitute of defenses, is bankrupt, that it has prejudiced and incompetent leadership, weak and defecting allies, disunity in allied nations and in the United States itself, and extols the virtues of the enemies—cannot successfully challenge the verdict of a jury which finds him guilty of a crime."[88]

The Court relied on these "misstatements of the country's continued failure in battle" in sustaining Pelley's conviction, including Pelley's claims that the losses at Pearl Harbor were much greater than the FDR administration was reporting. Posterity would give significant academic credit to Pelly's factual claims,[89] for example, as Professor Stone concluded when he wrote that "Pelley's characterization of the scope of American losses at Pearl Harbor was actually more accurate than the administration's misleading reports,"* leaving only his opinion claims.

Eventually, the Supreme Court would clarify that media opinion statements—which can never be true or false, as they are entirely subjective—are not actionable unless they are "provable as false."[90] Further, "statements that cannot reasonably be interpreted as stating actual facts about an individual are protected."[91] There is no question that in 1940s America, Pelley's opinions were considered anathema socially and politically, but as John Stuart Mill advocated, there should be no law silencing the natural right to expressing opinion because "[w]e can never be sure that the opinion we are endeavoring to stifle is a false opinion; and if we were sure, stifling it would be an evil still."[92] Pelley intermixed truth and opinion, which must be tolerated in a society that is based on natural rights, no matter how unpopular.

Instead, the Seventh Circuit denied his appeal on this and several other occasions. One of these appeals included an accusation that the federal prosecutor blackmailed the defense attorney into rolling its punches by threatening to deport his German wife under the Smith Act.[93] The Supreme Court declined to hear an appeal on a few occasions, and Pelley received and served ten years in federal prison until he was conditionally paroled in 1952.[94] The condition was that he not engage in "political activities" for the balance of his life.[95]

The Great Sedition Trial of 1944 was one of the most redeeming moments in First Amendment law during this era. This is not because of results of the proceedings, but because it played out as a "Department of Justice experiment in imitation of a Moscow political propaganda trial"[96] and blew up in the government's face so badly that the Justice Department backed far off political prosecutions until the Second Red Scare in the 1950s.

---

* "We [the FDR administration] knew although the public didn't, at the time—that our majestic Pacific fleet had been knocked groggy and wouldn't be able to challenge the Japs for a long time—would be able only to execute a desperate delaying action." Donald M. Nelson, *Arsenal of Democracy: The Story of American War Production* (New York: Harcourt, Brace, 1946), 6; Stone, *Perilous Times*, 263.

With FDR, the press, and popular opinion wrapped up in wartime hysteria, Attorney General Biddle announced that twenty defendants who had "nothing in common [in terms of concert of action, timing, or geography] except a shared hatred of Jews, communism, and Roosevelt" were to be indicted under the Smith Act for "conspir[ing] to undermine the morale of the armed forces."[97] Evidence was first presented to a grand jury in 1941 and an indictment filed in 1942.[98] The government filed a superseding indictment in 1943, and that finally proceeded to trial in 1944.[99] The *New York Times* lamented how the proceedings were "running wearily."[100] In the article "Sedition Trial Even Now Is 'Only' in Its First Stage," "one of the few surviving reporters covering the mass sedition trial" described that the defendants were wearing the Imperial flower of Japan to mark the sixth month of their ongoing trial—with no end in sight—after years putting in a proper indictment.[101]

In the words of a defense attorney and a defendant writing a book on the topic in 1946, A *Trial on Trial: The Great Sedition Trial of 1944*: "[T]he Trial was conceived and staged as a political instrument of propaganda and intimidation of certain ideas and tendencies which are spoken of as isolationism, anti-communism, and anti-Semitism. . . . [A]t no time was the Department of Justice or the F.B.I. worried over the menace to the public safety or the war effort created by these thirty-odd defendants."[102]

These defendants were so unconnected that their viewpoints were often contradictory and mutually exclusive, holding one, two, or none of the descriptors cited above.[103] Somehow, though, the government intended to prove conspiracy, which requires the agreement of all members to a *common* criminal purpose or plan, plus an overt act in furtherance of the conspiracy.

Over the course of the trial, the defendants began treating it as a farce and wearing Halloween masks in the courtroom at times.[104] After the trial dragged on for eight months, with the prosecution halfway through its case, the matter was disposed.[105] The original judge, Edward C. Eicher, died from the stress of the trial, and the next federal judge to whom the case was referred declared a mistrial.[106] The *New York Times* reporter wrote, "Sedition Trial's Wrangles Come to an Abrupt Close," and he described how there were "no lamentations from any source" over the dismissal. Then he complained about the waste of $60,000 in court costs.[107]

The *Washington Post* lambasted the Court, writing that the trial would "stand as a black mark against American justice for years to come" and, in the article "Courtroom Farce," called for the government officials "responsible for this travesty" that is undermining confidence in American justice, to "end this sorry spectacle."[108] It withdrew its reporter.[109] Summing up public sentiment nicely, the *Saturday Evening Post* hailed "Let This Be Our Last Mass Trial."[110]

Through the political prosecution of the "American Hitler," William Pelley, the obduracy of Frank Biddle, the disaster of the Great Sedition Trial, and the new Smith Act, the government had laid the groundwork for a shift in the freedom of speech during wartime.

Of note in the Pelley trial is that he was correct about certain factual assertions regarding the outcome of battles and the impetus for the Japanese attack on Pearl Harbor. FDR's prosecution of Pelley acts just as a Wilson-era barrier to entering the marketplace of ideas that wartime governments put in place, and the publication of misleading reports acts to flood the market with bad information, the effect of which is to sift out truths rather than falsehoods, corrupting the market's truth-seeking function.

Totally baseless political *criminal* prosecutions seemed to become utterly disfavored in the United States after the farce of the Great Sedition Trial. Yet there was still the possibility of throwing a victim to the wolves, like Pelley, for opinion statements because a slightly less strict form of the sedition part of the Smith Act remains enacted in the U.S. Code to this day. Under the ominous title "Advocating Overthrow of the Government," it permits up to twenty years in prison for publishing or orally advocating—not conspiring, merely advocating—overthrow of the government by force.[111] During the Cold War, the Smith Act would be used to send a few more Paschal lambs to the slaughter.

Congress would remain relentless in satisfying the will of political majorities, suppressing communism throughout the Cold War through HUAC and trouncing the natural rights to free and private association. On the plus side, however, the embarrassment the Justice Department faced from its sheer incompetence in the Great Sedition Trial led to the retreat from attacking the freedom of speech in the criminal sphere.

Economic Liberties: The First and Second War Powers Acts and the Return of the War Boards

World War II mirrored World War I in many ways, but none more so than the stripping of economic liberties by executive or administrative fiat. FDR and Wilson, while comparable on free speech rights, were at least distinguishable based on the *results* of their political-speech policies. No such distinction can be drawn in their iron-fisted control of prices, wages, and labor. Using Soviet-style "two year" planning and "Control Materials Programs,"[112] the FDR administration converted the United States from a free market into a command economy.

Backdrop: Jurisprudence and Self-Ownership After the Depression

In the previous chapter discussing World War I, it was noted that outside of the national security jurisprudence applied during the war, there was robust protection for economic liberties at the Supreme Court level through the *Lochner v. New York* line of cases. However, in 1937, amid unprecedented political pressure, the Court reversed direction on protecting the natural right to contract and struck a significant blow to the principle of self-ownership in *West Coast Hotel v. Parrish*.

Lochner involved a suit under the Fourteenth Amendment Due Process Clause.[113] The petitioner ". . . permitted an employee working for him to work more than sixty hours in one week," in violation of a state law requiring New York bakery employees to work not more than fifty hours a week.[114] The Court struck down the law, reasoning that

[t]he statute necessarily interferes with the right of contract between the employer and employees, concerning the number of hours in which the latter may labor in the bakery of the employer. The general right to make a contract in relation to his business is part of the liberty of the individual protected by the Fourteenth Amendment [Due Process Clause] of the Federal Constitution. . . . The right to purchase or to sell labor is part of the liberty protected by this amendment, unless there are circumstances which exclude the right.[115]

In dissent, Justice Holmes claimed, "This case is decided upon an economic theory which a large part of the country does not entertain."[116] He went on to explain that he believed the Constitution does not ensconce the principle of self-ownership in the right to contract: "The liberty of the citizen to do as he likes so long as he does not interfere with the liberty of others to do the same . . . is interfered with. . . . [The] Constitution is not intended to embody a particular economic theory, whether of paternalism . . . or of laissez faire."[117]

Holmes's dissent ignores the Lockean and classical liberal influences on the Drafters of the Constitution that underpinned the inclusion of the Contracts Clause.[118] The Constitution also embodies the Natural Law principle of self-determination and self-ownership, ensconced not only in the Contracts Clause, but also in the Fifth Amendment requiring due process as a precursor to government interference with life, liberty, or property and prohibiting takings; and in the Thirteenth Amendment prohibiting owning another person or his labor.[119] Axiomatically, these principles extend to the economic realm. Although Holmes accused the majority of projecting its collective, personal economic theories onto the Constitution, "Holmes may well have been projecting his personal disbelief in constitutional constraints onto the Founders."*

---

* "Moreover, Holmes offered no factual evidence to support his pronouncements, which he apparently regarded as self-evident." James W. Ely Jr., "The Constitution and Economic Liberty," *Harvard Journal of Law & Public Policy* 35, no. 1 (2012): 29.

Unfortunately, for personal liberty, FDR's political beliefs were more akin to those of Justice Holmes, arguing that "economic laws are not made by nature . . . [but] by human beings."[120] This fallaciously presumes that the economic relationship between humans is not governed in some respects by immutable moral laws such as two plus two equals four and there is no such thing as a free lunch, not solely by governmental regulations, whether authoritative or majoritarian. One of those laws is a bargaining position of absolute self-ownership governing the disposition of all property and labor.

When the Depression hit in the 1930s, unemployment reached 25 percent, the national income rate declined by more than 50 percent,[121] and almost $400,000,000 had been lost in 1931 alone from bank failures.[122] FDR's New Deal contained swaths of new economic regulations, including price, wage, and hour fixes for labor.[123] The Court was not willing to abide this and began striking down New Deal legislation.[124] FDR, not willing to abide by the Supreme Court, introduced the Judicial Procedures Reform Bill of 1937, or court-packing stunt, to create new seats on the Court and to fill them with justices who agreed with his politics.[125] The plan had generated lukewarm-at-best support and virulent opposition;[126] but to avoid conflict and preserve integrity, the Court abandoned the *Lochner* line of cases, cutting the legal protections for economic liberties to nil.

Effectively, FDR's fantastic political threat had cowed the Supreme Court into producing a jurisprudence that had now constitutionally permitted the degree of governmental economic control that John Maynard Keynes's General Theory endorsed. The Court signaled its surrender to FDR's whim in two cases, *West Coast Hotel Co. v. Parrish* and *United States v. Carolene Products*. In 1937, the Court ruled in *West Coast* and upheld a minimum wage law in violation of the freedom to contract for a price a buyer is *willing* to pay.[127] In *Carolene Products*, the Court relegated economic rights and liberties to the realm of "rational basis" review, the least exacting standard of scrutiny that the Court can apply to a rights deprivation, ending the *Lochner* era, and ushering in a day of disastrous economic regulation.[128] The startling relegation of economic liberties to a category of protection far less than that accorded to civil liberties was manifested in the infamous Footnote 4.*

War Is Declared, and Powers Are Expanded

In declaring war on Germany and Japan, Congress took the exact same language used in World War I which this book has argued had been offensive to the Public Takings Clause: "[T]o bring the conflict to a successful termination, all of the resources of the country are hereby pledged by the Congress of the United States."[129] It is clearer this time that Congress is pledging the private resources of all who own them as well as the resources previously owned by the federal government.[130]

In order to supplement the president's power over the country's war economy, Congress passed two War Powers Acts, one in 1941 and one in 1942. FDR would use these Acts to their full extent over the course of the war, creating, expanding, and abolishing government agencies to control the economy.

Similar to the Overman Act of 1918, the First War Powers Act of 1941,[131] in Title I, permitted the president to reorganize and redistribute the federal bureaucracy "for the better utilization of resources and industries," as he "may deem necessary."[132] Title II provided the president a blank check, signed by Congress, to engage in contracts for prosecuting

---

* "There may be narrower scope for operation of the presumption of constitutionality when legislation appears on its face to be within a specific prohibition of the Constitution, such as those of the first ten Amendments, which are deemed equally specific when held to be embraced within the Fourteenth. . . .

"It is unnecessary to consider now whether legislation which restricts those political processes which can ordinarily be expected to bring about repeal of undesirable legislation, is to be subjected to more exacting judicial scrutiny under the general prohibitions of the Fourteenth Amendment than are most other types of legislation. . . .

"Nor need we enquire whether similar considerations enter into the review of statutes directed at particular religious, . . . or national, . . . or racial minorities. . . ; whether prejudice against discrete and insular minorities may be a special condition, which tends seriously to curtail the operation of those political processes ordinarily to be relied upon to protect minorities, and which may call for a correspondingly more searching judicial inquiry." United States v. Carolene Products Company, 304 U.S. 144, 152 & n4 (1938).

the war.[133] Title III expanded the Trading with the Enemy Act to permit the president total control over commerce with foreign nations, and the liquidation of foreign assets under U.S. jurisdiction for the purposes of vesting them in the United States and helping the war effort.[134] Title III slipped in a nonmailability and press-censorship provision, permitting the president to "cause to be censored . . . mail, cable, radio, or other means of transmission" when the communication was leaving the territorial United States.[135] Violations of Title III were punishable by imprisonment and fine.[136]

The Second War Powers Act of 1942[137] was longer and more forceful; however, it ended up being more just than either its immediate predecessor or the Overman Act. Title I gave the president the power to use any garage or motor vehicle facility in the United States and its territories, noncompliance with which was punishable under the law.[138] Title II odiously permitted the president or his agents to take "immediate possession" of any property "necessary for military . . . purposes" after "filing [a] condemnation petition."[139] The president had priority in production bestowed on his contract orders by Title III, which obviously would likely unconstitutionally impair the obligations of contracts.[140]

Further, the president was permitted to inspect the business records of any party to any commercial contract—without a warrant—to ensure compliance with the Act, and "the president may allocate any [shortage] material or facilities . . . as he shall deem necessary or appropriate . . . to promote the national defense."[141] Title III was also supported by a criminal penalty.[142]

However, despite all this, Title VI of the Act provided for protection of the property rights of Americans: It made the Fifth Amendment's rule for determining just compensation applicable to wartime takings of property; albeit, the president, rather than a court, did the actual calculating of the value of the taken property.[143] That is, of course, a violation of due process as the Fifth Amendment right is to a *judicially* determined amount, not a biased executive one. How can it be expected that the paying party in a condemnation action could determine the price and do so alone? These Acts, while clearly showing little regard for the natural right to be secure in one's property and possessions, thus imported a bit more constitutional protection to private property than had been previously given during wartime, but unconstitutionally rejected the constitutional norms.

Guns and Butter: The Return of the War Boards

America was facing copper shortages for the first year of the war, 1941: "[Y]ou can't fight much of a war without almost unlimited amounts of copper [for, among other things, bullets]."[144] Moreover, in the spring of 1940, a "fair part of the United States Army consisted of deteriorating World War I stocks."[145] "Under congressional peacetime appropriations," the size of the army had fallen to 227,000, and there were a total of 2,655 active planes.[146] At the time, the national debt stood at $41 billion when appropriations were doled out in 1940.[147] "The United States had no heavy tanks at all, [and] 144 medium tanks on hand or on order."[148] The Pearl Harbor attack decimated the Pacific fleet in December 1941. The fall of the Philippines in 1942 boded equally poorly for the Pacific theatre.[149] In January 1942, the German Kriegsmarine entered "Second Happy Time," on the Atlantic Coast, known as this because of the ease with which U-boats could sink U.S. ships.[150] As is best summed up, "The United States was still in the early stages of motorizing its horse cavalry regiments,"[151] outdated since World War I.

To the contrary, America's enemies were prepared for the fight: "The success of the Nazi drive across Europe proved what the military of other nations had long suspected: that the complete disarmament after World War I had given her the opportunity to design and build modern equipment."[152] The Nazi Wehrmacht, or Defense Force, consisted of a 4.5-million-man Heer, with six armored Panzer divisions of 3,600 armored vehicles that had decimated British and French armies.[153] The Germans were firing 105mm howitzers while we used .50 caliber machine guns.[154] Their air force, the deadly Luftwaffe, was estimated at 25,000 planes, nearly ten to one to our number of planes.[155] As discussed, the Kriegsmarine had a large head start on the U.S. Navy, and the Pacific fleet was not faring well against the Imperial Japanese navy. Donald M. Nelson, chairman of the War Productions Board aptly stated, "We were really in trouble."[156]

Before Pearl Harbor: 1939–41

Between 1939 and the attack on Pearl Harbor, "industrial preparations were directed by four successive agencies, each with a new increment of power."[157] The first agency was the War Resources Board (WRB), created to "make suggestions" for gearing up the civilian industry for war, which served from August 9th 1939 to November 24th 1939.[158] When the agency was announced in August, the navy and War Department representatives made clear that in the event of a "war emergency," the WRB would serve as the new War Industries Board.[159] There was a "stir of criticism" after the announcement because the people were "reluctant to abandon a policy of isolation."[160] Thus, after reporting, it was dissolved and never served its function as the central planning committee of the U.S. economy.[161]

The president was warned in 1940 that such "powerful superagencies" might make uncorrectable "blunders" in planning; nevertheless FDR's faith in bureaucracy would prove resolute.[162] FDR reactivated a World War I advisory body called the Advisory Commission to the Council of National Defense. It was a "heterogeneous body" of "men [and one woman] now engaged in private industry" that was also "in sympathy with the President's social objectives."[163]

The Advisory Commission was "theoretically the operating arm of a Cabinet level Council of National Defense," but in reality, what FDR made was "a nucleus War Resources Administration, with himself as *ex officio* chairman."[164] Two members were vested with the power to clear war contracts with "billion[s] of [government] dollars to spend," which Congress sanctioned in successive acts in June, September, and October 1940, following the fall of France.[165] The body added a division of labor, despite the "dozen government agencies" charged with labor, and stabilized prices through "voluntary cooperative pressure."[166]

Despite being hampered with incredible bureaucratic inefficiency, such that "the right hand could [not] find out what the left hand was doing, or planned to do at a given time," the body lasted until January 1941.[167] Additionally on September 8th 1939, FDR signed an executive order that activated a "super administrative services division" entitled the Office for Emergency Management (OEM).[168]

In January 1941, the industrial economy moved strongly toward "centralized direction" and "unified command," while the civilian economy suffered its first deprivations.[169] The Office of Production Management (OPM) replaced the Advisory Board in full on January 7th 1941.[170] However, until the creation of the *fourth* agency, the Supply Priorities and Allocations Board (SPAB), in August 1941, "[c]oordination and central direction" were not achieved in policy.[171] Similar to what happened during the Depression, Roosevelt was lampooned in the press for his alphabet soup–like creation of bureaus.[172]

"OPM had full power to 'formulate plans for the mobilization for all defense of the production facilities of the Nation, and to take all lawful action necessary to carry out such plans,'" including "'assuring'" that the appropriate amount of raw material was given to the government, that facilities were maximally used, and that defense production was "'expedited.'"[173] The OPM used priority in contract fulfillment power, compulsory ordering, and property requisitioning under congressional and executive authority.[174] However, the OPM was hampered by institutional issues: Namely, the management office had no requirements clearinghouse telling it what resources were needed by different sectors of the economy, and it could not handle the sheer mass of paperwork involved in running an entire economy.[175] Thus, to relieve the planning problem, the SPAB was created by executive order on August 28th 1941.[176]

These two agencies would "control the civilian economy" through elaborate limitations, mandatory curtailments, control orders, and rations.[177] In terms of labor, the OPM and the FDR administration took command of the labor resources of the country. Similar to World War I, in Los Angeles, the army took over one plant on strike, and any workers who ceased to do "essential work" had draft deferments removed, obviously disincentivizing leaving any industry.[178] By agreement between the unions and the government, no strikes were permitted, and hour and pay schedules were standardized.[179] An Office of Price Administration and Civilian Supply was created within the OPM, whose administrator was to have "'independent and complete control in determining prices.'"[180]

In a final, lasting stab of the Wilson administration's inability to accomplish its domestic economic objectives, "existing records of World War I experience were too incomplete and too poorly organized to serve as guides in the emergency then facing the nation."[181] That emergency was the defense preparations in 1940 and 1941 for World War II.[182] Economic preparation for war was bungled by successor agency after successor agency of FDR's bureaucratic shots in the dark. In order to counter this compounding failure, with each new agency introduced, the FDR administration "tighten[ed] control" of the "total [American] economy."[183] By the fifth and final agency's establishment, it was backed with the "full wartime powers of the President": The zenith of his legal authority.[184]

In his 1999 book, *Day of Deceit: The Truth About FDR and Pearl Harbor*, Robert B. Stinnett, a navy photographer who served in the same World War II aerial group as former President George H. W. Bush, used documents acquired from a Freedom of Information Act request to demonstrate definitively that FDR knew about the attack on Pearl Harbor in advance and let it go as part of his larger strategy to provoke the Japanese into war.[185] The smoking guns included several declassified, U.S.-decoded Japanese naval broadcasts, and spy communiqués which set forth a timetable, a census, and bombing plans for U.S. ships at Pearl Harbor, at least the contents of which were relayed to FDR and his aides.[186]

In large part, the book discussed a particularly damning piece of evidence called the McCollum Memo, a six-page document written in October 1940—fourteen months before the attack on Pearl Harbor—and addressed to two senior FDR military advisors outlining the steps for provoking the Japanese into making an overt act of war.[187] The National Archives turned it over in response to Stinnett's 1995 Freedom of Information Act request.[188] At least one FDR advisor endorsed the plan *in writing* in an attachment to the memo.[189] Although it is unclear whether FDR saw the memo itself, he adopted its recommendations in full and even used his executive order power to carry out the aims it suggested.[190]

The McCollum Memo's "means [by which] Japan could be led to commit an overt act of war" included eight specific recommendations to aggravate the Japanese.[191] Most of them included sending U.S. warships and submarines into "the Orient, Philippines, or Singapore" to indicate a U.S. military presence right in the heart of the Japanese Imperial sphere of influence, getting access to European-allied bases in the region and Australia, or using European alliances to inhibit or embargo Japanese trade (a strategy FDR effectively used).[192] However, one recommendation was curiously isolationist rather than bellicose: "Keep the main strength of the U.S. fleet now in the Pacific in the vicinity of the Hawaiian Islands."[193] Why, when attempting to provoke war, would the military want to leave the fleet in a centralized location? They needed a target so that "by these means" the Japanese would make war.[194]

The McCollum Memo was classified after World War II, and Dudley Knox, the superior who endorsed the plan in writing in an attachment to the memo, was awarded a Legion of Merit in 1945 for his accurate preservation of historical navy records from the Word War II era. Although the FDR-knew-about-Pearl-Harbor historical narrative had been relegated to conspiracy theory for almost sixty years, thanks to Stinnett's diligent work acquiring classified government documents it is now historical fact, and FDR's last noble lie was revealed. Of course, this was more than a lie; it made the president complicit in the deaths of 2,500 members of the U.S. military killed like sitting ducks on December 7th 1941. The infamy of which FDR later spoke was his own.

1942–45: The War Years

One month after Pearl Harbor, in January 1942, Roosevelt created a fifth and final agency, the War Production Board (WPB), to succeed

OPM and SPAB.[195] It lasted until 1945.[196] FDR delegated his entire authority under Title III of the Second War Powers Act to the chairman of the WPB, Donald M. Nelson, who admittedly held power "potentially greater than ever held by any other civilian, except a wartime President."[197] By the end of 1942, the "economy had been converted to war production."[198]

In 1942, the WPB considered civilian industry the biggest threat to full military production, thus "rapid contraction in civilian industry" was a short-term goal of the board.[199] The WPB accomplished that task via ominously named "L" and "M" orders, and the Controlled Materials Plan, which prohibited the manufacture of specific goods and the use of specific materials, respectively.[200] Many durable goods, gaming machines, radios, refrigerators, metal furniture, passenger cars, vacuum cleaners, toys, sewing machines, lawn mowers, kitchen utensils, windows, phonographs, and razor blades were curtailed or prioritized.[201] "[T]he production of nonwar . . . spare parts was also sharply curtailed."[202] However, there were harder impacts of the centralized American economy "not only in housing, but also schools, medical [and dental] care, retail shops, recreation facilities, and other localized services."[203]

Executive Order 9301 instituted a forty-eight-hour workweek for the duration of the war in any "place of employment."[204] With industries, labor, and government in line, the federal government had accomplished the centralized economic planning in the United States that the Soviet Union had been attempting since 1917. The centralization of control continued and was eventually peeled back after the victories in Europe and Japan.

Of note, however, is one aspect of the command economy that developed in 1943. The "czar" principle employed by the Obama administration began as commodity-division czars of the WPB, when it began to insist on being granted "a degree of autonomy that was equivalent to independent czardom." The vice president at the time, Henry A. Wallace, remarked that "establish[ing] commodity 'czars' seems to cause more confusion than the establishment of functional authorities."[205]

FDR candidly admitted he was perfectly willing to mislead and lie in order to accumulate power. He was also willing to violate constitutionally protected property rights for the same end. He needed power, so he started a war. He had a war on his hands, so he needed power.

7

The World War II Era

Quirin and the Japanese Cases

Now, therefore, by virtue of the authority vested in me as President of the United States, and Commander in Chief of the Army and Navy, I hereby authorize and direct the Secretary of War, and the Military Commanders whom he may from time to time designate, whenever he or any designated Commander deems such action necessary or desirable, to prescribe military areas . . . from which any or all persons may be excluded, and with respect to which, the right of any person to enter, remain in, or leave shall be subject to whatever restrictions the Secretary of War or the appropriate Military Commander may impose in his discretion.[*]

—FRANKLIN DELANO ROOSEVELT

---

[*] Franklin Delano Roosevelt, Exec. Order 9066, 7 Fed. Reg. 1407 (1942), authorizing the internment of Japanese Americans on the West Coast.

The Right to a Trial: Military
Tribunals and *Ex parte Quirin*

On July 2nd 1942, by presidential edict, the right to a civilian trial was removed for saboteurs, regardless of whether they were United States citizens:

> [A]ll persons . . . who give obedience to or act under the direction of any . . . [nation at war with the United States] and who during time of war enter or attempt to enter the United States or any territory or possession thereof . . . and are charged with committing or attempting or preparing to commit sabotage, espionage, hostile or warlike acts, or violations of the law or war, shall be subject to the law of war and to the jurisdiction of military tribunals; and that such persons shall not be privileged to seek any remedy . . . in the courts of the United States, or of its States, territories, and possessions.[1]

As discussed in chapter 3, the Treason Clause of the Constitution protects persons accused of giving aid and comfort to the enemy or waging war against the United States, alone, in groups, or under enemy direction.[2] Further, the Constitution "enshrines this in Article III, for the Judiciary to guard against encroachment of the protections provided for in the Treason Clause."[3] These textually demonstrable protections, however, were insufficient for the Supreme Court and FDR to halt the execution of one U.S. citizen without civilian trial, achieving likely the same result through an unnecessary flexing of executive muscles.

The Increasingly Relevant Case of the Eight Nazi Saboteurs and the U-boats in New York and Florida

Operation Pastorius began in Germany in early 1942.[4] Its directive was to train Germans who had lived in America to enter the United States and sabotage the U.S. war effort.[5] In charge of the missions was a former

U.S. resident and German American Bund member, Lt. Walter Kappe of Abwehr II.* Kappe recruited two army members and ten civilian workers who had lived in America to be part of a team of "secret agents."[6] The recruits were placed in an eighteen-day "crash course" sabotage school seventy-five miles outside Berlin in Gut Quenzsee.[7] There they learned how to blend in, to write correspondence in secret, to bomb the most effective places, and to use Jiu-Jitsu.[8]

After spy school eight of the twelve were split into two teams of four and sent to Lorient in the zone occupée in Vichy France.[9] On May 26th 1942, the first group—George J. Dasch, team leader; Ernest P. Burger; Heinrich H. Heinck; and Richard Quirin—left via U-202 for Long Island.[10] On May 28th 1942, the second group—Edward Kerling, team leader; Werner Thiel; Herman O. Neubauer; and Herbert H. Haupt—left via U-584 for Florida.[11]

The Long Island group landed on Amagansett Beach in East Hampton a little after midnight on June 13th, and the Florida group landed outside Jacksonville at Ponte Vedra Beach, Florida, on June 17th.[12] Each man wore a German military uniform.[13] Both groups, being under-trained, underprepared, and (as will be shown) staffed with the wrong men for the job, would face embarrassing failure, thus discouraging sabotage attempts on the U.S. East Coast for the duration of the war.[14]

The captain of the U-202, Hans-Heinz Linder, was no great fan of the beaches of Long Island because his submarine—on a secret mission where avoiding detection was key—became stuck on a sand bank.[15] Just before dawn, the submarine managed to break free undetected.[16]

The spy group, however, was detected. A Coast Guardsman walking along the beach happened upon the group while they were burying their insignia and sabotage equipment. One Nazi was reported to still be wearing his bathing suit.[17] After bungling a cover story about being a local fisherman, Dasch bribed the Guardsman with $260 to stay

---

* Defense Division 2 (Nazi Sabotage Unit).

quiet.[18] His group proceeded to New York City in civilian clothing.[19] The Guardsman had taken the money to get rid of the four men and reported the incident to his Coast Guard colleagues.[20] They proceeded to dig up boxes of explosives and Nazi uniforms on the beaches, and the hunt was on.[21]

The Florida group fared better on the beaches, landing successfully and traveling to Jacksonville undetected.[22] The group then split into pairs, Kerling and Thiel heading to Cincinnati, and Haupt and Neubauer embarking for Chicago.[23] Kerling and Thiel continued on from Cincinnati to New York City.[24] Haupt returned to his father's home in Chicago, where Hans, his father, under false pretenses, helped him get a job in a defense plant and obtain a car, and sheltered him.[25] Once they arrived in New York, Kerling reached out to his old roommate, Anthony Cramer, who, after guessing Kerling was a spy, helped him and Thiel hide some of their money.[26]

Dasch, while in his New York City hotel room, decided that he no longer wished to serve the Third Reich and planned to turn himself in to the FBI.[27] He confided in his co-conspirator Burger.[28] Dasch alerted the FBI to his presence via telephone on June 14th. On June 19th, Dasch, calling himself "Pastorius," turned himself in.[29] At first, his FBI interrogators did not believe him, but eventually they felt his story was credible.[30] After an East Coast manhunt, the remaining seven co-conspirators were arrested by June 27th 1942.[31]

On July 2nd 1942, FDR issued Proclamation No. 2561 *retroactively* ensuring that the Nazi saboteurs would never see the inside of a civilian courtroom. His order was published in the *Federal Register* on July 7th, and the military tribunal opened proceedings against the saboteurs the next day, July 8th.[32] The government was represented by Attorney General Biddle and the Army Judge Advocate General, Maj. Gen. Myron C. Cramer.[33] FDR-nominee Chief Justice Stone's son, Maj. Lausen H. Stone, headed the defense.[34]

During the trial, the defense team decided to engage in a legal tactic called a "collateral attack." Using the writ of habeas corpus, or other similar operations of law, a defendant can "attack" ongoing proceedings in one court using a different court. On July 28th 1942, all the defendants, except Dasch, petitioned for leave to file for a writ under the theory that *Ex parte Milligan* was the controlling case and that because civilian courts were open, access should be provided.[35] The district court denied leave in *Ex parte Quirin*, and the Supreme Court agreed to hear the case.[36] The Supreme Court heard oral argument *the next day*, on July 29th. In an act of extreme cowardice, the Court issued an unsigned, one-page order on July 31st, affirming the commission's legitimacy.[37]

While this collateral attack was ongoing and despite the "short time that [counsel] had to investigate this matter,"[38] the tribunal convicted the saboteurs around August 1st and sentenced them to death.[39] The sentence was carried out on August 8th for six of them: Dasch's and Burger's sentences were commuted to long prison terms for their roles in thwarting the plot.[40] The Supreme Court's "extended" opinion—providing the actual legal reasoning for the Court's decision—was filed months after the *per curiam* order and the executions, on October 31st.[41] By the time the dust had cleared in 1947, the Supreme Court had issued three opinions on the facts of this case, dealing with the saboteurs themselves and Haupt's father and Anthony Cramer, both of whom were convicted of treason.[42]

Wrongly Decided

In this case, the Supreme Court made one of many poor decisions rendered during this time period. There is a litany of constitutional problems with the *Quirin* case. The Nazi saboteurs were arrested, detained, and questioned by civilian authorities, mostly in the Southern and Eastern federal court districts of New York, which would have jurisdiction over the crime. This right to a regular trial is contained not only in Article III, section 2, of the Constitution but also in the Hague Conventions.[43]

Moreover, the order which excluded the Nazis from civilian courts was an *ex post facto*[*] presidential edict, without any congressional authority, issued five days after they had been arrested. The Constitution in Article I clearly states that no "ex post facto Law shall be passed."[44] While Article I traditionally constrains only congressional action and Article II constrains presidential action, in *Calder v. Bull*, a seminal Supreme Court opinion establishing the government's obligatory fidelity to Natural Law concepts, Justice Samuel Chase wrote, "Every law that alters the legal rules of evidence, and receives less, or different, testimony, than the law required at the time of the commission of the offence, in order to convict the offender [is an ex post facto law]."[45]

President Roosevelt's order creating the commission provided that the "Commission shall have power to and shall, as occasion requires, make such rules for the conduct of the proceedings . . . as it shall deem necessary for a full and fair trial of the matters before it. Such evidence shall be admitted as would, in the opinion of the President of the Commission, have probative value to a reasonable man."[46] Evidence, in all state and federal courts of law in the United States, must not merely be *probative*, but must also be *lawfully acquired* and *relevant*, so as to avoid introducing evidence that assassinates a defendant's character, tainting the jury with irrelevant prejudice.[47] This distinction between the evidentiary requirements of the Federal Rules of Evidence and military commission rules will prove of great import during the War on Terror.

And what of their citizenship? At the time the Supreme Court heard the case, Haupt, age twenty-two, asserted that he could avoid a military tribunal and was entitled to civilian trial because he was arrested and detained by civilian authorities, on U.S. soil, *while a U.S. citizen*.[48] Herbert Haupt was a U.S. citizen at the time he was captured. He presented a clear-cut case for treason by waging war and giving aid and comfort to the enemy. Traitors, because of the Treason Clause, can

---

[*] "After the fact," that is, retroactive.

never be constitutionally unilaterally killed (except, of course, in self-defense) by a superior or tried by military commission absent exigent circumstances.[49]

The Supreme Court dismissed Haupt's citizenship arguments in *Ex parte Quirin* in just two paragraphs, giving an opaque and circularly reasoned opinion on why his citizenship was unimportant.[50] Because he was not wearing his uniform, he was in criminal violation of the laws of war, and because the law proscribing treason says nothing about failing to wear a uniform, no civilian protections were afforded him because he was charged with a violation of the law of war, not treason. Of course, waging war against the United States is the hallmark of treason, and the Constitution's criminalization of treason supersedes any treaty. In the Court's opinion, Haupt was not entitled to the due process that the Fifth and Sixth Amendments guarantee to every person. The Nazi saboteurs, even the American among them, had their natural right to a fair and regularly constituted trial violated.

Most of all, the Court handily dismissed the *Ex parte Milligan* argument that the law of war "can never be applied to citizens in states which have upheld the authority of the government, and where the courts are open and their process unobstructed."[51] How did the Court get around this clear rule regarding the primacy of civilian courts for citizens? The Court ruled, "We construe the Court's statement as to the inapplicability of the law of war to Milligan's case as having particular reference to the facts before it. From them the Court concluded that Milligan, not being a part of or associated with the armed forces of the enemy, was a non-belligerent, not subject to the law of war save as-in circumstances found not there to be present and not involved here."[52]

The Court begs the question to be determined: The military tribunal in *Quirin* existed to determine whether the saboteurs were associated with the enemy. Therefore, unless the presumption of innocence is changed, the military tribunal would be unable to exercise jurisdiction without determining the verity of the indictment. The Court read *Milligan*, a jurisdictional case dealing with the predicate of which court's rule speaks in a certain area, and disingenuously converted it into a choice of laws case, where the question is merely to what law the defendant is subject *within* the court structure. Additionally, the *Milligan* Court clearly stated that the question was jurisdictional: "The controlling question in the case is this: Upon the *facts* stated in Milligan's petition, and the exhibits filed, had the military commission mentioned in it *jurisdiction*, legally, to try and sentence him?"[53] not whether the laws of war applied to him.

Overruled?

The Court, however, disgracefully fell into the wartime hysteria that had swept the nation in 1942 following the beating our armed forces had taken so far in the war. In a later case, the Court seemingly overruled *Quirin*, although not expressly, restoring *Milligan* as guiding the application of irregularly constituted military courts' jurisdiction to citizens.

In *Duncan v. Kahanamoku*, a civilian Honolulu stockbroker challenged his conviction by military tribunal for embezzlement.[54] He had been tried for embezzlement by a military tribunal because, in the wake of Pearl Harbor, FDR instituted martial law for all crimes in Hawaii, and so, military tribunals were convened for all judicial matters.[55] After the war ended, the Court held that the act which authorized martial law and thus, military commissions, "was not intended to authorize the supplanting of courts by military tribunals. . . . We hold that both petitioners are now entitled to be released from custody."[56]

In a particularly telling use, the Court cited *Quirin* twice, once for the proposition that procedural safeguards were important and the other in a footnote, articulating its understanding that *Quirin* stands for the broad principle that military commissions can try only certain types of captives—"enemy belligerents, prisoners of war, or others charged with violating the laws of war"—in line with the jurisdictional rules of *Milligan*.[57] The "*Milligan* Rule" was cited eight times.[58] Thus, a blow was struck in favor of liberty. As was said in *Milligan*, "The Constitution of the United States is a law for rulers and people, equally in war and in peace, and covers with the shield of its protection all classes of men, at all times, and under all circumstances."[59]

Executive Fiat: The Japanese Internment Camps

War hysteria hits the hardest along racial lines, and throughout the country, from the president to the military, there was a "pervasive American prejudice against 'Orientals'"; namely, that they were "unassimilable" and would adhere to their emperor.[60] Following the attack on Pearl Harbor, the FBI detained more than 9,000 aliens of German, Italian, and Japanese descent.[61] The approximately 890,000 remaining enemy aliens registered under the Smith Act were restricted from owning weapons, possessing radios, or moving freely.[62] The restrictions were lifted on Italian nationals.[63] German nationals were generally left to their own devices.[64] The Japanese, however, were interned in concentration camps for the duration of the war.

The Racial History of Executive Order 9066

"In the immediate aftermath of Pearl Harbor, there was no clamor for the mass internment of Japanese aliens and Japanese Americans";[65] however, FDR would sign Executive Order 9066 on February 19th 1942, just two and a half months after the Pearl Harbor attack, permitting the internment of U.S. citizens without cause. Why? Misinformation amplified by racial tension and wartime hysteria caused public sentiment to shift away from condemning internment toward extolling its utmost necessity in just two months.

Gen. John L. DeWitt was the army general in charge of the West Coast defense. In the wake of Pearl Harbor, he and Navy Secretary Frank Knox released several false reports of a Japanese fifth column,* naval and air force activity on the California coast.[66] False news reports

---

* *Fifth column* is a term that originated in the Spanish Civil War for subversive activities—a fifth column in addition to four columns of troops.

of fifth-column activity also permeated the marketplace of ideas, dispersing misinformation to fearful people.[67] Attorney General Biddle, General DeWitt, and FBI Director Hoover were staunch opponents of mass internment for logistical and legal reasons.[68] DeWitt even called the prospect of mass internment "damned nonsense."[69]

On January 25th 1942, however, public sentiment shifted with the release of the report by the commission on Pearl Harbor. The report placed blame for the Pearl Harbor incident on the shoulders of "persons of Japanese ancestry" for fifth-column activities in Hawaii that enabled the attack.[70]

Public sentiment went drastically in favor of internment. California Governor Culbert Olson and California Attorney General Earl Warren, future chief justice of the U.S. Supreme Court, entered the debate, calling for the internment of the Japanese.[71] DeWitt flipped on the issue, proclaiming that the "Japanese race is an enemy race"; "the racial strains [of Japanese Americans] are undiluted"; "[w]e must worry about the Japanese all the time until he is wiped off the map," and most famously, a "Jap's a Jap."[72] With such "enlightened" discussion from the upper echelons of the military hierarchy, there is no wonder that FDR found comfort in political cover and ordered such a massive rights deprivation to placate a hysterical public whose hysteria his agents flamed and upon which he capitalized so as to enhance presidential power.

On February 14th 1942, DeWitt openly called for the internment of all people of Japanese ancestry, despite their citizenship.[73] Biddle attempted to head off the impending order, but FDR silenced him and signed No. 9066 on February 19th, which

[a]uthorize[d] and direct[ed] the Secretary of War, and the Military Commanders whom he may from time to time designate . . . to prescribe military areas in such places and of such extent as he or the appropriate Military Commander may determine, from which any or all persons may be excluded, and with respect to which, the right of any person to enter, remain in, or leave shall be subject to whatever restrictions the

Secretary of War or the appropriate Military Commander may impose in his discretion. The Secretary of War is hereby authorized to provide for residents of any such area who are excluded therefrom, such transportation, food, shelter, and other accommodations as may be necessary, in the judgment of the Secretary of War or the said Military Commander, and until other arrangements are made, to accomplish the purpose of this order.[74]

"The public rationale for the decision, laid out in General DeWitt's final report on the evacuation of the Japanese from the West Coast, was that . . . the government had no reasonable way to distinguish loyal from disloyal persons of Japanese descent."[75]

Henry Stimson, the secretary of war, designated DeWitt to carry out this act, pursuant to Executive Order 9066 on February 20th 1942.[76] DeWitt wasted no time in bringing the West Coast under his thumb. His Public Proclamation Nos. 1 and 2, issued March 2nd and March 16th 1942, created military areas and warned of future possible evacuation for "classes of persons as the situation may require."[77]

Executive Order 9102 stepped up the internment process by creating a War Relocation Authority under the OEM to administer Order 9066 by orchestrating the removals.[78] More proclamations from DeWitt soon followed. Public Proclamation No. 3, which created curfews from 8:00 p.m. to 6:00 a.m. in Military Areas Nos. 1 to 6 (essentially the entire West Coast), was issued on March 24th 1942.[79] Shortly after, his Civilian Exclusion Order No. 1 began the exclusion of Japanese Americans from Puget Sound in Seattle.[80] Public Proclamation No. 4 forbade all Japanese Americans from migrating out of any military zone on the West Coast;[81] they would eventually be removed by compulsory measures. There would be fifty-six more exclusion orders by May 10th.[82] The imprisonment of 120,000 Japanese Americans would finish by August 7th, with the Japanese prisoners prohibited from leaving the camps.[83]

The devastation to the Japanese Americans was catastrophic. Citizens were ordered from their homes into hastily made camps and their liberty to move restricted by the color of their skin. In terms of the economic devastation of the West Coast diaspora:

> Upon return to their "home" towns, many found the belongings they had been forced to leave behind destroyed, vandalized, or missing. For the Issei [First Generation], their entire lives' earnings, the fruits of decades of hard work, were lost, and it was too late for them to start rebuilding their fortunes. About 20 percent of the surviving Issei were still below the poverty level in 1970. Men of the Nisei [Second Generation] could not complete their college educations because they had to work to support their families.
>
> The losses sustained by the Japanese Americans were great. According to a 1942 estimate by the Federal Reserve Bank of San Francisco, wartime property losses alone for Japanese Americans were by then in excess of $400 million.[84]

Executive orders, emergency "national security" actions, and a passive Congress took the most fundamental rights—to liberty and property—from a downtrodden American minority, including families with children. Tens of thousands of Italians and Germans were also detained, but released soon after because of a generally held belief that their racial stock was less inclined to adhere to the enemy.[85] The sound of such rationale—*based on racial stock*—whether employed to justify incarceration or liberation is utterly repugnant to the twenty-first-century ear and has largely been swept under the rug by FDR idolaters.

Hirabayashi and *Korematsu*

The Supreme Court was given the opportunity to review the actions taken pursuant to Executive Orders 9066 and 9102 in two cases, *Hirabayashi v. United States* and *Korematsu v. United States*. What ensued was the greatest human rights debacle in Supreme Court history since the *Dred Scott* case: The detention of 120,000 West Coast Japanese Americans, mostly citizens, despite not a single verified incident of espionage or sabotage, based solely on their ancestry, was given the imprimatur "constitutional."[86]

Kiyoshi Hirabayashi, a native-born U.S. citizen, was convicted under a federal statute that prohibited disobeying the curfew proclamation.[87] Hirabayashi broke curfew by being outside "the designated military area between the hours of 8:00 o'clock p.m. and 6:00 a.m."[88] He asserted that his Fifth Amendment due process rights had been violated.

The Court first noted the tactical error of this legal argument. Rejecting *Lochner*'s substantive due process, it held that the "Fifth Amendment contains no equal protection clause and it restrains only such discriminatory legislation by Congress as amounts to a denial of due process."[89] The curfew was found to be within the president's "war power," and the Court noted, "The fact alone that attack on our shores was threatened by Japan, rather than another enemy power, *set these citizens apart from others* who have no particular associations with Japan."[90]

The Court was wrong on two counts. First, due process encapsulates a semblance of equal protection: The process due to a Caucasian American is the same process due to a Japanese American. There is a natural right to equal protection under the laws, which is due any individual under judicial processing. Absent all governments' equal protection requirements, the laws would be so subjectively administered as to be authoritarian or meaningless. Further, the German Americans were not rounded up, despite the beating that the Atlantic Coast was taking from the Kriegsmarine. Individual rights and personal liberty would need to wait another day for this war to end and the FDR-cowed Court to assure their continued legal existence.

That day appeared as if it might have come in the fall of 1944 when Toyosaburo Korematsu's appeal reached the Supreme Court.[91] *Korematsu v. United States* was an appeal of an American citizen of Japanese descent who was convicted of "remaining in San Leandro, California," when a military order said he could not be there because of his race.[92] The opinion began by making a large advancement in civil liberties; it required strict scrutiny for racial classifications.[93] When the Supreme Court reviews a law that targets a particular group, depending on what type of group it is, the government action must meet a rational basis, intermediate, or strict scrutiny standard of review. Strict scrutiny review is the most exacting standard, requiring a compelling government interest and that the means of accomplishment be the least restrictive possible to achieve that interest. However, as the opinion turned, the government's action—the mass internment of more than a hundred thousand Japanese Americans without any individualized basis—was constitutional.[94] Korematsu's conviction was upheld.[95] The Court opined: "Compulsory exclusion of large groups of citizens from their homes, except under circumstances of direst emergency and peril, is inconsistent with our basic governmental institutions. But when under conditions of modern warfare our shores are threatened by hostile forces, the power to protect must be commensurate with the threatened danger."[96]

Thus, in the face of difficult and trying times, actions that were not justifiable under necessity, but were manifestations of racism, hysteria, and the "herd" mentality lamented in the Bourne essay, were made legal and constitutional. The counter-majoritarian branch, the Court, charged with halting the majority's encroachment on the civil and natural liberty of personal movement and use of property, had failed miserably in its delegated task. The "constitutional" internment was "the worst blow our liberties have sustained in many years," and *Korematsu* was a "disaster."[97]

Detaining more than a hundred thousand Americans without charge to investigate their "loyalty" is deplorable in itself.[98] However, this issue is compounded further by the demonstrable, patriotic adherence of many Japanese Americans to their country during the war. The 442nd Regiment, or the "Nisei"* Battalion, was composed of Japanese Americans whose families were interred during the war:[99] "The 442nd Regimental Combat Team

---

* "Second generation (immigrant)."

was the most decorated unit for its size and length of service, in the entire history of the U.S. Military. The four thousand men who initially came in April 1943 had to be replaced nearly 3.5 times. In total, about fourteen thousand men served, ultimately earning 9,486 Purple Hearts, 21 Medals of Honor[,] and an unprecedented eight Presidential Unit Citations."[100]

The Court, Congress, and FDR were judging the Japanese Americans by the color of their skin and not their actions.

Justice Murphy condemned the Court's decision to fall into "the ugly abyss of racism."[101] His vigorous dissent would destroy his personal friendship with FDR:

> No one denies, of course, that there were some disloyal persons of Japanese descent on the Pacific Coast who did all in their power to aid their ancestral land. Similar disloyal activities have been engaged in by many persons of German, Italian and even more pioneer stock in our country. But to infer that examples of individual disloyalty prove group disloyalty and justify discriminatory action against the entire group is to deny that under our system of law individual guilt is the sole basis for deprivation of rights. Moreover, this inference, which is at the very heart of the evacuation orders, has been used in support of the abhorrent and despicable treatment of minority groups by the dictatorial tyrannies which this nation is now pledged to destroy. To give constitutional sanction to that inference in this case, however well-intentioned may have been the military command on the Pacific Coast, is to adopt one of the cruelest of the rationales used by our enemies to destroy the dignity of the individual and to encourage and open the door to discriminatory actions against other minority groups in the passions of tomorrow.[102]

The Post-War: No Return to Reason

Although no relief may be afforded to Haupt or the saboteurs who likely would not have received a death sentence in civilian court, Congress repealed the War Powers Acts after the war, but not *until 1966*.[103] Title I of the Smith Act and the Espionage Act of 1917, however, remain in the U.S. Code today, changing form over the years and serving initially after World War II as the statutory basis for the congressional investigations of the Second Red Scare. The impending Cold War would impede the recognition of liberty after World War II, paving the way for oppression during the Second Red Scare.

The Japanese Americans did not fare too much better than Haupt in terms of restitution. The FDR administration announced the release of the Japanese Americans from internment on December 17th 1944, when it became apparent that the Allies would defeat Japan.[104] Further, one day after FDR announced the close of the internment camps, the Court abrogated the presidential power to issue such directives as Executive Order 9066 in *Ex parte Endo*, a Supreme Court case on a writ of habeas corpus from an interned Japanese woman, Mitsuye Endo:

> Detention which furthered the campaign against espionage and sabotage would be one thing. But detention which has no relationship to that campaign is of a distinct character. Community hostility even to loyal evacuees may have been (and perhaps still is) a serious problem. But if authority for their custody and supervision is to be sought on that ground . . . [congressional and executive action] offer no support. And none other is advanced. To read them that broadly would be to assume that the Congress and the President intended that this discriminatory action should be taken against these people wholly on account of their ancestry even though the government conceded their loyalty to this country. We cannot make such an assumption. As the President has said of these loyal citizens: Americans of Japanese ancestry, like those of many other ancestries, have shown that they can, and want to, accept our institutions and work loyally with the rest of us, making their own valuable contribution to the national wealth and well-being. In vindication of the very ideals for which we are fighting this war it is important to us to maintain a high standard of fair,

considerate, and equal treatment for the people of this minority as of all other minorities.

Mitsuye Endo is entitled to an unconditional release by the War Relocation Authority.[105]

In 1948, under the Truman administration, the government made its first stab at righting the wrong of Japanese American incarceration. The Japanese American Evacuation Claims Act was enacted on July 2nd 1948, providing for a limited redress of grievances.[106] However, the program administration of the law was "agonizingly slow," and only twenty-six thousand internees had been compensated by 1958.[107] In 1988, after years of Japanese American lobbying, President Reagan signed the Civil Liberties Act of 1988 into law, providing for a more realistic but still unsatisfactory compensation measure of $20,000 per individual and "discourag[ing] the occurrence of similar injustices and violations of civil liberties in the future."[108] Ensuring that "all eligible Japanese American recipients will receive their redress money," President George W. Bush expanded the compensation totals in 1992.[109] Liberty, too late for most and too little for all, had somewhat moved in a better direction.

The federal government's treatment of Japanese Americans during World War II showed its lack of fidelity to the Constitution in general and FDR's latent racism in particular. How safe are our liberties if this behavior can be lauded and unremedied?

Part 3

THE LONG WARS

1947–Present

The Cold War

The Truman Years, the Korean Conflict, and the Second Red Scare

[American] Communists are like maggots.[*]

—Rep. Emanuel Celler

Following World War II, the United States was drawn into what some would call World War III, the Cold War—the third major global conflict in fifty years. This one was "fought" between the Soviet Union and the United States from the end of World War II until the collapse of the Soviet Union in 1992. *Fought*, of course, is a misnomer because there was no actual direct fighting between the two major participants.

Traditional instruments of war like national armies, bombs, and guns were replaced with proxy armies, an arms race, spy games, and economic warfare. Several conflicts involved the United States against Soviet proxies, for example, the Korean War against North Korea and

---

[*] Remarks of Rep. Emanuel Celler (D-NY), 96 Cong. Rec. 13722.

China, the Bay of Pigs invasion of Cuba, the Vietnam War against the Vietcong, and conflicts in South America such as the invasions of the Dominican Republic and Grenada.

Clandestine operators came into existence during this period. In 1947, President Truman signed the National Security Act that reorganized the military into the Pentagon, the National Security Council, and the Joint Chiefs of Staff, while creating the CIA.[1] In 1952, Truman issued National Security Council Intelligence Directive, or Presidential Decision Directive No. 9, that created the National Security Agency (NSA).[2]

Attitudes on the home front reflected those of World War I and World War II. From the McCarthy era to COINTELPRO (FBI: Counterintelligence Program), from the McCarran Internal Security Act to the Pentagon Papers case, in a misguided belief that it could keep the home front secure from its enemies, Congress ceded more power to the presidency under Truman and Eisenhower. Eventually, the presidency reached a new height of power under Nixon and then collapsed when revelations came to light about the extent of his executive reach. Meanwhile, the Court maintained a lukewarm approach to limiting presidential power, restraining it at times and affirming it at others.

During World War II, Earl Browder led the Communist Party of the United States of America (CPUSA). "Under Browder's leadership, the CPUSA threw itself into the war effort."[3] The CPUSA even agreed to dissolve itself for a period of time and "cooperate[d] with capitalists."[4] "So long as American Communists pursued such a cooperative course and their patron remained an American ally, they were in no danger [from political prosecution]." However, the tides of political fortune changed in 1945 when the CPUSA reorganized with William Z. Foster, "a hardline Stalinist," at the helm. After FDR's death, the Soviet Union refused to honor the Yalta Conference and began imposing its will over Eastern Europe. Communists became a political liability as the Second Red Scare swept America following the Communist aggression in Eastern Europe and the fall of China to Communist forces.[5]

Truman, between his Marshall Plan and his foreign policy of Soviet "containment," "called upon the country to abandon more than a century of isolationism in favor of expensive overseas initiatives."[6] In order to swing the country to his viewpoint, he needed to use a noble lie to galvanize the hysterical and fearful American people into following his lead. "Given the tendency of the Americans to define international issues in moral terms and their historic fear of foreign radicalism, he . . . portrayed the undertaking as a crusade against communism."[7] What ensued was the Second Red Scare.

Truman needed to create an atmosphere of wartime fear and hysteria against communism: The "administration found it politically impossible to ignore GOP charges that it was doing too little to combat communism at home."[8] "Although convinced that domestic communism was a non-problem," which he once dismissed as "a contemptible minority in a land of freedom" that shrank in size from eighty-thousand to sixty-thousand between 1944 and 1948, and despite his Attorney General Tom C. Clark's statements that Americans "'have all been influenced in [their] thinking . . . by loud shouts from some quarters, notably the House Un-American Activities Committee,'" Truman "adopted a stringent loyalty-security program" and began mentioning the issue of communism in major campaign speeches.[9]

On March 21st 1947, Truman issued Executive Order 9835, setting the tone for the Cold War and the Second Red Scare over the next decade. Executive Order 9835 was an unprecedented legal measure that created the first loyalty program in the executive branch and established a Loyalty Review Board.[10] It led to the investigation of more than three million government employees, thousands of resignations, and the firing of more than three hundred as disloyal Communists.[11]

In Korea, the peninsula was divided into two different countries after the end of the Japanese occupation. The northern Democratic People's Republic of Korea chose Kim Il-Sung to lead it in a totalitarian, oppressive Communist government while the southern Republic of Korea selected Syngman Rhee, who maintained Western allies. The South and North were intent on reunification at any cost under their respective regimes and began engaging in border skirmishes, the North being the more victorious and better armed of the two.[12] Sensing American weakness in the Asian hemisphere because of the withdrawal of American troops and the victory of Communist Chinese forces over Chiang Kai-shek in the Chinese civil war, Soviet dictator Stalin approved of Kim's invasion of the South in April 1950, and on June 25th, North Korean forces crossed into South Korea.[13] In June 1950, the U.N. Security Council approved Resolution 83, permitting member states to provide military aid to South Korea, which Truman afforded.[14]

The McCarran Internal Security Act of 1950

Congress followed Truman's lead and cashed in on the political capital to be gained from prosecuting Communists rather than expending political capital to protect their civil liberties. They impermissibly silenced the one to feed the fears of the many. The infamous HUAC and McCarthy Committee's CPUSA, Hollywood, and U.S. Army hearings are the prime historic examples of the everyday congressional milking of the political cash cow of war hysteria. Almost three months into the Korean War, Congress passed the McCarran Internal Security Act of 1950.[15] With the passage of the McCarran Act, the follower became the leader as the Second Red Scare slipped out of Truman's control, becoming a beast of war hysteria unto its own.

The Act is divided into two titles. Title I, "Subversive Activities Control," which contemplates the suppression of Communist "activities" and "front" organizations in the United States, like the CPUSA, devoted to establishing an American "Communist totalitarian dictatorship."[16] Title II, "Emergency Detention," gave the president broad, unconstitutional, and unprecedented authority to incarcerate Americans and foreigners at the discretion of the president.[17]

Title I of the Act reads like a fascist repression statute. It prohibited members of Communist organizations from federal employment.[18] It denied passports to citizens who were members of the same.[19] It forced

Communist organizations and individual members thereof to register with the ominously named Subversive Activities Control Board (SACB).[20] It legally compelled all persons who published works or used broadcast airways to disclose their Communist affiliation.[21] It created the SACB to harass and spy on these organizations' activities.[22] It limited judicial review of board decisions.[23] Errors in registrations could result in $10,000 fines or five years in jail.[24]

But of all those things, first and foremost it gave eager and ambitious prosecutors a broad and deadly tool to use against Communists: The conspiracy to create a totalitarian dictatorship charge. The conspiracy charge is a prosecutor's greatest weapon. It doesn't really need to show much to prove the crime, only that there was agreement to do so, and one overt act in furtherance of the conspiracy by one of those who agreed. Moreover, when the conspiracy charge is on the table, hearsay testimony is admissible and no marital privilege applies when a spouse is accused of being part of the same conspiracy. The statute criminalized "substantially contribut[ing] to the establishment within the United States of a totalitarian dictatorship," punishable by up to ten years in jail or a $10,000 fine.[25]

Personally, I would not care for the United States to become a totalitarian dictatorship, and I am comfortable asserting that the vast majority of the country would agree with that in the marketplace of ideas. What is disquieting about this provision, however, is that the elements of the crime are not written proscriptively so as to exclude lawful and democratic means. Fascists and Communists, despite the asinine and widely unworkable and unpopular tenets of their philosophies, have as much right under the First Amendment as Republicans and Democrats to advocate for legal reforms sympathetic to their worldviews.

This Act is so broad, even attempting to promote or modify a constitutional amendment to make America totalitarian, as a peaceful measure of change, would be proscribed. If the tables were reversed, and the totalitarians were repressing the proponents of rights and democracy, one should hope that the guaranteed avenue of rewriting the social covenant would remain open to all those subject to it.

Title II, the "concentration camp" provision, is the totalitarian centerpiece of the McCarran Act. It authorized the arbitrary detention of *any* person—even a non-Communist citizen—*by the president* after a *presidentially declared* emergency. The Act permits the president, at his discretion and as he may certify, to declare an "Internal Security Emergency" when war is declared, there is an invasion, or a domestic insurrection occurs.[26] Thereafter, the president may, "acting through the Attorney General" and by issuing Justice Department warrants, detain anyone indefinitely.[27] Violations of the Act subjected the offender to a potential ten-year prison sentence and a $10,000 fine.[28] Detainees, however, would get the same judicial treatment as Guantanamo prisoners fifty years later and West Coast Japanese Americans five years before— their detention would be subject to the review of a Detention Review Board, a group of presidential appointees.[29]

The House considered the McCarran Act as H.R. 9490 on August 29th 1950.[30] The debate began by noting that a few years earlier, Congress failed the less offensive Mundt-Ferguson Communist Registration Bill of 1950, which was a reimaging of the 1948 Mundt-Nixon Bill, one of the authors of which was Rep. Richard Nixon (R-CA) who was, at the time, a young and eager member of the HUAC Committee.[31] The McCarran Act "does go considerably farther" than the original two attempts and "is a stronger bill."[32] One opponent of the bill, Rep. Emanuel Celler (D-NY), noted there were almost no opponents to the bill: "I fear me this bill will pass with a preponderating vote."[33] However, he went on to give a blistering attack on Truman's noble lie: "[T]he shadow of Russia and the sad events in Korea have highlighted a sort of fear, a hysteria that has gripped the Nation, and I shall say even has gripped many members of the House. I do hope that confusion will not track down our wisdom and that our hysterical feeling on anticommunism will not warp our judgment."[34]

Celler, even in attacking the Act's adoption of totalitarian "Communist techniques" and comparing it to the dreaded 1798 Alien and Sedition attacks, succumbed a bit to the hysteria.[35] Only a few sentences after his plea for sanity, he declared, "[American] Communists are like maggots."[36] Rep. Vito Marcantonio (L-NY), who had opposed the adoption of the Smith Act in World War II, opposed this "extreme assault upon the Constitution," comparing it to Jim Crow laws and the "edicts" of Mussolini and Hitler.[37] He made a pointed attack at the proponents of Truman's anti-Communist policy: "You are ripping [the Bill of Rights]; you are tearing [it] to pieces. You are using war hysteria to do it, and incidentally to promote an insane war policy about which there is so much confusion and which no one has as yet attempted in honesty to justify."[38]

Proponents of the Act, waxing jingoist, billed it as a "nonpolitical bill; it is an American bill for the protection and defense of this country."[39] The Act would not, as well, "in any way violate the civil rights or personal rights of any decent, God-fearing, loyal, American citizen."[40] Of course, the same man who made those remarks, Rep. Clarence Brown (R-OH), shortly thereafter noted: "Under this bill[,] I can conceive of a situation arising where some individual may be discriminated against a bit."[41] Rep. John E. Rankin (D-MS) dismissed Representatives Marcantonio and Celler's comments as "most amusing."[42] He further noted for the record many cases in the news involving Communist subversives, such as Julius and Ethel Rosenberg, who never had been "a member of a Christian Church" and sought to, in his opinion, "destroy the Christian religion—the Christian civilization."[43] He also lamented the lack of a "single Christian or a single white gentile among the Communists which [he] ha[s] just named [in the Congressional Record]," but ended on a patriotic note—"God save America."[44]

Rep. Usher L. Burdick (R-ND), who admittedly never expected Congress to be "legislating in a spirit of hysteria," had the last word on the House debate: "My desire to remain in office is not as strong as my desire to preserve the greatest democracy on earth. The clouds of hysteria will pass away some day and when the sun shines again on our institutions, our liberties, and this fair land, I hope our freedom, bought by such a terrible price, will not be supplanted by any form of dictatorship, or emasculated principles of free government."[45]

The Act passed the House in a vote of 354 to 20 and H.R. 9490 moved on to the Senate.[46]

The Senate debated the bill on September 12th 1950 as a separate piece of legislation, S. 4037.[47] The only serious debate was over adding self-serving detention amendments and deciding whether the registration process would be satisfactorily effective in combating the Communists compared to the FBI.[48] One of the few dissenters, Sen. Homer S. Ferguson (R-MI), lambasted the Act as "pure thought-control" and "a blueprint of dictatorship in America."[49] Eventually, the Senate vacated its version of the bill and passed H.R. 9490 in a vote of 70 to 7.[50]

The war hysteria that Truman tried to use as a tool to galvanize the people had spun out of his control. The worst abuses of World War II were being enacted to the sound of deafening applause. Moreover, the effect of this hysteria on the American people had been uniquely exacerbated by the previous forty years in a way Randolph Bourne could not have predicted. America had been in major, life-or-death global conflicts since the turn of the century, each time with its fear honed in to attacks on dissidents in order to superimpose domestic moral outrage onto distant international conflict. World War II was not even a decade past its end at the time. War hysteria appeared to have a cumulative effect on the American psyche.

Attempting to quell somewhat the beast he loosened, Truman made an empty gesture of vetoing a bill that had passed Congress by more than the majorities required to override the veto. His message to Congress on the matter gave them a serious dressing-down on the Act he believed would "put the Government of the United States in the thought control business" and "would make a mockery of the Bill of Rights." He continued,

> Instead of striking blows at communism, the [provisions of the Act] would strike blows at our own liberties and at our position in the forefront of those working for freedom in the world. At a time when our young men are fighting for freedom in Korea, it would be tragic

to advance the objectives of communism in this country, as this bill would do. . . .

[T]he application of the registration requirements to so-called Communist-front organizations can be the greatest danger to freedom of speech, press, and assembly, since the Alien and Sedition Laws of 1798.[51]

The House wasted no time responding to Truman's rather lengthy set of objections to the Act. It immediately moved to call the question, and Rep. John E. Rankin (D-MS), the only proponent of the bill to address Truman's message—even to speak at all—had this to say of its merits: "I have never heard so many misstatements in the same number of words. I am sure the President did not write it, and I doubt if he even read it. It sounds like Communist propaganda."[52] The House overrode the veto in a vote of 268 to 48.[53] The Senate engaged in longer debate, but nonetheless overrode the veto in a vote of 57 to 10.[54] Freedom subsumed to perceived security risk.

The Wrath of the Smith Act and the Escalating Korean Conflict

Chapter 6 discussed the Great Sedition Trial of the early 1940s and how the press at the time eventually begged "Let This Be Our Last Mass Trial."[55] Unfortunately, it was not our last mass trial.

Chapter 6 also discussed the Smith Act of 1940, which criminalized even being a *member* of a group advocating or showing the desirability of disloyal viewpoints such as overthrowing the government or even printing or editing material doing the same.[56] The Smith Act was a tool that not only could be used only against leaders rather than mere members, but also could lead to the entire political prosecution of a minority political faction. Yet as it was crafted, it did not apply only to Nazis and fascist sympathizers, but to Communists and other subversives.[57] Truman's legal infrastructure for abusing executive power in criminal prosecutions was already in place, left over from FDR's war. The criminal prosecutions under the Smith Act began in 1949.

Cold War Tension and the Great Communist Trial of 1949

"As early as 1946 the FBI and the Internal Security Section of the Justice Department's Criminal Division had begun assembling a case against the [Communist] [P]arty."[58] By 1948, that investigation yielded a "1,850-page prosecutive summary" which formed the basis for Attorney General Clark's order to obtain a grand jury indictment of the CPUSA leaders in that year.[59] Clark enlisted the U.S. Attorney for the Southern District of New York, John F. X. McGohey, to prosecute the case, despite warnings from his own attorneys that "the government would 'be faced with a difficult task in seeking to prove beyond a reasonable doubt . . . that the Communist Party advocates resolution by violence.'"[60]

"Worried that these indictments might disturb leftist liberals, and thereby undermine Truman's efforts to win them away from the third-party presidential candidacy of Henry Wallace, Justice Department officials arranged to keep the grand jury's action secret until after the Democratic National Convention."[61] On July 20th 1948, a federal grand jury in the Southern District of New York in Manhattan "handed up true bills" of indictment against the entire twelve-person board of the CPUSA for violations of the Smith Act. (Two days after, Wallace expressed support for them in the *New York Times*.)[62] The popular appellation for the case, the Foley Square Trial, came about because the case was held in Manhattan at the federal courthouse on Foley Square. The building was renamed the Thurgood Marshall United States Courthouse in 2001.

The Truman administration was adamant about a speedy trial for these defendants and wanted the case to begin trial proceedings by "September or October [of 1948]," not because of a concern over the defendants' civil liberties, but "so Democrats could exploit it during the campaign to answer Republican charges that Truman was soft on subversion."[63] Truman was expected to lose the election to the Republican ticket of New York Governor Thomas E. Dewey and California Governor (and later Chief Justice) Earl Warren, leaving responsibility for the impending end of nearly twenty years of unbroken Democratic White House rule squarely on Truman's shoulders. The administration did not get its wish for an October trial date, however. The defense attorneys—quite rightly—attacked the sufficiency of the indictment on the grounds that "anti-Communist hysteria [was] gripping the country" and managed to use William Z. Foster's failing health to delay the trial until January 17th 1949 and sever Foster from the other eleven defendants.[64] Of course, Truman's unexpected victory in the 1948 election demonstrates how unnecessary such a political farce was at the time in a practical sense in addition to being revolting in a constitutional sense. He won by more than two million votes, almost 5 percent, and this non-existent trial certainly was not the difference.[65]

The verdict was predetermined.[66] The CPUSA defendants were saddled from the outset with a then tenderfoot, cantankerous judge, Harold R. Medina, who, although beloved at my undergraduate alma mater, has been described by commentators, biographers, and Supreme Court justices as "combative, abrasive, sarcastic, hypersensitive, and an 'insufferable egoist.'"[67] In addition to having "substantial personal wealth and prep school-Princeton[-Columbia] background," Medina was an imperfect choice to sit as impartial judge for a politically motivated prosecution involving poor radicals because "there was also reason to believe Medina was biased against the defendants."[68] The belief was certainly confirmed throughout the course of the trial.[69]

From the outset, Judge Medina put his foot in his mouth. When he was ruling on whether to grant a defense motion to delay the trial, the prosecution objected on the grounds that it would let them continue their CPUSA activities. Medina noted, "If we let them do that sort of thing, they'll destroy the government."[70] A curious prospect: CPUSA membership had been shrinking; if they were left to carry on their CPUSA activities, they likely would become a smaller problem all by themselves and without the need for mass political suppression to further diminish their numbers. The marketplace of ideas was working and sifting out Communist ideology.

Moreover, Medina, who was sixty-one at the time of the trial and lived to be one hundred and two, was paranoid about his health after seeing the death of Judge Edward C. Eicher from a heart attack due to the stress of the Great Sedition Trial of 1944:

> [Medina] quickly concluded that the endless wrangling with defense counsel, in which he became involved almost from the first day, was part of a deliberate effort by what a sympathetic friend characterized as "the scum of the bar" to wear him down. Medina moaned publicly that the whole experience was just "more than any human being can stand."
>
> Animated by concern for his health, the judge developed an intense hostility toward the defense, which he expressed in a refusal "to have this trial carried on for the purpose of pushing out propaganda."[71]

While the defense attorneys' conduct certainly could be considered provocative, one of the most effective strategies to winning mass trials like these, as the Great Sedition Trial of 1944 showed, is making an absurdity of the proceedings. Medina, of course, would not hold the prosecution and the defense to the same standards in pushing out Communist propaganda. The prosecution's theory proving that the defendants advocated the violent overthrow of the government in contravention of the Smith Act asserted that before 1935, the CPUSA was devoted to the violent overthrow of the government per Leninist Marxism. It eschewed that during World War II because of the Nazi threat facing the mother country and then returned to former violent revolutionary tendencies in the post-war peacetime.[72] To prove it, they would need to introduce Communist "propaganda" into evidence:

> To prove [CPUSA schools on Communist philosophy indoctrinated violent revolution of the Proletariat], the prosecution relied mainly on articles, pamphlets, and books—especially on Marx and Engels's

The Communist Manifesto (1848), Lenin's *State and Revolution* (1917), Stalin's *Fundamentals of Leninism* (1929) and *Program of the Communist International* (1928). Much of this literary evidence was quite dated, and the government could offer no proof that American Communists were about to translate into action any of the ideas it contained. Nevertheless, literature was the heart of the prosecution's case. Government lawyers regarded the testimony of witnesses as only corroborative of their printed evidence and put them on the stand primarily to introduce and interpret Communist literature and explain how it manifested itself in the activities of the CPUSA.[73]

As Michael Belknap noted in *American Political Trials*, "The prosecution proceeded as if the party itself were the defendant, however. Only about ten percent of its evidence tended in any way to establish the complicity of the accused in the alleged conspiracy. The rest served only to build a case against the CPUSA."[74] Belknap's statement requires a bit more explication. In federal courts, for evidence to be introduced by either side into its case-in-chief, it must be relevant and not unfairly prejudicial. It must tend to prove the proposition for which it stands, and the prejudicial value must not substantially outweigh the probative or proposition-proving value.[75] Thus, only 10 percent of the evidence that was introduced at the trial even met the threshold that it tended to prove that Communists in general wanted to overthrow the government. Why introduce the rest? It had unfair, prejudicial value against the ideology but not against the defendants for the alleged crime. The trial was political theatre and propaganda for the government: An opportunity to showcase communism, bash it, and bash its leaders as "pinkos." "Indeed, some courts had held that calling a person a Communist was libel."[76]

When the defense got up to put on its case-in-chief, the trial continued the downward spiral into a kangaroo court. The defense team wanted to put on its own propaganda show and "'to show the whole body of Marxist-Leninist doctrine and from that let the jury decide whether . . . there is any teaching or advocacy of the overthrow of the government by force and violence.'"[77] Judge Medina would not allow this to happen; he "ruled that the defense might offer as evidence only those parts of books and articles which directly refuted the government's accusations."[78] This ruling condemned the entire defense strategy: "This, of course, rendered unworkable the defense strategy of disproving the charges against the defendants by showing the totality of what they taught and advocated."[79]

On cross-examination of defense witnesses, Medina permitted extraordinarily prejudicial behavior by the prosecution. "[T]he defendants were severely handicapped by the prosecution's principal cross-examination technique: asking defense witnesses to identify other individuals as members of the Communist party."[80] McGohey, on cross-examination, employed HUAC's favored technique of getting witnesses to name other Communists, making it the Justice Department's vehicle for attacking witness credibility. The bigger concern is what on earth did that have to do with proving they advocated trying to overthrow the government? Not only were these questions prejudicial, but utterly irrelevant. Nevertheless, Judge Medina "permit[ted] government lawyers to ask repeatedly for identification of other Communists having no apparent connection with the case and did let the jury consider witnesses' refusal to answer such questions in deciding how much weight to give their testimony."[81]

When the jury went to deliberate, Medina's instructions to them rejected any use of the First Amendment's "clear and present danger" test: "[I]f the defendants had violated the Smith Act, 'as a matter of law,' they had created 'sufficient danger of a substantive evil that Congress had a right to prevent to justify the application of the statute under the First Amendment.'"[82] Of course, the jury handed back convictions in a mere seven and a half hours on the narrow question of whether they had violated the Smith Act.[83] Ten of the defendants received five-year sentences. The eleventh, Robert Thompson, received a three-year sentence in light of his bravery in World War II that earned him a Distinguished Service Cross (D.C.S.).[84] Thompson was less than pleased with the outcome:

"Thompson promptly informed the press that he took 'no pleasure that this Wall Street judicial flunky has seen fit to equate my possession of the D.C.S. with two years in prison.'"[85]

After this sedition trial, however, the press did not assail the Justice Department or the judicial system, but approved of the outcome: "Most newspaper writers seem to find in the conviction of the eleven Communist leaders a source of satisfaction. . . . It is pleasant to indulge in such feelings of satisfaction."[86] No paper would demand that the government end mass political trials this time. However, the trial was just the first step—the defendants appealed.

Invasion and the Second Circuit Court of Appeals

The defendants had planted an appellate litigation strategy, however, in their objections to Medina's jury instructions. Medina's omission of the First Amendment question to the jury on "clear and present danger" created an issue of law that appellate courts review *de novo*. The defendants appealed, arguing that Judge Medina should have permitted them to use freedom of speech as a defense and that he committed reversible error by not instructing the jury on the "clear and present danger" test.[87] The Supreme Court had been favorably applying the "clear and present danger" test before this case,[88] so it seemed that Medina's error might result in a reversal.

Then the day following the conclusion of oral arguments, North Korea invaded South Korea, which "obviously shaped [the court's] treatment of the free speech issue."[89] The clarity of the war hysteria that faced the Court of Appeals is well demonstrated in the majority's apocryphal description of the CPUSA's activities:

> One may reasonably think it wiser in the long run to let an unhappy, bitter outcast vent his venom before any crowds he can muster and in any terms that he wishes, be they as ferocious as he will; one may trust that his patent impotence will be a foil to anything he may propose. Indeed, it is a measure of the confidence of a society in its own stability

that it suffers such fustian to go unchecked. Here we are faced with something very different. The American Communist Party, of which the defendants are the controlling spirits, is a highly articulated, well contrived, far spread organization, numbering thousands of adherents, rigidly and ruthlessly disciplined, many of whom are infused with a passionate Utopian faith that is to redeem mankind. It has its Founder, its apostles, its sacred texts—perhaps even its martyrs. It seeks converts far and wide by an extensive system of schooling, demanding of all an inflexible doctrinal orthodoxy.[90]

Because of the Korean conflict, the character of the case changed from a peacetime First Amendment case to a wartime subversion case. Accordingly, writing for the Second Circuit Court of Appeals, Chief Judge and famous jurist Learned Hand expectedly affirmed the convictions under the Smith Act, as well as its constitutionality.[91] In order to accomplish this herculean feat, Hand reformulated the "clear and present danger" rule to adopt a balancing test for First Amendment constitutionality:

The phrase, "clear and present danger," has come to be used as a shorthand statement of those among such mixed or compounded utterances which the Amendment does not protect. . . . It is a way to describe a penumbra of occasions, even the outskirts of which are indefinable, but within which, as is so often the case, the courts must find their way as they can. In each case they must ask whether the gravity of the "evil," discounted by its improbability, justifies such invasion of free speech as is necessary to avoid the danger. We have purposely substituted "improbability" for "remoteness," because that must be the right interpretation.[92]

Hand's reformulation converted the constitutional bias in favor of the freedom of speech, that Congress shall make *no* law abridging it, and replaced it with a balancing test of government and personal interests. Under that formulation, reaching the result of upholding the convictions was much easier.

As to the first matter, the constitutionality of the Smith Act under the First Amendment, the court held that "the Smith Act is constitutional, so limited."[93] However, it took some mental gymnastics to reach this conclusion. The defendants argued that the statute is so overbroad that it proscribes not only words inciting imminent, lawless action, but even innocuous speech. As Judge Hand stated in the majority opinion, the "words of the Act are unconditional and forbid advocacy or teaching of such a violent overthrow at any time and by anyone, weak or strong; literally, they make criminal the fulminations of a half crazy zealot on a soap box, calling for an immediate march upon Washington."[94] Clearly, this Act went well beyond the scope of the "clear and present danger" test, and the defense believed that this should be resolved through Congress rewriting the statute after the court strikes it down.

Instead, the court rewrote the statute from the bench, inferring that the statute was meant to reach only to the extent permitted by the First Amendment, similar to the Second War Powers Act of 1941, which permitted property takings to the extent permitted by the Fifth Amendment. The problem is, unlike the War Powers Act, the supposedly curative language was not even in the text of the statute. The court, however, considered this intent on behalf of Congress self-evident: "We have no such problem here, because there can be no doubt as to the intent; Congress has explicitly declared that it wished the words to govern all cases which they constitutionally could."[95] That is a particularly poor inference in light of the history of the Smith Act itself and Congress's intentions in previous wartime abridgments of the freedom of speech. Moreover, by upholding the convictions, the court had rendered meaningless the constitutional test. If these defendants were a clear and present danger to national security, it requires a vibrant imagination to envision what wouldn't be.

Judge Medina's jury instructions, "which took from the jury all questions regarding the constitutionality of the Act," were similarly upheld.[96] Although he refused to instruct them to make the actual determination of the clear "presence" or imminence of the danger, and the "degree of probability that the utterance will bring about the evil is a question of fact" within the province of a jury, and the "clear and present danger" test as Judge Hand formulated it is a question of fact, not a question of law, the actual balancing of interests was something within the court's province rather than the jury's.[97] Thus, for "these reasons the judge appears to us to have been right, when in the case at bar he took upon himself the duty of declaring that the defendants were guilty."[98] The court then added the qualifier for review, "if the jury found that they organized and supported the Party for the purpose, among others, of spreading the doctrine of violent revolution, that purpose to be realized as soon as it was feasible."[99] That question bears a striking similarity to the question of how imminently or presently the defendants might realize the desired lawless end. Therefore, what is seen here is an instance of question begging: The judge did not err in taking the question of presence or imminence from the jury because his determination was acceptable since the jury later made a finding regarding the feasibility of accomplishing the purpose.

The defendants appealed, and the Supreme Court agreed to hear a portion of their appeal.[100]

Dennis v. United States

The Supreme Court heard oral argument for *Dennis v. United States* on December 4th 1950. Ten days before the Supreme Court heard oral argument, on November 24th, General MacArthur promised an impressive victory on behalf of the U.S. Eighth Army in Korea, launching his Home-by-Christmas Offensive to end the war decisively.[101] It appeared that he could deliver given the U.S. forces' victories up to that point, and thus, war hysteria might abate. Nine days before the Supreme Court heard oral argument, on November 25th, the Eighth Army began the longest, most humiliating retreat in U.S. military history due to massive Chinese intervention in the war, and during a period in which the Chinese were inflicting heavy casualties on the retreating forces.[102] Just as the exigencies of war played out in the Second Circuit, the same considerations would taint the Supreme Court.

The Supreme Court waited to decide the case until June 4th 1951, when it became more obvious that the U.N. and Communist forces had deadlocked on the 38th Parallel. The Supreme Court, with the unmentioned background of the war against totalitarian China and North Korean Communist dictators, described the appellants thusly:

> [T]he Communist Party is a highly disciplined organization, adept at infiltration into strategic positions, use of aliases, and double-meaning language; that the Party is rigidly controlled; . . . Communists, unlike other political parties, tolerate no dissension from the policy laid down by the guiding forces, but that the approved program is slavishly followed by the members of the Party; that the literature of the Party and the statements and activities of its leaders, petitioners here, advocate, and the general goal of the Party, was, during the period in question, to achieve a successful overthrow of the existing order by force and violence.[103]

The Court began its analysis by drawing a false dichotomy: The "obvious purpose of the statute is to protect existing Government not from change by peaceable, lawful and constitutional means, but from change by violence, revolution and terrorism."[104] The statute stands for peace, law, and the constitutional order, while that which it stands against are the forces of violent, Communist revolution, and totalitarian terror. The false dichotomy is a fallacy wherein the proposition forces a binary choice when there are in reality many middle grounds and possibilities (especially relevant here given the breadth of the statute). It is the intellectual equivalent of forcing black and white onto what is actually gray. Accordingly, the Court broadly "reject[ed] any principle of governmental helplessness in the face of preparation for revolution, which principle, carried to its logical conclusion, must lead to anarchy."[105]

Chief Justice Vinson's opinion is one of the more fantastic examples of tortured reasoning in American jurisprudence. Take this line of reasoning, for example. He began by attempting to parse distinctions that delineate permissible speech from what the Smith Act covers—an admittedly "difficult" task, "the very language of the Smith Act negates the interpretation which petitioners would have us impose on that Act. It is directed at advocacy, not discussion."[106] Then, he went on to discuss the purposes of the First Amendment, which, for his argument to hold water, should line up with the distinction he just drew between advocacy and discussion: "The basis of the First Amendment is the hypothesis that speech can rebut speech, propaganda will answer propaganda, free debate of ideas will result in the wisest governmental policies. It is for this reason that this Court has recognized the inherent value of free discourse."[107]

The underlying premise of the First Amendment is an *adversarial* marketplace of ideas, where ideas *compete* for success. Speech can rebut speech. Propaganda is advocacy and discussion. It is impossible for that distinction to hold up over time. How can people discuss two opposing points of view in any form of competing ideas, or debate over the merits of opposite ideas without advocating for the merits of one perspective? Advocacy is essential to discussion because without it, the latter does not contain the adversarial ingredient that leads to an effectively functioning debate in the marketplace of ideas. Vinson's argument is nonsensical. His reasoning, while praising the value of "debate," leads to a Wilsonian distortion of the marketplace of ideas, not its efficient functioning the First Amendment protects.

For the majority, Vinson then concisely summarized the precedents to date that had advanced the freedom of speech: "Although no case subsequent to *Whitney* and *Gitlow* has expressly overruled the majority opinions in those cases, there is little doubt that subsequent opinions have inclined toward the Holmes-Brandeis rationale."[108] In previous chapters, this work has discussed the alliance between Justices Holmes and Brandeis in dissenting from the majority's evisceration of speech rights during the World War I and Red Scare First Amendment cases. Thus, despite recognizing that jurisprudence has developed in a way which would demand that the lower court be reversed, Chief Justice Vinson somehow managed to find his *Dennis* reasoning sound.

The majority also found Judge Hand's reasoning so sound that they adopted his formulation of the "clear and present danger" test outright.[109] And applying that test, they reasoned that the test "cannot mean that, before the Government may act, it must wait until the putsch [The Germanic term (now in American English usage) refers to a quick coup. One of Hitler's many coups was called (in English) the Beer Hall Putsch.] is about to be executed, the plans have been laid and the signal is awaited." Moreover, "[i]f Government is aware that a group aiming at its overthrow is attempting to indoctrinate its members and to commit them to a course whereby they will strike when the leaders feel the circumstances permit, action by the Government is required."[110]

In a completely unsurprising outcome, the Court determined that the leaders of the organization it presumed indoctrinated and spurred its members to subversive revolution, the CPUSA, were in fact guilty of Smith Act violations which were not protected by the First Amendment.[111] Citing the text quoted above, the record "convince[d] us that their convictions were justified on this score."[112] That sweeping conclusion is an interesting show of the majority's prejudice and the impact of war hysteria: The Court had "limited [the grant of *certiorari*] to . . . two questions," neither of which involved justifying the convictions but whether the First Amendment rendered parts of the Smith Act unconstitutional.[113]

In dissent, Justice Hugo Black concisely raised the voice of reason:

At the outset I want to emphasize what the crime involved in this case is, and what it is not. These petitioners were not charged with an attempt to overthrow the Government. They were not charged with overt acts of any kind designed to overthrow the Government. They were not even charged with saying anything or writing anything designed to overthrow the Government. The charge was that they agreed to assemble and to talk and publish certain ideas at a later date: The indictment is that they conspired to organize the Communist Party and to use speech or newspapers and other publications in the future to teach and advocate the forcible overthrow of the Government.

No matter how it is worded, this is a virulent form of prior censorship of speech and press, which I believe the First Amendment forbids. I would hold §3 of the Smith Act authorizing this prior restraint unconstitutional on its face and as applied.[114]

License to Persecute: The Second-Tier Offenders

The *Dennis* decision was a major blow to civil liberties. With the national leaders imprisoned and isolated, the CPUSA began to collapse, and "by 1953 that body was, according to the FBI, 'more or less inoperative.'"[115] Despite the functional impotence of the party and the failure of the government prosecution, as Justice Black pointed out, to tie the members to any actual overt act that could reasonably be interpreted as attempting to overthrow the government, the FBI and Justice Department took *Dennis* as a Supreme Court blessing to persecute the members of the Communist Party:

> The government added to the leadership problems of the CPUSA by prosecuting 132 additional Communists on Smith Act charges. Treating the Supreme Court's *Dennis* decision as a green light to move against the entire party [from 1951 to 1956], the Justice Department quickly secured indictments against national and state Communist leaders in New York and California. By July 1956, Los Angeles, Baltimore, Honolulu, Pittsburgh, Seattle, Detroit, St. Louis, Philadelphia, Cleveland, Denver, New Haven, and New York (twice) had hosted trials of "second string" Communist leaders for conspiring to violate the Smith Act, and other groups of Communists were awaiting trial in Boston and Puerto Rico.[116]

As the Justice Department was leading the American version of the purge of the Communist Party, juries were handing out convictions from war hysteria. The appellate courts stood silent: "[C]ourts of appeals upheld every Smith Act conviction that came before them. Twice the Supreme Court refused even to review such cases."[117] Recall as well that these indictments were handed down as late as 1956—Truman had put America in such a state of war hysteria and fear of Communist revolution that the Justice Department continued indicting Communists three years after the Korean Armistice, Stalin's death, and Truman's departure from the presidency in 1953.

The End of the Second Red Scare: The Warren Court

During the presidency of Dwight D. Eisenhower, the Supreme Court began to attack the legal bulwarks of the Second Red Scare as the exigencies of the Korean War began to fade. Additionally, in 1953, Earl Warren succeeded Fred M. Vinson as chief justice, bringing a new era of liberalism to the Court. In addition to marking the year in which the Warren Court began, 1953 was the year of the Korean Armistice and Stalin's death. However, it took until 1956 for the Red Scare to wind down, and in 1957, the Court reined in both Congress and the president in two successive decisions: *Yates v. United States* and *Watkins v. United States*.

Yates was a landmark Supreme Court opinion at the time.[118] It served as the most clear marking post that war hysteria would no longer be allowed to impose on the rights of political minorities. The *Yates* defendants were convicted in the Southern District of California under the Smith Act as second-tier Communist defendants following the *Dennis* decision.[119] The Los Angeles group appealed their convictions all the way to the Supreme Court, which issued a decision in 1957.[120]

In *Yates*, the Supreme Court held that convictions under the Smith Act require "advocacy of action to that end" of forcible overthrow of the government, not merely advocacy of forcible overthrow of the government as an abstract doctrine.[121]

Indeed, to accomplish this doctrinal end, the Court completely reshaped the meaning of Chief Justice Vinson's distinction between advocacy and discussion in *Dennis*:

It is true that at one point in the late Chief Justice's opinion it is stated that the Smith Act "is directed at advocacy, not discussion," but it is clear that the reference was to advocacy of action, not ideas, for in the very next sentence the opinion emphasizes that the jury was properly instructed that there could be no conviction for "advocacy in the realm of ideas." . . .

In failing to distinguish between advocacy of forcible overthrow as an abstract doctrine and advocacy of action to that end, the District Court appears to have been led astray by the holding in *Dennis* that advocacy of violent action to be taken at some future time was enough. It seems to have considered that, since "inciting" speech is usually thought of as something calculated to induce immediate action, and since *Dennis* held advocacy of action for future overthrow sufficient, this meant that advocacy, irrespective of its tendency to generate action, is punishable, provided only that it is uttered with a specific intent to accomplish overthrow. In other words, the District Court apparently thought that *Dennis* obliterated the traditional dividing line between advocacy of abstract doctrine and advocacy of action.[122]

To be entirely fair to the district court, despite Vinson's inclusion of what the Court considered apparently curative language, the former chief justice very clearly obliterated that distinction in *Dennis*, which *Yates* thankfully rehabilitated. The *Yates* decision is more properly read as overruling the *Dennis* case, efforts by the Court to save the former chief justice embarrassment at being overruled notwithstanding. That same day, the Supreme Court handed down a companion case to *Yates*, *Watkins v. United States*.[123]

In *Watkins*, the petitioner John T. Watkins was a career labor union leader and organizer who was subpoenaed by HUAC to testify.[124] When it was time to name names for the committee, he refused to do so and was held in criminal contempt of Congress.[125]

Writing for the majority, Chief Justice Warren noted that the text of the statute for contempt of Congress contains unusual narrowing language regarding how pertinent the question asked by a congressman is to the inquiry at bar: "Part of the standard of criminality, therefore, is the pertinency of the questions propounded to the witness."[126] Warren then went on to attack the pertinence of naming names to the inquiry of Communist activity: "[T]he authorizing resolution, the remarks of the chairman or members of the committee, or even the nature of the proceedings themselves, might sometimes make the topic clear. This case demonstrates, however, that these sources often leave the matter in grave doubt."[127] The majority concluded that Watkins "was thus not accorded a fair opportunity to determine whether he was within his rights in refusing to answer, and his conviction is necessarily invalid under the Due Process Clause of the Fifth Amendment."[128]

The *Yates* and *Watkins* decisions were twin stabs at the heart of the Second Red Scare legal infrastructure. In *Yates*, the Court's reading of the Smith Act was "narrowed to the point of making it virtually unenforceable."[129] It "took the 'teeth' out of the Smith Act," and "[a]fter the Yates case, there were [almost] no more prosecutions carried out to enforce the Smith Act."[130] The *Watkins* holding had far-reaching implications for reform to the congressional investigatory system, "plac[ing] fundamental restrictions on a Congressional investigatory power that in recent years has been asserted as all but limitless."[131] It permanently damaged the power of committees like HUAC and the McCarthy Committee to harangue individuals for public spectacle and political profit.

However, "[a]ll that glisters is not gold,"[132] and in 1959, the Vietnam War would become the focus of the American public. In the Vietnam-era cases *Scales v. United States* and *United States v. O'Brien*, the Court would leave the door open for future oppression.[133]

Property Rights and Presidential Power in the Korean War: *Youngstown Sheet and Tube Co. v. Sawyer*

The *Youngstown Sheet and Tube Co. v. Sawyer* case represents a modern landmark check by the Supreme Court on presidential power.[134] Justice

Black's 1952 opinion that the president's actions violated the Separation of Powers principle, integral to the Constitution, was "so simplistic,"[135] yet powerful in its implications for restraint on future executive action in wartime.

In 1950, when the North Korean military invaded the South in defiance of international peace treaties, President Harry Truman ordered American troops into the region. President Truman decided not to seek a congressional declaration of war and thus unlawfully bypassed Congress. His approach was not only unconstitutional; at the time, it was novel. President Truman applied to the newly formed United Nations for a resolution authorizing military force.

The Truman administration addressed the problem of post-war inflation with the creation of a new governmental agency called the Wage Stabilization Board.[136] The board sought to keep nationwide price levels down by diffusing labor quarrels and using other techniques. Despite the board's best efforts, the agency was unable to contain the strike of the United Steel Workers of America. The steel industry had rejected the proposed increases in hourly wages put forward by the Wage Stabilization Board, citing the inability to increase steel prices in response to higher wages.

President Truman, fully appreciating the importance of a reliable, efficient, and above all American steel industry in wartime, moved to avoid a potential military embarrassment. Similar to Wilson's and FDR's economic seizure actions in their respective world wars, on April 8th 1952, the president issued Executive Order 10340, directing the secretary of commerce to seize and operate the majority of American steel mills[137] in direct contravention of the Fourth and Fifth Amendments. The executive order did not cite a specific statutory provision asserting the power to execute this action; it "invoked generally the powers vested in the President by the Constitution and laws of the United States."[138]

Truman subsequently notified Congress of his actions, submitting to the fact that Congress possessed the power to supersede his order.[139]

Congress failed to act on the president's seizures. However, Congress *had already* acted on the possibility of similar situations with the passage of the Defense Production Act of 1950,[140] the Labor Management Relations Act of 1947,[141] and the Selective Service Act of 1948,[142] all of which "repeatedly," and affirmatively, "declined to authorize governmental seizures of property to settle labor disputes."[143] The steel industry filed suit in federal district court, seeking a declaratory judgment and injunctive relief. The district court judge issued a temporary injunction on the secretary of commerce's actions. The Court of Appeals stayed the injunction, and the Supreme Court agreed to hear the appeal.

In a 6-to-3 decision, the Supreme Court affirmed the district court's order, restoring the injunction upon the government and awarding control of the steel mills back to their rightful and lawful owners. In his majority opinion, Justice Hugo L. Black emphasized the obvious: The president may use only powers specifically given to him by the Constitution itself or powers authorized by Congress when exercising its enumerated legislative abilities. There was no statute that authorized the president to seize the mills, and the Constitution does not provide such an individual enumerated power to the president outright: "Authority to issue such an order in the circumstances of the case was not deducible from the aggregate of the executive powers under Article II of the Constitution; nor was the Order maintainable as an exercise of the president's powers as commander-in-chief of the armed forces. The power sought to be exercised was the lawmaking power."[144]

Despite the fact that, as Truman's attorney general argued, presidents in the past had exercised this kind of executive power,* the Court correctly held that the actions of President Truman were indeed illegal. Justice

---

* "The assertion of plenary, if not absolute, policy making authority did not originate with Truman. Lincoln, Wilson, Theodore Roosevelt, Franklin D, Roosevelt, and subsequent Presidents, including Clinton, George H. W. Bush and George W. Bush, all have made similar assertions of power." See Arthur H. Garrison, "National Security and Presidential Power: Judicial Deference and Establishing Boundaries in World War Two and the Korean War," *Cumberland Law Review* 39, no. 3 (2009): 662.

Black concluded his opinion with this: "The Founders of this nation entrusted the lawmaking power to the Congress alone in both good and bad times. It would do no good to recall the historical events, the fears of power and the hopes for freedom that lay behind their choice. Such a review would but confirm our holding that this seizure order cannot stand."[145] The president acted in a "total absence" of power in his attempt to circumvent the legislative process and control the private companies.[146]

Arguably the most well-known judicial concurrence in U.S. judicial history emerged from the *Youngstown* case. That opinion, a concurrence by Justice Robert Jackson, has come to be recognized as "the seminal decision defining presidential power within the separation of powers context."[147] Justice Jackson opined three separate power categories which the president can occupy at any one time:

1. When the President acts pursuant to an express or implied authorization of Congress, his authority is at its maximum, for it includes all that he possesses in his own right plus all that Congress can delegate. In these circumstances, and in these only, may he be said (for what it may be worth) to personify the federal sovereignty. If his act is held unconstitutional under these circumstances, it usually means that the federal [g]overnment as an undivided whole lacks power.

2. When the President acts in absence of either a congressional grant or denial of authority, he can only rely upon his own independent powers, but there is a zone of twilight in which he and Congress may have concurrent authority, or in which its distribution is uncertain. Therefore, congressional inertia, indifference or acquiescence may sometimes, at least, as a practical matter, enable, if not invite, measures on independent Presidential responsibility. In this area, any actual test of power is likely to depend on the imperatives of events and contemporary imponderables, rather than on abstract theories of law.

3. When the President takes measures incompatible with the expressed or implied will of Congress, his power is at its lowest ebb, for then he can rely only upon his own constitutional powers minus any constitutional powers of Congress over the matter. Courts can sustain exclusive Presidential control in such a case only by disabling the Congress from acting upon the subject. Presidential claim to a power at once so conclusive and preclusive must be scrutinized with caution, for what is at stake is the equilibrium established by our constitutional system.[148]

When the president has statutory authorization, his power is at its highest; law exists, and the president is empowered by the Constitution to enforce the law. When the president acts on his own, without congressional approval, he may execute only such powers that were given to him by the Constitution itself. He may not, for example, declare war on another country. However, as the commander in chief, the president is empowered through Article II of the Constitution to mobilize troops in preparation for war.

The most obvious situation in which the president lacks both congressional and constitutional authority is when he acts in complete contradiction to congressional action.[149] In a presidential-power category described by Justice Jackson as the "lowest ebb,"[150] the president "has no authorization to act in this type of situation, even in an emergency."[151] As Tara Branam wrote: "If the President's action is incompatible with the will of Congress, then the only possible justification for the action is that it is based on presidential authority derived from the Constitution. Where such a showing cannot be made, the presidential directive *must* be overturned."[152]

The courts have remained largely deferential to presidential action. *Youngstown* represents the only presidential executive order ever overturned in its entirety by the U.S. Supreme Court, and surprisingly, lower courts have struck down only two other presidential directives.[153]

Both lower court decisions[154] involved a presidential order in conflict with the National Labor Relations Act.[155] In the first case, in 1996, *Chamber of Commerce v. Reich*, the Court reprimanded President Clinton when he issued an executive order prohibiting the permanent replacement of striking workers.[156] The D.C. Circuit held that President Bill Clinton, although not claiming independent constitutional power, cannot claim broad statutory authority from a general statute when there exists another more specific statute which restricts the president.[157]

In the second case, in 2002, *Building & Construction Trades Department v. Allbaugh*, President George W. Bush signed an executive order which prohibited federal agencies from requiring or prohibiting project labor agreements on construction jobs that were federally funded.[158] The D.C. Circuit overturned that order. The Court, unlike the case with Clinton, found that Bush's directive lacked both independent constitutional power and statutory authorization. The Court invalidated the order as "beyond the scope of the President's authority."[159]

In practical terms, actions of previous presidents have emboldened the actions of future officeholders. The courts have not only the power but also the responsibility to restrain the president when he attempts to wield unauthorized power. As discussed below, modern presidents have repeatedly usurped legislative power at both the expense of Congress and the rights of individual citizens. For all the academic laurels heaped on Justice Jackson's concurrence and all the relief over stopping the president from stealing property, the Natural Law point has been missed. Under the Natural Law, the only moral property transfers are those which are fully and truly voluntary. I suspect that Jefferson would have argued that no government may give itself the power to seize or take property, and no majority may make it lawful for the government to do so to a minority because the ownership of property is a natural right—thus free from government interference.

Can a Treaty Trump Freedom?

Does the Constitution provide protection to individuals abroad? Do we enjoy freedoms guaranteed to us by the Bill of Rights when we travel to other countries? In 1957, the Supreme Court answered these questions, at least with respect to American citizens who are arrested by U.S. authorities overseas. In the case of *Reid v. Covert*, the Court ruled that the Constitution supersedes international treaties ratified by the Senate and that American citizens still enjoy protections abroad while in the custody of U.S. forces.[160]

A military tribunal convicted Clarice Covert, wife of a U.S. Air Force sergeant stationed in the United Kingdom, of murdering her husband. Mrs. Covert was brought before a court-martial under the Uniform Code of Military Justice, where she was tried, convicted, and sentenced to life imprisonment.[161] The military claimed it was given jurisdiction to prosecute Mrs. Covert by an executive agreement entered into between the president of the United States and the government of the United Kingdom, allowing for the U.S. military courts to exercise jurisdiction over offenses committed by American servicemen and their dependents in Great Britain. Covert petitioned a federal court for a writ of habeas corpus, and the case eventually reached the Supreme Court. The Court addressed two separate questions: (1) Does the ability of Congress "to make Rules for the Government and Regulation of the land and naval Forces" allow for the court-martial of civilian dependents of soldiers? and (2) Even if Congress had that power, do the Fifth and Sixth Amendments prohibit such an action?[162]

Answering in the negative to the former and in the affirmative to the latter, the Court held that U.S. citizen civilians abroad have the right to Fifth and Sixth Amendment constitutional protections.[163] Therefore Mrs. Covert was entitled to a civilian jury trial in an Article III court, not a military tribunal, which essentially consisted of her husband's peers. "No agreement with a foreign nation can confer power on the Congress, or on any other branch of Government, which is free from the restraints of the Constitution."[164]

This was not the original conclusion[165] of the Court, however. In *Reid v. Covert I*, the majority held that the provisions of Article III and other amendments do not apply to American citizens tried by the U.S. government in foreign countries.[166] It took until rehearing in *Reid v. Covert II*[167] for the Court to reverse its position and hold in its new opinion that civilian citizen military dependents could not be tried by military authorities.[168]

Remarkably, this is the only time the Supreme Court has reversed its previous decision after a petition for rehearing.[169] The Constitution should not be thrown to the wayside while Americans are abroad. If natural rights are truly inalienable, they do not disappear while one is outside the United States; they are inalienable. Justice Black summarized this notion beautifully: "[W]e reject the idea that when the United States acts against citizens abroad it can do so free of the Bill of Rights. The United States is entirely a creature of the Constitution. Its power and authority have no other source. It can only act in accordance with all the limitations imposed by the Constitution."[170]

The passage of a law through Congress and the ratification of a treaty by the Senate are the only ways in which enforceable federal law can be created. However, the Supreme Court has been consistent in its insistence that the government cannot supersede the Constitution. International treaties ratified by the Senate may supplement the Constitution, but they may not alter the protections and provisions already contained within its authority. The Supremacy Clause dictates a mandatory adherence to this principle.

With the modern rise of technology and transnational corporations, American citizens are increasingly overseas. How can it be logical or consistent with Natural Law principles for the U.S. government to apply the Constitution at home and disregard it abroad? It cannot. The Constitution was not designed to apply merely to individuals within the borders of the United States; rather, it was crafted to protect *from the government* the inalienable rights that all human beings possess regardless of location, status, or wealth.

As we have seen, the federal government has twisted and tortured the Constitution to its own ends of the acquisition of power and property even when it is not actively engaged in large-scale war. Is it any wonder that all war—violent war and cold war—makes this easier to accomplish? Let us look at what the feds did during the infamous Cold War of the twentieth century.

9

The Cold War

The Civil War in Vietnam

*Let historians not record that when America was
the most powerful nation in the world we passed
on the other side of the road and allowed the last
hopes for peace and freedom of millions of people to
be suffocated by the forces of totalitarianism.*[*]

—President Richard Nixon

The Vietnam War Under JFK and LBJ: Liberalization and Vacillation on the Freedom of Speech

Nearly two decades had passed since the end of the Second World War and the start of the Cold War. Most Americans regarded the Soviet Union and communism as "a threat to America and a menace to its principles."[1]

---

[*] President Richard Nixon, Address to the Nation on the War in Vietnam (November 3, 1969).

The administration of President Harry Truman, the decade before, moved the United States from a stance of neutrality to one of intervention in the containment of communism worldwide.[2] Under Truman and Eisenhower, the United States had already expended military and diplomatic aid in Vietnam, but the conflict did not hit the American political stage until 1959, after North Vietnam invaded Laos in December 1958. In President John F. Kennedy's term, the situation continued to escalate with several hundred American Special Forces "military advisors" arriving in May 1961.

By the time of the Kennedy assassination, the United States had committed more than sixteen thousand troops to combat in Vietnam.[3] Kennedy's successor, Lyndon B. Johnson, was committed to creating a "Great Society" domestically and pursuing globalism abroad.[4] Johnson felt compelled to fight a full-blown war in Vietnam, and in 1965 he authorized both air and ground combat operations against the North Vietnamese. America drafted its young men to fight a war in Southeast Asia. By the end of 1967, the number of American troops in Vietnam had increased to more than half a million.[5] The war brought with it the usual attempts by the government to trample upon individual civil liberties, particularly those of Communists. The Court both liberalized and vacillated over the freedom of speech, issuing decisions that tended to strike at attempts to prioritize security over freedom.

The change of chief justice from Fred Vinson to Earl Warren in 1953 was one of the starkest changes in Court leadership, matched only by the change from Earl Warren to conservative Chief Justice Warren E. Burger in 1969. Moreover, the Vietnam War was overwhelmingly unpopular with the American people, thus providing the Court some political cover to avoid giving wartime deference to Congress. However, as the conflict in Vietnam escalated, the advances in First Amendment jurisprudence made by the Warren Court succumbed to the demands of "national security" on the road to *Brandenburg v. Ohio*.

Kennedy and *Scales v. United States*

In *Scales v. United States*, the Court upheld the 1958 re-conviction of Junius Scales of the CPUSA for violating the (mere) membership provision of the Smith Act on First and Fifth Amendment grounds. Broadly assaulting the freedom of association, the Court held thusly:

> Little remains to be said concerning the claim that the statute infringes First Amendment freedoms. It was settled in *Dennis* that the advocacy with which we are here concerned is not constitutionally protected speech, and it was further established that a combination to promote such advocacy, albeit under the aegis of what purports to be a political party, is not such association as is protected by the First Amendment. We can discern no reason why membership, when it constitutes a purposeful form of complicity in a group engaging in this same forbidden advocacy, should receive any greater degree of protection from the guarantees of that Amendment.[6]

President John F. Kennedy commuted the sentence of Junius Scales, "the only American ever imprisoned under that clause of the Smith Act prohibiting membership" in a Communist organization, in December 1962.[7] The gambit gained him favor in East Coast political circles, with the *New York Times* "feel[ing] that the President acted with courage and wisdom, as well as in the best American tradition in granting it."[8] Conversely, the Court's decision was assailed by the *New York Times* editorial board when it was issued in June: "The sustaining of the Smith Act's membership clause, and the setting in motion of the ponderous Internal Security Act, can only serve again to divert public attention to the virtually non-existent internal Communist threat. The real Communist threat is abroad."[9] Thus, in the background to the new liberal attitude of the 1960s, there was mounting tension regarding legal repression in the escalating Vietnam War.

Noble Lies: The Gulf of Tonkin, Escalation in Vietnam Under LBJ, and *Albertson v. Subversive Activities Control Board*

President Kennedy was assassinated on November 22nd 1963, and Vice President Lyndon B. Johnson succeeded him. On August 2nd and 4th 1964, the United States raised a false flag operation in the Gulf of Tonkin by claiming that North Vietnamese naval ships attacked the USS *Maddox* based on deliberately misleading interpretations of NSA intercepts that showed no attack occurred.[10] Tonkin was LBJ's noble lie. As a result, LBJ had cause to begin a massive war in Southeast Asia. Between 1963 and 1968, U.S. troop levels in Vietnam went from 16,000 to 536,000.[11] The next ground phase of the Cold War, the Vietnam War, derailed the Warren Court's march toward a robust First Amendment jurisprudence in *United States v. O'Brien*. To its credit, though, the Warren Court did manage to ensure in its other First Amendment cases that a Third Red Scare did not result from the Vietnam War.

In 1965, the Supreme Court directly squared off with the Subversive Activities Control Board (SACB), the agency created under the McCarran Act for the sole purpose of harassing Communist organizations. If there were an agency that would be the source of dragging harmless, everyday political radicals through quasi-judicial trials, it would be the SACB.

In *Albertson v. Subversive Activities Control Board*, the Warren Court handily dealt the SACB a blow by taking all real power from it to perform its primary function, registering Communists:

> The risks of incrimination which the petitioners take in registering are obvious. Form IS-52a requires an admission of membership in the Communist Party. Such an admission of membership may be used to prosecute the registrant under the membership clause of the Smith Act, or under §4(a) of the Subversive Activities Control Act, to mention only two federal criminal statutes. Accordingly, we have held that mere association with the Communist Party presents sufficient threat of prosecution to support a claim of privilege.[12]

By making the fact of mere association a question subject to the Fifth Amendment privilege against self-incrimination, the Court effectively said to all Communists that filling out these forms may be avoided by asserting their Fifth Amendment rights! This was a large blow to the ease of access that ambitious anti-Communists would otherwise have to information about possible prosecutions.

United States v. Robel

The Warren Court followed up its decision in *Albertson* with a direct attack on the McCarran Act and the state's interest in national security in 1967 in *United States v. Robel*.[13]

Eugene F. Robel was a machinist in Seattle who was a member of the CPUSA.[14] He worked at Todd Shipyards Corp. from the time the CPUSA was designated a Communist-action organization under the McCarran Act in 1961.[15] In 1962, Secretary of Defense Robert McNamara designated the facility a "defense facility," which thereby made employment for any Communist-action organization member at the shipyard a criminal offense, *for the employee*.[16] Robel was charged with violating that section of the McCarran Act.[17] The district court dismissed the indictment, relying on the precedent in *Scales*.[18] The government initially appealed to the Ninth Circuit, which certified a direct appeal to the Supreme Court.[19]

The Supreme Court first noted that the portion of the McCarran Act under which Robel was convicted was "impossible to narrow its indiscriminately cast and overly broad scope without substantial rewriting." Therefore, the Court held that "it is precisely because that statute sweeps indiscriminately across all types of association with Communist-action groups, without regard to the quality and degree of membership, that it runs afoul of the First Amendment."[20] Just like that, the criminalization of being both a CPUSA member and a federal employee disappeared. The Court's next holding was utterly shocking.

Because the government asserted that Congress's independent war powers could justify this action, the Court had occasion to address the merits of the state's interest in national security. Chief Justice Warren's majority opinion on addressing that question resounds as one of the few Supreme Court precedents vehemently attacking the over-exercise of war authority:

> The Government seeks to defend the statute on the ground that it was passed pursuant to Congress' war power. The Government argues that this Court has given broad deference to the exercise of that constitutional power by the national legislature. That argument finds support in a number of decisions of this Court. However, *the phrase "war power" cannot be invoked as a talismanic incantation to support any exercise of congressional power which can be brought within its ambit.*
>
> "[E]ven the war power does not remove constitutional limitations safeguarding essential liberties." More specifically in this case, the Government asserts that [the McCarran Act] is an expression "of the growing concern shown by the executive and legislative branches of government over the risks of internal subversion in plants on which the national defense depend[s]."
>
> *Yet, this concept of "national defense" cannot be deemed an end in itself, justifying any exercise of legislative power designed to promote such a goal.* Implicit in the term "national defense" is the notion of defending those values and ideals which set this Nation apart. For almost two centuries, our country has taken singular pride in the democratic ideals enshrined in its Constitution, and the most cherished of those ideals have found expression in the First Amendment. *It would indeed be ironic if, in the name of national defense, we would sanction the subversion of one of those liberties—the freedom of association—which makes the defense of the Nation worthwhile.*[21]

The Court's language in this case was a landmark change in war powers jurisprudence. Even Justice Jackson's concurrence in *Youngstown* could not have had the limiting impact of this language. Compare this case to the *Korematsu* decision twenty-three years earlier: "Compulsory exclusion of large groups of citizens from their homes . . . is inconsistent with our basic governmental institutions. But when under conditions of modern warfare our shores are threatened by hostile forces, the power to protect must be commensurate with the threatened danger."[22] The Court had come far in reversing the trend of bowing to the phrase "national security" anytime it was used in a legal argument. However, as the war escalated and tensions on college campuses across the country rose, the Supreme Court would not be able to keep up its trend and slipped back toward the *Scales* jurisprudence.

United States v. O'Brien

In the 1968 case of *United States v. O'Brien*, the Supreme Court held that a criminal law against burning a draft card did not violate the free speech protections of the First Amendment.[23] The case was argued six days before the First Tet Offensive and decided shortly after the North Vietnamese began the Second Tet Offensive.

On March 31st 1966, David O'Brien stood on the steps of the South Boston Courthouse and burned his draft card as a personal protest against the war in Vietnam.[24] A crowd attacked O'Brien, and the FBI subsequently arrested him for destroying his draft card, a violation of section 462(b)(6) of the Military Training Act.[25] One year before O'Brien's arrest, Congress had amended the Military Training Act to penalize anyone who "forges, alters, . . . or in any manner changes" a Selective Service certificate. The statute also punished anyone who "knowingly destroys [or] knowingly mutilates" a Selective Service certificate.[26] O'Brien was indicted and then subsequently convicted by a jury for violating the Act.

The First Circuit upheld the conviction, and O'Brien appealed to the Supreme Court. In a 7-to-1 decision, the Supreme Court upheld the conviction and the statute as furthering a compelling governmental interest—maintenance of conscription records. Writing for the majority, Chief Justice Earl Warren rejected O'Brien's argument that the law was only passed to suppress the free speech of anti-war protesters. The Court, it would seem, was unmoved by the prospect of a statute restricting First Amendment protections if the government could prove that there was another constitutionally valid, motivating factor.[27] Chief Justice Warren wrote that "this Court will not strike down an otherwise constitutional statute on the basis of an alleged illicit legislative motive."[28]

This decision by the Court marks a large departure from the American tradition of free, unrestricted speech. The Court effectively licensed the government to arrest individuals in wartime who manifest disagreement with its actions.

O'Brien was just "expressing a simple but powerful political idea: his personal opposition to and refusal to participate in the ongoing and pro-active American military involvement in Southeast Asia."[29] Moreover, his simple destruction of *his own* draft card can hardly be said to dis-rupt the government's record-keeping. Under the Court's reasoning, the door was opened to the possibility for Congress to pass legislation which conflicts with one part of the Constitution but is valid under another. This decision is not logical. One part of the Constitution cannot guar-antee the validity of a statute when another part forbids it. A law *must* conform to all the parts of the Constitution in order to be legitimate. There cannot, and must not, be a way for the government to abrogate some rights in pursuit of others, lest no rights remain secure.

The Dawning of the Nixon Years: *Brandenburg v. Ohio*

Immediately after winning the 1968 presidential election, Richard M. Nixon promised to bring the Vietnam War to an honorable end. Taking the zeitgeist of the Nixon anti-war movement, the Court decided *Brandenburg v. Ohio* in 1969, unanimously overruling *Whitney v. California* and casting considerable doubt on the *Dennis* line of cases.[30] It held that for speech not to be protected by the First Amendment, it must be "directed to inciting or producing imminent lawless action and is likely to incite or produce such action."[31]

Clarence Brandenburg was convicted under Ohio's criminal

syndicalism statute, Ohio's two-for-one sedition and criminal syndicate act.[32] Brandenburg was a local leader of the Ku Klux Klan in Hamilton County.[33] At a meeting of the Klan with thirteen attendees—twelve members and one cameraman from a news crew—who were mostly armed, he gave the following speech:

> This is an organizers' meeting. We have had quite a few members here today which are—we have hundreds, hundreds of members through-out the State of Ohio. I can quote from a newspaper clipping from the Columbus, Ohio Dispatch, five weeks ago Sunday morning. The Klan has more members in the State of Ohio than does any other organization. We're not a revengent [sic] organization, but if our President, our Congress, our Supreme Court, continues to suppress the white, Caucasian race, it's possible that there might have to be some revengeance [sic] taken.
>
> We are marching on Congress July the Fourth, four hundred thousand strong. From there we are dividing into two groups, one group to march on St. Augustine, Florida, the other group to march into Mississippi. Thank you.[34]

Although certainly not an invitation that I would care to accept, it is a far cry from dredging up a massive popular revolt. The Court handled this issue by overruling *Whitney*, which eliminated the "clear and present danger" test and its rival, the bad tendency test, from Supreme Court jurisprudence and streamlined First Amendment jurisprudence into the "imminent lawless action" test.[35] Therefore, the Court held, "Measured by this test, Ohio's Criminal Syndicalism Act cannot be sustained."[36] The Court ruled that all innocuous speech is absolutely protected, and all speech is innocuous when there is time for more speech to resist or rebut it. The beginning of the Nixon years appeared as though there would be a shift toward a more liberalized state, but in reality it was a shift toward the secret-police state.

Nixon's 'Nam: The Vietnam War from the Late 1960s into the 1970s

When the Nixon administration took over in 1969, it promised "peace with honor" in the Vietnam War. America believed that "Nixon's the One" to end the war, and in that spirit he began the Paris peace talks and visited the South Vietnamese in July 1969 to mark the beginning of troop withdrawals. Taking action on his campaign promise, President Nixon announced the withdrawal of twenty-five thousand American troops from Vietnam in addition to the implementation of what Nixon referred to as the Vietnamization* of the southeastern Asian country. This turned out to be an oxymoron of sorts, as the latter part of the war saw the deaths of twenty thousand additional American soldiers and "several times the bomb tonnage [the military] had dropped in all of World War II."[37]

What was supposed to be a presidency of healing and renewal for the nation transformed America into an era of protest, scandal, and government abuse. Demonstrations raged across America, calling for the president to end the war immediately. Bombings of ROTC buildings and the arson of other university buildings nationwide rose dramatically.[38] Among the radical groups to shape out of the conflict, none gained more notoriety than the Weathermen. As a group that split off from the Students for a Democratic Society, the Weathermen declared social war not only on the conflict in Vietnam but also on the "entire imperialist system that made war a necessity."[39] In October 1969, the Weathermen charged into prominent Chicago neighborhoods waving flags, trashing cars, and breaking windows. In response, police shot six members and arrested approximately two hundred fifty. While many anti-war-movement supporters disapproved of these antics, America became fixated by the civil unrest taking the country by storm.[40]

In a speech targeted at responding to the nationwide protests, Nixon

---

*   Nixon wanted to turn ground combat generally over to the South Vietnamese.

addressed what he called the "Silent Majority," the segment of the population that was not protesting the war. Nixon told the nation that he refused to allow "the policy of this nation to be dictated by the minority who . . . try to impose [their view] on the nation by mounting demonstrations in the streets." This statement by Nixon truly exposes the feelings of the newly minted president. "Echoing the worst moments of Adams and Wilson, Nixon now claimed that a foe within the United States was even more dangerous to that national interest than the enemy in Vietnam."[41]

The White House became a headquarters for free speech suppression and the center for a litany of falsehoods to the American public. In the days before the largest anti-war demonstration in American history, the Vietnam Moratorium of November 1969, a deputy assistant to the president named Alexander Butterfield authored a memorandum outlining a plan to combat the message of protesters. Wires, letters, and news articles were needed, as Butterfield explained, to support the president's policies which denounced the undesirable character of groups planning to participate in the November Moratorium, even going as far to say that such individuals were providing "aid and comfort to the enemy."[42] In essence, the Nixon administration considered protesting Americans to be treasonous and dangerous.

In the spring of 1970, President Nixon seemingly reversed his campaign promise to end the war in Vietnam when he announced the bombing of sites in Cambodia as a tactic to cut off North Vietnamese supply lines. The country was outraged. Student protests exploded at colleges and universities nationwide, culminating in the walkout of more than 1.5 million students. That spring at Princeton University, final examinations were deemed optional so that students could use their time to travel to Washington, DC, and protest.

It is truly amazing how much power political activism and the possibility of backlash can influence the decisions of the federal government. James Madison discussed at length the power of factions in the *Federalist Papers*,[43] and the principles he writes about hold true throughout American history: The people themselves can provide a check on the tyranny of government. In January 1970, President Nixon had a monumental choice to make: Whether to expand the war even farther into the country of Laos. Protesters gathered in Washington[44] to protest the further involvement of the United States in Vietnam. They were met with police and military personnel who swept the downtown region, sprayed tear gas, and arrested almost seven thousand people. One commentator recounted the experience was more akin to "Saigon in wartime than Washington"[45] in peacetime. This set the stage for historic political scandal, including the infamous events of Watergate.

COINTELPRO and the Rise of Domestic Spies

By 1972, J. Edgar Hoover had been the director of the Federal Bureau of Investigation (FBI) for just short of forty years. He had served under six presidents and during almost twenty sessions of Congress. However, after his death, Congress "quickly decided that in a democracy no one should be able to amass the power that Hoover had" and soon passed legislation that limited future directors to a term of ten years.*

Although Director Hoover was responsible for the capture and prosecution of notorious criminals and corrupt politicians alike, it is now known that he instigated numerous illegal operations and directives. The most infamous of these has come to be known as COINTELPRO (Counter Intelligence Program).

After constant frustration with the federal court system limiting the investigative techniques of the Department of Justice as well its ability to prosecute radical political dissidents, Hoover initiated COINTELPRO to satisfy his "increasingly paranoid view of the world"[46] and keep tabs on select American groups and organizations, mainly ones with Communist tendencies. This program was authorized

---

* "Future FBI directors would serve ten-year terms—long enough to outlast whatever president appointed them and thus provide some political cover, yet not long enough to establish a separate power base." Garrett M. Graff, *The Threat Matrix: The FBI at War in the Age of Global Terrorism* (New York: Little, Brown, 2011), 56.

without the approval or even knowledge of either the president or the attorney general.[47]

In 1956 agents of the Bureau began to investigate organizations like the Ku Klux Klan, the Black Panthers, and the Socialist Workers Party, among others.[48] Techniques used by the FBI included anonymous phone calls, IRS audits, and other intrusive and sometimes illegal measures. In all, around seven different COINTELPRO operations existed at various times,[49] making up 2,370 implemented counterintelligence actions.[50]

Initiated by J. Edgar Hoover with the goal of repressing and disbanding protest groups, the objectives of COINTELPRO reportedly included the following:

1) Gathering information (intelligence);
2) Crafting a negative public image of the targeted group;
3) Interfering with the group's internal structure;
4) Instigating internal fighting and disagreement;
5) Limiting the group's access to public resources;
6) Constraining protest and assembly abilities; and
7) Interfering with specific individuals and their ability to participate in the group.[51]

On a cool night in Media, Pennsylvania, in March 1971, members of the Citizens' Commission to Investigate the FBI, a group under investigation by the COINTELPRO operation, broke into the Bureau's field office. The burglars stole more than a thousand "poorly secured" dossiers and other documents which outlined the setup of COINTELPRO. The organization subsequently took the confidential documents to the press, and the program was fully exposed to the American public. Hoover swiftly declared an end to the program and created guidelines for the future intelligence of domestic individuals and groups. It did not operate by normal law enforcement means such as legitimate prosecution (except in the case of the HUAC hearings in the Second Red Scare), but by violence, deception, police harassment, and intimidation.[52] COINTELPRO did not lead to a single criminal prosecution of any government officials, but instead to the creation of a special congressional committee in 1975 to investigate these crimes after that scandal was bolstered by Watergate. For the most part, the COINTELPRO operations were terminated in the early 1970s when the agents who facilitated the programs became weary of public exposure.[53]

The COINTELPRO directive epitomizes unconstitutional domestic government intrusion in the name of national security. There have been reports of FBI agents committing untold illegal and unconscionable behaviors: Causing anti-war activists to be evicted from their homes, disabling suspected people's cars, intercepting mail, breaking and entering, stealing documents, wiretapping phones, bugging conversations, and doing potentially more.[54] It is without question that Hoover was wrong to order such measures. The *Washington Post*, publishing an article on the constitutional assaults committed by the FBI in COINTELPRO, which, candidly, seem tame by contemporary standards of government lawlessness, stated sharply: "'The American Public needs to know what the FBI is doing' and 'needs to think long and hard about whether internal security rests . . . upon official surveillance and the suppression of dissent or upon the traditional freedom of every citizen to speak his mind on any subject, whether others consider what he says wise or foolish, patriotic or subversive, conservative or radical.'"[55]

The government cannot legally break into any private home, open any mail, or wiretap any telephones without probable cause and a warrant from a judge. Such an intrusion clearly violates the protections of the Fourth Amendment.[56]

The Pentagon Papers and Watergate

As if the public relations situation was not bad enough for the Nixon administration, things took a turn for the worse on June 13th 1971. Several newspapers, including the *New York Times* and the *Washington Post*, had published highly damaging and embarrassing documents that were substantially at odds with the government version of recent events.

These came to be known as the Pentagon Papers. "Suddenly the hidden intentions of American policymakers, at least through 1968, and their own understandings of the real situation in the Vietnam War, stood revealed."[57]

Four years earlier, the secretary of defense had commissioned the creation of a "History of United States Decision-Making Process on Vietnam Policy, 1945–1967."[58] Although the Papers contained mostly common knowledge, they also contained key, unknown-to-the-public aspects of the war; knowledge that "they could hang people for."[59] For example, the papers documented that President Truman, while still in office, rejected appeals from Ho Chi Minh for American assistance; that the United States was actively planning military operations in Saigon after the 1954 Geneva Conventions; that advisors to President Kennedy had not merely advised South Vietnamese troops but rather actively engaged in direct military operations; that the Gulf of Tonkin Resolution had been rushed, even "rammed" through Congress under obviously false pretenses; and finally that, unbeknownst to the American people, American troops had knowingly dropped bombs on thousands of Vietnamese civilians.[60] And in a bitter and ironic twist of events, the Papers revealed to the American public "that the enemy knew what we [the public] were not permitted to know."[61]

Quite possibly the "Edward Snowden" of his day, Daniel Ellsberg became in essence an American fugitive when the government revealed that he had been responsible for leaking the Pentagon Papers to the press. Ellsberg was a Harvard-educated bureaucrat who served in the Department of Defense under then Secretary of Defense Robert S. McNamara. Ellsberg later left the government to work for the Rand Corporation, a nonprofit think tank initially formed to offer research and analysis to the U.S. government and armed forces. Spending time in Vietnam and subsequently becoming instrumental in the compilation of the Pentagon Papers, Ellsberg increasingly gained an adverse prospective of the war in Vietnam. As Professor Geoffrey Stone recounted: "He concluded that Vietnam had never been a war of 'aggression from the

North,' as the government had claimed, or even a 'civil war.' Rather, it was 'a war of foreign aggression, American aggression.'"[62]

After learning that a friend had become employed by the *New York Times*, Ellsberg decided to take action and sent over a redacted copy of the Papers to the newspaper. Upon initial receipt of the Pentagon Papers, the leadership at the *Times* debated the lawfulness and ethics of publishing the Ellsberg treasure trove.[63] The threat of publication took the Nixon administration by complete surprise, since the Department of Justice and the attorney general had never heard of the Pentagon Papers.

Things escalated quickly, however, when the Justice Department filed a complaint with the federal district court in Manhattan seeking an injunction against the *New York Times* publishing the materials. Judge Murray Gurfein* granted a temporary injunction against the *Times*, ruling that harm resulting from not publishing the article was far outweighed by the "irreparable harm that could be done to the interests of the United States Government if [the documents were published and the government] should ultimately prevail [in the case]."[64]

In granting the government's request for an injunction, the Court, for the first time in the history of the Republic, *prevented* a newspaper from publishing *truthful* information. This egregious move by Judge Gurfein has come to represent an abhorrent attack upon the freedom of the press and the First Amendment. The Constitution expresses no "right" to know what the government is up to, but it does guarantee the right of free speech and the right of the press to publish information to the public: Even information damning to the government. "[The] Framers were committed to minimal, 'watch dog' government, and saw rights as 'retained by the people' to be safeguarded against infringement by government."[65]

The federal government does things in secret all the time. The public's "right to know" is the "derivative"[66] of First Amendment protections.

---

* Judge Gurfein was appointed by President Nixon.

However, when the government is truly acting unconstitutionally, persons who know this must have the lawful right to bring the situation to the light of day.[67] Information attesting to such activity must have the ability to come to light. The federal government has received its power from the States and they in turn from the people: When government fails to remain faithful to its purpose and constitutional directive, the people deserve to know. As Justice Louis D. Brandeis famously stated, "Publicity is justly commended as a remedy for social and industrial diseases. Sunlight is said to be the best of disinfectants; electric light the most efficient policeman."[68]

After the injunction was granted, Ellsberg led the life of a fugitive. Several journalists interviewed him in secret locations around the nation. In one of those interviews Ellsberg responded to a question by news anchor Walter Cronkite:

> I think the lesson is that the people of this country can't afford to let the President run the country by himself . . . without the help of Congress, without the help of the public. . . . What these studies tell me is we must remember this is a self-governing country. We are the government. . . . [W]e cannot let the officials of the Executive Branch determine for us what it is that the public needs to know about how well and how they are discharging their functions.[69]

After hearing additional arguments on a motion by the *Times* to reconsider, Judge Gurfein had a substantial change of heart and removed his injunction, ruling that the Espionage Act of 1917 was never intended to interfere with the right of a newspaper "to vindicate the right of the public to know" the truth.[70] Yet he stayed his vacation of his injunction, pending appeal.

This case and a companion case, dealing with an injunction the government sought and obtained upon the *Washington Post*, made their way to the Supreme Court in *New York Times Co. v. United States*.[71] By 1971, the Court had changed in ideological makeup since the Earl

Warren–Court days. A Nixon appointee, Warren Earl Burger, was now chief justice, and most commentators expected the Court to rule in the government's favor. However, in a 6-to-3 decision, the Court rejected the validity of the injunctions upon the newspaper companies. Justice Hugo Black noted: "Every moment's continuance[72] of the injunctions against these newspapers amounts to a flagrant, indefensible, and continuing violation of the First Amendment." The Court rejected the claim that national security is a logical ground for limiting the freedom of the press: "[T]he word 'security' is a broad, vague generality whose contours should not be invoked to abrogate the fundamental law embodied in the First Amendment."[73] There can be no balance between the Constitution and civil liberties; there is only the bias of freedom over security via protection from the government.

The publication of the Pentagon Papers marked a historic validation of the press in America, and the story remained in the mainstream media for months.

What happened to the heroic whistle-blower? Daniel Ellsberg voluntarily turned himself in to federal officials in Boston on June 28th 1971. He was subsequently indicted under the Espionage Act of 1917. To the Nixon Justice Department, the Supreme Court's decision to protect the press had no bearing on the vindication of Ellsberg; he had committed a crime against the government under the 1917 law.

However, Nixon, wishing to discredit Ellsberg even further, ordered, authorized, or acquiesced in the use of federal agents to break into the office of Ellsberg's psychiatrist in September 1971.[74] When District Court Judge Matthew Byrne received word of this, he dismissed all charges against Ellsberg because "the 'unprecedented' government misconduct offended the 'sense of justice' and 'incurably infected the prosecution of this case.'"[75] Nixon's plan backfired.

A year and four days after the Pentagon Papers were first published came Watergate. Several senior administration officials were incarcerated and the president resigned for their involvement in the cover-up of a break-in at the Democratic National Headquarters in the Watergate

Hotel, taking down the Nixon administration in 1974.[76] Subsequent revelations showed that the Nixon administration and Attorney General John Mitchell's illegal political spying program was aimed at electoral victory.[77]

Nixon's Legacy: Attacks on Presidential Power

The Non-Detention Act of 1971

One attempt to apologize for the detention and concentration of Japanese Americans during World War II was the Non-Detention Act of 1971. It was meant to symbolize a promise of "never again" would the president be allowed to order the mass detention of civilians pursuant to an emergency. Unfortunately for Congress, however, doing that wouldn't require a limitation on independent presidential power, but an amendment to the McCarran Internal Security Act's concentration camp provision which expressly permitted the president to do exactly that. Thus, Congress passed the 1971 Non-Detention Act to amend the McCarran Act.[78]

While this book typically affords a deeper analysis of the text of national security statutes, the Non-Detention Act requires very little explanation; the bill simply says: "No citizen shall be imprisoned or otherwise detained by the United States except pursuant to an Act of Congress."[79] Essentially, the Act amended the McCarran Act so that Congress, not the president, needed to declare the emergency. This Act would become increasingly important in the Global War on Terror thirty years later. The Act merely transferred the legal ability to assault due process from the president to the Congress. It did nothing to uphold natural rights or constitutional norms.

The War Powers Resolution of 1973

In terms of U.S. casualties, the Vietnam War was the fourth deadliest conflict in U.S. history.[80] What most Americans would consider to be a lawful war with real national security consequences was in fact a military conflict executed *without* a formal declaration of war from

Congress.[81] In response to this outrageous expansion of unconstitutional power by three presidents (JFK, LBJ, and Nixon). Congress adopted the War Powers Resolution (WPR) in 1973.[82] In a move that indicated a reversal of past acquiescence on the part of Congress toward presidential use of military force,[83] the WPR purported to rein in the president's use of troops without a declaration of war.

The WPR stipulates that the president, as the commander in chief of the armed forces, may introduce the military into hostilities or situations where hostilities appear imminent "only pursuant to (1) declaration of war, (2) specific statutory authorization, or (3) a national emergency created by an attack upon the United States, its territories, or its armed forces."[84] Furthermore, it requires that the president consult with Congress, when possible, before committing troops into conflicts and that the president report to Congress within forty-eight hours after troops are deployed into hostilities or in situations that show potential for imminent involvement with hostilities.[85]

The most substantial component of the law requires that the president withdraw troops after sixty days of hostility unless Congress has declared war or authorized a thirty-day extension or is physically unable to meet as a result of an armed attack on the United States.[86] The president is able to extend the sixty-day period by another thirty days if he can show that doing so is in the best interest of the armed forces' safety.[87]

Although not ruling explicitly on the validity of the WPR, the Supreme Court has been unambiguous in its interpretation that the constitutional separation of powers *must* be respected. But in *Morrison v. Olson*,[88] the Court held that by undertaking the duties of another branch, a branch of the federal government does not violate the Separation of Powers Doctrine unless it attempts to increase its own powers at the expense of another branch.[89]

The WPR is unconstitutional. Some schools of thought argue that the resolution is unconstitutional because Congress has relieved the commander in chief powers from the president and claimed them for itself. Congress may *only* authorize or de-authorize military offensives. It may not conduct war or otherwise impede on the enumerated powers of the executive.[90] However, that is a classic case of correct result based on wrong reasoning. It is unconstitutional because it permits the president to take offensive military action without a declaration a war. Quite contrary to the classical version of War Powers Resolution unconstitutionality, Congress is unconstitutionally giving its power to the president, not overreaching and restricting the president's powers. The Constitution could not be clearer: Only Congress may declare war and provide for the armed forces; the president is the commander in chief and may conduct offensive war only with the express permission of Congress.[91]

The Church Committee and the Foreign Intelligence Surveillance Act of 1978

During the Ford administration, in the wake of the COINTELPRO, the Pentagon Papers, Watergate, and Nixon's resignation, the Senate created a special committee to investigate government intelligence operations.[92] The committee was named for its chairman, Sen. Frank F. Church (D-ID). The committee sat during 1975 and 1976, publishing fourteen reports and airing out the dirty laundry of the NSA, FBI, and CIA.* The agencies' activities ranged from opening and photographing hundreds of thousands of pieces of mail, to assassinating foreign leaders, to establishing IRS abuses, to exploiting COINTELPRO. Its work inspired the creation of a special secret court to grant warrants for intelligence officials in violation of the Fourth Amendment.[93]

Thus, in response to decades of expansive executive action in regard to intelligence gathering,[94] Congress passed the Foreign Intelligence Surveillance Act (FISA) in 1978.[95] The Act was poised to address

---

* The full text of the Church Committee's reports is available in many places online. The Assassination Archives and Research Center, for example, provides them at "Church Committee Reports," http://www.aarclibrary.org/publib/contents/church/contents_church_ reports.htm.

presidents who had been increasingly asserting "national security" interests in rationalizing their disdain for the Fourth Amendment.[96]

Under FISA, the government was authorized to monitor the communication of foreign entities and individuals who were agents of them, without a court order, for up to one year, *unless* the surveillance acquired the contents of any communication to which a United States person[97] was a party. If the communication involves a United States person, judicial authorization is required within seventy-two hours of the government's initial action.[98]

FISA also establishes a special federal court, known as the Foreign Intelligence Surveillance Court.[99] A secret court with a secret judge, the court was made up initially of seven, and now eleven, federal district court judges, appointed by the chief justice, who hear requests by the federal government for wiretap authorizations against suspected foreign intelligence agents inside the United States. If an authorization request is denied, the government may *not* apply to a different FISA judge. It may, however, appeal to the Foreign Intelligence Court of Review to address grievances.*

The government must have probable cause of criminal behavior, and it must particularly describe the place to be searched or the person or thing to be seized for a judge to authorize a search warrant upon an individual or entity. FISA, however, established a new, different, and lesser standard. Under FISA an individual under suspicion need be an agent of a foreign power. Therefore, the government would only have to show a FISA Court judge probable cause that an individual was such an agent. Under the Act, this alone was sufficient for the judge to issue a warrant. The FISA Court and many parts of the Act itself have been amended repeatedly in the wake of the September 11th 2001 terrorist attacks. The current federal government has irreverently disregarded the Constitution in its effort to "protect" America and abused this special court structure

---

* This is very rare. The first request to be appealed occurred in 2002. See In re Sealed Case No. 02-001, 310 F.3d 717 (2002) (per curiam).

to conduct unprecedented, Big Brother–type data-mining operations of all persons in America.

The common thread of constitutional excess in the Cold War era is secrecy. The government insisted upon secrecy for itself, yet openly punished it for groups it hated and feared. The ancient right to be left alone suffered a great setback. Soon, the feds would look to more military violence.

10

Before 9/11

America and Global Terror from 1980–2001

*"Oceania was at war with Eastasia"**

—GEORGE ORWELL

The United States' relationship with the Islamic world is a product of its modern role in the international community. After World War I, the United States and Britain engaged in an open door policy, like the one in China, with respect to Middle Eastern oil.[1] During World War II, Churchill and FDR signed an Anglo-American Petroleum Agreement in 1944, partitioning Middle Eastern oil.[2]

During the Cold War and through its role as Israel's ally, the United States rose as a Middle Eastern power. In 1953, the CIA and Britain's MI6 orchestrated the overthrow of the elected prime minister of Iran to impose an absolutist rule under the Shah and the military.[3] In 1957, President Eisenhower raised the stakes against the Soviet Union,

---

*   George Orwell, *1984* (New York: Signet Classics, 1950), 180–81.

declaring "the United States regards as vital to the national interest and world peace the preservation of the independence and integrity of the nations of the Middle East," which Congress affirmed, promising military and financial aid to nations threatened in the Middle East.[4] During the Carter administration in 1979, revolutionaries overran the U.S. embassy in Tehran, resulting in the Iranian hostage crisis.[5] America had sown enmity abroad that soon would stop taking the form of state and quasi-state aggression, transfiguring into the more inconspicuous visage of terrorist jihad.

The Ronald Reagan and George H. W. Bush Administrations: The First Blows of Global Terrorism and the Seeds of al Qaeda

The 1986 Berlin nightclub bombing in Germany stands in stark contrast to the remainder of the 1980s, which was a time of relative peace for Americans from terrorist attacks. Terrorist organizations would begin challenging the United States on its soil in the next decade.

During the 1980s, however, the Soviet Union was attempting to subjugate Afghanistan.[6] The United States, playing the proverbial white knight, covertly intervened for the Islamic mujahideen—Afghani jihadists fighting against the Soviet Union encroaching on their soil—with substantial monetary and weapons support.[7] Osama bin Laden "heard the call" for jihad and joined the mujahideen in 1979.[8] By 1984, he had formed the Maktab Khadamat (MAK), or Afghan Services Bureau, to raise support from around the world for combating the Soviets.[9] The mujahideen began recruiting in the United States through MAK.[10] One notably successful recruiter was the "Blind Sheikh" Omar Abdel-Rahman, who operated out of a mosque on Atlantic Avenue in Brooklyn, New York.[11]

George H. W. Bush became president in January 1989. The Soviet Union completed leaving Afghanistan a month later in February 1989.[12] Afghanistan plunged into seven years of sectarian violence and civil war.[13] That same year, 1989, bin Laden founded al Qaeda to carry out global jihad.[14] Bin Laden and his mujahideen-turned-al-Qaeda force traveled to Saudi Arabia, his homeland.[15] Iraq invaded Kuwait in 1990, and bin Laden offered his soldiers as mercenaries to King Fahd Al Saud against the vastly superior Iraqi army.[16] The king declined bin Laden's offer, opting for the United States to station troops in Saudi Arabia instead.[17] Bin Laden began recruiting members and speaking out against the House of Saud for profaning the Holy Land by permitting infidels (U.S. troops) there.* Eventually, bin Laden was banned from Saudi Arabia, and he moved al Qaeda to the Sudan in 1992, remaining there until 1996.[18] America created an enemy in its former ally—the former mujahideen newly branded as al Qaeda.

The Clinton Administration: The War on Terror Begins and the Executive Claims New Powers

All presidents must legally swear to "preserve, protect, and defend the Constitution of the United States," creating an affirmative duty on the president as chief law enforcer to preserve freedom and as commander in chief to prevent force from assaulting security.[19] In the recent wave of 1990s nostalgia, the William J. Clinton administration years have been hailed as a centrist utopia of peace and prosperity. Despite his economic accomplishments compared to his two successors, President Clinton failed in responding to the threat of global terrorism, paving the way for the attacks of September 11th 2001 and the ensuing decade-plus-long war on freedom.[20]

---

* "The latest and the greatest of these aggressions, incurred by the Muslims since the death of the Prophet . . . is the occupation of the land of the two Holy Places—the foundation of the house of Islam, the place of the revelation, the source of the message and the place of the noble Ka'ba, the Qiblah of all Muslims—by the armies of the American Crusaders and their allies. (We bemoan this and can only say: 'No power and power acquiring except through Allah')." Osama Bin Laden et al., "Bin Laden's Fatwa," PBS Newshour, August 23, 1996, http://www.pbs.org/newshour/updates/military/july-dec96/fatwa_1996.html. "Yet, it was the symbolic presence of the U.S. Marines on the Arabian Peninsula that enraged Osama bin Laden." Richard Miniter, *Losing Bin Laden: How Bill Clinton's Failures Unleashed Global Terror* (Washington, DC: Regnery, 2003), 2.

In his 1997 book about the Clinton administration, former senior aide and my former Fox News colleague Dick Morris recalled a conversation with the president about where Clinton would sit in history, in which Clinton ruefully conceded that he was in the middle of the pack in terms of presidential greatness.[21] History will judge the Clinton administration harshly for its inattention to the dawn of international terrorism.[22] Moreover, it will blame Clinton personally for laying the legal foundation for George W. Bush's rendition and torture programs, for doing the same for Obama's drone programs, and for having a negligent national security infrastructure during his term.

The War on Terror began for the United States in 2001, when the Bush administration was "authorized" to use military force to root out terrorism anywhere in the globe, but it began for the opposing al Qaeda force in 1992. The first al Qaeda attacks on U.S. targets took place in 1992 and 1993, with a more blatant, formal declaration of war, or fatwah, being issued by bin Laden in August 1996 and again in 1998.[23]

The 1993 World Trade Center Bombings

On September 1st 1992, Pakistani radical Ahmed Ajaj was caught entering the United States. His partner, Ramiz Yousef, an al Qaeda–trained radical, was traveling with him.[24] Ahmed's uncle Khalid Sheikh Mohammed and he had conspired with other radicals in America, including the "Blind Sheikh" Rahman, in a plan to attack the World Trade Center, carrying out bin Laden's jihad.[25] In an utterly macabre foreshadowing, the radicals bombed the World Trade Center on February 26th 1993, a little over one month into Bill Clinton's presidency, killing six Americans and wounding more than a thousand persons.[26] The FBI rounded up all the conspirators who were in America.[27]

In the ensuing criminal prosecutions in the Southern District of New York, the conspirators were convicted of several crimes, including seditious conspiracy to levy war. In *United States v. Rahman*—the Blind Sheikh's 1999 appeal from those convictions to the U.S. Court of Appeals for the Second Circuit—one co-conspirator, El Sayyid Nosair ("the first al Qaeda operative to be arrested by America," whose legal fees were being paid by bin Laden financial fronts),[28] asserted that because he was a U.S. citizen, the Treason Clause requires the testimony of two witnesses who must support his conviction for levying war against the United States.[29]

The court clearly defined the defendants' conduct as "levying war [against the United States]," which other circuit courts have tended to term terrorist acts.[30] Moreover, the Second Circuit noted: "It is undisputed that Nosair's conviction was not supported by two witnesses to the same overt act. Accordingly the conviction must be overturned if the requirement of the Treason Clause applies to this prosecution for seditious conspiracy."[31] However, citing *Ex parte Quirin*'s reasoning that citizenship alone won't give Treason Clause protections, the Second Circuit denied their defense, and the Supreme Court denied *certiorari* the following year in 2000.[32]

Two months after the Oklahoma City bombing in 1995, on June 21st of that year, President Clinton issued Presidential Decision Directive 39, creating the precedent for a system of extraordinary rendition that permitted U.S. personnel to become complicit in torture. The Bush administration would use the directive as a legal excuse to do the same. "Return of the suspect[ed terrorists] by force may be effected without the cooperation of the host government."[33] Meanwhile, "the White House was [still] dismissive [of bin Laden]."[34]

Clinton and al Qaeda 1996–2001: Afghanistan, Khobar Towers, the Embassy Bombings, and the USS *Cole*

By 1996, al Qaeda became an arm of the Taliban's defense ministry in the Islamic emirate of Afghanistan.[35] Al Qaeda had five thousand fighters in the Taliban army, including one thousand of the elite Brigade 055 unit.[36] Under Taliban governmental blessing, bin Laden's army "establish[ed] military camps where fighters were trained to battle the Northern Alliance as well as conduct terrorist operations outside Afghanistan."[37] Moreover, by 2001 "the Taliban militia had become so subject to the dominion and control of al Qaeda that it could not pursue independent policies with respect to the outside world."[38] "[The Taliban have] proved themselves subservient to al Qaeda."[39] This organ of government declared war in 1996.[40] Despite the clear associations, the Bush administration would sidestep the state-actor issue to avoid "giving rights" to war prisoners.

On June 25th 1996, an explosion "tore off the front of the [Khobar Towers] compound and was felt twenty miles away in Bahrain," killing nineteen American servicepersons.[41] Clinton did not address this as an intelligence or military matter.[42] Moreover, Clinton's attention was diverted elsewhere because he was in the midst of the Filegate and Whitewater scandals, and his former business partners had just been indicted in the latter of those.[43] Obviously, this was a recipe for disaster.

"[T]he Clinton [a]dministration not only failed to follow potentially productive leads but in some instances made the investigators' job more difficult."[44] Clinton initially reacted with ire, promising justice and itching for a full-scale invasion of Iran.[45] He met with a Saudi prince and wrote to King Fahd; Vice President Gore banged on a negotiating table during a temper tantrum, demanding information from a Saudi prince.[46] However, Clinton "lost interest" in the investigation.[47] "[T]he president barely mentioned the case in meetings with Saudi leaders."[48] FBI Director Louis Freeh, distrusting Clinton, waited until George W. Bush was in office to proceed: Then he sought an indictment of the co-conspirators in federal court in 2001.[49] Eventually, when Freeh presented his findings to Sandy Berger, Clinton's national security advisor, they were dismissed as "hearsay" and buried.[50]

Al Qaeda attacked the U.S. embassies in Tanzania and Kenya on August 7th, the eighth anniversary of the entrance of American forces into Saudi Arabia.[51] Twelve Americans and more than two hundred others would die. Clinton publicly responded on that morning, posing almost Bush-like and turning vindictive: "We will use all the means at our disposal to bring those responsible to justice, no matter what or how long it takes," but again he would lose interest.[52]

After issuing a capture-but-don't-intentionally-kill order, Clinton took military action, but it was an abject failure, "the greatest foreign policy blunder of the Clinton Presidency":[53]

> Investigators quickly discovered that bin Laden was behind the attacks. On August 20, Clinton ordered cruise-missile strikes on a bin Laden camp in Afghanistan and the al-Shifa pharmaceutical plant in Sudan. But the strikes were at best ineffectual. There was little convincing evidence that the pharmaceutical factory, which administration officials believed was involved in the production of material for chemical weapons, actually was part of a weapons-making operation, and the cruise missiles in Afghanistan missed bin Laden and his deputies.[54]

Clinton was first assailed in the press, perhaps unfairly,[55] for wagging the dog: The Monica Lewinsky scandal overlapped (the let's-blame-let's-exonerate-them affair from January 1998 to February 1999), and Clinton's opponents attacked him for distracting from that "real issue" with this military gaffe.[56] Clearly, President Clinton was distracted by the scandal.[57]

Second, Clinton was assailed for the poor outcome of the missile strikes in Afghanistan and Sudan. In total, six jihadists were killed. The press dubbed the pharmaceutical plant "the aspirin factory": The plant had been producing aspirin and animal vaccines, "operating under a U.N. license and had been extensively inspected by a U.N. task force only months before."[58]

Clinton was "pissed" about the result and halted a planned second missile strike in light of the press's opprobrium.[59] Instead, he issued an executive order on August 20th, freezing bin Laden and al Qaeda's American assets.[60] Losing interest, Clinton continued his "usual" vacillation over whether it was worth the political consequences to kill bin Laden by a covert operation.[61] The Clinton Justice Department and FBI, however, went after all the co-conspirators that they could find. The trial, popularly known as the Embassy Bombings Case, lasted from January 2001 to May 2001.[62] The defendants were convicted, and in 2010, their convictions were upheld when the Supreme Court denied their petition for *certiorari*.[63]

On October 12th 2000, the USS *Cole* was in Aden Harbor, Yemen, on a routine refueling mission.[64] Two suicide bombers in a small motorboat rammed into the side of the ship, exploding themselves and killing seventeen sailors.[65] The FBI and State Department were dispatched to the scene.[66]

At the time, Clinton was more interested in the escalating Israeli-Palestinian conflict, as the *Washington Post*'s John Harris stated, "[T]he escalation between Israelis and Palestinians took the edge in preoccupying senior administration officials."[67] Clinton's address on the topic promised justice but quickly sidestepped and reframed the issue, claiming the terrorists were trying to disrupt the Israeli-Palestinian peace process.[68] The FBI and State Department officials investigating on the ground started a "war" with each other early on that only escalated, resulting in an FBI official being recalled at an ambassador's request and an attempt to run the investigation from across the Atlantic in New York. Notwithstanding all this, investigators linked the bombing to bin Laden.[69]

The Early George W. Bush Administration on Counterterrorism

Before 9/11, President George W. Bush simply did not "feel that sense of urgency."[70] Vice President Dick Cheney, who had "confidently assumed the national security portfolio for a president who had virtually no experience in the area," was stuck in an outdated, Cold War mind-set of the Middle East.[71] Thus, the Bush administration downgraded terrorism as a national security priority:

> One of the first official acts of the current Bush administration was to downgrade the office of national coordinator for counterterrorism on the National Security Council—a position held by Richard Clarke. Clarke had served in the Pentagon and State Department

under presidents Reagan and Bush the elder, and was the first person to hold the counterterrorism job created by President Clinton. Under Clinton, he was elevated to cabinet rank, which gave him a seat at the principals' meeting, the highest decision-making group for national security.[72]

Before the 9/11 attack, the Bush administration cut counterterrorism funds, denied requests for more counterterrorism agents, threatened to veto additional counterterrorism spending, ignored numerous warnings about imminent attacks, and declared focusing on bin Laden a mistake.[73] Later investigations would reveal, however, that at least seven months before 9/11, the Bush administration began domestic spying operations.[74]

Were George H. W. Bush and Bill Clinton too tepid or too willing to use military violence for the wrong purposes? We may never know, but we do know that their uses of violence were grounded in the unchecked use of it by their predecessors.

11

The George W. Bush Administration

The Global War on Terror and Privacy in the Post-9/11 World

*[A]t just this moment [of fanatical, state-induced jingoism] it had been announced that Oceania was not after all at war with Eurasia. Oceania was at war with Eastasia. Eurasia was an ally.**

—GEORGE ORWELL

O n September 11th 2001, bin Laden, al Qaeda, and his co-conspirators attacked the United States. During these attacks, suicide bombers struck the famous Twin Towers of the World Trade Center and the Pentagon, killing nearly three thousand people on American soil.[1] It was hailed as a second Pearl Harbor, except the kamikaze pilots came at the start of the

---

* George Orwell, *1984* (New York: Signet Classics, 1950), 180.

war rather than the end. America would react much like it did after Pearl Harbor. War hysteria reared its ugly head as freedom vanilla replaced French vanilla in cafeterias in the style of Wilsonesque-nomenclature propaganda.[2] Civil rights and natural rights would be openly assaulted by a government sworn to protect them in one of the longest wars in American history. Randolph Bourne's decried jingoism would return to the sounds of trumpets blaring and the sight of flags waving. The familiar phrase "Remember the *Lusitania*," which became "Remember Pearl Harbor," became "Remember 9/11." Anti-Muslim and anti-Arab sentiment filled the country as America waxed hysterical, crying for "us" to "get those towelheads."

Unlike what happened after Pearl Harbor, however, the Bush administration would not order a "review of how they could have been so badly surprised" because the results would have shown "a colossal bureaucratic failure, combined with inattention and a lack of political will at the top."[3] However, the endemic bureaucratic problems with counterterrorism strategy were remnants of the Clinton administration. Clinton left his successor with years of unresolved tangles between the CIA, FBI, State Department, and NSA over information sharing and had failed to develop a successful strategy against bin Laden for eight years.[4] Nonetheless, the Bush administration's home-front execution of the war was characterized by "warrantless wiretapping, mass arrests of Arabs, Pakistanis, and other Muslim immigrants[, inhumane torture programs,] and a prodigious rollback of the civil liberties of American citizens."[5] The executive branch, through the use of the noble lie and the organs of state powers, would abjure liberties in creating a modern police state under the guise of fighting a War on Terror, starting with our ostensible enemy, then moving on to personal vendetta and perpetual, aimless war.

Bush's Wars: Congress, the Authorization for Use of Military Force of 2001, and H. J. Res. 114

After September 11th, the Bush administration was clear in its terms of surrender: The Afghanistan government had to extradite bin Laden and his top associates and shut down terrorism within its borders.[6] Before the diplomacy began, however, Bush was supplied with what he needed from Congress: Authority to use his power as commander in chief over the entire globe to conduct a War on Terror, a war without a stated goal, a war without end.

On September 14th, Congress passed the Authorization for Use of Military Force (AUMF), giving the president specific statutory authorization within the meaning of the 1973 War Powers Resolution to carry out military operations against whom or whatever the president determined perpetrated or harbored persons who perpetrated the 9/11 attack, but not a declaration of war. The AUMF notably left out any geographical or legal restrictions on who or where the president may pursue anyone or anything he determines to be affiliated with 9/11 terrorists. Bush's quagmires and policies in conducting his authorized war would prove to be an affront to constitutional and natural liberties. Under the guise of wartime necessity and the AUMF, President Bush would commence the largest expansion of executive reach since President Wilson, inching toward the zenith of power of the imperial or unitary executive.[7]

The Afghanistan Theatre Under the AUMF

On September 18th, President Bush communicated his surrender terms to the Taliban via Pakistani back channels, and they were received somewhat warmly.[8] However, the Taliban's control of Afghanistan was loose after years of civil war, and al Qaeda was for all intents and purposes its standing army with the country serving as the flagship of the sixty-seven-nation organization.[9] Bush prepared for war, signing the AUMF that had been passed four days earlier.[10] On September 20th, an *Ulema** of more than a thousand Afghan imams** gave a more tepid response than what was received via back channels, calling for independent U.N. investigation, urging bin Laden to leave the country, and declaring that if America attacked Afghanistan to reach the al Qaeda forces there, there would be a world war in the form of jihad.[11] That night, addressing a joint session of Congress, President Bush demanded that bin Laden be extradited to the United States and that all terrorist camps in Afghanistan be destroyed.[12]

The Taliban toughened their stance with saber-rattling rhetoric. On September 21st, their envoy gave what was described as their final answer: "No, no, no!" with a deputy adding, "[M]ake no mistake: Afghanistan, as it was in the past—the Great Britain, he came, the Red Army, he came—Afghanistan is a swamp. People enter here laughing, are exiting injured."[13] The Taliban left open the option for cooperation if evidence was presented to them demonstrating bin Laden's complicity.[14]

The Taliban reached out on October 5th, offering to try bin Laden in an Afghani court and reiterating the condition precedent of evidence.[15] The Bush administration confirmed such evidence existed on a confidential basis via third-party Pakistani back channels that same day,[16] presumably because of the sensitive intelligence nature of the findings and the administration's desire to avoid the embarrassment of revealing that its intelligence evidence pre-dated September 11th.[17] In 2006, a federal court would admit as evidence a summary of testimony given by co-conspirator Khalid Sheikh Mohammed affirming al Qaeda's involvement in 9/11.[18]

However, the United States rejected the Afghani offer around noon on October 7th.[19] Bush was intent on bin Laden being turned over to the United States unconditionally[20] and causing such destruction in its pursuit of him that all eyes—including history's—would focus on what Bush did after 9/11, not what he failed to do before 9/11. America began its bombing campaign that night. On October 14th, the Taliban offered to

---

*   "Grand Council of Clerics."

** "Clerics."

turn over bin Laden to a neutral country if the bombing stopped and evidence was presented.[21] Bush rejected it.[22] On October 16th, they offered to turn him over to a third country without the evidence.[23] Bush rejected it.[24] He would countenance no embarrassment; intelligence secrets must be kept, and bin Laden was due in U.S. court. Congress had already given Bush the go-ahead, so they were powerless to press him to accept a deal. By December 2001, Operation Enduring Freedom resulted in U.S. ground forces in control of Afghanistan, and al Qaeda had fled the country to Waziristan/Pakistan and the southern Afghan mountain regions.[25]

It seemed as though victory was decisively won quickly; however, the Afghanistan front would turn into a Vietnam-like, stalemated quagmire, lasting well into the second term of Bush's successor, and only *apparently* later, in 2013, would the United States leave (as the Taliban caused civilian casualties to rise 23 percent).[26] Bin Laden escaped to Pakistan and survived until his murder on May 2nd 2011.[27] And as far as creating "enduring freedom" through nation building, the *New York Times* reported in August 2013 that even though Facebook and Twitter have reached the Afghani youth, they are "bound to their society's conservative ways."[28] U.S. troops had now been fighting directly in Middle Eastern wars for almost a decade and will probably be there for at least another.

In retrospect, the AUMF did not give a president the power to stamp out global terrorism. Such a feat cannot be accomplished so long as there are radicals in the world and American imperial impulses, but the power to mire U.S. forces anywhere in the world so long as a connection could be made to 9/11. This is an unprecedented power given to the executive to conduct war anywhere, at any time at all, with whomever crosses his pursuit of "justice."

Essentially, Congress delegated its power to declare war to the president—an action contrary to two hundred years of separation of powers principles regarding warfare,[29] and repugnant to the social compact which guarantees a specific form of government. Congress cannot pass the buck for deciding to go to war onto the executive branch by granting it absurdly broad discretion which swallows the rule of allocating that decision to Congress in the first place. It did, however, learn to declare war by not declaring war, but "authorizing" military force, thereby reducing its own political accountability. Even assuming that the Afghanistan part of the Global War on Terror was just because al Qaeda was a state actor, nothing can justify the Bush administration's personality-driven, militarily unnecessary, and morally unjustifiable entrance into its endless, bellicose quagmire.

The Iraq Theatre: The Noble Liars

Like the presidents before him, and most closely in image to Wilson, Bush decided to use the noble lie to create a second theatre in the Terror War that was neither necessary nor just. According to Gen. Hugh Sheldon, then chairman of the Joint Chiefs of Staff, from the night of 9/11, Defense Secretary Donald Rumsfeld and Deputy Defense Secretary Paul Wolfowitz were gunning for an invasion of Iraq, despite there not being "one iota" of evidence demonstrating Iraq had any responsibility in 9/11.[30] Involvement in 9/11 was the *one* requirement the AUMF would impose on Bush before he could unleash the U.S. military on any target in the globe besides invoking constitutional self-defense. He needed something else.

The Bush administration was relentless in its pursuit of a pretense for linking Iraq to 9/11. Wolfowitz and Rumsfeld had been pressing for a full topple of Saddam since they were advising in the Gulf War.[31] As part of the perversion of Clinton's rendition program, discussed in chapter 10, Vice President Dick Cheney ordered the CIA to render extraordinarily and brutally torture enemy combatants formerly being interrogated by the FBI.[32] These interrogation sessions resulted in clearly unreliable information, but the victims of CIA rendition and torture programs would admit, under duress, to such erroneous things as "al Qaeda and Saddam working together on WMDs."*[33] Nevertheless, it would take

---

* "Weapons of Mass Destruction," as in those possessed by the U.S. government.

"'unrelenting pressure'" and "more than a dozen visits to the CIA by Cheney and his chief of staff, Scooter Libby—to produce enough [questionable] 'evidence' of an active Iraqi WMD program to pull off their plans for an Iraq invasion."[34] Secretary of State Colin Powell used torture evidence that was later recanted in petitioning the U.N. on February 5th 2003 for sanctioning an anticipated assault on Iraq.[35]

On October 2nd 2002, clear victims of terror war hysteria Speaker John D. Hastert (R-IL) and House Minority Leader Richard A. Gephardt (D-MO) introduced House Joint Resolution 114, also known as the Iraq War Resolution: A separate AUMF (but not a declaration) authorizing military action against Hussein because he had weapons of mass destruction, and he was "harboring terrorist organizations," and "members of al Qaida . . . are known to be in Iraq."[36] Congress passed it on October 10 and 11th 2002.[37] After failing to build a broad or robust international coalition into 2003, and after U.N. Inspector Hans Blix's February 14th 2003 report directly refuted Colin Powell's February 5th case to the U.N. that Hussein had WMDs, the United States declared war on Iraq on March 19th.[38]

After eight years of nation building in Bush's second quagmire, the Iraq Theatre finally closed on December 18th 2011, costing 655,000 lives, 5,000 of them Americans, and the American people 2.2 trillion borrowed-and-not-yet-repaid dollars on the whim of a callous, naive president and his controlling, neocon advisors.[39] But Bush's largest blunder was his home front assault on personal freedom.

The Right to Privacy in the Global War on Terror

After lying about Iraq and WMDs, the Bush administration's biggest lie was that 9/11 justified or somehow compelled the creation of a vast, unprecedented, and almost unimaginable in scope NSA spying program. The First, Fourth, and Fifth Amendment protections in the Constitution render such a program illegal *per se*. Additionally, the administration lied about when it started domestic spying—domestic spying programs were active before 9/11.[40] It *did not* stop 9/11 or the Boston bombing eleven years later, and thus is as repugnant to good policy as it is to civil liberties. The full extent of domestic spying during the Bush administration is unknown to the public even today, but as reports roll out, it appears more and more expansive and oppressive.

The President's Surveillance Programs

In the wake of September 11th, Bush's first move was to broaden the authority granted to the NSA director under Executive Order 12333. Gen. Michael V. Hayden, then director of the National Security Agency, declared on September 26th 2001, "[A]ny Afghan telephone number in contact with a U.S. telephone number on or after 26 September was presumed to be of foreign intelligence value and could be disseminated to the FBI."[41] However, the "targeting of communication links with one end in the United States was a more aggressive use of E.O. 12333 authority than that exercised by former Directors."[42] The real action began in October.

On October 2nd, Hayden and Cheney communicated by passing messages via CIA Director George Tenet.[43] Cheney was interested in seeing what more the NSA could do to prevent terrorism. Hayden, replying with "a wink and a nod," said "'[n]ot with my current authorities.'"[44] Cheney was also unhappy because the FBI had "to get [warrants]" before it could engage in "domestic eavesdropping."[45] The Bush administration, not willing to be hampered by a lack of legal authority, quickly put its monarchist lawyer, John C. Yoo, on the case.[46] Yoo responded speedily, drafting a memo almost overnight which outlined "the president's inherent surveillance powers"—powers never granted in the Constitution or by statute, powers never before claimed, and powers that were never intended to be granted to an unchecked executive.[47]

Following Yoo's indefensible advice, Bush signed an order on October 4th 2001 that was drafted by Cheney's legal counsel, David Addington.[48] That order created the President's Surveillance Program, known publicly as Terrorism Surveillance Program, and to the NSA as code name STELLARWIND.[49] It was known more aptly as "'the vice president's special program.'"[50] Regardless of the name, as the program name has changed frequently over the course of the war, it refers to the unconsti-tutional fishing expedition that is the NSA's warrantless dragneting of telephony and Internet metadata and content, generally known to the public at the time of this writing.

From the outset, the Justice Department expressed unease about the program,[51] even though one of its own endorsed its legal underpinnings. Pursuant to the program, the NSA was permitted to collect telephony and Internet metadata *and* content—even that which was purely domes-tic.[52] Attorney General John Ashcroft signed off on the program without assessing its constitutionality or lawfulness. He asked Yoo to do that assessment three weeks later.[53]

This was the broadest known expansion of presidential spying powers in history.[54] Between October and November 2001, telecom-munications companies (save for Qwest, discussed hereafter) began voluntarily and secretly sharing data about their customers with the federal government.[55] In 2002, these disclosures would become part of formal agreements between the government and telecommunications providers.[56] It also set off one of the biggest almost-scandals in the Bush presidency later in 2004.

The PATRIOT Act of 2001: Offensive Portions of the Act

During Congress's war hysteria phase, it passed the USA PATRIOT Act of 2001,[57] an act that civil libertarians have railed against for the better part of thirteen years. "One of the most striking features of the USA PATRIOT Act is the lack of debate surrounding its introduc-tion."[58] Despite the fact that "many provisions of the Act relating to electronic surveillance" had been debated and rejected in previous congressional sessions, and even though House members were given a mere *fifteen minutes* to read this three-hundred-plus-page bill, the PATRIOT Act passed the House by a vote of 357 to 66.[59] This was not unlike its predecessor, the 1938 Congress, which created a Special Un-American Activities Committee after rejecting a similar legislative attempt to create one the previous year, before hysteria set in; or, unlike the 1950 Congress, which passed the McCarran Act after rejecting the 1948 Mundt-Nixon bill.[60]

The heading of this section of this work, "Offensive Portions of the Act," is a bit of a misnomer. In fact, every section of the Act is offensive to the Constitution for some reason or another. This discussion is limited to the most relevant provisions, determined by the demonstrable impact they have had on society (this is not to say the other provisions have had no impact, just that they relate less to privacy and more to other rights). Specifically, this discussion relates to selected portions of Title II of the Act, which purports to give the government unnatural, unconstitutional, and illegal authority to perform electronic surveillance. And it relates to the creation of the material support for terrorism offense created under Title VIII.[61]

As much as one would like to read the PATRIOT Act to understand the nuances of it,* that would prove a fruitless endeavor. Many portions of the offensive portions of the Act are simply listing modifications to the Foreign Intelligence Surveillance Act (FISA) or other various provisions of the U.S. Code without context; for example, Section 201 of the PATRIOT Act reads:

(2) by inserting after paragraph (p), as so redesignated by section 201(3) of the Illegal Immigration Reform and Immigrant Responsibility Act of 1996 (division C of Public Law 104–208; 110 Stat. 3009–565), the following new paragraph:

"(q) any criminal violation of section 229 (relating to chemical weapons); or sections 2332, 2332a, 2332b, 2332d, 2339A, or 2339B of this title (relating to terrorism); or."[62]

---

* For example, the Fox television show *Arrested Development* made a rather humorous reference to this in an episode where a defense attorney for the Bluth family, Wayne Jarvis, was now prosecuting them for the same crimes for which he was previously defending them. What was the excuse for the lawyer's clearly illegal and unethical behavior? Michael Hurwitz, *Arrested Development*, produced by Ron Howard, Culver City, CA: Fox Television Broadcast, 2004.

As an attorney, a former judge, and a law professor, I have absolutely no way to comprehend what this actually does without looking up eight different provisions of the U.S. Code. But I have done so. Looking up that one section of the bill took more than fifteen minutes. To read the entire Act—including the statutes it amends so as to understand it—consumes at least twenty hours. I have done so.

However, as the Electronic Privacy Information Center concisely explains: "Section 201 added crimes of terrorism or production/dissemination of chemical weapons as predicate offenses under Title III, suspicion of which enable the government to obtain a wiretap of a party's communications. Because the government already had substantial authority under FISA to obtain a wiretap of a suspected terrorist, the real effect of this amendment is to permit wiretapping of a United States person suspected of domestic terrorism."[63]

Moreover, this section is particularly invidious because the government is getting the typically more-difficult-to-get wiretap warrants rather than basic search warrants. Thus, the descriptions of the various provisions may not flow directly from the Act itself, but from interpretation of its sinews that stretch deep into various other acts at fifteen different titles of the U.S. Code.[64]

Section 206 of the Act—a portion that reads just as opaquely as Section 201—relates to "roving surveillance authority."[65] This has been nicknamed the "roving wiretaps" provision. Section 206 gives the federal government the authority to "intercept . . . any communications made to or by an intelligence target without specifying" the particular places or things to be searched.[66] The Fourth Amendment to the Constitution provides that "[t]he right of the people to be secure in their persons, houses, papers, and effects, against unreasonable searches and seizures, shall not be violated, and no Warrants shall issue, but upon probable cause, supported by Oath or affirmation, and particularly describing the place to be searched, and the persons or things to be seized."[67]

Clearly, there is a misalignment between the requirements which Section 206 purports to make law and the supreme law of the land.[68]

This provision affects more youth-oriented Web traffic, such as "libraries, university computer labs and cybercafes."[69]

The more invidious attack on individual rights came in the form of secrecy. The previous incarnation of FISA required third parties (such as common carriers and others) "'specified in court-ordered surveillance' to provide assistance necessary to accomplish the surveillance."[70] After the enation of Section 206, the government did not need to specify from what third party it was compelling data disclosure.[71] For instance, the government could (and later it was revealed it did) compel Internet and telephone carriers to turn over all the "business records" that the government requires, such as the metadata and content of hundreds of millions of innocent telecommunication transactions that occurred in the United States in the last few years—and compel them to do it *pursuant to an operation of law.*

Relatedly, Section 210 of the Act enabled the government to access the duration of a call and the time it was placed and ended, any "telephone or instrument number or other subscriber number or identity, including any temporarily assigned network address," and "any credit card or bank account number" paying for the provided service.[72]

The key phrase "pursuant to an operation of law" is standard, boilerplate content of every contract agreement. It is used to create an exception to the obligation of a party to a contract to keep secret the contents or workings of the agreement. Thus, when that phrase appears in almost every Internet company's contract, it permits Section 206 disclosure, in addition to what is specified in a valid warrant. This is a key distinction that has become more and more relevant in the wake of Edward Snowden's 2013 revelations about NSA spying.

Section 204, which is just as opaquely written as Sections 210 and 206 (you can see a theme developing here), permitted the government to obtain "stored voice-mail communications, like e-mail . . . through a search warrant rather than through more stringent wiretap orders."[73] This works in tandem with Section 209 of the Act, which permits nationwide warrants to issue from federal courts. Essentially, an administration-friendly judge in the Circuit for the District of Columbia could issue a secret search warrant for a San Diego resident's voice mails.

One of the more invidious portions of the Act is Section 213, the "sneak and peek" warrant provision. Law enforcement must provide notice to the person whose place or things have been searched. This requirement flows from the Fourth Amendment's consideration of the reasonableness of a search or seizure. Under Section 213, warrants issued pursuant to this section or "*any other* rule of law to search for and seize any property or material that constitutes evidence of a criminal offense in violation of the laws of the United States" may be executed by sneaking and peeking.[74] So really what sort of notice does Section 213 require? What government officials determine is "within a reasonable period of [the warrant's] execution."[75] Obviously this section is unconstitutional on its face and has since been somewhat abrogated.

Sections 214 and 216 work in tandem as well. "Section 214 removes the pre-existing statutory requirement that the government prove the surveillance target is 'an agent of a foreign power' before obtaining a pen register/trap and trace order under the FISA."[76] Broadly, the government can track with whom you communicate under the FISA, without making any showing of the "foreign" part of the Act. Essentially, it puts all persons in the United States, citizens and non-citizens, on the same legal footing as foreign spies.

Section 216 expands the traditional definition of a pen register. The term *pen register* originates in old telegram and telephone company practices and referred to the outgoing call log a telephone company kept on customers for billing purposes. After Section 216, it means a lot more: "[A] device or process which records or decodes dialing, routing, addressing, or signaling information transmitted by an instrument or facility from which a wire or electronic communication is transmitted" but for the actual content.[77] This expanded definition broadly includes telephony and Internet data.

Section 215, aka the library records provision or the business records provision, has drawn the attention of intense media scrutiny in recent days. If one were to pinpoint the most offensive, abhorrent portion of the PATRIOT Act, it would be Section 215. Section 215 permits the government to access "business records, medical records, educational records and library records without a showing of 'probable cause.' . . . [T]he government only needs to claim that the records may be related to an ongoing investigation related to terrorism or intelligence activities."[78] These "business records" include *all* the data maintained or kept by all third-party custodians—it refers quite literally to every business record, including what would appear on a monthly phone or Internet or credit card bill. Finally, Section 218 of the Act changed the requirement for seeking FISA warrants, lowering the bar from obtaining foreign intelligence being "the purpose" to "a significant purpose."[79]

The PATRIOT Act, Title V, §505, aka the National Security Letter provision, permits the federal agents, on their own and without any warrant, to compel a third party like a service provider to turn over stored electronic communications without notice to the owner of the communications; except, rather than under FISA's standard of demonstrating the communicator is an "agent of a foreign power," the government merely needs to meet the "broad standard of relevance [of the sought material]" to investigations of "terrorism or clandestine intelligence activities."[80] This marks a return to the practice of writs of assistance, whereby British soldiers could use general warrant authority *to authorize themselves* to enter the home of any colonist in the pre-Revolutionary War era.[81]

As Randolph Bourne lamented in 1918, with the swing of war hysteria, the criminalization of ideas comes in tow. In the quasi-war with France, it was criticism of the government in the Alien and Sedition Acts; in World War I, it was the disaffection of patriotism provision of the Espionage and Sedition Acts of 1917 and 1918; in World War II and the Cold War, it was the Smith Act's criminalization of sedition; and in the War in the Middle East, it was the material support for terrorism crime.[82]

Title VIII, §805 of the PATRIOT Act gave the government authority and broad power to punish any "service [that would in some manner help terrorists], including . . . expert advice or assistance . . . except medicine or religious materials."[83] Denying priests and doctors to the enemy goes against hundreds of years of battlefield and treaty law and common decency on behalf of clerics and doctors serving in uniform.

Moreover, *assistance* is an incredibly broad term. Does the New Jersey gas attendant who unwittingly pumps a few gallons into a jihadist's car heading for New York City provide assistance? What about the bank tellers who handle many customers a day and unknowingly cash a check for a terrorist? Do they provide material, "expert" aid? What about the TSA agent who stamps a suicide bomber's passport—that certainly would be a specialized, material form of assistance. What about doctors who provide the directly criminalized "expert medical" assistance to the wounded or attorneys who defend them?[84] This statute, just like the many Sedition Acts that preceded it, contains a potential fifteen-year prison sentence![85]

The statute is broad enough so that even a cleric who gives an unrelated religious message to a jihadist provides material support through religious comfort. Analogizing to Catholicism, it is broad enough to criminalize a priest giving confession or last rites to an enemy soldier. It does not merely criminalize urging them on to crusade or jihad by bellowing battle cries of "Deus vult."* Certainly this criminalizes more behavior than imminent, lawless action as per the First Amendment standard set by the Supreme Court in the 1969 case *Brandenburg v. Ohio* and its progeny. Therefore, it circumscribes too many behaviors across too many classes of people to be a valid law.

Unsurprisingly, as America enters its second decade of Middle Eastern wars (at this writing, an entire generation of people under age twenty-one has seen nothing but war after emerging from infancy—at

---

* *Deus vult*, "God wills it," was the rallying cry of the First Crusade. Pope Urban II bellowed it out at a sermon at the Council of Clermont, bringing the kings of Europe into a long and bloody struggle in the Middle East. "Medieval Sourcebook: Urban II: Speech at Clermont 1095 (Robert the Monk version)," in James Harvey Robinson, ed., *Readings in European History*, vol. 1 (Boston: Ginn and Co., 1904), 312–16, http://www.fordham.edu/halsall/source/urban2a.html.

least thirteen years by the time you read this), the PATRIOT Act is by and large still good law with minor modifications and will be such until at least 2015,[86] despite its facial unconstitutionality and invalidity under the Natural Law.

Total Information Awareness and the 2004 FBI-Justice Department Mutiny

By January 2002, with the PATRIOT Act and the President's Surveillance Program in tow, the Bush administration made its final moves toward achieving the Orwellian horror state. In a hidden subsector of a project of the Department of Defense, President Bush, Vice President Cheney, and project director Vice Adm. John M. Poindexter sought to achieve "Total Information Awareness" by "constructing a computer system that could create a vast electronic dragnet, searching for personal information as part of the hunt for terrorists around the globe—including the United States."[87] Poindexter was a disgraced naval officer whom Congress took down in the 1980s Iran-contra scandal.[88] This particular task of creating Total Information Awareness was to be carried out by the Information Awareness Office.[89]

This program's mission was to

> . . . provide intelligence analysts and law enforcement officials with instant access to information from Internet mail and calling records to credit card and banking transactions and travel documents, without a search warrant.
>
> Historically, military and intelligence agencies have not been permitted to spy on Americans without extraordinary legal authorization. But Admiral Poindexter, the former national security adviser in the Reagan administration, has argued that the government needs broad new powers to process, store and mine billions of minute details of electronic life in the United States.[90]

Obviously, this "Orwellian" program, hidden far from the disinfecting sunlight of congressional and judicial review, never really disappeared.[91] As the 2013 revelations about PRISM and the FISA Court orders have demonstrated, Total Information Awareness has been achieved. Big Brother continues to maintain a treasure trove of personal data on all persons in America since circa 2009.

The media picked up this story on November 14th 2002—despite earlier reports*—when the late William Safire of the *New York Times* wrote a not-so-incendiary-but-rather-true piece about the project in 2002.[92] Responding in 2003, the wartime Congress feigned making a fuss over this mass intrusion on the personal information of Americans. Mark Williams wrote,

> Washington's lawmakers ostensibly killed the TIA project in Section 8131 of the Department of Defense Appropriations Act for fiscal 2004. But legislators wrote a classified annex to that document which preserved funding for TIA's component technologies, if they were transferred to other government agencies, say sources who have seen the document, according to reports first published in *The National Journal*. Congress *did* stipulate that those technologies should only be used for military or foreign intelligence purposes against non-U.S. citizens. Still, while those component projects' names were changed, their funding remained intact, sometimes under the same contracts.[93]

The motto of Admiral Poindexter's office was *Scientia est Potentia*, "Knowledge is power."[94] The government hid its aim in plain sight: Strengthening the health of the state by acquiring power. Knowledge is power, and total knowledge in the hands of the state's imperial president is almost total, monarchical power over the individual. There are no

---

* John Markoff had been writing about it since February and right up until a few days before Safire wrote his article. John Markoff, "Chief Takes Over New Agency to Thwart Attacks on U.S.," *New York Times*, February 13, 2002, http://www.nytimes.com/2002/02/13/us/chief-takes-over-at-agency-to-thwart-attacks-on-us.html; see endnote 87.

secrets in the post-9/11 world. Financial, medical, or just personal, they are available to the government at a keystroke.* "War is the health of the state" because it provides the executive branch with the political capital to advance its powers and to reach deeper into the depths of jingoist fear and manufacture that fear into honed rage. PATRIOT Acts and Freedom Fries provide the executive the powers to do what it wishes while the people sign away their liberties to the state. They both assign and alienate their rightful and natural powers to the state, engrossing the state and strengthening its power over the individual and his liberty through manipulation and deception: Noble lies.

The Information Awareness Office was just one subset of the President's Surveillance Program; the PSP included many items under code name STELLARWIND, such as the Terrorist Surveillance Program.

In the fall of 2003, James B. Comey Jr. "arrived at the Justice Department . . . as Justice's number two [under Attorney General John Ashcroft]," replacing Jay S. Bybee, who became a federal appellate judge.[95] Then Office of Legal Counsel (OLC) head Jack Goldsmith brought Comey "into the loop" on February 19th 2004 on the scope of the President's Surveillance Program. On March 4th 2004, "Comey met with Ashcroft for an hour to raise the legal team's myriad concerns."[96] Comey "believed there had clearly been at least two felony violations of surveillance law."[97]

"Senior officials . . . usually received their briefing from [the vice president's counsel David S.] Addington or from Vice President Cheney

---

* In fact, some government officials or subcontractors have been using this power to spy on love interests, with the practice garnering its own intelligence community shorthand acronym, LOVEINT. The *Atlantic* noted that there have been thousands of individuals affected by unreported NSA compliance incidents. Conor Friedersdorf, "Lawbreaking at the NSA: Bring On a New Church Committee," *Atlantic*, August 16, 2013, http://www.theatlantic.com/politics/archive/2013/08/lawbreaking-at-the-nsa-bring-on-a-new-church-committee/278750/; Mike Masnick, "NSA Admits Okay, Okay, There Have Been a Bunch of Intentional Abuses, Including Spying on Love Interests," *Tech Dirt*, August 23, 2013, http://www.techdirt.com/articles/20130823/18432024301/nsa-admits-okay-okay-there-have-been-bunch-intentional-abuses-including-spying-loved-ones.shtml; Siobhan Gorman, "NSA Officers Spy on Love Interests," *Wall Street Journal*, August 23, 2013, http://blogs.wsj.com/washwire/2013/08/23/nsa-officers-sometimes-spy-on-love-interests/.

himself—an odd situation, given that the vice president's office didn't legally have any surveillance oversight."[98] Two days after the March 4th meeting with Ashcroft, "the Justice Department first presented its concerns to the White House. Addington was furious."[99] The Justice Department told the vice president's office to drop its concerns, stating, "Bush was 'free to overrule [us] if he wants.'"[100] They were finished with the criminal, illegal, and unconstitutional actions of the vice president's office that served to do nothing but aggrandize the power of the president at the expense of constitutionally guaranteed individual privacy.

The situation continued to escalate. Cheney called in the CIA and the NSA to badger Comey and the Justice Department into line.[101] The intelligence community pressed Comey, claiming "[i]f the program didn't continue, thousands would die, and it would be all Jim Comey's fault."[102] The meeting was a tense moment in the Bush White House:

> At one point, Comey said he couldn't find a legal basis for the program. Yoo's original memo, he explained, was specious on its face. "Others see it differently," a scowling Cheney replied.
>
> "The analysis is flawed—in fact, fatally flawed. No lawyer reading that could reasonably rely on it," Comey said, his hand sweeping across the table dismissively.
>
> Addington, standing in the back of the room, spoke up. "Well I'm a lawyer," he snapped, "and I did."
>
> Responded Comey, "*No good lawyer.*"
>
> The room went silent.[103]

In the wake of this meeting, FBI Director Robert S. Mueller III reviewed the legal arguments and joined the side of his Justice Department bosses Goldsmith, Comey, and Ashcroft.[104]

The situation came to a head when the senior officials in charge of the Justice Department and FBI had a showdown with the White House Office of Legal Counsel and the president himself in "an uprising of epic proportions."[105]

Attorney General John Ashcroft was hospitalized shortly after his March 4th meeting with Comey, leaving Deputy Attorney General Comey as acting attorney general.[106] Ashcroft was medicated for severe pain and kept under heavy sedation during his stay in a Washington, DC, hospital. His wife, his medical proxy, requested that no one be allowed to speak to him. David Ayres, the chief of staff to John Ashcroft, interrupted Comey on his drive home to inform him that the president had personally violated Ashcroft's wife's wishes that he not be disturbed by telephone calls and had sent his chief counsel, Alberto R. Gonzales, and his chief of staff, Andrew H. Card Jr., to visit Ashcroft and demand that he reauthorize the STELLARWIND program, per the legal FISA/PATRIOT Act requirement(s).[107] Comey immediately got in touch with Mueller, and the two sped to the George Washington University Hospital to intervene.[108] Mueller "ordered his agents [guarding Ashcroft] to use force, if necessary, to prevent the Secret Service and the White House from removing Justice Department officials from the hospital room," anticipating Gonzales and Card's "likely" move to have Secret Service agents ready to assist them.[109]

Mueller, Goldsmith, and Comey arrived first and were waiting by Ashcroft's hospital bed when Gonzales and Card arrived shortly afterward.[110] Ashcroft "chided" the administration officials for their misleading behavior earlier and Yoo's unethical memorandum: "You drew the circle so tight I couldn't get the advice I needed" and indicated that the signature would need to come from acting Attorney General Comey, not him.[111] Gonzales and Card and their colleagues departed, defeated.

Mueller and Comey had enough—attempting to go behind Comey's back to manipulate the infirm Ashcroft was a bridge too far. They began the mutiny: "Across the upper ranks of the Justice Department and the Bureau, letters of resignation were drafted."[112] The officials were prepared to engage in a walkout on a president—"one of the most explosive Washington scandals in recent memory"[113]—because "they would not tolerate having the president continue a program that was illegal."[114]

Ashcroft's chief of staff delayed the walkout on Thursday, March 11th 2004, the final day to reauthorize the program, citing the attorney general's health and the effect on it of the planned resignations.[115] This bought the Cheney team enough time to maneuver until the delay expired on Monday.[116] "The crisis was never mentioned [to Bush]."[117]

At the Friday morning briefing, the Mueller-Comey team discovered that "Addington had rewritten [the PSP] authorization . . . so that it no longer had to be signed by the attorney general and instead was okayed by Gonzales's signature."[118] President Bush pulled Comey aside for a personal meeting.[119]

Comey and the president dined, and the president argued that Comey should let Bush handle the PSP "burden."[120] Comey retorted that morally he could not do it.[121] "Bush knew so little of what had transpired that week; his advisors had never let on."[122] Comey first relayed to President Bush that his FBI director was about to resign over the illegal program, and Bush flinched.[123] Mueller and Bush met thereafter, and Bush gave the final word: "The commander in chief told the FBI director at the end of their discussion, 'Tell Jim [Comey] to do what Justice thinks needs to be done.'"[124]

Of course, this was a temporary victory: "Some of the questions about the [NSA]'s new powers led the administration to temporarily suspend the [PSP] operation [in 2004] and impose more restrictions."[125] Almost a decade later and with the benefit of hindsight, Ashcroft, Comey, and Mueller's efforts to preserve lawful and constitutional government were for naught.

Political Prosecutions in the Bush Era: The IT CEO and the Notre Dame Professor

As Bourne described, with the tide of war hysteria comes the persecution of different viewpoints and dissenters. This work takes specific focus on two of these cases: The "insider trading" prosecution of former Qwest CEO and vice chairman and then later chairman of the National Security Telecommunications Advisory Committee, Joseph P. Nacchio, and the refusal to permit Professor Tariq Ramadan to enter the United States to take up a teaching post at my *alma mater*, the University of Notre Dame.

Nacchio was indicted for insider trading, and according to Scott Shane of the *New York Times*:

> As part of his defense, Mr. Nacchio claimed that he had knowledge of top secret contracts with the N.S.A. and other government agencies that made the company's financial prospects brighter than was publicly known. Prosecutors denied the claims[, and objected to the defense].
>
> At the time of the claimed meeting at the N.S.A.'s Fort Meade, Md., headquarters on Feb. 27, 2001, Mr. Nacchio was chairman of the National Security Telecommunications Advisory Committee, whose members included top executives of most of the major communications companies. Like nearly every chief executive in the industry, he had been granted a security clearance to work with the government on secret projects.
>
> In the court papers, Mr. Nacchio's lawyers said he and James F. X. Payne, then Qwest's head of government business, spoke with N.S.A. officials about the agency's Groundbreaker project, in which the agency's non-secret information technology would be contracted to private companies.
>
> At the same meeting, N.S.A. officials made an additional proposal, whose exact nature is not made clear in the censored documents.
>
> "The court has prohibited Mr. Nacchio from eliciting testimony regarding what also occurred at that meeting," one of the documents states. Another passage says: "The court has also refused to allow Mr. Nacchio to demonstrate that the agency retaliated for this refusal by denying the Groundbreaker and perhaps other work to Qwest."[126]

Joe Nacchio's testimony goes into more detail. In the spring of 2000 and spanning into 2001, he met Gen. Harry D. Rutledge Jr., manager of the National Communication Systems, and James F. X. Payne.[127] The two planned to have Qwest build fiber optic intranet facilities for overseas and domestic military installations, potentially a very lucrative long-term contract (especially considering the long-term deployment of the U.S. military overseas).[128] Joe Nacchio relied on those business opportunities, which Qwest was uniquely capable of handling, in signing his company's SEC guidance filings and conducting his business trades during 2000 and 2001.[129]

However, in February 2001, Nacchio refused to comply with a government demand to become part of a "potentially illegal surveillance program—and when he declined, [the NSA] punished the company by dropping a contract worth hundreds of millions of dollars."[130] His colleagues in telecommunications and his new so-called friends in government tried to talk him into staying with the program. To this day, Nacchio is prohibited from saying what the NSA demanded of Qwest. But Joe Nacchio believed in his heart that he was being asked by the government to break federal law.

Thereafter, in the spring, Qwest's classified contracts dried up. The Bush administration, through the SEC and the Justice Department, then decided to discredit the dissenter and deter other CEOs from following suit. Like William Pelley during World War II, he was maliciously prosecuted. The administration accused him of pumping and dumping his investors—trading based on material inside information because he didn't have any solid long-term investments on his books for fiber optics business opportunities.[131]

Refusing to sacrifice the privacy of millions of clients landed Nacchio seventy months in prison.[132] He was released on September 21st 2013 and is writing a book about the terrors of justice.[133] Joe Nacchio is not bitter. But he is busting with awful truths he cannot reveal.

Nacchio was not alone in being persecuted—scholars, with all the trappings of the First Amendment attached to their work, were no safer than businessmen.

Engaging in a "McCarthy-like attempt to keep prickly ideas out of the country," the Bush administration State Department refused to give a Swiss citizen and anti-jihadist Islam scholar, Professor Tariq Ramadan, a visa whereby he could accept a teaching post at Notre Dame.[134] The INS claimed that he had "used a 'position of prominence within any country to endorse or espouse terrorist activity.'"[135]

In the 2006 case *American Academy of Religion v. Chertoff (American Academy of Religion I)*, a federal court in the Southern District of New York heard the suit of Professor Tariq Ramadan against the Department of Homeland Security and the State Department for his "continued exclusion . . . from the United States."[136] He challenged both the statute under which his temporary visa was cancelled (one of the many portions of the PATRIOT Act which pertains to aliens) and the validity of the government's actions under the First Amendment.

Professor Ramadan was not some radical terrorist imam; he was an incredibly renowned scholar of peace in Islam:

> Ramadan is a Swiss-born scholar of Arab descent. He holds Masters Degrees in Philosophy and French Literature and a Ph.D. in Islamic Studies, all from the University of Geneva. After receiving his Ph.D., Ramadan taught Islamic Studies and Philosophy at the University of Fribourg in Switzerland. Since July 2005, Ramadan has served as a Senior Research Fellow at the Loahi Foundation in London and a Visiting Fellow at Oxford University.
>
> Ramadan is a well-known scholar of the Muslim world. He has published more than 20 books, 700 articles, and 170 audio tapes, most of which focus on the subject of Muslim identity and the practice of Islam in the Western world, particularly Europe. Ramadan is perhaps best known for his vision of an independent European Islam. Specifically, Ramadan encourages Europe's Muslims to "reject both isolation and assimilation," and instead explore "the possibility of a 'third path' that would allow European Muslims to be both fully European and fully Muslim." Ramadan also advocates the development of an Islamic feminism and condemns the harsh penalties prescribed by the Islamic penal code. He shuns violence as a form of activism and has consistently spoken out against terrorism and radical Islamists.[137]

Professor Ramadan spoke at conferences and gave lectures in the United States several times from 2000 to 2003, once even delivering a speech *at the State Department* in 2003.[138] Professor Ramadan accepted "a dual appointment as the Henry R. Luce Professor of Religion, Conflict and Peacebuilding and [as] Professor of Islamic Studies in the Classics Department" at the University of Notre Dame and applied for an appropriate visa.[139] Initially, the visa was approved, but a month later the Department of Homeland Security "cancel[ed] [the] visa."[140] The government curiously argued in court that Professor Ramadan "'has never had a visa revoked, a visa application denied, or any other adverse action taken against him.'"[141]

As a result of the government's action, Ramadan had to decline the Notre Dame position in December 2004 and was unconstitutionally blocked from entering the United States to give lectures.[142] Applying for a second visa, he was literally told that his application "'would take at least two days but no more than two years.'"[143] His First Amendment rights were completely violated, and his natural right to speak the ideas he had studied and researched over a lifetime had been revoked behind the cloak of a bureaucratic game.

The Court was faced with a technical issue: The government had not granted him a visa, but it also had not actually denied Professor Ramadan a visa, thus the issue was not ripe for decision. So, the judge issued a writ of mandamus, ordering the Departments of State and of Homeland Security to make a decision within ninety days:[144]

If the Government has a legitimate and bona fide reason for excluding Ramadan, then it may exclude him, but it must do so by acting on the pending visa application, not by studying Ramadan's application indefinitely, while hoping for more supportive evidence to appear in the future. Ramadan's voluminous books, articles and speeches provide more than an adequate basis for review. His frequent visits to the United States, including a visit to the State Department in October 2003, provide ample first-hand insight into Ramadan's views.[145]

This set the stage for *American Academy of Religion v. Chertoff* (*American Academy of Religion II*) in 2007.[146]

In *American Academy of Religion II*, the district court faced the same claims with a final agency determination, which eliminated the ripeness issue. The government "officially denied the visa and gave its reason: Professor Ramadan had contributed money to an organization which provided material support to Hamas, a terrorist group."[147] In a deplorable decision, the district court granted summary judgment to the government on both the First Amendment claim and the constitutionality of the portion of the PATRIOT Act that rendered Professor Ramadan inadmissible to the United States.[148] The court cited the typical excuses: Institutional competency and deference to the executive on political questions.[149]

However, even this was not the end of the issue. The plaintiffs appealed the decision in the 2009 case, *American Academy of Religion v. Napolitano* (*American Academy of Religion III*).[150] The Second Circuit Court of Appeals overturned the district court's decision, holding that the State Department should have given Professor Ramadan a "reasonable opportunity to demonstrate, by clear and convincing evidence, that he did not know, and should not have reasonably known" that his money ended up in the hands of Hamas.[151] The court vacated the district court's decision and remanded for further proceedings.[152] The issue became moot, however, in 2010, when "Secretary of State Hilary Clinton issued Ramadan his visa."[153]

Other Battles in the Courts 2004–7: Declarations of Unconstitutionality with Respect to the PATRIOT Act

Several federal district courts recognized the unconstitutionality of various provisions of the PATRIOT Act. The decisions relating to Fourth Amendment rights were largely overturned by more cowed circuit courts, but the judiciary attacked the material support for terrorism charge.

The first judicial strike at the constitutionality of a provision of the PATRIOT Act came in 2004, in the case *Humanitarian Law Project et al. v. Ashcroft.*[154] The district court for the Central District of California ruled that the material support provision of the PATRIOT Act was unconstitutional because it was "impermissibly vague."[155]

In 1997, Madeleine Albright designated the Kurdistan Workers Party (PKK) a foreign terrorist organization.[156] The PKK is "the leading political organization representing the interests of the Kurds in Turkey, [and] was formed approximately 25 years ago with the goal of achieving self-determination for the Kurds in Southeastern Turkey. It is comprised primarily of Turkish Kurds."[157] The PKK engages in political advocacy and grassroots organization to assist Turkish Kurds in their seventy-five-year struggle against human rights abuses.[158] The plaintiffs in this case were "five organizations and two United States citizens" who sought to "support [only] the lawful, nonviolent activities of the PKK."[159] The plaintiffs in *Humanitarian Law Project* sought to have the court enjoin the federal government from criminally charging them under the material support statute because it is impermissibly vague,[160] a facial challenge (as opposed to an as-applied one) which would render a law unconstitutional in all applicable circumstances.

The void for vagueness doctrine holds that a law must be written "sufficiently clear so as not to cause persons of common intelligence . . . necessarily [to] guess at its meaning and [to] differ as to its application."[161] Thus, a criminal statute which purports to make gang assemblies illegal, but is written so broadly as essentially to prevent more than a few people from assembling together in public, is written too vaguely to be a valid law.

The *Humanitarian Law Project* team won this victory under that doctrine, on the grounds that the law itself proscribed more behavior than intended or may lawfully be proscribed, and that protected First Amendment activity was infringed by this statute:

> [T]he Court concludes that the term "expert advice or assistance," like the terms "training" and "personnel," is not "sufficiently clear so as to allow persons of 'ordinary intelligence a reasonable opportunity to know what is prohibited.'"

. . . The "expert advice or assistance" Plaintiffs seek to offer includes advocacy and associational activities protected by the First Amendment, which Defendants concede are not prohibited under the USA PATRIOT Act. Despite this, the USA PATRIOT Act places no limitation on the type of expert advice and assistance which is prohibited, and instead bans the provision of *all* expert advice and assistance regardless of its nature. Thus, like the terms "personnel" and "training," "expert advice or assistance" "could be construed to include unequivocally pure speech and advocacy protected by the First Amendment" or to "encompass First Amendment protected activities."[162]

As it stood at the end of the Bush years, *Humanitarian Law Project* was a modest success for liberty.

In 2004, in *Doe v. Ashcroft (Doe I)*, a federal court in the Southern District of New York found that the "compulsory, secret, and unreviewable production of information required by the FBI's application of [National Security Letters] violates the Fourth [and First] Amendment[s]."[163] This effectively invalidated the power of federal agents to authorize themselves to seize records.

The court first decided not to view the statute in a vacuum, recognizing the perils of the overlapping provisions of the PATRIOT Act: "[The NSL provision] does not represent a discrete, stand-alone instance of legislation. Rather, it is but one point in a constellation of other laws, a part and pattern of a larger congressional design generally interrelated by the common purpose of facilitating various forms of investigations and law enforcement proceedings."[164] The court held that the NSL provision was an unconstitutional restraint on free speech, reasoning that the "blanket rule swearing everyone concerned to secrecy forever" could not survive First Amendment review.[165]

In 2005, a federal court in the District of Connecticut heard a similar case over an NSL request for library records in *Doe v. Gonzales (Doe II)*.[166] This district court, reasoning along now familiar lines, granted a preliminary injunction that prevented the government from enforcing the NSL provision against the plaintiff recipient of such request.[167]

In light of the legal setbacks of *Doe I* in 2004 and *Doe II* in 2005, Congress and President Bush nominally modified the material support crime and the NSL provision.

In the Intelligence Reform and Terrorism Prevention Act of 2004, Congress added some fluff to the definition of material support, purporting to winnow the class of activity proscribed by the "ambiguous expert advice or assistance" language.[168] In reality, however, the new language merely ensured that the expert advice would be derived from "scientific, technical, or other specialized knowledge," which in no meaningful way modified or narrowed the term *expert*.

When Congress and President Bush reauthorized the PATRIOT Act in 2005, it contained an illusory modification to the NSL provision.[169] Accordingly, in the 2006 case *Doe v. Gonzalez* (*Doe III*), the Second Circuit Court of Appeals overturned *Doe I and II* because the modifications to the statute rendered the *Doe* decisions moot and remanded the matter back to the district court.[170]

When the district court received the case again in 2007, it held that the illusory changes did not make the law constitutionally valid. "Instead of [creating] a categorical, blanket prohibition on disclosure with respect to the issuance of any NSL, . . . [it] now calls for a case-by-case determination of the need for a nondisclosure order to accompany an NSL."[171] The *Doe IV* decision found that "[s]pecifically, the statute provides that a recipient of an NSL is barred from disclosing that the FBI 'has sought or obtained access to information or records' . . . if the Director of the FBI, or his designee, 'certifies' that disclosure 'may result' in 'a danger to . . . national security . . .' 'is unconstitutional . . . because it functions as a licensing scheme that does not afford adequate procedural safeguards.'"[172]

In simple terms, the court held that in America the FBI may not decide who can lawfully speak about its clandestine domestic spying operations. The Second Circuit affirmed this decision in part in *Doe V*.[173] The

Second Circuit "modif[ied] the District Court's injunction by limiting it to enjoining FBI officials from enforcing the nondisclosure requirement of [the NSL provision] in the absence of Government-initiated judicial review," which means review by a trial judge in secret, without counsel present, thus not full and open proceedings.[174] Effectively, the Second Circuit gutted the decision while "affirming" parts of it.

In the 2007 case *Mayfield v. United States* (*Mayfield I*), a completely innocent man was stalked by the awesome mechanisms of the PATRIOT Act's Fourth Amendment legal machinery.[175] He filed suit in a federal court in the District of Oregon seeking a declaratory judgment that the FBI had violated his Fourth Amendment rights:

> . . . Mayfield is an American citizen born in Oregon and reared in Kansas. He [was] liv[ing at the time] with his wife and three children in Aloha, Oregon, a suburb of Portland. Mayfield [wa]s 38 years old, a former Army officer with an honorable discharge, and a practicing Oregon lawyer. Prior to his arrest, he had not traveled outside the United States since 1994, and he had never been arrested for a crime. [His suit against the federal government] allege[d] that FBI examiners were aware of Mayfield's Muslim faith and that this knowledge influenced their examination of Mayfield's fingerprints.[176]

The FBI received a fingerprint from the Spanish police after the Madrid train bombing in 2004, in which "terrorists' bombs exploded on commuter trains, murdering 191 persons, and injuring another 1600 persons, including three United States citizens."[177] The fingerprint was misidentified under questionable circumstances by an FBI agent and also by an independent contractor (who had been "reprimanded on at least three occasions for erroneously 'identifying' fingerprints").[178] An FBI senior agent then verified the questionable match in view of the fact that "Mayfield is Muslim."[179]

The FBI proceeded to turn Mayfield's life into Winston Smith's vision of the world in *1984*:

[They placed] electronic listening devices ("bugs") in the "shared and intimate" rooms of the Mayfield family home; executed repeated "sneak and peek" searches of the Mayfield family home, occurring when the family was away from the home and performed "so incompetently that the FBI left traces of their searches behind, causing the Mayfield family to be frightened and believe that they had been burglarized;" obtained private and protected information about the Mayfields from third parties; executed "sneak and peek" searches of the law office of Brandon Mayfield; and placed wiretaps on Mayfield's office and home phones.[180]

They took everything including his children's homework[181]— what relevance that could possibly have to a terrorist plot is beyond fathoming. The Spanish police cleared Mayfield of any involvement, arrested several Moroccan suspects, and "'refused to validate'" the FBI's results.[182] The FBI was more prejudicially focused on the fact that Mayfield "attended a mosque" and "advertised his legal services in . . . the 'Muslim Yellow Pages.'"[183]

Mayfield was arrested and held incommunicado from his family on May 6th 2004.[184] His family was told Mayfield was "being held as a primary suspect on offenses punishable by death, and that the FBI had made a 100% match of his fingerprint with the Madrid train bombing fingerprint."[185] The FBI stated this after Spanish authorities had stated definitively that the fingerprint in question was not Mayfield's. The FBI disgraced him publicly by leaking his alleged (and bogus) involvement in the Madrid train bombing.[186] However, following Spanish authorities properly identifying the fingerprint as that of an Algerian suspect, he was released on May 20th 2004.[187]

The *Mayfield I* court found that two provisions of FISA, which were modified by the PATRIOT Act, were unconstitutional.[188] When the government seeks to search a criminal suspect's home or place of business, it must get a warrant and demonstrate probable cause before a neutral magistrate. The FISA Act, however, "contains a 'foreign intelligence standard' of probable cause which requires a showing that the target may be an agent of a foreign government and the place or facility to be searched is being used in furtherance of espionage or terrorist activities."[189] As modified by the PATRIOT Act Section 218, however, the FISA standard is now the amorphous "significant purpose" standard, which broadly would permit spying on Americans for domestic terrorism, clearly not the purpose of FISA and under the purview of the more exacting Fourth Amendment standard.[190]

The court recognized this, striking down the provisions of law modified by Section 218 of the Patriot Act, noting that for "over 200 years, this Nation has adhered to the rule of law—with unparalleled success. A shift to a Nation based on extra-constitutional authority is prohibited, as well as ill-advised."[191]

However, in 2010 in *Mayfield II*, after successful settlement of all but one issue, the Ninth Circuit Court of Appeals vacated the *Mayfield I* decision, restoring those two provisions touched by Section 218 to law.[192] The court stated that because Mayfield had reached a settlement with the government, he no longer had standing to sue. The reasoning? His settlement with the government made after *Mayfield I*, which specifically left open his ability to pursue his Fourth Amendment claims, somehow meant that "his [Fourth Amendment privacy] injuries already have been substantially redressed by the Settlement Agreement."[193]

Secrets for Some: Alteration of Declassification Procedure, Executive Order 13292, and the *New York Times* Sits On and Then Releases Data Collection Information

In 1995, President Clinton adopted information procedures that took a brave step toward government transparency. Executive Order 12958 created information declassification procedures aimed at revealing the secrets the U.S. government had been keeping under the veil of state secrecy.[194] According to Clinton's fourth chief of staff, John D. Podesta, discussing the "unprecedented effort" to open government documents to researchers:

[T]he notion of open government—the fundamental tenets of the Freedom of Information Act—are really part and parcel of our First Amendment rights. And I think it's worth going back and reminding you just exactly what those tenets really are that form the basis of that Act: that *disclosure* is the general rule, not the exception; that *all* individuals have equal right of access; that the burden is on the *government* to justify the withholding of a document, not on the person requesting it; and that individuals improperly denied access to documents have the right to seek injunctive relief in the courts.[195]

After making playful references to the search for aliens in government documents (Podesta was after all speaking at a National Press Club meeting sponsored by the Sci Fi Channel), Podesta got to the meat of what Executive Order 12958 did: "Before President Clinton signed that executive order, a tiny minority of classified documents—only 5%— had a fixed classification date. Since the signing of that order, more than 50% of those documents are now marked for declassification in ten years or less."[196] This was an amazing achievement against the bulwark of the entrenched defense bureaucracy.

"But even more significantly: during the five years that the executive order was in place, its policies resulted in the declassification of over 800 million pages of historically valuable records, with . . . hundreds of millions more pages to be declassified in the next few years."[197] The order contained an automatic declassification procedure after twenty-five years,[198] thus setting a minimum bar of eventual transparency.

One of the "[s]cholars, historians, journalists, [or] everyday researchers around the world" Podesta foretold would use these declassified revealed documents acquired through the Freedom of Information Act (FOIA) was a previously cited author, Robert B. Stinnett.[199] Stinnett's work, *Day of Deceit*, proved a legitimate and convincing case based on released government documents that the FDR administration actively engaged in a cold war with Japan during 1940 and 1941, intending to lead to the predicted attack on Pearl Harbor.[200] Stinnett thanked

"Congressman John [E.] Moss [(D-UT)], the author of America's Freedom of Information Act (FOIA)" in his dedication because of the significance of the FOIA.[201]

The FOIA was carried out in a manner not meant to obfuscate its purpose, per Clinton's order—a president being transparent. Despite the fact that "[m]ainstream TV has not been forthcoming," legitimate sources in the "mainstream print media [have] given *Day Of Deceit* very fine reviews. That includes *The New York Times*, *The Wall Street Journal*, *San Francisco Chronicle*, et al."[202]

This story is relevant for two reasons. First, because the mainstream media kept ideas that would change the image Americans have adopted of FDR out of the mainstream media. This repression of unpalatable thoughts about the propriety of war actions is similar to how the *New York Times* manipulated the American people between 2004 and 2005. The paper, badgered by the federal government, kept stories about abuses of the Orwellian President's Surveillance Program from publication.[203] Second, that era of open, transparent government was abruptly slammed closed in 2003 when President Bush revoked Executive Order 12598 and replaced it with Executive Order 13292.[204]

Executive state secrets and classification orders have existed since 1863. Gen. Ambrose Burnside issued General Order No. 38 in 1863, criminalizing communication with the enemy.[205] FDR gave secret classification the presidential imprimatur in 1940 with Executive Order 8381, preventing "general dissemination of information relative" to "Certain Vital Military and Naval Installations and Equipment."[206] Using their executive order power, several presidents modified the control of public information, waxing and waning the manipulation of the marketplace of ideas. President Eisenhower, after initially expanding the class of materials that came under classification procedure, narrowed it slightly in 1953.[207] President Carter in 1978 limited what could be classified, but President Reagan reversed that trend in 1982.[208] In 1993, the Government Accounting Office realized it could save hundreds of millions of dollars by declassifying material,[209] and thus Clinton's executive transparency order was born.

According to a Congressional Research Service Report from 2009, Bush's Executive Order 13292

- eliminate[s] the Clinton order's standard that information should not be classified if there is "significant doubt" about the need to do so;
- treats information obtained in confidence from foreign governments as classified;
- authorizes the Vice President, "in the performance of executive duties," to classify information originally;
- adds "infrastructures" and "protection services" to the categories of classifiable information;
- eases the reclassification of declassified records;
- postpones the starting date for automatic declassification of protected records 25 or more years old from April 17, 2003, to December 31, 2006;
- eliminates the requirement that agencies prepare plans for declassifying records;
- cancels the order requiring the Archivist to create a "government wide database of information that has been declassified," and instead requires the "Director of the Information Security Oversight Office [ISCAP]. . . [to] coordinate the linkage and effective utilization of existing agency databases of records that have been declassified and publicly released"; and
- permits the Director of Central Intelligence to block declassification actions of the ISCAP, unless overruled by the President.[210]

This manipulation of the marketplace of ideas has existed since President Wilson set the precedent of noble lies in the First World War.[211] Since then, almost every president has taken up the mantle of keeping secrets and the American exceptionalism narrative without question. This is another form of manipulation of the marketplace of ideas, whereby the executive even created Rumsfeld's famed "known unknowns"[212] by removing information from the complete set of what is known to exist, if the content is known or not, in the marketplace of ideas.

Moreover, Vice President Cheney himself described this specific expansion of the vice president's powers as creating a secret, unilateral classification authority.[213] And why did the vice president need so much authority for declassification procedures? Surely the person of the president, embodied in his imperial executive, was enough authority. Vice President Cheney could not get access to classified information he wanted because of the constrictions on Executive Order 12598. He needed the president to create an exception to his own rules for the vice president!

Private entities also manipulate the marketplace of ideas in times of war. Many recollect that William Randolph Hearst used yellow journalism to sensationalize the internal Spanish colonial problems in Cuba and push the United States into the Spanish-American War, for the paper's profit.[214] More narrowly, the media cannot withhold vital information from the marketplace of ideas that underlies the basis for which people make informed political decisions, while claiming First Amendment protection at the same time. The Fourth Estate exists to do the opposite of that.

Eight years before the *Guardian* dropped the Edward Snowden bombshell in 2013, the *New York Times* shocked the world by revealing that the NSA, "[u]nder a presidential order signed in 2002, . . . has monitored the international telephone calls and international e-mail messages of hundreds, perhaps thousands, of people inside the United States without warrants over the past three years in an effort to track possible 'dirty numbers' linked to Al Qaeda."[215] The article referenced a "temporary suspen[sion]," of the program in 2004,[216] undoubtedly due to the FBI-Justice 2004 James Comey–led Mutiny that was hushed up until the summer of 2007.[217]

However, the *New York Times* had created its own "known unknown" about the War on Terror and the powers of the government: "The White House asked the *New York Times* not to publish this article, arguing that it could jeopardize continuing investigations and alert would-be terrorists that they might be under scrutiny. After meeting with senior administration officials to hear their concerns, the newspaper delayed publication for a year to conduct additional reporting. Some information that administration officials argued could be useful to terrorists has been omitted."[218]

The *Times* editors held the story for *an entire year* because the president's men *asked* them to do so, and during that year, George W. Bush was reelected to the presidency.

The editors of the *Times* knew since 2004 that "the number monitored in this country may have reached into the thousands over the past three years"[219]—a modest revelation compared to the hundred-million-plus bombshell the *Guardian* would drop a few years later during the Obama administration. However, as one of the authors, Eric Lichtblau, later admitted in 2008, he and his colleagues received the same scare tactics as those that were used on Comey in the Justice-FBI Mutiny: "The clichés did their work; the message was unmistakable: If the *New York Times* went ahead and published this story, we would share the blame for the next terrorist attack."[220]

PRISM Takes the Torch: The Protect America Act of 2007 and the 2008 FISA Court Amendments

By September 2006, the Bush administration was in bad shape. Its own Justice Department and FBI had mutinied in 2004; the *New York Times* discredited the administration's surveillance program in December 2005; *Doe I–IV* was in consideration from 2004 to 2007; *Mayfield* was an ongoing public embarrassment between 2004 and 2007; *Rasul, Padilla,* and *Hamdan*—major Supreme Court blows to the Guantanamo rendition and torture regime—were all handed down between 2004 and 2006; Abu Ghraib was a public scandal between 2003 and 2004; "Scooter" Libby was indicted for leaking classified information in October 2005 (which Cheney authorized under his new Executive Order 13292 powers);[221] the House of Representatives fell to the Democrats in 2006; and Bush fired Rumsfeld the following day and replaced him with Robert

Gates, the best friend of Bush's father. Bush and Cheney did not have the political capital to maintain their vast data and military empire that dug into every aspect of American lives.

The executive could no longer be answerable for such a program as the PSP—the American people wouldn't stand for it.[222] Thus, President Bush "decided not to reauthorize these activities and the final Presidential Authorization expired on February 1, 2007" in order to "work on the transition of authority" to a body that can't be held accountable: The judiciary.[223] And thereby, "[c]ertain activities that were originally authorized as part of the PSP have subsequently been authorized under orders issued by the Foreign Intelligence Surveillance Court (FISC)."[224]

The picture wasn't that simple, however. The president needed Congress to approve the shift of accountability; FISA and the power to modify federal court jurisdiction belonged expressly to a Congress which has always jealously guarded those prerogatives. Thus, through two acts of Congress, political accountability shifted away from the executive to the judiciary through the collusion of the political branches. This was accomplished through the Protect America Act of 2007 and the FISA Amendments Act of 2008, which bridged the gap from unconstitutional executive program to executive program with the imprimatur of a secret Article III court.[225]

The Protect America Act of 2007 was one of the many totalitarian acts that Bush signed into law. The Act modified FISA to permit the "acquisition" of information, so long as "reasonable" procedures were in place for gaining electronic intelligence information on people "reasonably believed to be located outside the United States" with a "significant purpose" of acquiring foreign intelligence information, regardless of citizenship, and *pursuant to the directive of the Director of National Intelligence and the Attorney General*.[226] The Fourth Amendment certainly had a different bar for governmental interference with private communications. Moreover, it conscripted the assistance of "service provider, custodian, or other person (including any officer, employee, agent, or other specified person of such service provider, custodian, or other person) who has access to communications, either as they are transmitted or while they are stored" in complying with the executive directives.[227]

The Protect America Act included an "appeals" mechanism, however: "The court's review [would] be limited to whether the Government's determination is clearly erroneous." Moreover, that determination was limited to whether the Justice Department and NSA's "procedures are reasonably designed to ensure that acquisitions conducted . . . do not constitute electronic surveillance."[228] The Act passed in the Senate in a vote of 60 to 28, and in the House in a vote of 227 to 183.

The FISA Amendment Acts of 2008 added a new Title VII to the FISA.[229] The Act iterated the same compulsory requirements of the Protect America Act; however, it contained a new, invidious twist in Section 702 that continued the deepest data mining of the now-defunct PSP:

(h) DIRECTIVES AND JUDICIAL REVIEW OF DIRECTIVES.—

(1) AUTHORITY.—With respect to an acquisition authorized . . .[by] the Attorney General and the Director of National Intelligence . . . , in writing, an electronic communication service provider to—

(A) immediately provide the Government with all information, facilities, or assistance necessary to accomplish the acquisition in a manner that will protect the secrecy of the acquisition and produce a minimum of interference with the services that such electronic communication service provider is providing to the target of the acquisition; and

(B) maintain under security procedures approved by the Attorney General and the Director of National Intelligence any records concerning the acquisition or the aid furnished that such electronic communication service provider wishes to maintain.

(2) COMPENSATION.—The Government shall compensate, at the prevailing rate, an electronic communication service provider for

providing information, facilities, or assistance in accordance with a
directive issued pursuant to paragraph (1).

(3) RELEASE FROM LIABILITY.—No cause of action shall lie in any
court against any electronic communication service provider for providing any information, facilities, or assistance in accordance with a
directive issued pursuant to paragraph (1).[230]

Not only was the government going to compensate the telecommunications and Internet companies for their betrayal of essentially all
American data they had while keeping their mouths shut, it also released
them from criminal and civil liability. The FISA Court merely had the
power to review for some vague unlawfulness and whether the conduct
was "electronic surveillance," whatever that amorphous term means.[231]

The new Acts accomplished the PSP's goals and practical effects
under the secret eye of the FISA Court, which later revelations would
show had significant trouble dealing with the NSA's brazen lawlessness.
The new NSA program created pursuant to this accountability-shifting
Section 702 of the FISA Amendments Act, the Protect America Act of
2007, and Section 215 of the PATRIOT Act was entitled PRISM and
would be continued into the presidency of Barack H. Obama.[232] On the
day the FISA Amendments Act was signed into law, the ACLU filed suit
in what would become *Clapper v. Amnesty International*.[233]

The record of the George W. Bush administration for protection of
fundamental liberties is as poor as those of John Adams, Lincoln, and
Wilson. Yet most Americans went along—until they learned about torture. Remember torture? It was the use of it by Saddam Hussein that Bush
claimed justified invading Iraq—until he, too, used it, as we shall now see.

12

The George W. Bush Administration

Render and Torture

*The degree of civilization in a society can
be judged by entering its prisons.*[*]

—ATTRIBUTED TO FYODOR DOSTOYEVSKY

B efore the Clinton administration, extraordinary rendition was a tool the CIA and FBI had used a total of three times.[1] Extraordinarily rendered people are "kidnapp[ed] . . . and [spirited] out of their sanctuaries, either for trial in America or in their country of origin."[2] However, under Clinton's secret Presidential Decision Directive (PDD) 39, the CIA would begin spiriting these suspects to "Jordan, Syria, Morocco, or Egypt, all of which have legal systems that employ torture as a matter of course."[3]

---

[*] Commonly, perhaps erroneously, attributed to Fyodor Dostoyevsky. Regardless of its accuracy, the attribution captures the heart of Dostoyevsky's later work on the miserable conditions society imposes on prisoners who have been convicted in some way of violating the state's wishes. See Fyodor Dostoyevsky, *The House of the Dead* (1862).

251

Clinton personally authorized more than seventy such renditions in his tenure: "[I]n [the few] cases" where suspects were ordered to appear in U.S. court, they made trial; the rest were more valuable for intelligence and sent to "third countries where they would have no legal rights."[4]

Vice President Gore, Richard Clarke, and Madeleine Albright were "strong support[ers]" of the program, joining in President Clinton's "intense" interest in it.[5] Egypt's most famous terrorist, Talaat Fouad Qassem, was "seized in Croatia, flown to the USS *Adriatic*, a navy warship, interrogated, then flown to Egypt for [torture and] execution."[6] Egypt's secret police, the Gihaz al-Mukhabarat al-Amma, is widely known for its brutal torture regime, "real Macho interrogation . . . enhanced interrogation techniques on steroids" and was used by both Presidents Bush and Clinton.[7]

Congress attempted to end this program in 1998. The Foreign Affairs Reform and Restructuring Act slipped in a passage making it the policy of the United States not to "expel, extradite, or otherwise effect the involuntary return of any person to a country in which there are substantial grounds for believing the person would be in danger of being subjected to torture, regardless of whether the person is physically present in the United States."[8] Clinton vetoed the bill in late October,[9] paving the way for Bush and Cheney's unprecedented expansion of the program that made torture a matter of course for the United States in dealing with state enemies.

Bush's Supreme Court: The Office of Legal Counsel

Cheney, being Bush's right and left hands when it came to national security, rejected the slightly less constitutionally antithetical, Clintonesque law enforcement approach of using prosecution and investigation to end terrorism via rendition.[10] In the wake of 9/11, "Cheney began drawing up plans for ambitious global kidnapping . . . operations in which certain elements of the CIA would initially take a leading role."[11] Further, "according to former CIA and State Department officials, [Cheney] began effectively directing a global manhunt using a mesh of Special Operations Forces and operatives from the CIA."[12]

The Bush administration shut off its rendition efforts from "US military commanders and even CIA station chiefs around the world," welding executive power into the hands of the president and his advisors, removing the lower and middle institutional echelons of executive advice and power.[13] Bush was carrying out his war with the tack of Wilson or FDR in stripping civil liberties. However, Wilson's propaganda would become the literal truth of American prison systems. Prisoners would be sexually and physically abused at the hands of U.S. and U.S.-led-third-party interrogators operating under the color of unilateral executive permission. In turn, this would become al Qaeda's propaganda, but unlike Wilson's, it would be true.

The Bush administration expanded upon Clinton's PDD 39, which would not be declassified until 2007,[14] with a secret body of laws in the Office of Legal Counsel (OLC) and other agency memoranda. Under the Bush administration's imperial or unitary executive theory of government, classified, senior-aide-written memoranda such as these are the "conclusive statements" of constitutionality and law for the federal bureaucracy's conduct: "OLC effectively functioned as an internal Supreme Court for the executive branch—a secret Supreme Court."[15]

President Bush, in claiming this power to interpret the Constitution in *secret*, was robbing the judiciary of a governmental function that has been well established since the 1803 case of *Marbury v. Madison*: The federal judiciary under the Supreme Court and the Court itself constitute the final and absolute arbiters of constitutionality, not the president and his advisors.[16] Bush and those who served at his pleasure were creating legal doctrine contrary to long-standing Supreme Court jurisprudence similar to Wilson's National War Labor Board. This was a power similar to that which kings of England once held before it was taken away because of abuse.

The Torture Memos

The Torture Memos, as they are collectively referred to, comprise a cache of classified OLC, White House, and internal Department of Defense documents authorizing and creating the legal standards for "constitutional" torture, as oxymoronic as that sounds.[17] Of the more notable documents, two memos were written by then Assistant U.S. Attorney General Jay S. Bybee and one letter by John Yoo. Of the remaining authorizations and documents, some were written by Defense Secretary Donald Rumsfeld (one of which included an unpleasant little "joke" about elongating stress position duration).[18]

The first document, Standards of Conduct for Interrogation under 18 U.S.C. §§2340–2340A, (OLC standards), is a memorandum from Bybee to Attorney General Alberto Gonzales.[19] Title 18, Section 2340 of the U.S. Code defines torture, and Section 2340A criminalizes torturing or attempting to torture under the color of lawful authority.[20] This statute represents the principle embodied in the Constitution that no one shall be subjected to "cruel and unusual punishments."[21] Section 2340 defines torture as intentional behavior by a governmental person "intended to inflict severe physical or mental pain or suffering (other than pain or suffering incidental to lawful sanctions) upon another person within his custody or physical control."[22] The law further criminalizes prolonged mental duress torture such as threats against the person or life of the individual or another person.[23] Also prohibited is the use of "procedures calculated to disturb profoundly or affect the senses or the personality."[24]

Bybee's memo offered a "creative" interpretation of that statute, which vastly expanded the powers of the executive over the physical person and inherent dignity of war prisoners, reviving the tradition of English royal torture warrants.[25] The OLC standards gave a medieval interpretation of what the anti-torture statute meant:

> Physical pain amounting to torture must be equivalent in intensity to the pain accompanying serious physical injury, such as organ failure,

impairment of bodily function, or even death. For purely mental pain or suffering to amount to torture under Section 2340, it must result in significant psychological harm of significant duration, e.g., lasting for months or even years. . . . *We conclude that the statute, taken as a whole, makes plain that it prohibits only extreme acts.*[26]

Bybee, who now sits on the U.S. Court of Appeals for the Ninth Circuit, authored one of the most morally groundless, ethically repugnant, logically dubious, and constitutionally challenged sentences in American history, and George W. Bush probably rejoiced when it was read to him.

Further, the memo adopted the conclusion that in the course of conducting the war, "enforcement of the statute would represent an unconstitutional infringement of the President's authority to conduct war."[27] The president's authority to conduct war, according to Bybee, Yoo, and their colleagues, superseded the natural right to be free from punishment without conviction, the human right to be governed by the plain meaning and traditional understanding of the law, and the constitutional right to due process.

The memo noted that the Torture Victims Prevention Act of 1991, which was signed into law by President George H. W. Bush and created a right of action in U.S. courts against *foreign* officials who tortured individuals, would not apply to U.S. officials—and certainly not the president—but that the standards and case law would provide guidance.[28] Cases under the torture statute itself could provide no guidance, as the first prosecution under it began in 2006.[29] The precedent of an imperial presidency that Bush set, expanding upon Clinton, would be used by his successor to assert an even more extreme question regarding the natural right to life. He would use it to justify murder.

In reaching the conclusion that torture must involve pain akin to organ failure, Bybee began by explaining that "Section 2340 makes plain that the infliction of pain or suffering per se, whether it is physical or mental, is insufficient to amount to torture."[30] The memo compared severity of pain that rises to the legal level of torture not to police interrogations, prisoner of war interrogations, or any sort of legal or procedural context involving confinement, but to the medical definition of an "emergency condition" for insurance health benefit reasons.[31] This statute provided restrictive enough language to provide a basis, albeit a totally irrelevant and frivolous one, for a broad definition of how severe pain must be for it to constitute torture.[32] It is inconceivable that the congressional drafters of an insurance benefit statute, pre-Obamacare, thought they were defining torture.

Even more curiously, in looking to what would rise to mental torture under the Act, Bybee would note that the prolonged prong of the torture statute required a definition of *prolonged* which the U.S. Code did not provide.[33] Bybee would again ignore the guidance of any sort of police or war interrogation common law, which provides an extensive body of cases on when and how "prolonged" mental duress could constitute cruel and unusual punishment, and instead looked to the dictionary, which provided the broader definition that Cheney and Bush were seeking.[34]

In all, Bybee would conclude that seven conditions would constitute torture, some of which, as will be discussed below, clearly contradicted even these minimally human standards: "(1) severe beatings using instruments such as iron barks, truncheons, and clubs; (2) threats of imminent death, such as mock executions; (3) threats of removing extremities; (4) burning, especially burning with cigarettes; (5) electric shocks to genitalia or threats to do so; (6) rape or sexual assault, or injury to an individual's sexual organs, or threatening to do any of these sorts of acts; and (7) forcing the prisoner to watch the torture of others."[35]

Relying on international decisions, the memo would, however, justify using stress positions, sleep deprivation, sensory deprivation, hooding, and diet reduction, despite precedent calling these cruel and unusual punishment.[36]

Moreover, the Bybee torture memo managed to find an extensive list of U.S. precedents where "the defendant tortured the plaintiff" and stuffed the precedents into an appended list.[37] Notably on that list was

Daliberti v. Republic of Iraq, where the D.C. District Court found that *five days* of enduring diet restriction and sleep deprivation, stripping, threatening extreme physical duress, and blindfolding were "more than enough" to fall within the ambit of the Torture Victim Prevention Act.[38] America was about to step into such illustrious human rights company as Hussein's Iraq, which George W. Bush many times stated he invaded in order to put an end to Saddam's "torture chambers" and "rape rooms."[39] The memo would also instruct its readers that they could invoke necessity and the principle of national self-defense to justify their actions, subjecting their decisions to a utilitarian and arbitrary moral calculus that could theoretically justify any behavior by government agents.[40]

Bybee's second torture memo was even more chilling. Entitled "Interrogation of al Qaeda Operative," it specifically authorizes ten "interrogation" methods: "(1) attention grasp, (2) walling, (3) facial hold, (4) facial slap (insult slap), (5) cramped confinement, (6) wall standing, (7) stress positions, (8) sleep deprivation, (9) insects placed in a confinement box, and (10) the waterboard."[41] Some portions of it regarding the use of insects are blacked out even today.[42] Detainees would be subjected to such treatment by CIA operatives and to far worse treatment at the hands of third parties to whom they were rendered.

The third memo of importance is an untitled letter from Yoo to Gonzales.[43] Essentially, it outlined the legal arguments for avoiding international criminal jurisdiction under the Convention Against Torture because of a more restrictive U.S. intent requirement, justifying the programs under international law.[44] Now no obstacle—natural, constitutional, or international—could obstruct the president's exercise of unbridled power over the personhood of his war prisoners.

The Cheney Program: Under the Color of Law

Much like the World War Congresses, the War on Terror Congresses have been unceasingly adherent to the executive in matters of national security.* In the beginning, the Bush administration's rendition and torture program was an "ad hoc operation with prisoners stuffed into shipping containers." However, Cheney's secret interrogation program would expand quickly upon Clinton's use of PDD 39 "authority":

> Eventually the CIA would build up its own network of secret "black sites" in at least eight countries, including Thailand, Poland, Romania, Mauritania, Lithuania and Diego Garcia in the Indian Ocean. But in the beginning, lacking its own secret prisons, the Agency began funneling suspects to Egypt, Morocco and Jordan for interrogation. By using foreign intelligence services, prisoners could be freely tortured without any messy congressional inquiries.
>
> . . . The administration also unilaterally decided to reduce the Gang of Eight members of Congress [privy to intelligence briefings] to just four: the chairs and ranking members of the House and Senate intelligence committees. Those members were prohibited from discussing these briefings with anyone. In effect, it meant that Congress had no oversight of the . . . program. And that was exactly how Cheney wanted it.[45]

The United States was in illustrious company: Mauritania did not abolish slavery until 1981 and didn't criminalize owning slaves until 2007, the very last country to do either.[46]

However, the Bush administration, driven by the idea of a completely imperial executive, soon discovered that the CIA would have too many lawyers and too much oversight for their liking; they wanted a clandestine war.[47] Rumsfeld, who had become jealous of Cheney's standing at the forefront of defense policy, advocated a more independent use of the military to avoid any congressional oversight because war acts wouldn't show up in the intelligence briefing of covert acts.[48] Cheney agreed, and

---

* Later on, in President Obama's second term, however, this would show signs of changing.

the administration would use the war power in this manner to claim state secrecy in "the most controversial and secret activities."[49]

In order to carry out these operations, the Joint Special Operations Command (JSOC), the most elite of the Special Forces, would rise under Rumsfeld, Cheney, and the presidential war power to become the administration's personal, global, secret police.[50] Rumsfeld and Cheney would build up JSOC to conduct operations that the CIA had been doing—but without the accountability and with the reach of a global battlefield—and downgrade the CIA's role. The CIA's fall from grace was precipitated by its refusal and inability to fall into lockstep on invading Iraq by providing the necessary intelligence to justify war.[51]

Because the CIA could not produce intelligence suggesting Iraq had WMDs or was linked to 9/11, Rumsfeld and Cheney switched the responsibility for that to Rumsfeld's Defense Department in March 2002.[52] JSOC personnel and Rumsfeld, observing the tactics used by the CIA, decided they were insufficiently gruesome to elicit more effective responses.[53] That's when the United States created its own torture program, extrapolated from the Special Forces' dreaded Survival, Evasion, Resistance, and Escape (SERE) program.[54]

"The SERE program was created to introduce US soldiers, sailors, and airmen to the full spectrum of torture that 'a totalitarian evil nation with a complete disregard for human rights and the Geneva Convention' could use on them if captured."[55] SERE was built on the lessons of "Communist China, North Korea, the Vietcong, Nazi Germany, and scores of other regimes and terror groups."[56] Over the course of 2002, the administration would reverse engineer an interrogation program from the SERE program.[57] The CIA was the primary administrator of the Cheney Program, but eventually JSOC would usurp it and run a parallel program because of the benefits of "greater flexibility and far less oversight." Despite later denying it, congressional leadership, such as then House Minority Whip Nancy Pelosi, was briefed on tactics being used.[58]

In December 2002, CIA Director George Tenet claimed that the United States had already detained more than three thousand suspected al Qaeda operatives in secret prisons in more than a hundred countries.[59] President Bush publicly admitted that the CIA and JSOC secretly subjected about one hundred detainees to torture.[60] Later reports would put the number of persons tortured under the "enhanced" techniques at 136, but "[t]here may be many more individuals."[61] The International Committee of the Red Cross would later report what would happen to military detainees upon processing for military custody:

> The detainee would be photographed, both clothed and naked prior to and again after transfer. A body cavity check (rectal examination) would be carried out and some detainees alleged that a suppository (the type and effect of such suppositories was unknown by the detainees) was also administered at that moment.
>
> The detainee would be made to wear a diaper and dressed in a tracksuit. Earphones would be placed over the ears, through which music would sometimes be played. He would be blindfolded with at least a cloth tied around the head and black goggles. . . .
>
> The detainee would be shackled by [the] hands and feet and transported to the airport by road and loaded onto a plane. He would usually be transported in a reclined sitting position with his hands shackled in front. The journey times . . . ranged from one hour to over twenty-four to thirty hours. The detainee was not allowed to go to the toilet and if necessary was obliged to urinate and defecate into the diaper.[62]

Moreover, once a detainee's initial processing was complete, the treatment only got worse. The Bush administration's secret prisons were torture mills. In his most recent book, *Dirty Wars*, Jeremy Scahill provides incredible detail about the treatment and selections of prisoners.

Between 2002 and 2003, the render and torture program was primarily a CIA operation.[63] These extraordinarily rendered individuals would be locked in solitary confinement, sometimes for years on end, with their families knowing nothing of where they were.[64] Masked men interrogated them:[65]

During the course of their imprisonment, some of the prisoners were confined in boxes and subjected to prolonged nudity—sometimes lasting for several months. Some of them were kept for days at a time, naked, in "stress standing positions," with their "arms extended and chained above the head." During this torture, they were not allowed to use a toilet and "had to defecate and urinate over themselves." Beatings and kickings were common, as was a practice of placing a collar around the prisoner's neck and using it to slam him against walls or yank him down hallways. Loud music was used for sleep deprivation, as was temperature manipulation. If prisoners were perceived to be cooperating, they would be given clothes to wear. If they were deemed uncooperative, they'd be stripped naked. Dietary manipulation was used—at times the prisoners were put on liquid-only diets for weeks at a time.[66]

Prisoners were also told that no legally enforceable rules applied to their detention, and some were waterboarded.[67] Like the Soviet Union's secret police, the CIA and JSOC made rendered individuals simply disappear.[68] Detainees were also selected arbitrarily, without regard to whether they were "complicit," "innocent," "knowledgeable," or "truly clueless."[69]

However, the military interrogations were the most brutal and unquestionably wrong acts of the Bush administration's exercise of war power. Because the CIA's operations were "not harsh enough," Cheney created the parallel JSOC secret interrogation operation.[70] The JSOC operation was run out of many camps, but this discussion will focus on a few of the better-documented incidences: One from the infamous Guantanamo Bay (Gitmo) Detention Center, which this writer visited in 2003, and the other at Camp "Nasty-A—Military Area" (NAMA), a former Hussein torture facility the JSOC occupied and resurrected, leaving the "meat hooks that hung from the ceiling during the Iraqi dictator's reign of terror in place for their use,"[71] and some from the military prison in Bagram, Afghanistan.

Mohamedou Ould Slahi was captured, rendered in Jordan at the behest of U.S. officials.[72] While there, he was starved until he "looked like a ghost" and subjected to interrogation about his role in the Millennium Plot (a planned attack on Los Angeles International Airport and the USS *The Sullivans* that law enforcement foiled).[73] Prisoners like Slahi who were rendered to Jordan were "interrogated with 'electric shocks, long periods of sleep deprivation, forced nakedness, and made to sit on sticks and bottles,' the latter being 'a form of sexual violence,' according to another former Jordanian detainee."[74]

Other prisoners rendered from U.S. custody to places like Jordan suffered far worse fates. One al Qaeda operative, Binyam Mohamed, was rendered to Morocco for "'unspeakable torture'":

> "They took the scalpel to my right chest. . . . Then they cut my left chest. This time I didn't want to scream because I knew it was coming," Mohamed said, "One of them took my penis in his hand and began to make cuts. He did it once, and they stood for maybe a minute, watching my reaction. One of them said it would be better to cut it off, as I could only breed terrorists."
>
> Mohamed said he signed the confessions put in front of him, and then endured SERE-style "brainwashing." . . .
>
> [Military] [c]omissions prosecutors ridiculed such claims. "If we examine Binny's [penis]," one joked while relaxing at a bar, "It'll be to look for [his defense counsel's] teeth marks."[75]

The rendition and torture program had obviously violated all legal and ethical boundaries for custodial care, including genital mutilation and threats of castration.

Slahi was then transferred to U.S. custody at a former Soviet installation, the Bagram Theater Internment Facility in Afghanistan, in June 2002 via a process the same as the one the CIA used for new detainees; the FBI would receive custody of him in Gitmo a month later.[76] He was given the same respect a person in civilian custody would receive in accord with due process; according to the president that respect was not a right that Slahi had by virtue of his humanity, but a benefice of the president.[77]

The president and his army could take it away. And in February 2003, they did: Slahi was transferred to military custody.[78] Jess Bravin in his book *The Terror Courts* detailed the military's abhorrent treatment of Slahi:

[Y]elling, strip searches, shaving the head and beard, and twenty-hour days. Water would be poured on Slahi's head to "enforce control." He could be ridiculed, placed in a mask, made to wear signs with Arabic labels like "liar," "coward," or "dog." Dogs could be brought in "to bark and agitate" him. Slahi himself could be forced to act like a dog— collared, barking, and performing tricks.

He could be treated as a woman and forced to wear a burka or con- fronted with a female interrogator in "close physical contact." The plan called for preventing Slahi from praying or, alternatively, forcing him to worship a stag idol. Violating such "religious taboos" would "reduce the detainee's ego and establish control," the plan explained. . . .

. . . [The torture program] was designed, the document said, to "replicate and exploit the 'Stockholm Syndrome' between detainee and his interrogators." Successfully implemented, "the subject feels that he is about to be killed," the NCIS [Naval Crime Investigative Service] chief psychologist, Michael Gelles, wrote regarding a similar special projects plan. . . .

Other female interrogators removed their camouflage tops and rubbed their breasts against the shackled prisoner, fondled his genitals, insulted him, and laughed at him. Photographs of the reproductive process, of vaginas and birth canals and babies, were plastered on the walls. A woman interrogator ridiculed him for failing to impregnate his wife.[79]

The constitutional and human rights violations abounded. In any U.S. criminal jurisdiction, doing that to a prisoner would be torture, abuse, and sexual abuse. Inmates are given robust protection from having their worship restricted, let alone being forced to worship a false idol.[80] Another Guantanamo inmate, Qahtani, was subjected to the military's "Varsity plan": A torture scheme approved by Rumsfeld that "focused on sexual and excretory humiliations, including forced enemas."[81] His military prosecutors jocularly referred to him and others subjected to similar treatment as "'enema combatant[s].'"[82]

Ahmed al-Darbi was subjected to JSOC's version of the Cheney Program, the one that used the broader extension of presidential war powers rather than civilian covert authorities like the CIA employed. In 2004, Darbi finally trusted investigators enough to talk about his abuse:

> Two CITF [Counterintelligence Task Force] agents interviewed Darbi over two days. The Bagram he described was a chamber of horrors, and he personally had witnessed soldiers torturing an Afghan man named Dilawar, a taxi driver mistakenly held as a terrorist. From his own cage, Darbi had watched a screaming Dilawar suspended from his arms for two days, his feet dangling above the ground, as soldiers beat him. Dabi said he heard—correctly, it turned out—that Dilawar died soon thereafter.
>
> Darbi's own experience involved continuous pain, degradation, and fear. "His hands were cuffed above his head, his face was sprayed with water and pepper was blown onto his face. He was dragged and thrown against walls. The dragging and being thrown were considered normal things that occurred [every] day," the agents wrote.[83]

His interrogators threw used toilet paper at him, made him defecate in public streets, threatened to sodomize him on multiple occasions, and put their genitals near his face.[84] At one point, an interrogator showed Darbi a condom and offered to demonstrate its use on him.[85] "Inmates [at Bagram] often were subjected to enemas."[86] Two prisoners would die at Bagram under interrogations and accountability and oversight systems (or a total lack thereof) created under the color of authority of the president's war powers and in clear contravention of the Torture Statute and Due Process Clause.[87]

Camp NAMA provided another macabre image of JSOC torture mills in action. After being captured, the combatant would be "place[d] . . . under the guard of soldiers he had just been trying to kill" for three days.[88] Unsurprisingly, incidents of mistreatment followed.[89] When the captives were finally interrogated, it got worse:

> The interrogations [in the punishment for some reason room] often incorporated extremely loud music, strobe lights, beatings, environmental and temperature manipulation, sleep deprivation, twenty-hour interrogation sessions, water and stress positions, and personal, often sexual, humiliation. The forced nudity of prisoners was not uncommon. Almost any act was permissible against the detainees as long as it complied with the "No Blood, No Foul" motto. But, eventually, even blood was okay.
>
> One former prisoner—the son of one of Saddam's bodyguards—said he was made to strip, punched repeatedly in the spine until he fainted, was doused with cold water and forced to stand in front of the air conditioner and kicked in the stomach until he vomited. Prisoners held at other facilities also described heinous acts committed against them by interrogators and guards, including sodomizing detainees with foreign objects, beating them, forcing water up their rectums and using extreme dietary manipulation—nothing but bread and water for more than two weeks in one case.
>
> Members of the task force would beat prisoners with rifle butts and spit in their faces. One member of the task force reported that he had heard interrogators "beating the s— out of the detainee." . . . On at least one occasion, they abducted the wife of a suspected insurgent being hunted by the task force "to leverage the primary target's surrender." The woman was a twenty-eight-year-old mother of three who was still nursing her six-month-old baby. After interviewing numerous members of the task force at NAMA, Human Rights Watch

concluded, "the abuses appear to have been part of a regularized process of detainee abuse—'standard operating procedure.'"[90]

The evidence points conclusively to a systematic, presidentially approved, vice presidentially directed, top-to-bottom, unilateral program to vitiate the natural, constitutional, and lawful right to be free from torture and cruel and unusual punishments. These were Bush's Japanese prison camps, but he didn't have FDR's equivalent of a World War II victory over a tyrant who attacked the United States to secure a relatively popular place in mainstream history.

Although not done pursuant to any order, the CIA's version of the program contributed to the largest public human rights shaming the U.S. government has experienced in recent memory. The policy of essentially restrictionless torture, endorsed by the CIA, led to the creation of a culture of zero-restriction treatment among the Military Police (MPs) at the "U.S.-run gulag," Abu Ghraib.*

Detainee treatment at Abu Ghraib became public in 2004, discussed below, causing immeasurable global damage to the credibility of the United States as a defender of natural and civil liberty. According to the initial Abu Ghraib investigator, Army Maj. Gen. Antonio M. Taguba, the prison's MPs engaged in similar treatment to the JSOC camps described above, but also in much more heinous treatment of which there was video or photographic evidence, including "'a video of a male American soldier in uniform sodomizing a female detainee,'" and images of "'torture, abuse, rape and every indecency.'"[91]

Even under the broadest reading of the Constitution, war powers

---

* "Several Army and Department of Defense investigations found that the CIA presence may have contributed to the abuse committed by military police. 'There was at least the perception, and perhaps the reality, that non-DOD agencies had different rules regarding interrogation and detention operations,' an investigation report by Lt. Gen. Anthony R. Jones concluded. 'Such a perception encouraged soldiers to deviate from prescribed techniques.'" Michael Scherer and Mark Benjamin, "Other Government Agencies," *Salon*, March 14, 2006, http://www.salon.com/2006/03/14/chapter_5/. See Jeremy Scahill, *Dirty Wars: The World Is a Battlefield* (New York: Nation Books, 2013), 160.

do not permit the president and his military agents knowingly or even negligently to permit torture. The president and his senior officials enormously expanded war powers to effect inhumane and shameful treatment upon U.S. prisoners[92]—truly among those in society most at the mercy of the government and its agents—while concentrating power in the hands of a few depraved individuals who carried out this systematic regime of torture under an ideological, imperial, unitary presidency.[93] These detainees were not just tortured with programs designed from the best of totalitarian torture regimes for the purposes of war under the president's power to defend the realm—or necessity as Bybee's memos strain to argue—but in no small part to provide a basis for one of the most unjustifiable wars in U.S. history.

That is the penultimate height of power of the noble lie and the imperial presidency, done chillingly with medieval brutality. The zenith of the imperial president's war power would be achieved by Bush's successor, Barack H. Obama: The unilateral "right" to adjudicate by secret fiat whom of his "subjects" are enemies of the state and then *to execute them without trial*.

Bush's Obstinacy on the Power to Torture: Jack Goldsmith, the Detainee Treatment Act of 2005, and *Hamdan v. Rumsfeld*

Bush's power and sanction of torture would be challenged by the other two branches of the government—Congress and the Supreme Court— and his own advisors in the OLC.

The President's Advisor Tries to Kill the Policy

In 2004, Abu Ghraib's regime of systematic prisoner abuse became a widely public matter when a segment about it aired on CBS's 60 *Minutes*.[94] After that, there was increasing public pressure for investigation of the abuses in the detainee program, and the other branches would challenge the Bush administration's power to torture. Moreover, Jay S. Bybee, the former head of the OLC, was appointed to sit on the Ninth Circuit Court of Appeals in 2003 (before his Torture Memos became public). His departure from OLC left an opening that would be filled first by the other Torture Memo author John Yoo and then by Professor Jack Goldsmith in October 2003.[95]

Goldsmith, as it would later be revealed in a 2007 *New York Times* article, had been attempting to get OLC to rescind Yoo's August 2002 opinion;[96] he believed the legal reasoning to be poor at best.[97] After Abu Ghraib, he gained the momentum to do so, and he withdrew Yoo's memo after it was leaked.[98] It was the first time an administration had reversed its own OLC memo on a grave matter.[99] However, Goldsmith resigned in June 2004, citing the fact that his colleagues in the administration doubted his "reliability" after the withdrawal of Yoo's memos.[100] The next acting OLC head, Daniel Levin, expanded the definition of torture so it was consistent with what the prior Yoo opinion authorized[101] and thus consistent with Cheney's wishes.

In 2005, the next OLC acting head, Steven Bradbury, wrote three Torture Memos, effectively reauthorizing the previously permitted Yoo torture procedures.[102] After Jack Goldsmith resigned, the Senate would not confirm anyone as the full-time head of OLC.[103]

The Detainee Treatment Act of 2005 and the Non-Veto Veto

In May 2005, the *New York Times* brought to light the "brutal" circumstances surrounding the deaths of two detainees at JSOC's Bagram Prison and Abu Ghraib.[104] Shortly thereafter, the public demanded better respect of human rights from the president and the Pentagon, but as was just discussed, the Bush administration was none too keen to give up such a power once seized. Congress, however, rose to the occasion.

In 2005, Congress passed the Detainee Treatment Act of 2005 (DTA).[105] The Act created "Combatant Status Review Tribunals," whose decisions were appealable to a regular circuit court.[106] The Act prohibited the president and the armed forces from using the reverse-engineered SERE techniques, yet it approved the techniques in the Army Field Guide, which are torturous, and thus unlawful, yet infinitely more humane and less degrading.[107] What has become of us as a people that we now discuss *gradations of torture?*

The DTA granted combatants anywhere held by the Department of Defense or in U.S. custody generally the writ of habeas corpus, which the Constitution mandates only Congress may suspend in times of rebellion and had been unavailable to detainees by executive fiat.[108]

President Bush made the nominal concession of signing the Act into law, but in his signing statement declared the following:

> The executive branch shall construe . . . the Act, relating to detainees, in a manner consistent with the constitutional authority of the President to supervise the *unitary* executive branch and as Commander in Chief and consistent with the constitutional limitations on the judicial power, which will assist in achieving the shared objective of the Congress and the President, evidenced in Title X, of protecting the American people from further terrorist attacks. . . . Finally, given the decision of the Congress reflected in . . . [the part of Act pertaining to habeas corpus], shall apply to past, present, and future actions, including applications for writs of habeas corpus, described in that section, and noting that section 1005 does not confer any constitutional right upon an alien detained abroad as an enemy combatant, the executive branch shall construe section 1005 to preclude the Federal courts from exercising subject matter jurisdiction over any existing or future action, including applications for writs of habeas corpus, described in section 1005.[109]

President Bush, known for sounding tongue-tied, engaged in Orwellian doublespeak. Somehow, Bush believed that he had the power to suspend the writ of habeas corpus for persons in U.S. custody because the constitutional authority of the unitary president, per the Bush administration, is limitless over the individual in wartime. The signing statement should be read as what it is: A veto. The president conducted himself accordingly.

Hamdan v. United States: The Supreme Court Is Angered

Before the Detainee Treatment Act, in 2004, the Supreme Court recognized that the Constitution protected the right to habeas corpus to all detainees under U.S. control in the first detainee case, *Rasul v. Bush*.[110] Eight hours after hearing combined oral argument on April 28th 2004 for the second and third detainee cases to reach the Supreme Court, *Rumsfeld v. Padilla* and *Hamdan v. United States*, the Abu Ghraib scandal hit the news.[111] During oral argument earlier that day, responding to a pointed line of questions on the ordered torture of "'harmless, detained enemy combatant[s],'" Deputy Solicitor General Paul Clement tritely stated to the Court, "'Well, our executive doesn't [order torture].'"[112]

In 2006, the Supreme Court heard *Hamdan v. Rumsfeld*.[113] The *Hamdan* Court held that Common Article 3 of the Geneva Conventions applies in full to detainees in U.S. custody.[114] Common Article 3 prevents "outrages upon personal dignity, in particular, humiliating and degrading treatment," as well as violence against a person in custody that is "cruel treatment and torture."[115]

President Bush responded to what he saw as encroachments on his imperial, unitary prerogative. In a 2007 executive order and totally ignoring *Hamdan*, he announced that based on his and congressional action and pursuant to "the authority of *the President to interpret the meaning and application of the Geneva Conventions*," Common Article 3 applies to detainees, subject to his interpretation.[116]

Unsurprisingly, the president "hereby determine[d] that a program of detention and interrogation approved by the Director of the Central Intelligence Agency fully complies with the obligations of the United States under Common Article 3."[117] Moreover, in July 2007, Bradbury authored an OLC memo which would—in a footnote—state that in light of the Military Commissions Act of 2006, discussed above, the president may reassert "his pre-*Hamdan* conclusion that Common Article 3 does not apply to the armed conflict against al Qaeda," or "lawfully . . . reassert his pre-*Hamdan* interpretation of the treaty" by administrative interpretation.[118]

Five days before President Bush's second term in office was to end, Bradbury issued an OLC memo recanting the Bush view of the allocation of war powers between the president and Congress. That is the largest concession any branch of government could get from Bush on the power to torture.[119] His successor would make modest concessions, scaling back the rendition and torture program to more Clintonesque levels.*

Perhaps the legacy for which George W. Bush will best be remembered is his use of torture. For all his silly-sounding and amoral efforts to redefine and hide it, its potency shall always stick to Bush's name. Yet no practice in the history of humanity has been more consistently condemned. As we shall see, he even tried to make it a tool for prosecutors.

---

* The debate over torture presents a perfect opportunity to demonstrate the difference between neoconservative and classical liberal philosophy. In the Republican Party, there are neoconservatives and classical liberals. Both sides want less government intrusion into the economy because of a robust belief in property rights and markets, but classical liberals believe that these rights against interference extend from personhood, which axiomatically encapsulates the private and personal realm. Thus, neoconservatives can justify majoritarian stripping of personhood rights like the right to bodily integrity, which precludes torture, trouncing social natural rights like privacy, and oppressing the rights of gays to marry whom they love. Classical liberals consider such incursions unnatural and abhorrent.

13

The George W. Bush Administration

The Right to Trial

Those who wrote our constitutions knew from history and experience that it was necessary to protect against unfounded criminal charges brought to eliminate enemies and against judges too responsive to the voice of higher authority. The framers of the constitutions strove to create an independent judiciary but insisted upon further protection against arbitrary action. Providing an accused with the right to be tried by a jury of his peers gave him an inestimable safeguard against the corrupt or overzealous prosecutor and against the compliant, biased, or eccentric judge.[*]

—Duncan v. Louisiana

---

[*] Duncan v. Louisiana, 391 U.S. 145, 156 (1968) (White, J.).

The Revival of Military Commissions and the Right to Trial

FDR convened a military commission in 1942 and, within a month and a half, executed all but two of the defendants brought before it, German saboteurs, including one U.S. citizen who asserted the Treason Clause as a defense.[1] This treatment contravened constitutional law and the Hague Conventions and was seemingly overruled in *Duncan v. Kahanamoku*.[2] President Bush expanded unconscionably upon this precedent and created a system of military commissions that would be an incredible example of the power the Bush administration believed the president had over human rights, and of utter incompetence. Bush wanted an imperial judiciary accountable to him in secret, not a federal one with transparency.

The American Star Chamber Court: The Pink Palace Court

In order to perfect his unitary imperium, President Bush worked through military orders and the Department of Defense to carry out prosecutions, resulting in a battle with the Supreme Court and Congress over treatment and the civil rights of detainees in U.S. jurisdiction that would last well into his successor's presidency. "The Bush Administration . . . acted as though 9/11 had forever changed the constitutional order, creating a permanent state of emergency where legislative and judicial powers must yield to executive policy decisions."[3] And in that permanent state, the American Star Chamber court, the Pink Palace court, was born.*

---

* The Pink Palace is the name of the Gitmo building wherein the trials were held. Bravin coins the term *Pink Palace Court* in his book the *Terror Courts*, which is a reference to the Star Chamber Court, a similar Middle Ages English kangaroo court which handed down secret sentences in secret trials. See Jess Bravin, *The Terror Courts: Rough Justice at Guantanamo Bay* (New Haven, CT: Yale University Press, 2013), 181, 185, 203, 213, 219, 294, 333.

Military Order of November 13, 2001

In the days following 9/11, the Bush administration's then OLC head Robert Barr began floating the idea of military commissions in the style of FDR's Nazi saboteur trial.[4] Vice President Cheney's legal counsel, David S. Addington, also reached a similar conclusion independently.[5] John Yoo's aide, Deputy Assistant Attorney General Patrick F. Philbin, authored a November 6th 2001 memo (relying on *Quirin*) which would claim: "The President both has inherent authority as Commander in Chief to convene military commissions and has received authorization from Congress for their use to the full extent permitted by *past executive practice*."[6] Philbin shrewdly used as his precedent not the familiar phrase "as permitted by law," but the Cheney-inspired "as permitted by past executive practice." And how did Philbin get around the *Milligan* rule that had been reinforced after *Quirin*?

By ignoring contrary Supreme Court precedent and stating, "We believe that the broad pronouncements in *Milligan* do not accurately reflect the requirements of the Constitution and that the case has properly been severely limited by the later decision in *Quirin*."[7] So the executive branch overrode the Supreme Court, despite Attorney General John Ashcroft's strenuous objections, both constitutional and practical.[8] This time, the prosecutions would not have the added legitimacy of at least being carried out by the attorney general, as Frank Biddle had done in the 1940s when FDR ordered the prosecution of the submarine saboteurs by military tribunal and not a federal court or regularly constituted court-martial.[9]

At the same time, William (Jim) James Haynes II, general counsel for the Department of Defense and a former Cheney-Addington acolyte from the elder Bush's administration, began work on a military commission order.[10] When the order was circulated to the more independent (not political appointee) Judge Advocate Generals for the three military branches, they reacted with "'disbelief,'" one calling it "'insane'":

> [Haynes's] draft declared it "not practicable" for military commissions to follow "the principles of law and the rules of evidence" that

defined American justice. Other than directing that trials be "full and fair," the eighteen-hundred-word order made no reference to basic elements of due process—proof beyond a reasonable doubt, presumption of innocence, the right to remain silent. The only standard was that evidence hold "probative value to a reasonable person"—a unisex updating of the FDR order's language, which referenced the "reasonable man." Instead of separating the roles of judge and jury, the order merged them into a single finder of law and fact, a commission headed not by a judge but a "presiding officer" who could be overruled by the other members.

There was no requirement that any member of the commission be a lawyer. Instead lay officers from infantry, artillery, or other units would conduct a trial that could order a defendant executed.[11]

In crafting his opinion, Haynes ignored the mountains of precedent from U.S. military commissions from the 1840 Mexican war to the Civil War, where under general orders all commissions abided by "'the same general rules as courts-martial in order to prevent abuses which might otherwise occur;' to the in Europe after World War II that operated similar to "courts-martial and providing a review of each conviction."[12]

Further, Federal Rule of Evidence 403 requires that a judge weigh the probative value of evidence *against* its prejudicial value.[13] For example, evidence introduced into a robbery trial about how the defendant unrelatedly assaulted a person ten years before has little probative value, but would tend to be probative of a propensity to commit crimes of violence. At the same time, however, it is also highly prejudicial so a judge will likely exclude it. In this "court" room, no such balancing is necessary, and the minute probative value of that assault would make it admissible. This was done because the president expected "rapid convictions and executions," not due process, to be imposed.[14]

On November 13th, Vice President Cheney saw President Bush at a luncheon, and the latter orally approved the order, despite "little involvement" on Bush's part.[15] The order was not put through the typical vetting process that executive proclamations go through, but was taken directly to Bush's office, where he simply "flipped to the last page [and] signed his name" before dashing off to meet Russian President Vladimir Putin.[16]

Moreover, objectionable parts of the draft were not removed, but classified evidence was ensured not to be shown to unauthorized defendants or defense attorneys, and appellate review was nowhere in sight.[17] Accordingly, Bush created a kangaroo court under the ominously termed edict Military Order of November 13th.[18]

The Commissions Begin and Then Bungle

On March 21st 2002, Secretary of Defense Rumsfeld signed Military Commission Order No. 1 to effectuate Bush's order, which, after a hard fight within the Pentagon, included the *presumption of innocence* as a judicial guarantee.[19] On February 7th 2002, Bush cleaned up any international law issues by denying that the Geneva Conventions applied to the current conflict.[20] What ensued was a political struggle for the remainder of Bush's term over getting his own bureaucracy to try someone using these commissions (which would take years to do), and between Bush and the other branches over where the judicial power lay, despite the fact that the Constitution clearly gives it to the judiciary. The monarchist theories employed by the OLC in rendering its advice had long been "overwhelmingly rejected by the legal community."[21]

Haynes appointed Army Col. Fred L. Borch to be the first chief prosecutor for the commissions to be carried out at Gitmo.[22] He, in turn, appointed Lt. Col. Stuart Couch head of the Planning and Finances prosecutions team. The administration chose Gitmo because it had a unique legal arrangement with the government of Cuba that avoided having literal American sovereignty attached to it, only "complete jurisdiction and control."[23]

Though it was clearly a bogus distinction, John Yoo and Patrick Philbin believed it sufficient to avoid the "interference" of "[j]udicial review" or the Geneva Conventions because it was the "'legal equivalent of outer space.'"[24] Thus, in January 2002, Camp X-Ray became active in Gitmo.[25] Almost immediately there were mistreatment claims, and Rumsfeld casually demurred.[26] Moreover, Couch and CITF legal counsel representatives began raising concerns that evidence obtained during interrogation would be inadmissible.[27] Evidence obtained under torture is subject to exclusion in court under both international law and Supreme Court precedent.[28]

Other concerns plagued the commissions' work beyond admissibility and legal ethics: *The prisoners had committed no crimes!* The commissions had no criminal code to work from and needed to figure out with what to charge the criminals they were holding.[29] This is logically absurd: Imagine being arrested and then being told later that your charging officials will come up with criminal conduct to describe something you did and then figure out a way to punish you. The commissions' offices had trouble with obtaining interagency cooperation from intelligence agencies regarding turning over evidence to the prosecutors, but nonetheless they decided to try the Justice Department to get help in figuring out this conundrum.[30] What ensued was a rebuke.[31]

The commissions office bureaucrats developed a few theories to prosecute the al Qaeda detainees, so they brought on a (publicly) unnamed specialist who had completed a "one-year advanced degree in the subject."[32] He devised a theory on which the prosecutions "hinged" that all al Qaeda members were in a conspiracy to commit the 9/11 attacks, and they could be charged thusly.[33] The problem is that the conspiracy charge does not work for armed forces. First, international law does not assign conspiracy war crime status,[34] and while normally international law is not relevant to U.S. law, it has significantly more weight when it comes to international armed conflict than to other, more mundane matters. Second, if all al Qaeda conspired to commit the war crime of 9/11, down to the lowest Afghani fighter, then all the U.S. military would be responsible for the war crimes the Bush administration perpetrated against detainees throughout the course of both wars in the black site prisons.

Thus, U.S. military and international law have enshrined the command responsibility doctrine, whereby the commanding officials bear responsibility for their inferiors. The Bush administration's legal theory made inferiors responsible for other inferiors' conduct because they had the same commanding officer. The alternative theory of prosecution was criminalizing membership in al Qaeda, which Haynes, in a rare showing of constitutional deference, dismissed as Orwellian "thoughtcrime."[35] The executive's agents created a new crime contrary to law in order to hold enemies accountable.

In March 2003, amid bureaucratic issues from above, below, and other agencies, and ethical concerns from staff over using torture testimony and serious questions of constitutionality, Borch and the commissions prosecutions office had a total breakdown in functionality:[36] The imperial ministry couldn't even carry out its own unconstitutional orders. Moreover, in 2004, there were accusations that Borch was biased in his prosecutions and was not ensuring due process.[37] One prosecutor accused him of "'repeatedly'" saying, "'[T]he military panel [jury] will be handpicked and will not acquit these detainees.'"[38] In April 2004, Col. Robert L. Swann would replace Borch as head of commissions prosecutions.[39] He would clash with Couch over Couch's insistence on investigating detainee treatment and not trying abuse cases.[40]

However, outside this system, civilian attorneys had been working to attack collaterally the Gitmo detainees' status through habeas petitions.[41] The Supreme Court was beginning to pay attention, and the executive unitary theory and an imperial president would soon be tested in the forum that President Bush most feared.

The Supreme Court Against Congress and the President

The Warning Volley: *Padilla, Hamdi,* and *Rasul*

There is nothing that a judge hates more than when an attorney, knowingly or because he was duped by his client, makes a material misrepresentation to the court. Between April 20th and 28th 2004, the Supreme Court heard oral argument in three cases: *Rumsfeld v. Padilla,*

Hamdi v. Rumsfeld, and *Rasul v. Bush*.[42] After the close of arguments on the 28th, when the U.S. government's lawyers vehemently denied torturing detainees, the Abu Ghraib scandal broke on TV.[43] On June 28th, the Court handed down its opinions in all three cases, giving a clear warning shot to the executive branch that the judiciary would be stepping in. President Bush was dismissive of the cases and minimized their importance in public, proceeding with his Pink Palace court.[44]

José Padilla is a native-born U.S. citizen.[45] As he stepped off his flight from Pakistan to Chicago O'Hare, federal agents apprehended him under a material witness warrant, permitting them to detain him as a material witness in an ongoing proceeding.[46] The ongoing proceeding was the grand jury investigation in the Southern District of New York into the 9/11 attacks.[47] Padilla was transferred to Justice Department criminal custody in New York City.[48] He moved to vacate the warrant against him on May 22nd, but his petition would have to wait.[49]

On June 9th, President Bush issued an order designating Padilla—a citizen detained peacefully on U.S. soil and being processed in open, working courts who had never been accused of engaging in acts of violence—an enemy combatant and directing Rumsfeld to seize Padilla from the custody of U.S. marshals in Manhattan and detain him in military custody under the Department of Defense.[50] The president claimed his inherent war powers, and the AUMF permitted him to do so.[51] Padilla was moved to a South Carolina brig, where he would be held for three and a half years with no access to family or an attorney from June 2002 to March 2004.[52] While on U.S. soil in South Carolina, he was tortured by his military interrogators:

> Padilla alleged that he was subjected to prolonged isolation; deprivation of light; exposure to prolonged periods of light and darkness, including being "periodically subjected to absolute light or darkness for periods in excess of twenty-four hours"; extreme variations in temperature; sleep adjustment; threats of severe physical abuse; death threats; administration of psychotropic drugs; shackling and

manacling for hours at a time; use of "stress" positions; noxious fumes that caused pain to eyes and nose; loud noises; withholding of any mattress, pillow, sheet or blanket; forced grooming; suspensions of showers; removal of religious items; constant surveillance; incommunicado detention, including denial of all contact with family and legal counsel for a 21-month period; interference with religious observance; and denial of medical care for "serious and potentially life-threatening ailments, including chest pain and difficulty breathing, as well as for treatment of the chronic, extreme pain caused by being forced to endure stress positions."[53]

Padilla's lawyer, filing as a third party, sought a writ of habeas corpus from Judge Michael Mukasey, a future Bush attorney general and then the chief judge of the Southern District of New York, the place from which Padilla had been unlawfully kidnapped by the military. Judge Mukasey ruled that the Southern District of New York had jurisdiction to issue the writ, but that the president had the authority to detain Padilla.[54] The Second Circuit affirmed on the jurisdictional question but reversed on the question of presidential authority.[55] The Supreme Court granted *certiorari*.

However, Padilla was effectively denied relief. Chief Justice William Rehnquist, writing for the majority, held that the Southern District of New York did not have jurisdiction to hear the case. The Court held that the proper respondent was not the defense secretary, but the brig commander, and thus jurisdiction was proper within the District of South Carolina.[56]

Accordingly, the Court did not reach the question of whether the president had the "authority to detain Padilla militarily" because the case was decided on jurisdictional grounds.[57] This particular issue was thorny because the challenge to presidential authority was made under the Non-Detention Act of 1971.[58] This means that if the president had the authority to detain Padilla under the AUMF, then the AUMF was congressional assent to detention within the meaning of the Non-Detention

Act of 1971. Astute readers will remember that the resultant implication is that legally (not constitutionally) the president has authority to detain citizens *to the extent permitted by the McCarran Act.* In *Padilla,* the Supreme Court made sure to leave no precedent to the opposite effect, specifically avoiding that issue. There were two cases to announce. The next one was a landmark.

Rasul v. Bush was the next terrorism case reported that day. Shafiq Rasul was subjected to similar torturous treatment as Padilla.[59] The Court's rage at President Bush's unconstitutional usurpation of its judicial power and his treatment of detainees would be expressed.[60] The collective defendants were "2 Australian citizens and 12 Kuwaiti citizens who were captured abroad during hostilities between the United States and the Taliban," now housed in Gitmo.[61] The detainees filed for writs of habeas corpus in the district court of the District of Columbia, which held that "'aliens detained outside the sovereign territory of the United States [may not] invok[e] a petition for a writ of habeas corpus,'" which the D.C. Court of Appeals affirmed.[62] The Court reversed:[63]

> But in any event, *nothing* in . . . *any of our other cases* categorically excludes aliens detained in military custody outside the United States from the "privilege of litigation" in U.S. courts. The courts of the United States have traditionally been open to nonresident aliens. *Cf. Disconto Gesellschaft v. Umbreit,* 208 U.S. 570, 578 (1908) ("Alien citizens, by the policy and practice of the courts of this country, are ordinarily permitted to resort to the courts for the redress of wrongs and the protection of their rights"). And indeed, 28 U.S.C. §1350 explicitly confers the privilege of suing for an actionable "tort . . . committed in violation of the law of nations or a treaty of the United States" on aliens alone.[64]

Thus, the Court handily dismissed the administration's arguments that based on Supreme Court precedent, militarily detained aliens may be categorically denied access to court. And what of the president's extension of military jurisdiction under the war power? Would that pre-clude review? No, "[t]he fact that petitioners in these cases are being held in military custody is immaterial to the question of the District Court's jurisdiction over their . . . claims."[65] Chief Justice Rehnquist and Justices Scalia and Thomas dissented, calling the majority opinion "an irrespon-sible overturning of settled law in a matter of extreme importance to our forces currently in the field" that Congress ought to resolve.[66] The majority, however, had supplied the Constitution a victory: The writs may issue, and detainees may access civilian courts.

The Court's last detainee case that day was *Hamdi*. However, the court's makeup would again realign with Justices Stevens and Scalia join-ing in dissent, while Justice O'Conner took the plurality.[67] What was the complicating factor? The appellant was a U.S. citizen—the exact question the Court avoided in *Padilla*. Yaser Esam Hamdi was born in Louisiana, moved to Saudi Arabia as a child, then ended up in Afghanistan for about two months in 2001.[68] Northern Alliance fighters captured Hamdi in Afghanistan and turned him over to U.S. officials as an enemy combat-ant.[69] The government interrogated him in Afghanistan, transferred him to Gitmo on January 2002, then upon discovering he was a citizen, moved him in April 2002 to the South Carolina brig that held Padilla.[70] His father sought to effect the issuance of a writ of habeas corpus in the Eastern District of Virginia.[71] The district court granted standing to the father and ordered that Hamdi be given access to counsel.[72] The Fourth Circuit reversed.[73]

Writing for the plurality, Justice O'Connor avoided the question of whether the Constitution gave the president plenary power to detain indi-viduals, narrowly answering "whether the Executive has the authority to detain citizens who qualify as 'enemy combatants.'"[74] O'Connor performed a constitutional balancing of Hamdi's right to be free from detention without congressional authorization against the government's war author-ity.[75] Her reasoning is uncomfortable: First, the Suspension Clause of the Constitution requires that Congress actually suspend the writ of habeas corpus to avoid having detention challenged on those grounds.

The AUMF in no way contains the words *habeas, corpus, writ, suspension*, or *detain*. Moreover, security, which is what the war power guarantees, is a consequent good, not an *a priori* right, like the right against unlawful detention: They cannot be balanced. Nevertheless, taking a unique view of the Suspension Clause, O'Connor concluded that the AUMF was an act of Congress that permitted detention and thus, while not expressly saying it, somehow did not offend the Suspension Clause of the Constitution.[76] The plurality opinion held that due process requires that "a citizen-detainee seeking to challenge his classification as an enemy combatant must receive notice of the factual basis for his classification, and a fair opportunity to rebut the Government's factual assertions before a neutral decision-maker," not a trial or a habeas hearing, and possibly a McCarran Act tribunal.[77]

Justice O'Connor also left open the door for the McCarran Act to be reintroduced into American national security law almost forty years after the Nixon era put it to rest. The Fourth Circuit had held that the president had the authority to detain Hamdi pursuant to an act of Congress,[78] which means that the Non-Detention Act of 1971 does not prevent McCarran Act detentions. Justice O'Conner attempted to hedge her language as much as possible in implicitly reviving the McCarran Act: "[T]he AUMF is explicit congressional authorization for the detention of individuals in the narrow category we describe (assuming, without deciding, that such authorization is required), and that the AUMF satisfied [the Non-Detention Act's] requirement that a detention be 'pursuant to an Act of Congress' (assuming, without deciding, that [the Non-Detention Act] applies to military detentions)."[79]

O'Connor's "narrow category" is also quite unclear. In the following sentences she referenced the broadest language of the AUMF—which the reader has seen can be stretched to almost no limit—and narrowly to Afghani Taliban fighters.[80] The language of the case leaned toward the latter, but we can only hope it would not be read as the former. She also refused to narrow the category by distinguishing between citizens and non-citizens, on U.S. soil or abroad.[81]

Justices Scalia and Stevens's dissent takes the proper view of the case:

Where the Government accuses a citizen of waging war against it, our constitutional tradition has been to prosecute him in federal court for treason or some other crime. Where the exigencies of war prevent that, the Constitution's Suspension Clause, Art. I, §9, cl. 2, allows Congress to relax the usual protections temporarily. Absent suspension, however, the Executive's assertion of military exigency has not been thought sufficient to permit detention without charge. No one contends that the congressional Authorization for Use of Military Force, on which the Government relies to justify its actions here, is an implementation of the Suspension Clause. Accordingly, I would reverse the judgment below.[82]

The Suspension Clause is a binary power, as Justice Scalia properly recognized, not a constitutional indication of the seriousness of a balancing interest. Congress did not suspend the writ in the AUMF—indeed, if one looks to the only example of Congress suspending the writ (in 1863), the lawmakers took the care to be so express as to title the Act "An Act relating to Habeas Corpus, and regulating Judicial Proceedings in Certain Cases."[83] Clearly, congressional precedent and the plain text of the AUMF lend more credibility to Justices Scalia and Stevens's dissent rather than Justice O'Connor's plurality.

Overall, June 28th 2004 was a good day for liberty compared to the executive-military tyranny that preceded it. But the Court gave the president some wiggle room to save face: Bush himself could establish military tribunals, but they must afford traditional due process rights, thus legitimizing them as a respecter of civil rights and national security.

However, the president and the Defense Department generally were dismissive of the Court's rulings, particularly *Rasul*, and proceeded with their prosecutions.[84]

In order to appear to satisfy the Supreme Court's ruling, Deputy Defense Secretary Paul Wolfowitz signed an order on July 7th 2004, creating Combatant Status Review Tribunals (CSRT), which he contended afforded the detainees confrontation rights and limited rights to see the evidence being put against themselves.[85] However, "[t]he

Tribunal is not bound by the rule of evidence such as would apply in a court of law. Instead, the Tribunal shall be free to consider any information it deems *relevant and helpful* to a resolution of the issue before it."[86] Being "relevant and helpful" is a low bar compared to balancing prejudice and probative value for each piece of evidence. In criminal courts in civilized nations, whether civilian or military, evidence is to be admitted only if its probative value outweighs its prejudicial value. Under this new scheme, no respect is paid to limiting the prejudicial effect of evidence or really, the due process a civilized people would expect.

The *Hamdan* Case Begins

On August 4th 2004, the Pink Palace court would open arraignments for the first four cases. This is, of course, almost three years after the accused were first detained, during all of which time the federal courts were open and operating—so much for the right to a speedy trial.[87] The first of these new prosecutions would be against Salim Hamdan.[88] After a challenge involving the impartiality of the judges that caused delays, which was of course resolved in the judges' favor, the first commission hearing began on November 7th.[89] However, while the attorneys were quibbling over issues regarding the composition of the judicial panel, a bailiff slipped the presiding officer, Col. Peter Brownback, a note. Brownback called an indefinite recess: Hamdan's collateral habeas attack in D.C. district court had won, and the court issued an order to the government to justify his confinement.[90] The commissions were halted.[91] However, on July 15th 2005, the D.C. Circuit Court of Appeals reversed the district court, and the commissions resumed.[92] On November 7th 2005, the Supreme Court granted *certiorari* to Hamdan, posturing for a direct square-off with the president over the constitutionality of his commissions.[93]

Congress Steps In Between the Court and the President

On December 30th 2005, however, Congress stepped in—during the pendency of Supreme Court proceedings—and enacted legislation that aimed to prevent the Supreme Court from hearing Hamdan's appeal.[94] The Detainee Treatment Act, discussed above, also contained a second provision in it that incentivized Bush to sign: A jurisdictional limitation. Pursuant to Article III of the Constitution, except where the Supreme Court is given original jurisdiction, Congress decides where the jurisdiction of federal courts begins and ends.[95] The Act was intended to prevent "the Bush Administration from abusing prisoners [but it] became, in final form, a license for further excess."[96]

Besides dealing with treatment as such, the Act did two things with respect to jurisdiction. First, except as provided for within the Act, "no court, justice, or judge, shall have jurisdiction to hear or consider" writs of habeas corpus or "any other action against the United States or its agents relating to any aspect of . . . detention" for persons properly designated enemy combatants and in military custody.[97] Second, the Act gave "exclusive jurisdiction" to hear appeals from commissions or CSRTs to the D.C. Court of Appeals—the same court that had overturned Hamdan's habeas petition in the first place.[98]

The Supreme Court has always been touchy about its jurisdictional relationship to Congress. As Justice Frankfurter once wrote, "Congress need not establish inferior courts; Congress need not grant the full scope of jurisdiction which it is empowered to vest in them; Congress need not give this Court any appellate power; it may withdraw appellate jurisdiction once conferred and it may do so even while a case is *sub judice*."[99] Thus, even if proceedings are ongoing in a case, Congress can strip jurisdiction from the Court, as it did in one case, *Ex parte McCardle*, discussed in chapter 4, during the Reconstruction era.

The Supreme Court was in a precarious situation as far as hearing Hamdan's case. In the previous set of detainee cases, it had given a gift to the president to correct his actions, but that gift was thrown back with jurisdiction stripping: If the Bush administration could not have the power to process terrorists as it wished, no branch of government would. Meanwhile, hundreds of detainees were being held without trial and were being tortured. In briefing on the case to the Supreme Court, the government's lawyer, Paul Clement, "told the justices that Congress had revoked their authority to hear Hamdan's case and must therefore dismiss it."[100] The die was cast.

Stevens Strikes Back: *Hamdan v. Rumsfeld*

Oral arguments took place on March 28th 2006.[101] Salim Hamdan was not a combatant or a general, but was bin Laden's driver.[102] As Charlie Swift, Hamdan's attorney, often observed, "[T]he Allies didn't prosecute Hitler's driver."[103] Because Chief Justice Roberts, when he was Judge Roberts, had been on the Circuit Court panel that denied Hamdan's petition, he disqualified himself. With one of the three dissenters in *Rasul* out of play, things were looking up for Hamdan. However, there was still the question of whether the Court even retained the power to hear the case in light of the Act. Further, between oral arguments and the decision, the Pentagon would take a PR shellacking. On June 10th 2006, three Gitmo detainees committed suicide, and Commandant Rear Adm. Harry Harris Jr., the commanding officer at Gitmo, dismissed it as a jihadist PR move—"an act of asymmetrical warfare waged against us."[104] Subsequently, there were "growing international calls for the camp to be closed down."[105]

Justice Stevens announced the majority opinion on June 29th 2006.[106] The Court found that the Detainee Treatment Act of 2005 did not strip its jurisdiction in *this* case, that the AUMF and Detainee Treatment Act do not authorize military commissions, and that the commissions' procedures violated the domestic Uniform Code of Military Justice as well as the Geneva Conventions, Common Article 3 of which applied to the current conflict with al Qaeda.[107]

In dealing with the Detainee Treatment Act, the Court handily dismissed the jurisdictional issue. While the Act does strip jurisdiction, it does not do so for pending, or *sub judice* cases filed prior to the date's enactment: "[I]f a statutory provision 'would operate retroactively' as applied to cases pending at the time the provision was enacted, then 'our traditional presumption teaches that it does not govern absent clear congressional intent favoring such a result.'"[108] Thus, Congress's attempt to limit the Court's power to adjudicate fell flat on its face.

With respect to the merits, the Court was less forgiving. Justice Stevens began by noting that the Military Commission Order No. 1 signed by Rumsfeld "permit[s] the admission of *any* evidence," sworn, unsworn, hearsay, and coercion induced were all admissible and that the defendants had limited rights to see the evidence against them.[109] Further, he noted that based on the Uniform Code of Military Justice, "the rules applied to military commissions must be the same as those applied to courts-martial unless such uniformity proves impracticable."[110] He then gave deference to the president's determination that civilian court rules were not practicable here but stated that there was no similar determination for courts-martial rules, and thus, Hamdan's treatment was unconstitutional under domestic law.[111]

Additionally, the majority applied the Geneva Conventions' Common Article 3 to all detainees:

> Common Article 3, then, is applicable here and, as indicated above, requires that Hamdan be tried by a "regularly constituted court affording all the judicial guarantees which are recognized as indispensable by civilized peoples." While the term "regularly constituted court" is not specifically defined in either Common Article 3 or its accompanying commentary, other sources disclose its core meaning. The commentary accompanying a provision of the Fourth Geneva Convention, for example, defines "'regularly constituted'" tribunals to include "ordinary military courts" and "definitely exclud[e] all special tribunals."[112]

In other words, these special commissions that operate by none of the civilized guarantees of the world violate what are the most recognizable set of international laws incorporated into the Uniform Code of Military Justice and recognized by almost every country. Bush's powers to defy the Constitution and laws of war seemed to be at an end. As Jess Bravin eloquently put it: "[Bush] had created a permanent offshore system of summary justice by extrapolating his constitutional function as 'commander in chief of the Army and Navy' into the power to do whatever he wished in the name of national security. The Constitution contemplated no such thing, the Court said."[113]

However, Bravin also noted that the Court's opinion merely meant that Bush needed to "seek congressional authorization before deviating from existing military statutes."[114] In fact, "because the . . . military order violated acts of Congress [the Uniform Code of Military Justice], Stevens found no need to go further."[115] And indeed, he shouldn't have— the Supreme Court does not decide questions of constitutional law if a case can be decided on less solemn grounds. Thus, expecting the executive to take the second warning volley as an opportunity to fix its own house, Stevens did not reach "whether the commissions Bush envisioned would be constitutional even with congressional authorization."[116] "Vice President Cheney now demanded that legislation authorizing commissions be passed immediately."[117]

The Return of the Congress: The Military Commissions Act of 2006

Congress and the Supreme Court were due to go another round in Bush's presidency over the issue of commissions, which would continue well into his successor's second term. On October 17th 2006, a few months after *Hamdan* was handed down, President Bush signed the Military Commissions Act of 2006, attempting to overrule *Hamdan*.[118]

In the wake of *Hamdan*, the Bush team went into full spin control, trying to justify its unrightful and unlawful kangaroo court: "Reluctantly, Bush played his trump card: the CIA prisoners. Pass the commissions bill or, he implied, [Khalid Sheikh Mohammed] might walk free. Before a White House audience seeded with 9/11 families, Bush suggested that it was the Supreme Court—rather than his own administration—that had blocked bringing them to trial."[119]

Khalid Sheikh Mohammed was the mastermind of 9/11, and he had been sitting in Gitmo waiting for a commission trial for almost *five years*. At any point in time the Bush administration could have turned him over to civilian courts in the Southern District of New York, where the crime was actually committed, where the effects of 9/11 were primarily felt, and where the U.S. attorneys had already built an entire civilian case, and achieved justice for those families.[120]

But that would interfere with Bush's regime of centralizing power through fear and war hysteria. Especially with midterm congressional elections coming up,[121] that was a possibility of a check on his wartime powers Bush could not abide. Thus, Bush threatened: His justice or no justice. The Republican-controlled Congress would have no problem bolstering the power of their party's wartime president, even at the expense of liberty.

The Act made some improvements on the military commissions, such as excluding torture statements, but overall was an endorsement of Bush policies. First, as far as torture statements, if the "degree of coercion" was disputed, the evidence could be admitted based on its probative value.[122] Moreover, hearsay evidence was admissible unless "unreliable or lacking in probative value."[123] That means the panel, which was also performing the role of fact finder traditionally assigned to juries, would need to assess the reliability of witnesses and the probative value of evidence before contemplating a verdict. Moreover, it stripped habeas jurisdiction from all courts for all claims retroactively and in the future, except for the D.C. Court of Appeals per the 2005 Act, via altering the habeas corpus jurisdiction statute.[124] Notably, Senator Barack Obama (D-IL) voted against the Act.[125]

With congressional approval and all nuisance habeas petitions being funneled into one favorable court, commissions resumed in February 2007 under the leadership of Col. Morris Davis, who replaced Swann as chief prosecutor in 2006 when Swann retired.[126] The first slated case was the Australian David Hicks, who entered a PATRIOT Act "material support for terrorism" plea and served a suspended sentence in Australia.[127] However, the Hicks plea took a lot of wind out of Davis's sails due to internal office politics, and his policy that waterboarding testimony was not admissible led to conflicts with Haynes and Pentagon higher-ups.[128] He did not last long as prosecutor. The *fourth* chief prosecutor, Col. Larry Morris, took over in October 2007.[129]

Boumediene v. Bush

Lakhdar Boumediene was another Gitmo detainee whose family had filed third-party petitions for writs of habeas corpus. The D.C. Circuit Court of Appeals denied his habeas petitions.[130] On April 2nd 2007, the Supreme Court denied *certiorari*, citing a desire to avoid creating new constitutional law.[131] However, on June 29th 2007, the Court reversed itself and granted *certiorari*.[132] The Court was again squared off with President Bush and Congress in the 2008 case of *Boumediene v. Bush*. This time, however, the Court was fed up and fired up and would not stop short.

The Court, with Justice Kennedy writing for the majority, began by distinguishing its analysis in the previous four cases: "Petitioners present a question not resolved by our earlier cases relating to the detention of aliens at Guantanamo: whether they have the *constitutional* privilege of habeas corpus, a privilege not to be withdrawn except in conformance with the Suspension Clause."[133] The previous cases, they claimed, dealt with the *statutory* jurisdiction of habeas corpus, which Congress may amend, but not the *constitutional right* to the writ.

Kennedy proceeded to address the relationship between *Hamdan* and the Military Commissions Act: "[W]e cannot ignore that the MCA was a direct response to *Hamdan*'s holding that the DTA's jurisdiction-stripping provision had no application to pending cases. The Court of Appeals was correct to take note of the legislative history when construing the statute, and we agree with its conclusion that the MCA deprives the federal courts of jurisdiction to entertain the habeas corpus actions now before us."[134]

It seemed like a loss for liberty: The Court had no jurisdiction to hear the claim, a condition precedent to reaching the merits of any case without dismissing it. However, while habeas jurisdiction is statutory, it is a constitutional right that cannot be abridged simply by saying no court may hear it. Thus, Congress must take the extraordinary step of suspending habeas corpus under the terms set in the Suspension Clause, lest the constitutional language be rendered meaningless.

The jurisdictional issue was not that simple, however. Although the Court arguably lacked *subject-matter* jurisdiction, or jurisdiction over the merits of the habeas claim because of the Commissions Act, it also had an issue of *personal* jurisdiction: As John Yoo so kindly pointed out, Cuba is not sovereign U.S. territory, and the U.S. Supreme Court's jurisdiction over persons ends at the limits of U.S. sovereignty. The Supreme Court had to establish both personal and subject-matter jurisdiction.

Kennedy dismissed Yoo's absurd claims by distinguishing between de jure (by law) and de facto (by the facts) sovereignty. By law, yes, Cuba was sovereign, but "[t]here is no indication, furthermore, that adjudicating a habeas corpus petition would cause friction with the host government. No Cuban court has jurisdiction over American military personnel at Guantanamo or the enemy combatants detained there. While obligated to abide by the terms of the lease, the United States is, for all practical purposes, answerable to no other sovereign for its acts on the base."[135]

The Court then held that because the Court and the Constitution's jurisdiction extended to the de facto U.S.-sovereign territory of Cuba, the Suspension Clause of "the Constitution has full effect at Guantanamo Bay. If the privilege of habeas corpus is to be denied to the detainees now before us, Congress must act in accordance with the requirements of the Suspension Clause."[136] The Court then read the Military Commissions Act as a jurisdiction-stripping statute, not a suspension;[137] therefore, "MCA §7 thus effects an unconstitutional suspension of the writ."[138]

The Court's holding restored accountability and preserved the legitimacy of U.S. courts. Those "officials whose primary motive was redistributing powers from the legislative and judicial branches to the executive," had lost their day in court.[139] Unfortunately, however, this battle would extend well into the next presidency. The young senator who voted against the 2006 Act would wind up signing into law its successor act.

14

The Obama Administration

A Midterm Review of the Middle East, Torture, and Trials

Meet the new boss, same as the old boss.[*]

The Bush administration hobbled out of office after narrowly avoiding prosecution for war crimes and did so with the opprobrium of the American people: At the end of the Bush presidency, a third of the country approved of Bush's job and two-thirds disapproved of the job he did.[1] That was before we knew the less-than-full extent of what happened during his administration that we do at this writing in 2014.

The American people, however, would not be fooled again![2] They voted out the old Republican autocracy and would then bring about

---

[*] The Who, "Won't Get Fooled Again," recorded March 16, 1971, http://thewho.com/album /whos-next/.

295

change. There was hope for the future in an intelligent new Democratic presidential candidate: Barack H. Obama, the legal scholar and young senator from Illinois. He was being inaugurated while the Cheney-Bush administration was on its way back to Texas, and Yoo was back at UCLA Berkeley Law School. Obama promised to reject Bush-era war hawkishness by ending the Middle Eastern wars quickly, closing Guantanamo, and running a more transparent government. His high-handed talk and personal credibility earned him a Nobel Peace Prize within days after he took office.

Bush was the great "tragedy,"[3] but Obama has become the great hypocrite. He took on the mantle of his predecessor's wars and expanded on his powers just as Bush had expanded on Clinton's.[4] Despite his promises to rebuild our international relations after the Bush years, our allies find him an "unreliable partner."[5] President Obama, the ebullient and intelligent new face on the oldest of despotic institutions—commander in chief in a time of war—took the power even further: The unilateral ability to claim a citizen's life without judicial process.

Obama's Wars

In 2010, Bob Woodward of the *Washington Post*, one of the reporters who broke the Watergate scandal in the 1970s, published a book on Obama's alteration of Afghanistan and Iraq war policy in the Pakistani Theatre entitled *Obama's Wars.*[6] The book title was, like Obama's Nobel Peace Prize, premature. Obama continued the Bush odyssey into perpetual war, giving Bush's neoconservative wars the neoliberal, bipartisan imprimatur.[7] Specifically, he advanced the presence of the United States in Somalia, Yemen, Pakistan, and Libya, bringing the United States into a total, unending war in the Middle and Near East—and he did it in secret.[8]

Moreover, he attacked the natural right of people to elect their own government in the same fashion as the predecessor he denounced and claimed further war powers. The Bush-Obama Wars maintained the health of the state in terms of fear and government power, however,

Obama would also claim he could wage a geographically unlimited war on terror through the AUMF.

The Somali Theatre

A perfect example of the total lack of change in foreign policy between the Bush and Obama administrations is the Somali Theatre of the Middle and Near East Wars.

The Bush Administration

Following the Battle of Mogadishu in 1993 where U.S. forces under Clinton took a demoralizing loss in the Black Hawk Down incident, and the subsequent U.N. withdrawal in 1994, Somalia returned to its "perpetual state of civil war."[9]

During the Bush years in late 2002 and 2003, U.S. intelligence officials made contact with Mohamed Afrah Qanyare, a Somali warlord, to "'[discuss] intelligence business.'"[10] Al Qaeda had hit Kenya in November, and they believed that the same cell responsible for those attacks and the 1998 embassy bombings was operating in Somalia.[11] Although "[r]adical Islam was new to Somalia and was not widespread before the launch of the Global War on Terror," the Bush administration saw "the governmentless nation of Somalia [as] prime territory for al Qaeda [and its leaders fleeing Afghanistan] to set down new roots." "[E]minent analysts of the country's affairs" considered the threat of an al Qaeda takeover minimal or nonexistent.[12]

Thus, Operation Black Hawk was born: A U.S. "old-fashioned proxy" war being carried out by brutal Somali warlords whose power the United States expanded.[13] The U.S. plan was simple:

> Instead of strengthening the Somali government, [Somalia's then foreign minister] said, "they started cooperating with the warlords, thinking that the best way to combat terrorism was to help the warlords become stronger, and chase away the fundamentalists from Somalia. That backfired. . . ."

> Although US forces did not immediately move into Somalia . . .
> the expanded US base at Camp Lemonnier in Djibouti was rapidly
> becoming a hub in the Horn of Africa for JSOC and the CIA.[14]

This plan "caused a radical backlash in Somalia."[15] JSOC was set to back up the CIA and its warlords.[16]

Warlords like Qanyare went crazy with the free rein of the Bush era's hunting program, "engag[ing] in an all-out targeted kill and capture campaign against anyone—Somali or foreign—they suspected of being a supporter of any Islamic movement."[17] Somali captives were rendered via the U.S. navy to Ethiopian prisons and tortured using "electric shocks," then returned to "the Somaliland gulag."[18] "[I]n many cases, [the warlords] were chopping [suspected Islamists'] head[s] off and taking the head[s] to the Americans."[19] The error rate for warlords was rumored to be as high as seventeen civilians to three "targets."[20] It was a "[n]o mercy" program, in the words of Qanyare.[21] And it was facilitated by the U.S. government.

The United States' Somali program, however, "open[ed] the doors . . . for al Qaeda to step in," creating a problem where there was once none in a foreign country.[22] "By 2004, the [Central Intelligence] Agency's outsourced Somalia campaign was laying the groundwork for a spectacular series of events that would lead to an almost unthinkable rise in the influence of al Qaeda in the Horn of Africa."[23]

The warlord alliance was detested because "they were killing Somalis in the service of a foreign power."[24] The United States was growing more and more obsessed with perpetual war and "want[ed] to start an open war in Mogadishu." "It was this horrific era that gave birth to the Islamic Courts Union (ICU)."[25]

The ICU was a non–al Qaeda response to the years of brutal warlordism.[26] In 2004, several local Sharia courts formed under Sheikh Sharif Sheikh Ahmed to fight back against the oppressive warlord agents of the United States and Ethiopia, Somalia's longtime enemy and U.S. ally.[27]

Philosophically speaking, the Somali people were the closest thing to a State of Nature in 2004. They began to organize spontaneously into a system of laws and adjudication across tribal lines—they were creating a social compact. The United States and Ethiopia flooded in weapons and backed the warlords (sometimes with JSOC personnel) in order to prevent this order from establishing. The U.S.-Ethiopian forces were thwarting the voluntary social compact of another country, a violation of the right to enforce the Natural Law, and the American people and Western press did not know the gravity of this.

In February 2006, the CIA-warlord alliance responded by creating the Alliance for the Restoration of Peace and Counterterrorism with a six-month goal to wipe out the ICU and the terrorists.[28] An open declaration of war between the warlords and the ICU followed.[29] During the war with the CIA warlords, the ICU made uneasy allies with the terrorist organization Harakat al Shabab al Mujahideen (al Shabab)—but did not permit them to join the courts.[30]

In "just four months . . . [the ICU] d[rove] out the CIA's warlords."[31] The ICU took control of the Somali capital, Mogadishu, on June 5th 2006.[32] Much like our Founding Fathers had their Tory neighbors and England out of their land to enforce their social compact and natural rights, the ICU prevailed over the mercenary-warlord forces of the CIA in a surprising victory. Like King George III, George Bush II was stunned by the sting of loss, "[W]e will strategize more when I get back to Washington [from Texas] as to how to best respond to the latest incident there in Somalia."[33]

The ICU took down roadblocks and other governmental military institutions that were inhibiting commerce and brought a "modicum of stability" to Somalia.[34] Food prices dropped in the starved country, crime rates dropped, and people "felt safer than they had at any point in sixteen years."[35] The Bush administration elected "not [to] allow" this multi-group, consent-based government to continue.[36] It contemplated killing Sheikh Sharif and made a deal with the Devil.[37] The United States got Somalia's "historical enemy" Ethiopia to invade, bringing a cavalcade of "horror and chaos" to Somalia.[38]

In 2006, the U.S. government was "nobly" lying through its teeth in characteristic fashion as the United States saber-rattled about al Qaeda being in bed with the ICU.[39] Ethiopia's warlord era was over, but its occupation had begun in the new year of 2007. Al Shabab, one of the only Somali groups sympathetic to al Qaeda, began an insurgency against the U.S.-Ethiopian foreign overlords, ruling from thousands of miles away.[40]

The 2007 campaign/occupation involved a "concentrated campaign of targeted assassinations and snatch operations by JSOC [and Ethiopians] in Somalia," which had the benefit of "producing few significant counterterrorism results."[41] The United States and the proxy Ethiopians were wiping out a bunch of civilians through machine-gun strafing and running a terror campaign.[42] They tapped Sheikh Sharif to become a new leader, despite planning to kill him and usurping his government a few months earlier. The occupation was ugly:

> By early February 2007, the Ethiopian invasion had become an occupation, which was giving rise to widening unrest. . . . The occupation was marked by indiscriminate brutality against Somali citizens. Ethiopian and U.S.-backed Somali government soldiers secured Mogadishu's neighborhoods by force, raiding houses in search of ICU loyalists, looting civilian property, and beating or shooting anyone suspected of collaboration with antigovernment forces. They positioned snipers on the roofs of buildings and would reportedly respond to any attack with disproportionate fire, shelling densely populated areas and several hospitals. . . . Extrajudicial killings were widely reported, particularly during the final months of 2007. Accounts of Ethiopian soldiers "slaughtering" men, women and children "like goats"—slitting their throats—were widespread, Amnesty International noted. Both Somali Transitional Government forces, led by exiles and backed by the United States, and Ethiopian forces were accused of horrific sexual violence. Although forces linked to al Shabab were also accused of war crimes, a large portion of those reported . . . were committed by Somali government and Ethiopian forces.[43]

Whether American or not, people have natural rights that differ from and overlap with their constitutional and statutory rights—the Natural Law is discoverable through reason, and the rights it conveys are reposed in the bosom of all humanity. One of those rights is self-determination. Clearly, respect for natural liberty from Americans *who had no business there* would have worked out better for Somalia and the ICU. The United States and its proxies had usurped the Somalis' natural right to form a governmental compact, killing more than six thousand civilians and imposing despotic law without the consent of the governed[44]—a typical outcome of U.S. proxy war taking the background in civil conflicts.

"[A]l Shabab emerged as the vanguard against foreign occupation."[45] As Jeremy Scahill pointedly noted in his book *Dirty Wars*, "Every step taken by the United States benefited al Shabab."[46] The insurgency bombed the prime minister's house, killed hundreds of U.S. proxy troops, and brought the expert fighters—the former Afghani mujahideen, al Qaeda—into the mix.[47] In 2008, the Ethiopians left, and the transitional government under the rebranded Sheikh Sharif was labeled as turncoats and scalawags.[48]

Al Shabab, despite a hard-line Sharia philosophy, won cultural support to defeat the Somali government, soon "control[ling] more land than any other al Qaeda-affiliated group in history."[49] They established Sharia courts to fill the absent judicial system and brought "food, money," and water.[50] They negotiated with clan leaders for bloodless takeovers and dismantled roadblocks, which, as discussed earlier, were economic dampers—"checkpoints here historically used by warlords as tools of extortion rather than security."[51] All in all, America was losing the culture war to al Qaeda because of Bush's *stupidity* and his agents' *brutality*.

The Obama Administration

What would Bush's successor do with the benefit of hindsight? Despite the clear learning experience of the Bush administration, Obama made considerable headway, as a Russian foreign minister would point out, handling "the Islamic world like 'a monkey with a grenade.'"[52]

Upon taking office, Obama immediately shifted funding to another foreign mission in Somalia, the African Union Mission (AMISOM), in order to counter the growing and widely successful al Shabab insurgency.[53] He wanted JSOC to get "more aggressive" in Somalia and shipped weapons to the Sharif government.[54] The Speaker of the Somali Parliament at one point even called for, among others, Ethiopian troops to come back to support the Sharif government.[55] Propping up a government without the consent of the governed was proving to be Obama's game as well.

In 2010, al Shabab joined with local militias and al Qaeda international by conflating "its embrace of the terror group with resistance against foreign aggression."[56] Warlords switched sides based on internal politics, showing the utter lack of cogency to the plan of foreign intervention.* Suicide bombings continued.[57]

Continuing through 2011, the render-then-interrogate program was a large part of Obama's war in Somalia.[58] However, the assassinate-and-intervene plan was having success in Somalia. By August, al Shabab was in a "weakened state" losing the war and had almost no money due to military losses and a drought; but it had Mogadishu.[59] It appeared "on the ropes."[60] With the economic devastation, winning the culture war would have been possible through tactics similar to how al Shabab rose in the first place—some people need water, not bombs.

The United States, however, opted for the route of perpetual war and "total savagery throughout the country."[61] Al Shabab engaged in a strategic retreat and then came out again, attacking the U.S.-backed AMISOM mission with guerilla terrorist tactics. It also began to use al Qaeda to strengthen its hold over the hearts and minds of the Somali people. "[Al Qaeda high-up Abu Abdullah al-]Muhajir and his allies distributed food, Islamic books and clothes at the [Somali refugee]

---

* In *Dirty Wars*, Scahill used the example of "career jihadist commandeer" Ahmed Madobe, whom "JSOC nearly killed . . . in 2007." Scahill, *Dirty Wars*, 394; ibid., 202–22. He became an American-Somali-backed warlord after being released from Ethiopian custody in 2009. Ibid., 394–95.

camp [they were visiting], which housed more than 4,000 people."[62] The al Qaeda delegation also brought an ambulance. . . . [Muhajir] handed out bags full of Somali shillings, equaling about $17,000."[63]

The sobering realization is that despite what party is elected, the ways of creating perpetual war under noble lies—foreign influence in civil wars, assassinations, clandestine paramilitary, and covert military operations—remain the same. This is how Obama carried out Bush's foreign policy: He expanded on it with minor modifications. Thus, the theme throughout this section is that Obama did little else but endorse Bush-era policies and enlarge the executive power at the expense of the civil liberties of hundreds of millions of Americans.

The Yemeni Theatre

Bush bears at least half the blame for the disaster that continues to be Somalia, but Obama primarily is to blame in three other theatres: Waziristan, Libya, and the one discussed here, Yemen.

Ali Abdullah Saleh had been president of North Yemen and then unified Yemen since the Carter administration. He was a shrewd power broker and knew how to keep himself and his family ruling Yemen across the administrations of six different American presidents and avoided going "the way of the Taliban" by using terrorism and instability to scare the United States into helping him.[64] In 2001, Saleh decided to be forthcoming and helpful to the United States, and he traveled to visit Bush and Cheney.[65] He granted permission to the United States to fly drones freely in Yemeni skies.[66] Saleh carried out a good-faith raid for the United States (which failed miserably) to get some terror suspects, and U.S. military "trainers" were sent to him.[67] Bush had enlisted a second proxy ally. By 2002, the United States was running drone assassinations and enlisting local tribal leaders with Saleh "to kill people it designated as terrorists, in any country, even if they were US citizens."[68]

In 2003, several terrorist attacks in Yemen resulted in a crackdown on terrorism and several hundred arrests and incidents of violence.[69] However, between 2004 and 2010, Saleh was engaged in a civil war against the Houthi minority with the support of U.S. drones and Special Forces, and Saudi Arabia.[70] He "consistently used allegations of Iranian support for the Houthis and deliberately conflated them with al Qaeda."[71] This laid the groundwork for the "sleeping giant" al Qaeda in the Arabian Peninsula (AQAP) to come into being in the Obama years.[72]

Several al Qaeda leaders escaped prison in Yemen in 2006 and began building up AQAP.[73] By 2008, a few months before Obama took office, they had launched "a massive kamikaze attack on the US Embassy in Sana'a[, Yemen]," to which the campaigning Obama responded war hawkishly.[74] "JSOC teams carried out unilateral, direct actions against al Qaeda suspects in Yemen. These operations were never mentioned in public."[75] By January 2009, the stage was set: AQAP was a full force, and JSOC was working in Yemen.[76] Would Obama divert from his predecessor's imperial whimsy?

In the first year of the Obama presidency, "the security situation deteriorated significantly."[77] Obama adopted a plan that was "'heavily militarized, [and] heavily focused on directly neutralizing the threat, instead of kind of draining the swamp.'"[78] JSOC took the lead in the new Yemeni theatre, and the United States sent over more military trainers following a defeat of Saleh's forces by al Qaeda in summer 2009.[79] By December 2009, the U.S. proxy was ingratiating the enemy to the local population, and Saleh was destabilizing. Scahill used the case of Sheikh Saleh bin Fareed as an example of how factions who would otherwise be allies against terrorism turned into anti-American fighters because of the aggressive U.S. policy—which had nothing to do with 9/11.

Bin Fareed was a powerful tribal leader. His territory included the town of al Majalah. On December 17th 2009, Fareed learned that al Majalah was the subject of an aerial attack, ostensibly by the Yemeni government, which claimed credit for the attack, but in reality the attack was the "opening salvo in America's newest war."[80] Bodies were everywhere in the massacre: "Five pregnant women were killed."[81] The town was "littered" with cluster bombs that had U.S. markings on them, including serial numbers.[82] The United States covered up the incident and let Yemen take the blame, calling al Majalah an al Qaeda terrorist camp.

Bin Fareed would have none of it. He hosted a large conference of tribal leaders "to show their solidarity with the victims of the missile strike."[83] When members of al Qaeda asked to speak at it, he prohibited them, and when they violated his wishes, he unsuccessfully *tried to kill the al Qaeda recruiters*.[84] The al Majalah massacre was becoming a rallying cry for opposition against foreign missiles from the skies.[85]

By January 2010, JSOC was moving at a two-dozen-operations-a-month pace in Yemen, and the regional instability coupled with the rise of AQAP, in which the United States played no small part, began to garner media and administration attention.[86] It was "The Year of the Drone."[87] Obama "formaliz[ed] the process for conducting assassinations against terror suspects," permitting three executive organs of government—the National Security Council, CIA, and military—to maintain active and open kill lists that he personally approved.[88] That year the CIA took its first attempt at killing the imam Anwar al-Aulaqi by drone.[89] Through 2010, however, the Yemeni forces continued to kill civilians ineptly while letting al Qaeda forces escape, much to the chagrin of the equally challenged JSOC.[90]

By 2011, the Arab Spring had hit Yemen, and thousands of protesters were in the streets of Sana'a seeking President Saleh's ouster.[91] The United States was getting involved in Libya's civil wars but was concerned over potentially losing Saleh and AQAP's advances in southern Yemen, so it continued to run the strategy of "bomb[ing] [AQAP] out of existence."[92] The United States "was shifting tactics. With the Saleh regime severely weakened, the Obama administration calculated that it had little to gain from that alliance at this stage. The United States would double down on its use of air power and drones, striking in Yemen at will to carry on its campaign against AQAP. The Obama administration began quick construction of a secret base in Saudi Arabia."[93]

America became like the terrorists it had fought to kill: "'The US sees al Qaeda as terrorism, and we consider the drones terrorism,' [major tribal leader Mullah Zabara] said. 'The drones are flying day and night, frightening women and children, disturbing sleeping people. This is terrorism.'"[94] President Obama said it best, "[N]o country on Earth . . . would tolerate missiles raining down on its citizens from outside its borders."[95]

The Waziristani (Pakistani) Theatre

The U.S. presence in Pakistan, or more accurately the war in Waziristan (a tribal region of northern Pakistan) is the subject of intense investigation (as relatively little is known about its proceedings) and is the subject of significant treatment by commentators.* Much as they did in Yemen, covert and clandestine operators would carry out the war with drones hovering high above.[96] Unlike Yemen, however, the Pakistani government cared about sovereignty, and the United States had to conduct its Pakistani war in a more limited manner, so as not to appear to be at war with Pakistan.[97]

In 2002, the Pakistani and U.S. officials then in power brokered an arrangement where the United States could engage in hot pursuit of terrorist suspects entering Pakistani territory, and that was the extent of U.S. involvement.[98] However, "[e]veryone in Pakistan knew the CIA [and JSOC were] operating extensively in the country—every drone strike was a stark reminder—but the US military could not be perceived to be in the country for any purpose other than training Pakistani forces."[99] And there it was: A *third* secret war theatre.

The plan to get deep into Pakistan with the global War on Terror "stalled as a result of the ongoing fight for control of Pakistani operators between the CIA and the Pentagon," as late as 2008.[100] After years of drone wars, when the Bush administration finally got its act together enough to carry out the war with ground forces, it was a few months

---

* Bob Woodward of the *Washington Post*, for example, has written an entire book on Obama's ramping up and revamping of the Pakistani strategy he inherited from Bush. See Bob Woodward, *Obama's Wars* (New York: Simon & Schuster, 2010).

until the guard changed to President Obama, and the SEAL team's first attack was a blunder, resulting in many civilian deaths—men, women, and children—displeasing Pakistan.[101]

After taking office, "Obama began striking Pakistan almost weekly."[102] He gave theretofore unauthorized access to sensitive government facilities to Blackwater drone contractors and broadened the acceptable zone of military action in Pakistan.[103] He even let the conflict spill over into nearby Uzbekistan.[104] That's the world under the AUMF. What did Uzbekistan have to do with 9/11?

The extent of the U.S. clandestine involvement in Pakistan and the unbridled liberty with which it acts there are not fully known. However, the 2011 "curious case of Raymond Davis" sheds some light.[105] Davis, a clandestine operative reporting to JSOC with diplomatic immunity under a nonsense cover, was conducting intelligence in the streets of Lahore when the ISI, the Pakistani intelligence services, decided to send him a message. As he was traveling on January 27th, two young men on a motorcycle pulled in front of him:.

> At some point, Davis pegged the two guys on the motorcycle in front of him as a threat. As he told it, one of the men brandished a firearm in a menacing way. Davis grabbed his Glock 9 and fired five shots through his front windshield, with deadly precision, taking down Muhammed Faheem, who was on the back of the bike. One shot hit him in the head, just above his ear. Another pierced his stomach. The driver of the motorcycle, Faizan Haider, hopped off the bike and started to flee. Davis, Glock in hand, stepped out of his car, aimed and fired five more shots. Haider fell thirty feet from his motorcycle. At least two shots hit him in the back. He later died in the hospital.[106]

"The postmortem report indicated that both men who were killed by Davis were shot from behind."[107] Davis's nonsense cover was that he worked for the Regional Affairs Office as "a bureaucrat who stamped passports and performed administrative duties—essentially a pencil pusher."[108] President Obama, nobly lying, proudly claimed Davis as a member of our diplomatic corps.[109] However, a later search of his car by the Pakistani police would reveal a spy kit worthy of James Bond, including makeup, surveillance equipment, extra ammunition, various IDs, ATM cards, night equipment, and a cache of other spy tools.[110] Moreover, his background wasn't exactly the run-of-the-mill, Ivy League diplomat—Davis was "a seasoned Special Forces operator," with experience from the Green Berets to JSOC, to Blackwater in Pakistan, from laundering money to conducting clandestine operations.[111] Needless to say, the plain evidence belied his and Obama's cockamamie diplomat line.

Of course, as Scahill pointed out, "accept[ing] this version of the story would require believing" a completely absurd series of events: "[T]hat an administrative staffer at the consulate would, by chance, be so cool-headed . . . so skilled with a glock . . . [that] with an assassin's precision, [he would kill] . . . two assailants by firing his weapon from behind the steering wheel through the windshield of his car."[112]

Was this paper-shuffling diplomat in any way fazed by this encounter? Did he call the police to assist him? No:

> According to eyewitnesses, after shooting the two men, Davis returned calmly to his vehicle and took out a military grade radio. He called for backup.
>
> Before getting back into his vehicle, onlookers in the crowded intersection watched as Davis walked over to the blood-soaked bodies of the two men he had shot and photographed them. As crowds began to descend on the streets, the potential for a mob was forming. Traffic police called out for Davis to stop. He ignored them, got back in his car—the windshield riddled with bullet holes made by his own Glock—and sped off.[113]

The backup that he radioed operated with equally reckless disregard for the rule of law. As soon as it hit traffic, the backup vehicle hopped up on a median and "punched it," "darting into oncoming traffic."[114]

Predictably, the backup vehicle "slammed into the motorcycle of a Pakistani man, Ibadur Rehman." The man was crushed.[115] The vehicle continued to the scene, but it fled after the occupants realized Davis was already gone.[116]

By February the case was a nightmare for the United States. Davis played the diplomatic immunity line and claimed he fired in self-defense.[117] The case, the intrusion upon sovereignty, and the blatancy of the U.S. lies incensed the Pakistani people. The widow of one of the men, Shumaila Kanwal, recorded a video of herself demanding revenge on the Americans—"'blood for blood. . . . No deals.'"[118] Shumaila had swallowed rat poison before the video, protesting her husband's killing.[119] It was recorded as a death message to ensure justice for his murderer. "Back in Washington," however, "the full weight of the Obama administration was being thrown behind the cause of his freedom."[120]

The administration's lie machine was in full swing, and "Obama, Kerry, and other US officials publicly characterized Davis as a diplomat" and pressured the media into suppressing the story.[121] The *New York Times*, true to form since withholding the Total Information Awareness–program story in 2004, withheld the fact that Davis was an active CIA agent at the time of his capture.[122] Also true to form, the *Guardian*, despite CIA and MI5 pressure not to print the story, went ahead and let the people know the truth.[123] However, as Glenn Greenwald pointed out in a piece for *Salon*, "The NYT's Journalistic Obedience," in this case the *Times* was not merely concealing a story; it was contributing to spreading false propaganda for the government—the exact antithesis of the function of a free press.[124]

Once the CIA-Davis link was officially reported, the ISI began cracking down on CIA agents in Pakistan, and "dozens of 'contractors' fled the country."[125] Relationships between the ISI and the CIA had soured to an unprecedented level.[126] This was a total disaster because without operations and war in Pakistan, there was no chance of winning in Afghanistan. America's global war machine depended on the critical link of ISI compliance and Pakistani subservience.

ISI, CIA, and military officials from both countries met in a luxury beach resort in Muscat, Oman, and began to hammer out a deal for blood money.[127] Of course, this was despite the fact that the families and the dead widow had been adamant in insisting upon justice by law rather than bribes. The U.S.-Pakistani cabal came up with a plan to use a provision of Sharia law, *diyyat*, in order to receive a pardon from the family in exchange for money.[128]

The family's reluctance to accept such an arrangement was also no obstacle:

> [At the first day of Raymond Davis's trial,] . . . instead of witnessing the presentation of evidence, the testimony of eyewitnesses or the questioning of Davis, the family members were ordered to sign papers pardoning the American. "I and my associate were kept in forced detention for hours," claimed an attorney for the family of Faizan Haider. Each of the family members was brought before the judge and asked if he or she pardoned Davis. Under intense pressure, all of them answered yes. The judge then dismissed the case against Davis and ordered his release. "This all happened in a court and everything was according to law," [the Punjabi Law Minister] declared.[129]

The United States paid $2.3 million to the families of his victims and to some people in the local government at Lahore. Hillary Clinton "praised the arrangement."[130] Pakistani sovereignty was a convenient fiction for a government selling the sovereignty of its people to an American government that had no pause for even a moment in seizing it.

The Libyan War

In 2011, the world tossed the American perpetual war machine a freebee—the health of the state would be supported by the toppling of an ancient enemy from the days of Reagan: Col. Muammar Qaddafi. The Libyan civil war and the ill-fated prospect of rebel success in the war provided convenient "window dressing to cover a western military intervention that was supposedly for humanitarian purposes."[131]

The phrase "ancient enemy" is a bit questionable. Ronald Reagan called Qaddafi the "mad dog of the Middle East" who aimed to achieve a global "Moslem fundamentalist revolution."[132] Indeed, in 1986 Qaddafi's government supported the Berlin discotheque bombing and later supported the 1988 Lockerbie bombing. Reagan launched strikes in Libya aimed at killing Qaddafi on April 15th 1989, merely six days after calling him a mad dog. To President Bush and Prime Minister Tony Blair, however, Qaddafi was an ally and an asset.

In 2003, Qaddafi began courting the West and renounced terrorism.[133] In response and eyeing Libyan oil, Bush lifted economic sanctions in 2004.[134] Moreover, Libya became part of Bush's rendition and torture program, with victims telling their stories for the "first time . . . because until last year [2011] they were locked up in Libyan prisons."[135] Secretary of State Condoleezza Rice made public that the administration was "restoring full diplomatic relations with Libya" in 2006 and opened an embassy.[136] By 2008, Qaddafi had paid for the victims of the Lockerbie bombing, and President Bush engaged in the unprecedented step of speaking directly to Qaddafi over the phone. They were on the road to "full normalization of diplomatic relations between the United States and Libya."[137]

By August 2009, well into the Obama administration and with the blessing of Secretary of State Hillary Clinton, the McCain-led senatorial delegation to Libya hailed him as "an important ally in the war on terrorism" and "a peacemaker in Africa."[138] A little more than two years later, his "allies" ensured that he would be ousted and killed by rebels.

Then the Arab Spring came; in February 2011, Libyan rebels under the National Transitional Council began fighting against Qaddafi. Initially, many senior Libyan politicians defected, and the rebels gained large swaths of territory in the east, but Qaddafi was quick to respond and by March, it appeared that he was going to win. Reacting to the asymmetrical fighting between Qaddafi's professional army and air force, and Libyan rebels trying to topple his government, the U.N. Security Council adopted a resolution that created a no-fly zone over Libya.[139]

President Obama had a problem: The United Nations is not Congress and can't commit U.S. troops to war. The Security Council resolution was not enough to declare war formally. Obama began by following the requirements of the War Powers Resolution of 1973 (WPR): "When Mr. Obama first announced American military involvement in Libya, he notified Congress within 48 hours, as prescribed by the War Powers Act."[140] However, that was the end of his legal compliance.

Obama's OLC acting head, Caroline D. Krass, "told the president that he had to abide by the act's requirements."[141] This would have interfered with Obama's power to operate unilaterally in global war, so "the White House counsel [Robert F. Bauer] decided to pre-empt the Justice Department's traditional role."[142] Similar to the OLC and White House counsel splitting over the Torture Memos, "[a]s the war powers deadline approached, Mr. Bauer held a series of White House meetings at which he contested the Office of Legal Counsel's interpretation [of the WPR] and invited leading lawyers from the State Department and the Pentagon to join him in preparing competing legal opinions for the president."[143]

Needless to say, Obama selected Bauer's opinion: "[T]he billion-dollar bombing campaign in Libya does not amount to 'hostilities' under the War Powers Act."[144] This is, of course, absurd. The WPR broadly uses the term *hostilities* to avoid the distinction between *war* and policing *actions* or the many other euphemisms for war that presidents claim create a distinction between their "limited" armed conflicts and the previous four thousand years of war history. For example, as was discussed earlier, Vietnam was a war in every real sense but not a legal one. After notifying Congress, the president has sixty days to get authorization, and if it is not provided thereafter, then thirty days to end hostilities. According to Yale Law School Professor Bruce Ackerman writing in the *New York Times* on June 20th 2011: "Last Sunday was the 90th day of bombing in Libya, but Mr. Obama—armed with dubious legal opinions—is refusing to stop America's military engagement there."[145]

On March 19th 2011, with no formal declaration of war and in violation of the WPR, the United States and its allies shot cruise missiles, enforced the no-fly zone, began toppling an evil dictator, and promised what would become a catchphrase of the Obama administration's lies: "[N]o boots" on the ground.[146] On March 24th, boots did hit the ground, and hostilities continued when NATO took over, which, of course, would involve American boots and troops. NATO action also is not an exception to the War Powers Resolution. It doesn't matter what a treaty says—the power to declare war rests solely with the Congress, regardless of whether it is called hostilities, action, intervention, or war. By October, the United States had killed Qaddafi through its proxies and its clandestine operators.

In an August 2011 article, John Barry detailed the *fourth* U.S. secret theatre in the Middle and Near Eastern Wars:

> The U.S. military has spent about $1 billion so far and played a far larger role in Libya than it has acknowledged, quietly implementing an emerging "covert intervention" strategy that the Obama administration hopes will let America fight small wars with a barely detectable footprint. . . .
>
> But behind the scenes, the U.S. military played an indispensable role in the Libya campaign, deploying far more forces than the administration chose to advertise. And at NATO headquarters outside Brussels, the U.S. was intimately involved in all decisions about how the Libyan rebels should be supported as they rolled up control of cities and oil refineries and marched toward the capital, Tripoli.[147]

The United States provided CIA, intelligence, surveillance, Special Forces support, drones, refueling ships, missiles, air support, bombs, and NATO to support the rebels[148]—another clandestine, proxy civil war. Boots were definitely on the ground on October 5th 2013 when—despite Libya's claims that it gave no permission to impede on its sovereignty and that Libyan government officials "have vowed for months that their new government would never countenance Western military action on Libyan soil for any reason"—U.S. Special Forces operators captured accused terrorists Abu Anas al-Libi and Nazih Abdul-Hamed al-Ruqai.[149]

And for all of America's drones and planes, how is Libya faring post-Qaddafi? On the eleventh anniversary of 9/11, AQAP and radical militants attacked the U.S. embassy in Benghazi, killing the U.S. ambassador and three State Department contractors hired to protect him.[150] "Protests and strikes . . . have throttled Libya's daily oil production to one-tenth its capacity, jeopardizing the national economy."[151] "[N]ational military and police forces remain largely impotent."[152]

Torture and Unlimited Rendition

George Washington once said, "Should any American soldier be so base and infamous as to injure any [prisoner] . . . I do most earnestly enjoin you to bring him to such severe and exemplary punishment as the enormity of the crime may require."[153] In that spirit, on January 22nd 2009, President Obama signed Executive Order 13491, "Ensuring Lawful Interrogation."[154] In large part the world believes that Obama has fundamentally changed the game forever on American torture regimes.

However, this is an important misunderstanding of what Obama did. There is a difference between saying, "The president does not have the power to torture" and saying, "The president does not torture." One denies the premise; the other grants it, but shows the president is electing not to exercise the power. Obama's order suffers from two fatal flaws: The Army Field Manual Appendix M loophole and the veil of secrecy.

Obama's order states, "[A]n individual in the custody or under the effective control of . . . the United States Government, or detained within a facility owned, operated, or controlled by a department or agency of the United States, in any armed conflict, shall not be subjected to any interrogation technique or approach, or any treatment related to interrogation, that is not authorized by and listed in Army Field Manual 2-22.3 (Manual)."[155]

However, Appendix M of the Army Field Manual (with amendments from the Bush era) permits the isolation of prisoners; forty straight hours of interrogation with four-hour rests; "goggles, blindfolds and handcuffs" for up to twelve hours; and "physical stress."* Moreover, as the Human Rights Watch reported in 2012, individuals who were rendered to third countries, such as Libya, were still being released well into 2011.[156]

Thus, despite all the puffery of the order, American soldiers can certainly be so base as to strike prisoners and do much worse. Of course, this is all still shrouded in secrecy: "The Pentagon, even in the more transparent Obama era, has been rather testy about allowing human rights observers free access to any of the detention facilities at Bagram or the right to interview prisoners—though it has invited observers to tour its new prison."[157] Even in the Obama era, several witnesses have complained of Bush era–like torture at the hands of U.S. officials at Bagram.[158] Moreover, the government eschewed the American "rich history of military ethics dating back to General George Washington."[159]

And what about punishment for the enormity of the crime? What ever happened to the commanding U.S. officials who ordered war crimes committed by institutionalizing prisoner abuse? Nothing. The Obama administration hushed up Abu Ghraib photographs, gave immunity to officials, and performed a giant cover-up.[160] The American presidency has shifted over the last two hundred years from giving exemplary punishment for the enormity of the crime of torture to facilitating it, then sweeping it under the rug. Obama's record on torture is not quite as clean as his acolytes make it out to be.

The Right to Trial: Commissions Stand

President Obama voted against the Military Commissions Act of 2006 when he was a senator and while campaigning pledged in a speech at the Woodrow Wilson Center, "As President, I will close Guantanamo, reject

---

* Sarah Childress, "Six Reasons the 'Dark Side' Still Exists Under Obama," PBS Frontline, April 22, 2013, http://www.pbs.org/wgbh/pages/frontline/criminal-justice/six-reasons-the-dark-side-still-exists-under-obama/; Nat Hentoff, "Torture Under Obama," Cato Institute, February 17, 2010, http://www.cato.org/publications/commentary/torture-under-obama.

the Military Commissions Act, and adhere to the Geneva Conventions. Our Constitution and our Uniform Code of Military Justice provide a framework for dealing with the terrorists."[161] And in 2008, it seemed as though he had the political impetus to do so: The international community hated Gitmo, the people of the United States were against Gitmo, and the Supreme Court had declared in *Boumediene* that the latest attempt to isolate Gitmo from judicial review was unconstitutional.

By the time Obama entered office, the detainees had been held for almost seven years without trial (the sole exception being David Hicks, who is free at this writing). Obama, however, would prove similar to his predecessor: "He was reluctant to surrender executive powers that his predecessor had claimed," giving Gitmo and the Pink Palace court "a bipartisan imprimatur that virtually ensures they will be a fixture of American law for years to come."[162] Or in the words of former Gitmo Chief Prosecutor Col. Morris Davis, "Obama 'has now embraced and kissed on the lips the whole Bush concept [of military commissions]. He failed to keep a single promise he made in that speech [at the Wilson Center].'"[163]

Initially, the Obama administration showed signs of a commitment to the Constitution and a willingness to wind down the Bush legal regime of rendition, indefinite detention, torture, and unfair prosecution. In his second day in office, President Obama issued three executive orders: 13491, 13492, and 13493. Executive Order 13491 set the Geneva Conventions' Common Article 3 as the "minimum baseline" for detainee treatment and compelled all interrogations to follow the Army Field Manual, rather than the system set out in Yoo's draconian and medieval OLC memos.[164] Executive Order 13492 ordered a review of Gitmo detainees to ascertain their statuses (due for transfer, for prosecution, etc.).[165] Executive Order 13493 created a task force to develop policies on disposing of the Gitmo cases.[166] He also "suspended commissions proceedings indefinitely."[167] Administration officials saw this as a good opportunity to make a "clean break with Bush's legal experiments."[168] However, it went downhill from there.

By May 2009, Obama had reversed his position: "Following months of pressure from Defense Department and National Security officials, according to three knowledgeable sources, Obama changed course and announced that his administration would resurrect the Bush-era military commissions he had vowed to oppose."[169] In his May 15th 2009 press release, Obama's position was significantly different from the vitriolic distaste for military commissions he had previously espoused:

> Military commissions have a long tradition in the United States. They are appropriate for trying enemies who violate the laws of war, provided that they are properly structured and administered. In the past, I have supported the use of military commissions as one avenue to try detainees, in addition to prosecution in Article III courts. In 2006, I voted in favor of the use of military commissions. But I objected strongly to the Military Commissions Act that was drafted by the Bush Administration and passed by Congress.[170]

The hypocrisy characteristic of the Obama administration had begun to show. On November 13th 2009, however, Attorney General Eric Holder announced at last that Khalid Sheikh Mohammed would be tried with half of the other 9/11 conspirators in federal district court in New York City.[171]

Military Commissions Act of 2009

Obama, having now flipped on the issue, set the stage for Congress to force his hand. On October 28th 2009, Congress sent its first act to the new president for the continuation of military tribunals: The Military Commissions Act of 2009, which Obama signed into law on October 28th 2009. The Act made concessions to the Supreme Court. The Act limited hearsay and coercion testimony and improved the ability of the defense to obtain witnesses and present its case.[172] It also included prohibitions on double jeopardy.[173] However, it still fell "far short of the requirements imposed by the Constitution and Geneva Conventions."[174]

It did not bar all coercion testimony and generally "retained many of the structural flaws that had hobbled [commissions] since 2001."[175]

National Defense Authorization Act for Fiscal Year 2012

The National Defense Authorization Act for Fiscal Year 2012 (2012 NDAA) was another nail in the coffin of constitutional norms. The NDAA included three provisions which are constitutionally repugnant and render the commissions system permanent. First is Section 1021, which states: "Congress affirms that the authority of the President to use all necessary and appropriate force pursuant to the Authorization for Use of Military Force includes the authority for the Armed Forces of the United States to detain covered persons . . . pending disposition under the law of war."[176] This detention, however, could be indefinite, on U.S. soil, and extends so far as to cover U.S. citizens, *in even their private homes*, as well as aliens—clearly a violation of constitutional due process. Section 1022 requires that foreigners, not citizens or lawful resident aliens, be held in military custody rather than civilian custody.[177] Thus, they may be military prisoners subject to military jurisdiction and not subject to outside civilian jurisdiction. The 2012 NDAA included Section 1027, which prohibits using defense funds to transfer Guantanamo detainees off base.[178] They are permanently there until Congress or their home country funds their transfer, or the president disposes of their cases via adjudication. Amnesty International noted, "The bill will make President Obama the first President since the red scare in the McCarthy era to sign a law to introduce indefinite detention in the US. It will keep the detention facility at Guantanamo Bay open, potentially forever."[179]

All in all, the detainees at Guantanamo have been waiting more than a decade for trial. Their rights to due process, personhood, speedy trial, and fair adjudication have all fallen flat on their faces in the wake of Bush and Obama with hundreds of individuals left in uncertain and indefinite detention—a fate to which America never subjected its worst enemies before this War on Terror.

And what did America get out of all of this? Certainly not the speedy and satisfying prosecution of the 9/11 masterminds, and certainly not peace or justice: "[T]he maximum number of prisoners that the US military intends to prosecute, or has already prosecuted, is 20—or just 2.5 percent of the 779 men held at the prison since it opened in January 2002."[180] Khalid Sheikh Mohammed was transferred back to Gitmo for military trial, despite Attorney General Eric Holder's public promises and private objections.[181] A decade later we still have nothing to show for this clearly failed, irreparable experiment besides a litany of monumental civil rights violations.

One of the hallmarks of due process—the basic fairness which the Natural Law and the Constitution require the government to exercise whenever it is adverse to any person—is fidelity to rules and procedures that are generally acceptable and universally applicable. The procedures also must be in place *before* adversity began. The persistent efforts of the Bush administration to reject these norms has brought much woe and no justice.

15

The Obama Administration

A Midterm Review of Exponentially Expanded Drone Intervention and Privacy Attacks

The Telescreen received and transmitted simultaneously. Any sound that Winston made, above the level of a very low whisper, would be picked up by it; moreover, so long as he remained within the field of vision which the metal plaque commanded, he could be seen as well as heard. . . . You had to live—did live, from habit that became instinct—in the assumption that every sound you made was overheard, and, except in darkness, every moment scrutinized.*

—GEORGE ORWELL, 1984

---

* George Orwell, 1984 (New York: Signet Classics, 1950), 3.

The Drone Wars: Unmanned Aerial Vehicles and the Right to Life Under the Obama Administration

Many people lay the blame at Bush's feet for beginning weaponized drone warfare, but in reality it was President Clinton who began the U.S. weaponized drone program.[1] After an aerial drone spotted bin Laden in October 2000, President Clinton was frustrated that he could not simply push a button to end the life of the man who had sullied his foreign policy and national security records. President Clinton "gave orders to create an armed drone force."[2] That program came to fruition under President Bush when on June 18th 2004, the first weaponized drone struck in Waziristan. Up until September 4th 2001, the Department of Defense and CIA were still reluctant to utilize these creepy super-weapons, even to kill bin Laden.[3] After September 11th, that all changed for the Pentagon and the CIA, and like the render and torture program, something which began under Clinton and expanded under Bush, would exponentially increase in power under the Obama administration.

Prior to President Clinton, President Reagan had reiterated President Gerald Ford's and President Jimmy Carter's ban on assassinations in Executive Order 12333.[4]* This order, very plainly, proscribed assassination, an undefined term. After the Khobar Towers bombing in 1996, discussed in chapter 10, Clinton issued a Presidential Finding, or Memorandum of Notification, modifying the order proscribing assassinations.[5] It now included an exception when capture was infeasible and for specific people, which, of course, included bin Laden and his captains.[6] After 9/11, the Bush administration amended Clinton's Finding to remove the restrictive list of names and non-feasibility-of-capture requirement.[7] After that, the assassin machines known as weaponized

---

* President Ford signed Executive Order 11,905 in 1976, banning political assassinations, which President Carter expanded on in Exec. Order No. 12,036, 43 Fed. Reg. 3674 (1978); see Exec. Order No. 11,905, 41 Fed. Reg. 7703 (1976).

drones grew into Obama's favorite war machine. Of course, because of the definitional flexibility, drone operations later would be classified not as assassinations but as "targeted strikes."

Despite the Pentagon and CIA's love for drones, Bush himself was reluctant to use the weapons.[8] Conversely, Bush's successor would not have the same distaste for assassinations: "Obama had already authorized as many drone strikes in [his first] ten months [in office] as Bush had in his entire eight years in office."[9] At this writing, Obama has authorized almost seven times as many: About 320 strikes to Bush's 52, killing more than three thousand people.[10] Around 2 percent of those killed were high-level terrorist targets[11]—hardly a sufficient number of military targets to justify the attacks under international and domestic law conceptions of military proportionality in civilian-soldier death ratios.

The drones have been effective in their purpose, serving as killing-spying machines, but have engendered virulent hatred against the United States and continue to cause "mass trauma among civilians," which means constant "fear of attack, severe anxiety, powerlessness, insomnia and high levels of stress."[12]* Essentially, World War I shell shock has been visited on the Waziristanis/Pakistanis, Yemenis, and any other zone where the U.S. drone program haunts the skies. And what is the result? In Afghanistan, Pakistan, and Yemen, our drones' "reign of terror" has infuriated local populations and "proven vastly more effective than al Qaida in turning Muslims against the United States."[13] "The result was to guarantee an ever mounting desire for revenge."[14]

The use of these weapons, as general war machines, lacks substantial or set guidelines from the U.S. military hierarchy. President Obama, when facing reelection and the (short-lived) prospect of a loss to Republican Mitt Romney, scrambled to create guidelines for their use by future presidents.[15] However, since he won reelection, this effort has fallen by the

---

* There was a large, remarkable piece written on the topic in 2012, *Under the Drones*. Shahzad Bashir and Robert D. Crews, eds., *Under the Drones: Modern Lives in the Afghanistan-Pakistan Borderlands* (Cambridge, MA: Harvard University Press, 2012).

wayside, seeing as how Obama's non-transparent, *ex camera* discretion is no doubt, to him, the equivalent of formal, published guidelines.

Moreover, as the U.S. government pushes forth with proxy and drone wars throughout the globe, the president has claimed a new and awesome power. *President Obama claimed the unnatural and unconstitutional right to decide unilaterally which Americans shall die.* What was the basis for this power? No one knew before March 2013; it was a state secret hidden away as an ominous Justice Department "White Paper."

The Four (Known) Killing Cases: Anwar al-Aulaqi, Samir Khan, Abdulrahman al-Aulaqi, and Jude Mohammed

Using his fleet of drones, Obama killed four U.S. citizens between 2011 and 2013: Anwar al-Aulaqi, Samir Khan, Abdulrahman al-Aulaqi, and Jude Mohammed—only one of which he claims to have done intentionally. Anwar al-Aulaqi and Samir Khan were killed together following several attempts on al-Aulaqi's life. A few weeks later, al-Aulaqi's teenage son, Abdulrahman, was struck supposedly unintentionally. Jude Mohammed, one of the new wave of ex-patriot jihadists, was killed in a drone strike. Of these four, Obama has only admitted to targeting Anwar al-Aulaqi directly, relegating the rest to collateral damage. Thus, this section focuses mostly on the Anwar al-Aulaqi case.

Anwar al-Aulaqi was an "all-American boy."[16] He was born in New Mexico to proud parents who raised him in America until he was nine years old and then in Yemen as a moderate American Muslim.[17] "In 1991, he returned to the United States [from Yemen], where he earned a bachelor's degree at Colorado State University, wed a Yemeni cousin, and later received a master's degree in Educational Leadership from San Diego State University."[18] After 9/11 he became an American media star, "called upon by scores of media outlets to represent a 'moderate' Muslim view of the 9/11 attacks," even addressing a *Pentagon* luncheon.[19] Before he went to Yemen he had no U.S. criminal charges besides two patronizing prostitution complaints (which it is speculated were setups) and weak allegations of ties to 9/11 that the FBI dismissed.[20]

However, when the post-9/11 war hysteria came, "the crackdowns on Muslims and the wars abroad in Muslim countries" drove al-Aulaqi to leave for England in 2002.[21] Specifically, he was personally being stalked and interrogated by the FBI over his possible involvement in 9/11.[22] He left London for Yemen permanently in 2003, meeting up with his uncle Saleh bin Fareed.[23] With no publicly revealed evidence of criminal behavior, the United States branded him a terrorist in 2010 and began its CIA assassination plans.[24]

The CIA went through all manner of plans to kill Anwar al-Aulaqi, stretching from drones to the absurd. One plan to kill him used a Danish double agent who had his trust. That agent was supposed to set him up with a Croatian wife whose luggage would be bugged with a tracer and then blown up by drone missiles.[25] That plot failed, but "the United States got its man when, on September 30, 2011, a drone fired a 'barrage of Hellfire missiles' at his car."[26]

His car also carried Samir Khan, a "proud" traitor from Queens and fellow ex-patriot jihadist who was killed as collateral damage in that strike.[27] Khan was an incredibly popular, teenage, radical Islamic jihadist blogger by 2005.[28] He was subjected to FBI surveillance and eventually left the United States to join AQAP, lying to his parents about attending a university in Yemen.[29] Khan became editor of the AQAP publication *Inspire* and worked mostly as an online facilitator and translator.[30]

A few weeks after the missiles took out Anwar and Samir, the third American citizen was killed. Abdulrahman al-Aulaqi, Anwar's sixteen-year-old son, was killed in Yemen.[31] He had sneaked out of his safe home in northern Yemen for the purpose of "see[ing] his father."[32] "When Obama was briefed on Awlaki's location in Jawf and was told that children were in the home, he was explicit that he did not want any options ruled out."[33] Anwar was killed before Abdulrahman was able to see him.[34] Shortly after his father's death, Abdulrahman went out with some cousins to join other families barbecuing outdoors. There he was "cut up to pieces" and killed by a drone.[35] The victims of that strike were buried in a single grave. Why? "[T]hey were blown up to pieces by the drone

. . . [such that] they could not [sort] them into separate graves."[36] "The people who were there could recognize only the back of Abdulrahman's hair."[37] After initially feigning ignorance, the government accepted responsibility for Abdulrahman's murder.[38]

The fourth and final citizen, twenty-three-year-old Jude Mohammed from Raleigh, North Carolina, was wanted by the FBI for his jihadist activities and was "killed with about 12 other insurgents in what the C.I.A. calls a 'signature strike'" in May 2013.[39]

The Targeting "Due" Process: CIA Adjudication

How exactly did Obama arrive at the conclusion he could kill these Americans, including a child? It certainly wasn't done in compliance with a trial court decision or some similar operation of law. Tara McKelvey wrote an article on the process for *Newsweek* in 2011 entitled, "Inside the Killing Machine."[40] Relying on that work, a law student summarized the process succinctly:

> An individual must meet the CIA's legal standard in order to be classified as a terrorist that is subject to targeted killing. Pursuant to a secret fifty-page Department of Justice white paper outlining the terrorist classification process, approximately ten CIA Counterterrorism Center attorneys receive a "'two page document,' along with 'an appendix with supporting information, if anybody want[s] to read all of it.'" The attorneys then prepare a "cable" that "often run[s] up to five pages." Senior attorneys will review the cable for errors, such as if "'the justification [in approving a person for lethal operation] would be that the person was thought to be at a meeting [but was not].'" The cable is then sent to the CIA's General Counsel, who approves it. At any given time, there are about thirty individuals approved for targeting.[41]

President Obama himself approves the final orders to kill.[42]

The issues are multifold and relate to basic, elementary Fifth Amendment rights. First, no one outside the administration knows what this White Paper says in full, so no one can legitimately argue the standard by which targets are to be judged. Second, there is so little attention paid to the adjudication of guilt before the assignment of a death sentence—the process described here isn't even a tenth of what is due for the average capital offense trial. Third, there are no adversarial lawyers or notice in this system: The bomb is the notice.

The DOJ White Paper and State Secrets: The McMahon Betrayal

Obviously, organizations like the ACLU and the Center for Constitutional Rights (CCR) were up in arms about this issue. They had to litigate to get this "power" declared extra-constitutional. However, they didn't even know over what they were suing: The legal justification itself, the infamous DOJ White Paper, was classified. In *New York Times Co. v. U.S. Dep't of Justice*, the ACLU, CCR, and *New York Times* sued when their Freedom of Information Act request for the justification was denied.[43]

U.S. District Court Judge Colleen McMahon of the Southern District of New York wrote one of the most interesting and honest opinions of our time:

> However, this Court is constrained by law, and under the law, I can only conclude that the Government has not violated FOIA by refusing to turn over the documents sought in the FOIA requests, and so cannot be compelled by this court of law to explain in detail the reasons why its actions do not violate the Constitution and laws of the United States. The Alice–in–Wonderland nature of this pronouncement is not lost on me; but after careful and extensive consideration, I find myself stuck in a paradoxical situation in which I cannot solve a problem because of contradictory constraints and rules—a veritable Catch-22. I can find no way around the thicket of laws and precedents that effectively allow the Executive Branch of our Government to proclaim as perfectly lawful certain actions that seem on their face incompatible with our Constitution and laws, while keeping the

reasons for its conclusion a secret. But under the law as I understand it to have developed, the Government's motion for summary judgment must be granted, and the cross-motions by the ACLU and the *Times* denied.[44]

The ACLU and the *New York Times* argued that the government had disclosed so much information about the process that the White Paper described, it had waived the benefit of classified status.[45] The court, while recognizing that there was some merit to the argument, turned it down because the government spoke about the justification in broad generalities, one of the tenets of the classified data waiver test.[46]

Then the government rebuffed and publicly humiliated the judge who had just given them a gift. One month after the *Times* opinion, the government declassified a redacted version of it and leaked that version to NBC News: It was too sensitive to share with a federal judge in secret, but politically potent enough to share with friends in the media. Other courts chimed in after the release of the redacted version of the White Paper, ordering it to be declassified.[47] To this day, the full memo remains classified, as the Obama administration has yet to comply with the declassification orders.

The *al-Aulaqi* Case

Anwar al-Aulaqi's father, Nasser al-Aulaqi, sued to enjoin the federal government from lethally targeting his son before Anwar was killed. In *al-Aulaqi v. Obama*, the judge dismissed the case on standing grounds, issuing no real decision on the merits.[48] After their son was murdered, Nasser and Samir Khan's family refiled under *al-Aulaqi v. Panetta*, which at the time of this writing is pending disposition.

Judge Bates Dismisses the Case

In dismissing the case, U.S. District Court Judge John Bates issued two holdings. First, that Nasser al-Aulaqi lacked standing to sue because he wasn't Anwar or a properly interested third party.[49] Second, that the case presented a non-justiciable "political question,"[50] a doctrine under which the judiciary may decline to issue a ruling on the merits of a politically charged legal question where it prefers not to rule one way or the other.

The first holding makes sense and likely will be remedied in the ongoing *Panetta* legislation. However, the second holding, referencing that "courts are functionally ill-equipped to make the types of complex policy judgments that would be required to adjudicate the merits of plaintiff's claims," shows the aversion of judges to standing between the political branches during wartime.[51] Think about it: A father asks a court to prevent the president from killing the father's uncharged, untried, unconvicted, non-violent son, and an American federal judge who took an oath to uphold the Constitution declines to hear the case. How far we have come after these Bush-Obama years from even a hopeful expectation of rudimentary due process.

Wrongly Decided: The Due Process Clause and the Treason Clause

Judge Bates's second ruling is seriously inconsistent with the Constitution. While the courts have a common law doctrine to avoid hearing cases that challenge their equality with the other two branches and avoid some cases they shouldn't hear, the political question doctrine cannot be used as a shield against courts failing to discharge their constitutional obligations pursuant to Article III before patently unlawful, irreversible, and lethal action is taken by the government.

The Fifth Amendment to the Constitution provides that "[n]o person shall be held to answer for a capital, or otherwise infamous crime, unless on a presentment or indictment of a Grand Jury, except in cases arising in the land or naval forces, or in the Militia, when in actual service in time of War or public danger . . . nor be deprived of life, liberty, or property, without due process of law."[52] The Supreme Court in *Baldwin v. New York* expressly set the only acceptable process of law for capital federal offenses: Full trial.[53] Al-Aulaqi never even had a violent offense on his U.S. record,[54] but the president decided that he should die. That is not due process under the substantial (fairness) or the procedural (a jury decides facts) requirements of the Fifth Amendment.

Moreover, people in al-Aulaqi's position—that is, the government is essentially accusing them of treason—have even more protections. In Article III of the Constitution, the Founding Fathers ensconced a protection against this: "If nothing else, the Treason Clause—and its specific allocation of the responsibility for resolving treason cases to every branch *other* than the Executive—means that the President, and those who serve at his pleasure, should not act as prosecutor, defense counsel, judge, jury, and executioner, especially in secret."[55]

The simple appearance of the Treason Clause within the Article concerning the judiciary and not the president makes abundantly clear that the president and military and intelligence community may not adjudicate treason cases. Taking it a step further, that means the CIA can't then determine a citizen is levying war against his country (jihad) and then execute him without due process. It is unconstitutional on the face of the Fifth Amendment and Article III, and it is murder.*

Addressing a crowd at Northwestern University School of Law, Attorney General Eric Holder gave an astoundingly inarticulate retort to critics of the executive removing the judiciary from the killing selection process: "Some have argued that the President is required to get permission from a federal court before taking action against a United States citizen who is a senior operational leader of al Qaeda or associated forces. This is simply not accurate. 'Due process' and 'judicial process' are not one and the same, particularly when it comes to

---

* "Thus, the President may not invoke the laws of war regarding legal combatants to justify his actions domestically, which creates an unavoidable tug-of-war between the AUMF and the foreign-murder statute. And because the AUMF cannot reasonably be interpreted to repeal the foreign-murder statute, it is difficult to avoid the conclusion that any C.I.A. operative that executed President Obama's order to kill al-Awlaki is guilty of murder under the foreign-murder statute. An equally unavoidable conclusion is that certain high-ranking executive officials, including the President, would share in that criminal culpability." Philip Dore, "Greenlighting American Citizens: Proceed with Caution," *Louisiana Law Review* 72, no. 1 (2011): 286.

national security. The Constitution guarantees due process, not judicial process."[56]

Mr. Holder should take note of Article III of the Constitution, guaranteeing that anyone who levies war against his country, like an al Qaeda jihadist, can be ruled a traitor only by a federal court. Moreover, the Fifth Amendment would demand a full trial, not agency review.

Holder's speech did have one bit of solace for due process. *Within* the executive, the alleged terrorist would receive the legal equivalent of due process: The accused would be killed only "after a thorough and careful review." President Obama himself is the final arbiter of these decisions. This is such hogwash, it is astounding that the speaker is the federal attorney general.

While the jurisprudence of targeted killing is far from settled—one district court opinion not on point with another pending is hardly a body of law—the precedent set is rather dangerous. Does a president who murders care about privacy?

Domestic Drones and Privacy

Drones aren't weapons solely for the use of the federal government against the enemies of the state; they are coming into everyday American neighborhoods and cities. Congress passed and President Obama signed into law the FAA Modernization and Reform Act of 2012.[57] The Act commanded that the secretary of transportation "develop a comprehensive plan to . . . accelerate [safely] the integration of civil unmanned aircraft systems into the national airspace system."[58] This has the effect of requiring "the FAA to expedite the process of authorizing both public and private use of drones in the national navigable airspace."[59] Pursuant to that Act, the FAA began issuing Certificates of Authorization to certify agencies and individuals who may operate drones in U.S. airspace.[60] The FBI and several local law enforcement agencies have been issued certificates to use drones for domestic criminal operations.[61]

It is important to note that a drone is not simply a Reaper or a Predator drone, although the most commonly associated image of a drone is of the large, windowless airplane as either of those types appears. The current consumer choices in drones span "many shapes and sizes, ranging from as large as a commercial airplane to as small as a hummingbird, and many cost less than a helicopter."[62] In fact, some "drones' small size and light weight enable them to fit in the trunk of a car, and many are designed to be hand-launched by one person."[63]

Moreover, drones provide a broad array of spying tools to the domestic consumer: "[T]hey can be equipped with still and video cameras, infrared cameras, heat sensors, and radar. Drones can also carry tear gas or weapons. In addition to conducting visual surveillance, drones have the electronic surveillance capability of using sophisticated instruments to measure infrared radiation emanating from houses, eavesdrop on cell-phone conversations and text messages by impersonating cell-phone towers, and spy on Wi-Fi networks through automated password cracking."[64]

Additionally, "stealth technology enables drones to hover above us, silently monitoring everything we do in areas exposed to the sky."[65]

Thus, when discussing drone technology, the reader ought to realize that the shock-and-awe sorts of weaponized drones used against foreign targets are not necessarily the same ones that will be used here in America. The presence of those weapons is much more detectable than the hummingbird-sized, FBI-owned ones which will be floating over neighborhoods and peeking into windows, or checking for speeders on highways—a much more invidious and clandestine circumstance. Making this picture even bleaker, the "'government has predicted that as many as 30,000 drones will be flying over U.S. skies by the end of the [present] decade.'"[66]

Local law enforcement agencies have already begun to push the envelope: "The Montgomery County Sheriff's Office in Texas has even considered arming a drone with rubber bullets and tear gas."[67] Imagine that: A peaceful protest broken up by a fleet of drones firing rubber bullets and tear gas. It reads like something right out of 1984—the only thing Orwell got wrong was that the Telescreen needed to be installed in the room for the government to control everything: Its agents could just turn on any computer camera without an indicator light.* President Obama and Congress signed an order expediting the process of letting law enforcement use this new, and often dangerous, technology, despite the fact that "[w]here aviation was in 1925, that's where we are today with unmanned aerial vehicles."[68]

The Right to Privacy: PRISM, FISA, and the Snowden Controversy

As a senator, Barack Obama was opposed to NSA terrorist surveillance programs unless authorized by the FISA Court, which he believed to have exclusive jurisdiction over foreign intelligence warrants.[69] As a president, he would give full-throated endorsement to Bush's police state–like domestic spying programs, picking up the torch of PRISM and using the Justice Department to continue litigation aimed at diminishing the advances made by district courts against the PATRIOT Act during the Bush years.

Hopelessly Without Change: Reauthorization and Expansion of the Worst Acts

President Obama, who championed transparency and ending the exigencies of the Bush era, ended up signing Bush's signature piece of legislation back into law until 2015: The PATRIOT Act.[70] What about the

---

* "This statutory mandate will inevitably reduce our privacy through increased aerial surveillance of neighborhoods and public places by law enforcement drones, bringing us ever closer to an Orwellian state." Robert Molko, "The Drones Are Coming: Will the Fourth Amendment Stop Their Threat to Our Privacy?" *Brooklyn Law Review* 78, no. 4 (2013): 1283. The FBI (and by virtue of that, presumably the military, NSA, and CIA) can activate a laptop camera or desktop plugged-in camera and watch what it sees in real time, or record what it sees. See Craig Timberg and Ellen Nakashima, "FBI's Search for 'Mo,' Suspect In Bomb Threats, Highlights Use of Malware for Surveillance," *Washington Post*, December 6, 2013, http://www.washingtonpost.com/business/technology/fbis-search-for-mo-suspect-in-bomb-threats-highlights-use-of-malware-for-surveillance/2013/12/06/352ba174-5397-11e3-9e2c-e1d01116fd98_story.html.

FISA Amendments Act? Reauthorized until 2017.[71] The Protect America Act? It became part of the FISA Amendments Act so that will be around until 2017 as well. Obama picked up right where Bush's pen left off, signing the same bills for more years. Since 2010, Obama's NSA has been cataloguing Americans' social networks, "exploiting its huge collections of data to create sophisticated graphs of . . . Americans' social connections that can identify their associates, their locations at certain times, their traveling companions and other personal information . . . 'without having to check foreignness.'"[72]

The Espionage Act of 1917: Reportergate, Edward Snowden, and PRISM

In the name of national security, more than any predecessor, Obama has fortified the Espionage Act of 1917 as a tool for domestic and political spying in contravention of constitutional constraints on the executive. As of May 2013, the Obama Justice Department had "used the Espionage Act of 1917 six times to bring cases against government officials for leaks to the media six times—twice as many as all their predecessors combined."[73] By June, that number had climbed to eight:

> NSA whistleblower Thomas Drake was charged under the law in April 2010 for retaining classified information on secret surveillance programs. The government claimed it was for the purpose of disclosure.
>
> For disclosing classified information on FBI wiretaps to a blogger, FBI translator named Shamai Leibowitz was charged under the Espionage Act.
>
> Pfc. Bradley Manning was charged with multiple violations of the Espionage Act in July 2010 after disclosing US government information to WikiLeaks.
>
> Stephen Kim, a former State Department contractor, was charged in August 2010 for revealing classified information on North Korea to Fox News reporter James Rosen. (Rosen was labeled an "aider, abettor and co-conspirator" in the leak.)

In December 2010, a former CIA officer, Jeffrey Sterling, was charged under the Espionage Act after he communicated with *New York Times* reporter James Risen about Iran's nuclear program in the 1990s. (The Obama Justice Department has fought in the courts to have a judge require Risen to testify against Sterling.)

John Kiriakou, a former CIA officer, was charged under the Espionage Act in January 2012 after he shared information related to a rendition operation with reporter Matthew Cole.[74]

The eighth is Edward Snowden.

Reportergate

The Obama administration went a bridge too far when it began hunting down media leaks by hacking into a reporter's e-mail accounts. When the Stephen Kim investigation reached into Fox News reporter James Rosen's e-mails, it set off a chain of events that revealed how far Obama was willing to go in outdoing Nixon.

Kim was passing classified information about North Korea's nuclear program to Rosen.[75] Holder recognized the leak after reading an article by Rosen about North Korea in 2009. Through a secret subpoena signed by Holder, they tracked Rosen's movements, phone calls, and e-mails since 2009.[76] After the Justice Department had built enough evidence against Kim by secretly stalking him, they needed to get *admissible* evidence, and after being turned down by two judges, they finally found a compliant judge to issue a secret search warrant.[77] Then the scandal avalanched. Later reports revealed that the Obama spy machine's phone record data acquisitions "included 'thousands and thousands' of calls in and out of the news organization [the Associated Press]."[78]

Meanwhile, what was the Obama administration's legal theory for this chilling and deplorable attack on the freedom of the press? The Espionage Act of 1917. The Act, which, as discussed, was only used against publications as a perversion of its intent, criminalized leaking classified information and was written so opaquely as to allow reporters who receive such information to be listed as co-conspirators or aiders or abettors. In its application for the search warrant of Rosen's e-mails, the government told a federal judge that Rosen had conspired to commit *espionage* when he *received true information*. This legal reasoning has supposedly been dead since the Pentagon Papers case.

Snowden and PRISM

Amid a growing post-September 11th intelligence network that relies heavily on private contractors to supplement government work, Edward Snowden singularly emerges as a contractor who posed an inherent bureaucratic risk to Obama's spymasters: He had access to troves of classified files on the NSA's warrantless spying programs, and the personal outrage at America's secret intelligence gathering.[79] In June 2013, after spending months having limited and encrypted communications with Glenn Greenwald of the *Guardian* and Laura Poitras, a documentary filmmaker, to build trust, Snowden released thousands of NSA files, many of which were marked Top Secret and had the most limited circulation among government documents within the federal government.[80] The government brought out the tool of the 1917 Espionage Act to go after Snowden.

Greenwald wasted no time publishing the documents and a series of articles that analyzed the NSA's unprecedented mass eavesdropping on roughly 113 *million* American persons (almost one-third of the U.S. population) without a warrant or probable cause.[81] Big Brother was alive and well in the revelations as many learned that U.S. citizens and residents, without any connection to terrorism activity or persons linked thereto, but merely customers of Verizon, the telecom giant, were also swept up in the NSA's program.[82]

PRISM, the NSA moniker for its mass surveillance program post-President's Surveillance Program (PSP) and FISA Amendments Act, hardly enters our analysis without predecessors—government spying programs on a large scale were revealed through the 1970s Church Committee findings of illegal and unconstitutional domestic eavesdropping. Though long thought dead since the Church Committee, they existed, and PRISM follows in their footsteps. Almost immediately after the 9/11 attacks, George W. Bush authorized the PSP, code name STELLARWIND, to monitor without warrant and in secret the electronic communications of millions of American persons.[83]

In 2005, after withholding the story for a year, the *New York Times* ignited a scandal when it reported the existence of one subset of the PSP, the Terrorist Surveillance Program, surveying mere thousands.[84*] In February 2007, Bush did not renew his PSP amid public clamor over privacy concerns and serious blows to the Bush legal regime surrounding its secret eavesdropping program in the summer of 2006.[85]

After turning over the documents in Hong Kong, Snowden quickly hid himself until he could make an Aeroflot trip to Moscow and seek asylum from other nations.[86] On June 23, Snowden left Hong Kong; the day before, the U.S. government unsealed a criminal complaint charging Snowden with, among other crimes, espionage.[87] The very nature of Snowden's leak, lifting the veil on a massive intelligence-gathering network that attacked constitutional limits, moved the caught-red-handed feds to charge him.

PRISM supplemented the NSA's already robust collection of communications, gathering information at servers from several major U.S. providers, including Microsoft, Yahoo, Google, Facebook, PalTalk, AOL, Skype, YouTube, and Apple.[88] The named service providers denied that the NSA via PRISM had "direct" access to their servers and later revised public statements on the matter specifically to note that access came only when specific orders were issued by the courts, a much clearer sign that information dissemination, if any, was involuntary.[89] The criminal

---

* Interestingly, Snowden cites the *Times*'s decision to withhold the story as a reason he approached the *Guardian* instead of the Gray Lady: He felt that withholding from the public such information for so long a time undermined the journalistic integrity and values behind traditional press and sought out a contemporary to which he could leak the documents. See Ewen MacAskill, "Edward Snowden: How the Spy Story of the Age Leaked Out," *Guardian* (UK), June 11, 2013, http://www.theguardian.com/world/2013/jun/11/edward-snowden-nsa-whistleblower-profile; Peter Maass, "Q. & A.: Edward Snowden Speaks to Peter Maass," *New York Times*, August 13, 2010, http://www.nytimes.com/2013/08/18/ magazine/snowden-maass-transcript.html.

complaint against Snowden twice charged him under the Espionage Act of 1917 for illegally leaking national defense and classified intelligence communications.[90]

Court Decisions

In other domestic courts, however, President Obama has fared more favorably than his predecessor in acquiring favorable judicial decisions and avoiding bad ones.

In the 2010 case *Holder v. Humanitarian Law Project*, Chief Justice Roberts opined for the Court that the material support statute, as amended by the Intelligence Reform and Terrorism Prevention Act of 2004, was not impermissibly vague as applied to a different organization than the Kurdish Workers' Party.[91] This decision effectively reversed the declaration of invalidity found in *Humanitarian Law Project et al., v. Ashcroft* because a facial challenge rests on the premise that there is no set of circumstances in which the law could be found valid based on the asserted claim. The Supreme Court's holding is the equivalent of saying the First Amendment is all right for some groups but not for all.

All is not good news for statists, however. In the 2013 case *In re National Security Letter*, U.S. District Court Judge Susan Illston in the Northern District of California ruled that the NSL provision of the PATRIOT Act "suffer[s] from significant constitutional infirmities. Further, those infirmities cannot be avoided by 'conforming' the language of the statute to satisfy the Constitution's demands, because the existing statutory language and the legislative history of the statutes block that result."[92] Accordingly, the court invalidated the entire review sections of the NSL part of the statute on First Amendment grounds, thus invalidating federal agent–written search warrants.[93]

The FISA Court Decisions

Secret Laws Uncovered: Declassified FISA Court Opinions

Before Snowden's massive intelligence leak, the federal courts had begun hearing suits aimed at forcing the Justice Department and NSA to disclose FISA Court cases where the government applied for access to information and the FISA Court granted the application.[94] The Freedom of Information Act lawsuits came from civil liberties and digital rights groups—ACLU, NYCLU, Electronic Frontier Foundation (EFF)— and sought to shed sunlight on the lack of transparency in the Justice Department and NSA's wiretapping procedures and results.[95]

The Justice Department announced in September 2013 it would declassify hundreds of documents on the broad array of the NSA's domestic surveillance programs, all aimed at counterterrorism investigations and limited in scope to investigating terrorism or suspected terrorists, by releasing FISA Court opinions and orders and some government submissions and compliance reports to the FISA Court.[96] The response came after a federal judge in Oakland ordered the Justice Department to disclose documents, not as a voluntary move by the Obama administration.[97]

Among the newly released documents were several FISA Court opinions that created a legal timeline of the NSA's authorization for warrantless wiretapping after the Bush-era program was revealed. Beginning in 2006, the FISA Court authorized the NSA to gather telephony metadata (data on calls and callers that resembles the envelope of a letter—address and name only, not contents of the communication itself) information without a warrant based on the information's "non-content" nature.[98] The FISA Court created a framework to allow for non-content data collection and privacy protection within which the NSA could operate in its data collection efforts.[99]

The very nature of the FISA Court undermines much of its ability to oversee effectively the government's actions taken in response to its orders and opinions, and never so clearly than in the subsequent opinions and orders also revealed in the Justice Department declassification of documents. By 2008, the FISA Court released a supplemental opinion, clarifying that the NSA had the authority to collect the telephony data sought under the PATRIOT Act's revision to the original FISA statute.[100]

The reason for the clarification became known in the 2009 and 2011 opinions by the FISA Court. Compliance incidents were reported by the

NSA; data that had no relation to counterterrorism investigations was caught in NSA's dragnet; and analysts in the NSA were cross-referencing non-content data with other databases that never should legally mingle with the fruits of warrantless data gathering.[101] The FISA Court found itself caught in a series of oversights, misrepresentations, and outright lies by the government as it tried to justify its actions to the court.

Finally, the FISA Court ordered a complete review of the NSA program, its oversight and compliance procedures, and any incidents where violations of the 2006 framework occurred. In 2011, just two years after that order, FISA Court declared the NSA's upstream data collection (a sibling of PRISM as discussed, *supra*) a violation of the Fourth Amendment.[102] The agency had overstepped its legal bounds severely, acquiring thousands upon thousands of communications of persons whose Fourth Amendment rights shielded their data from acquisition prior to a warrant.

The Lawfulness of the FISA Court Revisited

Under FISA's watch, "the NSA has captured and stored the *content* of trillions of telephone conversations, texts and emails, and can access that content at the press of a few computer keys."[103] Since its inception, the FISA Court has been the prime example of a slippery slope. The very legal standard the FISA Act forces upon it has proven disastrously malleable: "In 30 years, from 1979 to 2009, the legal standard for searching and seizing private communications—the bar that the Constitution requires the government to meet—was lowered by Congress from probable cause of crime to probable cause of being an agent of a foreign power to probable cause of being a foreign person to probable cause of communicating with a foreign person."[104]

The judges of the court can keep no record of proceedings before them and can use only NSA pens and phones during proceedings.[105] The court is plagued with both systemic and constitutional problems that relate to a fundamental bedrock principle of American judicial process: The adversarial system.

Courts decide questions of law and fact. The source of those facts is determined by assessing the validity and credibility of witnesses and evidence presented by two or more opposing sides in order to arrive at a true, valid conclusion. The adversarial process, the process of competition between lawyers and parties in any case, allows for testing the veracity of facts in a case and scrutiny of claims. The problem with the FISA Court is that there is absolutely no adversarial process.

This issue is a double-edged sword. First, it corrupts the truth-seeking function of courts, and second, it violates the constitutional requirement of a case or controversy.

As to determinations of veracity or falsity, without adversity, assertions by the government go unchallenged, and a judge is left without any basis on which to contest the government's assertions. The lack of factual adversity reduces the function of the court to determining matters of law. By being limited in this manner, the court is essentially reduced to applying the law to whatever factual hypothetical the NSA wishes to submit to the court as a government affidavit. As was pointed out by FISA Court Chief Judge Reggie B. Walton, a main problem is that the court can get facts *only* from the NSA.[106] This is the same agency that, as discussed earlier, Judge Bates admonished in an opinion for lying *in FISA Court submissions* to an extent that is criminal. This lack of adversity corrupts the truth-seeking function of the courts of law—an ethical and legal duty assigned to judges.

Realizing the obvious issues of truth-seeking that come from a court blindly accepting the assertions of one party without even hearing from the other, not to mention the potential abuses of judicial power that could arise out of such a scheme, the Framers of the Constitution "wrote into Article III of the Constitution the absolute prerequisite of the existence of a case or controversy before the jurisdiction of any federal court could be invoked."[107]

The Supreme Court has guarded this requirement consistently since the adoption of the Constitution, and the decisions of the Supreme Court have circumscribed what is a case or controversy. The Case or

Controversy Clause typically relates to the constitutional requirement of proving injury-in-fact to demonstrate standing. However, the concern here is even more fundamental. The FISA Court doesn't even hear controversies or cases. The "actual controversy" rule means that cases which are unripe (no controversy has yet arisen), moot (controversy is resolved), or in which the opinion would be tantamount to an advisory opinion may not be adjudicated. Advisory opinions are like those issued by the OLC of the Justice Department—they are untested by legal adversity and are positive statements meant to guide, not to resolve, a matter at hand.

Without even the contemplation of an adverse party, matters brought before the FISA Court (it would be insincere to refer to them as cases) are advisory. Think about it: There is no criminal defendant or *ex parte* proceeding with the party in an adverse state; there is no civil suit with a plaintiff or a defendant with an amount in controversy. There is the government, submitting uncontestable facts, and receiving an opinion which rubber-stamps its findings.

This reasoning works in reverse as well: If the FISA Court doesn't rubber-stamp the government's submissions, then "those court orders are non-binding and the government has ignored them."[108] As I have previously argued: "Unenforceable rulings that may be disregarded by another branch of the government are not judicial decisions at all, but impermissible advisory opinions prohibited by the Framers."[109] A non-binding opinion, issued in secret to one party, based solely on its version of the facts, with no test of credibility, is mere advice and an opinion in the literal sense of the word, not the legal sense of a disposition of a valid claim.

The FISA Court suffers from irreconcilable issues and is inculcated with Defense Department bureaucrats and administration officials who care nothing for civil liberties or oaths to uphold the Constitution or to tell the truth in court submissions. Obama's track record on privacy is even worse than his predecessor's. Overall, the United States has become the dreaded Orwellian world of Oceania:

So fierce was the anger in Berlin over suspicions that American intelligence had tapped into [German Prime Minister Angela] Merkel's cellphone that Elmar Brok of Germany, the chairman of the European Parliament's foreign affairs committee and a pillar of trans-Atlantic exchanges since 1984, spoke Friday of America's security establishment as a creepy "state within a state."

Since Sept. 11, 2001, he said, "the balance between freedom and security has been lost."[110]

He was mostly right: The constitutional bias in favor of freedom, at the expense of even the state's police power, has been eroded over the past century and has culminated in the current, creepy super-state.

Conclusion

I s the battle to retain personal liberty in a free society a losing one?
The events discussed in this work and the regular, consistent, and
systematic manner in which they have unfolded throughout our history would seem to cause a prudent student of these times to answer in
the affirmative. And yet, because freedom springs naturally from every
human heart, it would seem as well that the government could never
fully eradicate it, via war or pestilence or totalitarian systems.

In America, the government's swift brutality toward human freedom can deter even the brave. Jefferson himself predicted that in the
long march of history, power and order would become concentrated
in the government, and the personal liberty of individuals would be
diminished.

In this book, I have attempted to demonstrate not the inevitability of
Jefferson's prediction, but the need for eternal vigilance—another warning he gave us. We have seen how each president who chose to do so was
easily able to use the behaviors of his predecessors plus fear and loathing
to justify his own extra-constitutional behavior.

That rewarded and unchecked behavior needs to stop and remain
stopped. We are entitled to a government that stays within the confines

of the Constitution, and the Constitution was written to keep the government off our backs and out of our homes and away from our telephones and computers and bank accounts, and to keep the government transparent. A secret government knows no bounds in its exercise of secret powers, and it will use secretly exercised powers to acquire more power.

We have seen and have had enough of this.

We need to see courage and understanding. I sincerely hope that this book will stimulate both a grasp of the magnitude of the problem and a resolution to solve it. The problem is a government that does not believe in any natural or constitutional or legal restraints upon itself. The solution is to have people in government who do believe in the Natural Law; and to have systems in place to change and diminish the government, not grow it.

Because freedom lies in our hearts, while we live, it lives. But it must do more than just lie there.

Acknowledgments

My acknowledgment here of those who fortified this work is necessarily inadequate. Many friends and colleagues have helped me solidify the arguments advanced in this book. Some displayed great patience and tolerance as it dominated my work and influenced theirs, some challenged its conclusions and compelled me to strengthen my arguments, and some participated in its actual construction.

The thesis of this work was originally suggested to me by my ideological colleague, Llewellyn H. Rockwell, Jr. Lew's leadership of the Mises Institute has produced some of the finest scholarship on liberty in the United States today, and I was thrilled to take his idea and see where the research would lead us. For the germ of an idea, and for unwavering friendship and support, I am in Lew's debt.

My executive assistant at the Fox News Channel, Mary Kate Cribbin, and my personal producer at Fox, Michael Daniels, himself a talented lawyer, patiently and happily tolerated the endless diversions and schedule changes caused by my efforts to write this book. I am deeply grateful to them.

My team of tireless researchers labored very long and often tedious hours as we examined the law and verified the facts in the hundreds of constitutional episodes discussed in this book. Alexander Yarbrough, Ryan Merola, and Alfred Falzone, III were the able law students who worked as a team headed by my chief researcher, Randal John Meyer. Under Randal's superb work ethic and able leadership of his fellow students, they all continued to keep me very busy with mountains of finely distilled research to review.

My colleagues at Fox, with whom I share professional goals and aspirations, have always been a source of strength at providing the sounding boards needed to anticipate the reaction of many of my controversial views. Executive Vice President Bill Shine, Vice President and General Counsel Dianne Brandi, Vice President Suzanne Scott, my former Executive Producer at Fox and now a CNBC superstar producer Gary Schreier, Charles Gasparino who is the best investigative journalist in our business, and my other dear on-air colleagues, David Asman, Bret Baier, Bill Hemmer, Elizabeth MacDonald, Geraldo Rivera, Shepard Smith, Chris Stirewalt, Stewart Varney, and Juan Williams have all directly or indirectly encouraged this work.

Among my most effective cheerleaders is my editor at Thomas Nelson, and now HarperCollins, Kristen Parrish. This is my ninth book to be filtered through Kristen's gentle but firm hands. She is the incarnation of patience.

My new colleagues at Brooklyn Law School have given me the intellectual sustenance and professional platform to address this undertaking and its companion work teaching constitutional jurisprudence to very bright law students. At some point I discussed much of this work with my respected academic colleagues in constitutional theory, Professors William Araiza, Joel Gora, Susan Herman, and Nelson Tebbe. None of these great scholars agree with all my views, yet all of them continue to encourage all my work.

My happy teaching at Brooklyn would never have come about but for the rejuvenation of my college friendship with the now legal powerhouse who is Brooklyn's new Dean, Nicholas Allard. Nick channeled much of his boundless energy in support of my intellectual passion—examining the behavior of the government for bright future lawyers through the prisms of the Natural Law and the Constitution. His friendship and support and our new professional collaboration have been a gift.

I am indebted to Sen. Rand Paul, who took the time to read an early draft of this book and to make serious constructive criticisms. He is a champion of personal liberty who is currently the U.S. Senate's greatest defender of the Constitution. I am personally honored and deeply grateful that he has written the foreword to this work.

Of course, my work would have been known to only a few without the now nearly seventeen-year platform that my boss at the Fox News Channel, Roger Ailes, has given me. Roger is a giant and a genius and a man of endless generosity and understanding, whose faith in me has changed my life for the good, beyond my wildest dreams; and those life changes made this book—like its predecessors—possible. Quite simply, I love Roger; even when he takes me to the Fox News woodshed.

Yet, my happy dreams turned dark last year when Jim Sheil, my alter ego to whose memory this book is dedicated, died suddenly on March 19th 2013, as we were working on this book. Jim and I shared much of our lives with each other. Among that which we shared was a love of the printed word. Yet our philosophies and politics were like oil and water. He once joked that editing my books made him feel as though he were Hillary Clinton editing the works of Ron Paul. Jim's brilliance made all my work better, his fairness made me anticipate challenges, and his faith in me made me a better person. His life cut short devastated me, but gave me an editor and an advocate in Heaven. May the angels deliver him into Paradise, if they haven't done so already.

Notes

Chapter 1

1. Chester James Antieau, "Natural Rights and the Founding Fathers—The Virginians," *Washington & Lee Law Review* 17, no. 1 (1960): 50.
2. Ibid., 43.
3. The Declaration of Independence (1776).
4. Gordon S. Wood, *The Creation of the American Republic: 1776–1787* (Chapel Hill: University of North Carolina Press, 1998), 8, 14, 283–4, 289, 292, 348, 601–2, discussing the role of Hobbes and Locke in influencing the Founding Fathers and their philosophies; "Foundations of American Government," USHistory.org, http://www.ushistory.org/gov/2.asp.
5. U.S. Const. amend. IX.
6. Griswold v. Connecticut, 381 U.S. 479 (1965); Pierce v. Soc'y of Sisters, 268 U.S. 510 (1925).
7. John Locke, *The Two Treatises of Civil Government*, ed. Thomas Hollis (London: A. Millar et al., 1764), bk. 2, ch. 2, §4, http://oll.libertyfund.org/?option=com_ staticxt&staticfile=show.php%3Ftitle=222.
8. Ibid., bk. 2, §6.
9. Thomas Hobbes, *The Leviathan* (1651), bk. 1, ch. 8.
10. "[T]hough in the state of nature he hath such a[n] [unlimited] right, yet the enjoyment of it is very uncertain, and constantly exposed to the invasion of others: for all being kings as much as he, every man his equal, and the greater part no strict observers of equity and justice, the enjoyment of the property he has in this state is very unsafe, very unsecure. This makes him willing to quit a condition, which, however free, is full of fears and continual dangers: and it is not without reason, that he seeks out, and is willing to join in society with others, who are already united, or have a mind to unite, for the mutual preservation of their lives, liberties and estates, which I call by the general name, *property.*"

Locke, *Two Treatises of Civil Government*, bk. 2, §123, emphasis in original; see also bk. 2, §22.

11. Locke, *Two Treatises of Civil Government*, bk. 2, §126; see also, bk. 2, §§124–5, describing the lack of a written law and a judiciary.

12. Ibid., bk. 2, §§88, 127, 131.

13. Ibid., bk. 2, §131. Whether the consent is tacit, express, or implied is outside the scope of this work.

14. Lysander Spooner, *No Treason*, no. 1 (1867), http://lysanderspooner.org/node/44.

15. "George the Third called our ancestors traitors for what they did at that time. But they were not traitors in fact, whatever he or his laws may have called them. They were not traitors in fact, because they betrayed nobody, and broke faith with nobody. They were his equals, owing him no allegiance, obedience, nor any other duty, except such as they owed to mankind at large. Their political relations with him had been purely voluntary. They had never pledged their faith to him that they would continue these relations any longer than it should please them to do so; and therefore they broke no faith in parting with him. They simply exercised their natural right of saying to him, and to the English people, that they were under no obligation to continue their political [connection] with them, and that, for reasons of their own, they chose to dissolve it. What was true of our ancestors, is true of revolutionists in general. . . . This principle was a true one in 1776. It is a true one now." Spooner, *No Treason*, no. 1, §§13–14; ibid., describing a legal defense to treason.

16. "The difficulty is, what ought to be looked upon as a tacit consent, and how far it binds, i.e. how far any one shall be looked on to have consented, and thereby submitted to any government, where he has made no expressions of it at all. And to this I say, that every man, that hath any possessions, or enjoyment, of any part of the dominions of any government, doth thereby give his tacit consent, and is as far forth obliged to obedience to the laws of that government, during such enjoyment, as any one under it; whether this his possession be of land, to him and his heirs for ever, or a lodging only for a week; or whether it be barely travelling freely on the highway; and in effect, it reaches as far as the very being of any one within the territories of that government." Locke, *Two Treatises of Civil Government*, bk. 2, §119.

17. Murray Rothbard, "War, Peace, and the State," *Standard*, April 1963, https://archive.org/details/WarPeaceAndTheState. "The fundamental axiom of libertarian theory is that no one may threaten or commit violence ("aggress") against another man's person or property. Violence may be employed only against the man who commits such violence; that is, only defensively against the aggressive violence of another. In short, no violence may be employed against a non-aggressor. Here is the fundamental rule from which can be deduced the entire *corpus* of libertarian theory." Ibid., 2–3, emphasis in original.

18. Ibid.

19. Ibid.; see also n1.

20. Ibid.

21. "All State wars, therefore, involve increased aggression against the State's own taxpayers, and almost all State wars (all, in modern warfare) involve the maximum aggression (murder) against the innocent civilians ruled by the enemy

State. On the other hand, revolutions are generally financed voluntarily and may pinpoint their violence to the State rulers, and private conflicts may confine their violence to the actual criminals. The libertarian must, therefore, conclude that, while some revolutions and some private conflicts *may* be legitimate, State wars are *always* to be condemned." Ibid., emphasis in original.

22. Thomas Aquinas, *Summa Theologica, Second Part: Treatise on Law* (1265–74), 2274–75, http://www.ccel.org/ccel/aquinas/summa.pdf.
23. Ibid., 2268–79.
24. Locke, *Two Treatises of Civil Government*, bk. 2, §§4, 22.
25. William Blackstone, *Commentaries on the Laws of England, Book the First* (Oxford: Clarendon Press, 1765), 121, emphasis added, https://archive.org/details/BlackstoneVolumeI.
26. Randolph Bourne, "The State," AntiWar.com, http://www.antiwar.com/bourne.php.
27. Ibid.
28. Ibid.
29. Andrew P. Napolitano, *Theodore and Woodrow: How Two American Presidents Destroyed Constitutional Freedom* (Nashville: Thomas Nelson, 2012); Andrew P. Napolitano, *Lies the Government Told You: Myth, Power, and Deception in American History* (Nashville: Thomas Nelson, 2010).
30. Korematsu v. United States, 323 U.S. 214 (1944).
31. Abrams v. United States, 250 U.S. 616 (1919) (Clarke, J.).
32. The Overman Act, 40 Stat. 556 (1918); see *Opinions of the Judge Advocate General of the Army: April 1, 1917 to December 31 [1918]*, vol. 2 (Washington, DC: Government Printing Office, 1919), 605–6. "Like its predecessor, it delegated to the President virtually unrestricted authority with respect to the administrative machinery necessary to meet the war needs of the Federal Government. And like its predecessor, the effect was to give the President complete control over the functions, duties and powers of the executive agencies of the Federal Government insofar as matters relating to the conduct of the war were concerned." Nathan Grundstein, *Presidential Delegation of Authority in Wartime* (Pittsburgh: University of Pittsburgh Press, 1961), 15–16.
33. Glenn Greenwald, "NSA Collecting Phone Records of Millions of Verizon Customers Daily," *Guardian* (UK), June 5, 2013, http://www.theguardian.com/world/2013/jun/06/nsa-phone-records-verizon-court-order.
34. State v. Shack, 277 A.2d 369 (N.J. 1971). The *Shack* court held that migrant workers cannot alienate their own right to association by their contracting to work under circumstances which would give rise to such an alienation, such as contracting to work and live on land where the owner may exercise a right to exclude government assistance workers.
35. "This right to property in one's own body and its standing room must be considered *a priori* (or indisputably) justified by proponent and opponent alike." Hans-Hermann Hoppe, "Rothbardian Ethics," LewRockwell.com, 2002, http://www.lewrockwell.com/hoppe/hoppe7.html.
36. Andrew Byers, *Faith Without Illusions: Following Jesus as a Cynic-Saint* (Downers Grove: InterVarsity Press, 2011), 53.

37. "*Charity* gives every Man a Title to so much out of another's Plenty, as will keep him from extream want, where he has no means to subsist otherwise." Cited in George C. Christie, "The Defense of Necessity Considered from the Legal and Moral Points of View," *Duke Law Journal* 48, no. 5 (March 1999): 1010n183, emphasis in original; Locke, *Two Treatises of Civil Government*, bk. 1, §42.

Chapter 2

1. Douglas G. Smith, "An Analysis of Two Federal Structures: The Articles of Confederation and the Constitution," *San Diego Law Review* 34, no. 1 (1997): 249.
2. Alfred W. Blumrosen and Steven M. Blumrosen, "Restoring the Congressional Duty to Declare War," *Rutgers Law Review* 63, no. 2 (2011): 420.
3. Ibid.
4. Ibid.
5. David P. Szatmary, *Shays' Rebellion: The Making of an Agrarian Insurrection* (Cambridge, MA: University of Massachusetts Press, 1984).
6. U.S. Const. art. I, §8.
7. Ibid.
8. U.S. Const. art. I, §8, cl. 12.
9. David Ackerman and Richard Grimmett, *Declarations of War and Authorizations for the Use of Military Force: Historical Background and Legal Implications*, CRS Report RL31133 (Washington, DC: Library of Congress, Congressional Research Service, 2003), CRS-2, 4, updated January 14, 2014.
10. Ibid., CRS-6.
11. Youngstown Sheet & Tube Co. v. Sawyer, 103 F. Supp. 569 (D.D.C. 1952), *aff'd*, 343 U.S. 579 (enjoining President Truman from seizing steel mills during the Korean War pursuant to Exec. Order 10340).
12. War Powers Resolution of 1973, 50 U.S.C. §§1541–48 (2012).
13. Blumrosen and Blumrosen, "Restoring the Congressional Duty to Declare War," 412, emphasis added.
14. John R. Vile, *The Constitutional Convention of 1787: A Comprehensive Encyclopedia of America's Founding*, vol. 1 (Santa Barbara: ABC-CLIO, 2005), 224.
15. U.S. Const. art. II, §2, cl. 1.
16. Saikrishna Prakash, "Unleashing the Dogs of War: What the Constitution Means by 'Declare War,'" *Cornell Law Review* 93, no. 1 (2007): 51.
17. Ibid., 63.
18. Erwin Chemerinsky, *Constitutional Law: Principles and Policies*, ed. Vicki Been et al., 4th ed. (New York: Aspen Publishers, 2011), 290.
19. The Prize Cases, 67 U.S. 635, 668 (1863).
20. Prakash, "Unleashing the Dogs of War," 93.
21. "Comment: Congressional Control of Presidential War-making Under the War Powers Act: The Status of a Legislative Veto After Chadha," *University of Pennsylvania Law Review* 132, no. 5 (1984): 1217.

Chapter 3

1. John Bakeless, *Turncoats, Traitors, and Heroes*, 4th ed. (New York: Da Capo Press, 1959), 15–16.

2. "His espionage had begun months before the war broke out; but no one seriously suspected anything until after he gave his mistress the ciphered letter." Ibid., 11.

3. Ibid., 11–16, describing how his treachery was discovered; 11, describing his positions.

4. Glenn P. Hastedt and Steven W. Guerrier, eds., *Spies, Wiretaps, and Secret Operations: An Encyclopedia of American Espionage*, vol. 1 (Santa Barbara: ABC-CLIO, LLC, 2011), 192.

5. "First Traitor a Boston Doctor," *Washington Times*, June 26, 2008, http://www .washingtontimes.com/news/2008/jun/26/first-traitor-a-boston-doctor/; see *Journals of the Continental Congress—Articles of War*, vol. 2, ed. Worthington C. Ford et al. (Washington, DC: Government Printing Office, 1905), 111–23, (hereinafter cited as JCC II), http://avalon.law.yale.edu/18th_century/contcong_06-30-75.asp; "Congress had foreseen such cases. Article XXVIII provided that anyone communicating with the enemy should suffer such punishment as a court-martial might direct." Bakeless, *Turncoats, Traitors, and Heroes*, 19.

6. Hastedt and Guerrier, *Spies, Wiretaps, and Secret Operations*, 192.

7. JCC II; "Article LI limited the punishment a court-martial could inflict. It could give penalties of thirty-nine lashes or a fine of two months' pay and it could cashier the offender and that was all!" Bakeless, *Turncoats, Traitors, and Heroes*, 19.

8. *Journals of the Continental Congress—Articles of War*, ed. Worthington C. Ford et al. (Washington, DC: Government Printing Office, 1905), 111–23, (hereinafter cited as JCC), http://avalon.law.yale.edu/18th_century/ contcong_09-20-76.asp; Hastedt and Guerrier, *Spies, Wiretaps, and Secret Operations*, 192.

9. For example, "Paul Revere's American spy ring in Boston had noticed some suspicious leaks." Bakeless, *Turncoats, Traitors, and Heroes*, 16.

10. Central Intelligence Agency, "Intelligence in the War of Independence," last modified September 5, 2013 (hereinafter cited as CIA, "Intelligence in the War of Independence"), https://www.cia.gov/library/center-for-the-study-of-intelligence/csi-publications/books-and-monographs/ intelligence/.

11. "The Secret Committee, for instance, sought military information and aid." Ed Crews, "Spies and Scouts, Secret Writings, and Sympathetic Citizens," *Colonial Williamsburg Journal* 26, no. 2 (2004), http://www.history.org/foundation/ journal/summer04/spies.cfm.

12. CIA, "Intelligence in the War of Independence."

13. Ibid.

14. Hastedt and Guerrier, *Spies, Wiretaps, and Secret Operations*, 191; CIA, "Intelligence in the War of Independence," for contrasting viewpoint.

15. CIA, "Intelligence in the War of Independence."

16. Ibid., emphasis added.

17. Ibid.

18. Hastedt and Guerrier, *Spies, Wiretaps, and Secret Operations*, 191.

19. See below, the section The Alien and Sedition Acts of 1798.

20. Charles Francis Adams, ed., *The Works of John Adams*, vol. 1 (Boston: Little, Brown and Co., 1856), 224–25, http://oll.libertyfund.org/?option=com_ staticxt&staticfile=show.php%3Ftitle=2099&Itemid=27.

21. Ibid.

22. Ibid., 224.

23. Compare Adams, *Works of John Adams*, 225, "[W]ho shall levy war against any of the said colonies within the same, or be adherent to the king of Great Britain, or other enemies of the said colonies, or any of them, within the same, giving to him or them aid and comfort, are guilty of treason against such colony," with the Treason Act, 1351, 25 Edw. 3, c. 2, declaring treason to consist of levying war and adhering to the enemies of the king of Britain.

24. Adams, *Works of John Adams*, 225.

25. James Madison, *Federalist* No. 43, Library of Congress, January 23, 1788, http://thomas.loc.gov/home/histdox/fed_43.html.

26. James Willard Hurst, *The Law of Treason in the United States: Collected Essays*, no. 12, Contributions in American History (Westport, CT: Greenwood, 1971), 83, http://www.constitution.org/cmt/jwh/jwh_treason.htm. "[I]t used the familiar terms of the Statute of Edward III, with a suggestion of the evidentiary requirements of the Statute of 7 William III." Ibid.

27. Carlton F. W. Larson, "The Forgotten Constitutional Law of Treason and the Enemy Combatant Problem," *University of Pennsylvania Law Review* 154, no. 4 (2006), arguing that the Treason Clause applies to U.S. citizen-enemy combatants; Randal John Meyer, "The Twin Perils of the al-Aulaqi Case: The Treason Clause and the Equal Protection Clause," *Brooklyn Law Review* 79, no. 1 (2013).

28. Meyer, "Twin Perils," 234.

29. Ryan Patrick Alford, "The Rule of Law at the Crossroads: Consequences of Targeted Killing of Citizens," *Utah Law Review*, no. 4 (2011): 1203, 1205–6, 1215; Meyer, "Twin Perils," 237 nn50–52 and accompanying text.

30. The Treason Act, 1351, 25 Edw. 3, c. 2; United States v. Rahman, 189 F.3d 88, 112 (2d Cir 1999) (per curiam).

31. Hurst, *The Law of Treason in the United States*, 143.

32. Meyer, "Twin Perils," 238nn54–55; "Mindful of their status as traitors while fighting the rule of England, they sought to eliminate the potential for abusive prosecution of treason against groups with public grievances by including systemic, constitutional restrictions." Ibid.

33. U.S. Const. art. III, §3.

34. James Madison, *Federalist* No. 51, Library of Congress, February 6, 1788, http://thomas.loc.gov/home/histdox/fed_51.html.

35. Hurst, *The Law of Treason in the United States*, 155. "[T]he tradition expressed in the First Amendment is a much broader one." Ibid.

36. U.S. Const. amend. I.

37. "Thus the historic background of the treason clause furnishes specific evidence rather than a priori reasoning for assigning a higher value to the free and nonviolent play of controversy over public issues than to the broad prevention of possible danger to security of social institutions. Especially does it underline the importance of preventing the use of the criminal law as an instrument of competition for political power." Hurst, *The Law of Treason in the United States*, 165–66.

38. Andrew P. Napolitano, *Lies the Government Told You* (Nashville: Thomas Nelson, 2010), 2–9, describing the deplorable conditions of slaves owned by some Founding Fathers.

39. William Shakespeare, *Julius Caesar*, act 3, scene 1, http://shakespeare.mit.edu/julius_caesar/full.html.
40. Stanley Elkins and Eric McKitrick, *The Age of Federalism* (Oxford: Oxford University Press, 1993), 462; Gordon S. Wood, *Empire of Liberty: A History of the Early Republic, 1789–1815* (Oxford: Oxford University Press, 2009), 134–35.
41. Elkins and McKitrick, *The Age of Federalism*, 478.
42. Joseph J. Ellis, *His Excellency, George Washington* (New York: Random House, 2005), 225.
43. "Jan. 1, 1781: Mutiny of the Pennsylvania Line," History.com, http://www.history.com/this-day-in-history/mutiny-of-the-pennsylvania-line.
44. Israel Shreve to George Washington, January 20, 1781, in *George Washington Papers*, Series 4, General Correspondence, 1697–1799 (Washington, DC: Library of Congress), http://memory.loc.gov/cgi-bin/ampage?collId=mgw4&fileName=gwpage074.db&recNum=522.
45. Ibid.
46. Ibid.
47. Ron Chernow, *Alexander Hamilton* (New York: Penguin Press, 2004), 475–76; William Hogeland, *The Whiskey Rebellion: George Washington, Alexander Hamilton, and the Frontier Rebels Who Challenged America's Newfound Sovereignty* (New York: Scribner, 2006), 189.
48. T. S. Eliot, "The Hollow Men," ArtofEurope.com, http://www.artofeurope.com/eliot/eli2.htm.
49. Elkins and McKitrick, *The Age of Federalism*, 482.
50. Hurst, *The Law of Treason in the United States*, 269.
51. Geoffrey R. Stone, *Perilous Times: Free Speech in Wartime, from the Sedition Act of 1798 to the War on Terrorism* (New York: W. W. Norton, 2004), 21.
52. U.S. Congress, Senate, Washington's Farewell Address to the People of the United States, 106th Cong., 2d Sess., 2000, S. Doc. 106–21, p. 6, http://www.gpo.gov/fdsys/pkg/GPO-CDOC-106sdoc21/pdf.
53. Stone, *Perilous Times*, 21.
54. Ibid.
55. Ibid.
56. Ibid.
57. Ibid., 22.
58. John Adams, Special Session Message, May 16, 1797, the American Presidency Project, University of California, Santa Barbara, www.presidency.ucsb.edu/ws/index.php?pid=65636.
59. William Stinchcombe, "The Diplomacy of the WXYZ Affair," *William and Mary Quarterly* 34, no. 4, 3rd series (1977).
60. Ibid.
61. Ibid.
62. Ibid.
63. Ibid.
64. Ibid.
65. Randolph Bourne, "The State," AntiWar.com, http://www.antiwar.com/bourne.php.
66. Stone, *Perilous Times*, 21; 5 Cong. Ch. 67, July 7, 1798, 1 Stat. 578; 5 Cong. Ch. 64, June 30, 1798, 1 Stat. 575; 5 Cong. Ch. 63, June 28, 1798, 1 Stat. 575.

67. Stone, *Perilous Times*, 25.
68. Ibid.
69. Ibid., 26.
70. George Athan Billias, *Elbridge Gerry, Founding Father and Republican Statesman* (New York: McGraw-Hill, 1976).
71. Stone, *Perilous Times*, 28.
72. 1 Annals of Cong. 567–68; 570–72; 577–78; 596–97.
73. 50 U.S.C. §21.
74. Stone, *Perilous Times*, 28.
75. Ibid.
76. Ibid.
77. 50 U.S.C. §21.
78. 5 Cong. Ch. 54, June 17, 1789, 1 Stat. 566.
79. Cited in *American Eloquence: A Collection of Speeches and Addresses*, ed. Frank Moore, vol. 2 (New York: D. Appleton, 1895), 222.
80. Sedition Act, 1 Stat. 596, sec. 2 (1798).
81. Ibid.
82. Nancy Murray and Sarah Wunsch, "Civil Liberties in Times of Crisis: Lessons from History," *Massachusetts Law Review* 87, no. 2 (2002): 72.
83. Akhil Reed Amar, "Of Sovereignty and Federalism," Faculty Scholarship Series, *Yale Law Journal* 96, no. 7 (1987): 1502.
84. Alien and Sedition Acts, Library of Congress, http://www.loc.gov/rr/program/bib/ourdocs/Alien.html.
85. Paul S. Gillies, "Ruminations: The Trial of Matthew Lyon," *Vermont Bar Journal* 37, no. 2 (2011): 7; U.S. House of Representatives, "The Life of Representative Matthew Lyon of Vermont and Kentucky," History, Art & Archives, http://history.house.gov/HistoricalHighlight/Detail/36323?ret=True; "History of the Federal Judiciary: The Sedition Act Trials—Historical Background and Documents," Federal Judicial Center, http://www.fjc.gov/history/home.nsf/page/tu_sedbio_lyon.html.
86. Stone, *Perilous Times*, 49n130.
87. Gillies, "Ruminations," 9; U.S. House of Representatives, "The Life of Representative Matthew Lyon"; Federal Judicial Center, "History of the Federal Judiciary."
88. "William Paterson was an Associate Justice of the U.S. Supreme Court, who sat, under the Judiciary Act of 1789, as half of the Circuit Court. Vermont U.S. District Judge Samuel Hitchcock joined Paterson on the bench." Gillies, "Ruminations," 9; "History of the Federal Judiciary: The Sedition Act Trials—Historical Background and Documents," Federal Judicial Center; Stone, *Perilous Times*, 50.
89. Stone, *Perilous Times*, 51.
90. Ibid., 52.
91. Ibid., 52–53.
92. "Resolved . . . that whensoever the general government assumes undelegated powers, its acts are unauthoritative, void, and of no force; . . . that this government, created by this compact, was not made the exclusive or final judge of the extent of the powers delegated to itself, since that would have made its discretion, and not the Constitution, the measure of its powers." Jonathan Elliot,

ed., *The Debates in the Several State Conventions, on the Adoption of the Federal Constitution, as Recommended by the General Convention at Philadelphia, in 1787,* vol. 4 (Washington, 1836), 540.

93. Amar, "Of Sovereignty and Federalism," 1502.

94. "In the longer term . . . the Resolutions proved to be among the most influential extraconstitutional, nonjudicial texts in American constitutional history." H. Jefferson Powell, "The Original Understanding of Original Intent," *Harvard Law Review* 98, no. 5 (1985): 927.

95. Ibid.

96. Ibid., 930–31.

97. Ibid., 931, emphasis added.

98. "Through their power to select senators and presidential electors, state lawmakers helped sweep the high-Federalist friends of the Alien and Sedition Acts out of national office in the election of 1800, replacing them with Jeffersonians who allowed the repressive acts to expire." Akhil Reed Amar, *The Bill of Rights* (New Haven: Yale University Press, 2008), 6.

99. David F. Enicson, "the Nullification Crisis, American Republicanism, and the Force Bill Debate," Jof Southern History, vol. 61, no. 2, May 1995, 249

100. Thomas E. Woods, *Nullification: How to Resist Federal Tyranny in the 21st Century* (Washington, DC: Regnery Publishing, 2010), 87–89.

101. Ibid.

102. Ibid., 89.

103. Ronald Reagan, First Inaugural Address, January 20, 1981, http://www.bartleby.com/124/pres61.html.

Chapter 4

1. Zechariah Chafee Jr., *Free Speech in the United States* (Cambridge, MA: Harvard University Press, 1967), 5.

2. James Madison, *The Papers of James Madison*, vol. 2 (Washington: Langtree and Sullivan, 1840), 741.

3. U.S. Const. art. I, §9, cl. 2.

4. Amanda L. Tyler, "The Forgotten Core Meaning of the Suspension Clause," *Harvard Law Review* 125, no. 4 (2012): 901.

5. Brian McGinty, *The Body of John Merryman: Abraham Lincoln and the Suspension of Habeas Corpus* (Cambridge, MA: Harvard University Press, 2011), 1.

6. Ibid.

7. Ibid., 1–5.

8. Ibid., 1.

9. Ibid., 17.

10. Roger Brooke Taney: "I can see no ground whatsoever for supposing that the President, in any emergency, or in any state of things, can authorize the suspension of the privileges [sic] of the writ of habeas corpus, or the arrest of a citizen, except in aid of the judicial power." Ex parte Merryman, 17 F. Cas. 144 (C.C.D. Md. 1861) (No. 9487).

11. Ibid.

12. McGinty, *Body of John Merryman*, 116.

13. Ibid., emphasis in original. For a thorough discussion of the tension between civil liberties and authority in the Civil War, see William H. Rehnquist, *All the Laws But One: Civil Liberties in Wartime* (New York: Knopf, 1998).

14. McGinty, *Body of John Merryman*, 5.

15. *In re* Kemp, 16 Wis. 359, 382 (1863).

16. Tyler, "The Forgotten Core Meaning of the Suspension Clause," 901.

17. See Amanda L. Tyler, "Suspension as an Emergency Power," *Yale Law Journal* 118, no. 4 (2009): 638n177.

18. James G. Randall, *Constitutional Problems Under Lincoln* (New York: D. Appleton, 1926), 150, https://archive.org/details/constitutionalpr00randa.

19. Tyler, "The Forgotten Core Meaning of the Suspension Clause," 992; statement of Sen. Jacob Collamer, Cong. Globe, 37th Cong., 3d Sess. 1206 (1863) at 550, noting that by a suspension "the President would be in the exercise of his power rightfully in arresting men who had been guilty of no crime, for the purpose of securing against the commission of [acts] . . . dangerous to the Government."

20. See Act of March 3, 1863, ch. 81, §I, 12 Stat. 755, 7552, 12 Stat. at 755–56: "[A] list of the names of all persons [who are] citizens of States in which the administration of the laws has continued unimpaired in the said federal courts [and] who are now, or may hereafter be, held as prisoners of the United States, by order or authority of the [Executive], . . . as State or political prisoners, or otherwise than as prisoners of war."

21. Tyler, "The Forgotten Core Meaning of the Suspension Clause," 987.

22. Ibid., 990.

23. See Sanford Levinson, David C. Baum Lecture, "Was the Emancipation Proclamation Constitutional? Do We/Should We Care What the Answer Is?," *University of Illinois Law Review* 2001, no. 5 (2001): 1135.

24. "On April 27, 1861, President Lincoln simultaneously declared martial law and authorized Commanding General Winfield Scott to suspend the writ of habeas corpus in Union territories. . . . Lincoln proclaimed that all persons who discouraged enlistments or engaged in disloyal practices would be subject to trial in a military commission, regardless of whether they were citizens or military. Lincoln thought that military commissions were necessary because, according to him, state courts did not have the authority to convict war protesters." Anne English French, "Trials in Times of War: Do the Bush Military Commissions Sacrifice Our Freedoms?," *Ohio State Law Journal* 63, no. 4 (2002): 1228–29.

25. See *Merriam-Webster Dictionary*, s.v. "drumhead court-martial," http://www.merriam-webster.com/dictionary/drumhead%20court-martial.

26. Joseph A. Ranney, "Abraham Lincoln's Legacy to Wisconsin Law, Part 2: Inter Arma Silent Leges: Wisconsin Law in Wartime," *Wisconsin Lawyer* 82 (February, 2009): 14.

27. Gen. Ambrose Burnside, General Order No. 38 (1863).

28. Randall, *Constitutional Problems Under Lincoln*, 177.

29. Geoffrey R. Stone, *Perilous Times: Free Speech in Wartime, from the Sedition Act of 1798 to the War on Terrorism* (New York: W. W. Norton, 2004), 102.

30. Ranney, "Abraham Lincoln's Legacy."

31. Judge Humphrey H. Leavitt went on to say that "self-preservation" is the "paramount law," rising above even the Constitution. In such times no "one connected with the judicial department should in any way 'embarrass or thwart

the executive in his efforts to deliver the country from the dangers which press so heavily upon it.'" Stone, *Perilous Times*, 103–4.

32. Ranney, "Abraham Lincoln's Legacy," where the court would not take jurisdiction over a military commission's final judgment; Ex parte Vallandigham, 68 U.S. (1 Wall) 243 (Wayne, J.) (1863).

33. Ex parte Vallandigham, 68 U.S. (1 Wall) 243, 251 (Wayne, J.) (1863).

34. The Trial of Hon. Clement L. Vallandigham by a Military Commission: and the Proceedings Under His Application for a Writ of Habeas Corpus in the Circuit Court of the United States for the Southern District of Ohio (Cincinnati: Rickey & Carroll, 1863).

35. Ex parte Milligan, 71 U.S. 2 at 142.

36. Marouf Arif Hasian, *In the Name of Necessity: Military Tribunals and the Loss of American Civil Liberties* (Tuscaloosa: University of Alabama Press, 2005), 80.

37. Ibid., 100.

38. Ibid., 87.

39. Ibid., 88. James Speed was once characterized by Rehnquist as "one of the least competent Attorneys General in the history of that office." William H. Rehnquist, "Civil Liberty and the Civil War: The Indianapolis Treason Trials," *Indiana Law Journal* 72, no. 4 (1997): 933.

40. Hasian, *In the Name of Necessity*, 104.

41. Ex parte Milligan, 71 U.S. (4 Wall) 2, 120–21 (Davis, J.) (1866).

42. Bryant Smith, "Book Review: Ex Parte Milligan: In the Matter of Lambdin P. Milligan," *Texas Law Review* 9, no. 1 (1930): 122.

43. Hasian, *In the Name of Necessity*, 80–81.

44. Ibid., 88.

45. Ex parte McCardle, 74 U.S. 506 (1868).

46. Ex parte McCardle, 74 U.S. at 508.

47. Ibid.

48. U.S. Const. art. III, §2.

49. Ex parte McCardle, 74 U.S. at 514.

50. Ibid.

51. "The Army became involved in traditional police roles and in enforce politically volatile Reconstruction-era politics." Mark D. Maxwell, *The Enduring Vitality of the Posse Comitatus Act of 1878*, Office of the Judge Advocate General, the Pentagon 37 Jun Prosecutor 34 (2003).

52. Gary Felicetti and John Luce, "The Posse Comitatus Act: Setting the Record Straight on 124 Years of Mischief and Misunderstanding Before Any More Damage Is Done," 175 *Military Law Review* 86, 109 (2003).

53. Wrynn v. United States, 200 F. Supp. 457, 464 (E.D.N.Y. 1961) (quoting Gillars v. United States, 182 F.2d 962, 972 (D.C. Cir. 1950)).

54. *Wrynn*, 200 F. Supp. at 465 (quoting Sparks, National Development 1877–1885, in *The American Nation: A History*, vol. 23 [1907], 127).

55. 1879 Army Appropriations Bill, 20 Stat. 152, at §15 (1878). The Posse Comitatus Act was passed as part of this legislative package.

56. Sean J. Kealy, "Reexamining the Posse Comitatus Act: Toward a Right to Civil Law Enforcement," *Yale Law and Policy Review* 21, no. 2 (2003): 384.

57. Ibid., 388.

Chapter 5

1. Geoffrey R. Stone, *Perilous Times: Free Speech in Wartime, from the Sedition Act of 1798 to the War on Terrorism* (New York: W. W. Norton, 2004), 137, 155.
2. Plato, *The Republic*, in *Plato: Complete Works*, ed. John M. Cooper (Indianapolis: Hackett, 1997), 1020–22, §§382–83; 1050, §414.
3. Ibid.
4. See chapter 3, discussing the Alien Enemies Act.
5. While treason is defined and restricted in the Constitution, see U.S. Const. art. III, §3; it is criminalized at 18 U.S.C. §2381 and has been modified from time to time, e.g., §1038. The §1097 rules created the crimes of unlawful entry and theft of property or "records." 35 Stat. §§1038, 1097 (1909).
6. Harold Edgar and Benno C. Schmidt, Jr., "The Espionage Statutes and Publication of Defense Information," *Columbia Law Review* 73, no. 5 (1973): 939–40nn26–28.
7. Ibid., 939–40.
8. Defense Act, 36 Stat. 1804 (1911).
9. Edgar and Schmidt, "The Espionage Statutes and Publication of Defense Information," 940.
10. Ibid.
11. Espionage Act, Pub. L. 65–24, 40 Stat. 217 (1917) (codified at 18 U.S.C. §792).
12. Edgar and Schmidt, "The Espionage Statutes and Publication of Defense Information," 940.
13. Stone, *Perilous Times*, 147.
14. Edgar and Schmidt, "The Espionage Statutes and Publication of Defense Information," 940–41.
15. Stone, *Perilous Times*, 148.
16. Ibid.
17. Ibid., 148–49.
18. Edgar and Schmidt, "The Espionage Statutes and Publication of Defense Information," 964.
19. Ibid., 941.
20. Stone, *Perilous Times*, 150.
21. The Espionage Act, Pub. L. 65–24, 40 Stat. 217, 18 U.S.C. §792 (1917), sec. 3, http://www.digitalhistory.uh.edu/disp_textbook.cfm?smtID=3&psid=3904; Stone, *Perilous Times*, 147.
22. *Merriam-Webster Dictionary*, s.v. "disaffect," http://www.merriam-webster.com/dictionary/disaffect.
23. Stone, *Perilous Times*, 151.
24. The Espionage Act of 1917, sec. 3, emphasis added; Stone, *Perilous Times*, 151.
25. U.S. Const. amend. I, emphasis added.
26. Stone, *Perilous Times*, 147, 149–50.
27. Peter Grier, "Postmasters General, Kings of Political Patronage?" *Christian Science Monitor*, March 11, 2010, http://www.csmonitor.com/USA/DC-Decoder/Decoder-Wire/2010/0311/Postmasters-general-kings-of-political-patronage; United States Postal Service, "Reform Proposal," http://about.usps.com/publications/pub100/pub100_034.htm.
28. Stone, *Perilous Times*, 149–50.
29. Ibid.

30. Ibid., 149.

31. Ibid., 150.

32. Ibid., 149n*.

33. The Sedition Act, 40 Stat. 553 (1918).

34. Stone, *Perilous Times*, 184–85.

35. The Sedition Act, 40 Stat. 553–54 (1918).

36. Stone, *Perilous Times*, 184–85.

37. Stone's book, which this book often cites, decries this act as well. Stone, *Perilous Times*, 184–85.

38. Ibid., 189.

39. Ibid., 190.

40. Ibid., 189.

41. Ibid.

42. Ibid., 190.

43. Ibid., 191.

44. Ibid.

45. Declaration of War, Joint Resolution, 40 Stat. 1 (1917), emphasis added.

46. The Overman Act, 40 Stat. 556 (1918).

47. Ibid.; United States v. Kraus, 33 F.2d 406, 408 (7th Cir. 1929) (describing the president's very broad powers).

48. Ibid.

49. Lochner v. United States, 198 U.S. 45, 53 (1905) (Peckham, J.).

50. Ibid.

51. Lochner v. United States, 198 U.S. 45, 63 (1905) (Peckham, J.).

52. Richard B. Gregg, "The National War Labor Board," *Harvard Law Review* 33, no. 1 (1919): 45.

53. Ibid.

54. Melvyn Dubofsky, "Introduction," *Papers of the National War Labor Board, 1918–1919*, ed. Melvyn Dubofsky and Randolph Boehm (Bethesda, MD: University Publications of America, 1985), vi.

55. Gregg, "The National War Labor Board," 45–51.

56. Ibid., 54. The Supreme Court case referred to as being abrogated is Hitchman Coal & Coke Company v. Mitchell, 245 U.S. 229 (1917).

57. Gregg, "The National War Labor Board," 54.

58. Ibid., 55.

59. Ibid.

60. Dubofsky, "Introduction," vi.

61. Administrative History, microformed on Records of the War Industries Board, Record Group 61.1 (National Archives, Federal Records).

62. Ami J. Abou-Bakr, *Managing Disasters Through Public-Private Partnerships* (Washington, DC: Georgetown University Press, 2013), 144.

63. U.S. Const. amend. V, proscribing the taking of property for private use or without just compensation; see above.

64. United States v. Kraus, 33 F.2d 406, 408 (7th Cir. 1929).

65. Ibid., emphasis added.

66. "Constitutional Law—Contracts—Power of Government to Enforce War-Time Contract to Accept Agreed Profit—Recovery of Excess Profits," *Yale Law Journal* 39, no. 3 (1930): 423.

67. United States v. Kraus, 33 F.2d 406, 408 (7th Cir. 1929).

68. United States v. Kraus, 33 F.2d 406, 409–10 (7th Cir. 1929).

69. 1 Williston on Contracts §1:17 (4th ed. 2013).

70. Stone, *Perilous Times*, 137.

71. Cited in ibid., 156–57.

72. For example, Jim Powell, *Wilson's War: How Woodrow Wilson's Great Blunder Led to Hitler, Lenin, Stalin, and World War* (New York: Random House, 2005).

73. See below, nn 160–67 and accompanying text; see Brandenburg v. Ohio, 395 U.S. 444 (1969).

74. Billy Murray, "Over There," recorded June 28, 1917, http://www.firstworldwar .com/audio/overthere.htm.

75. Stone, *Perilous Times*, 153.

76. Compare ibid., 153 n*.

77. Ibid.

78. David Pietrusza, "Roiling the Mid-Term Waters: Recalling Woodrow Wilson's Disastrous 1918 Gaffe," DavidPietrusza.com, http://www.davidpietrusza.com/ wilson-1918-midterm-election.html.

79. Compare Stone, *Perilous Times*, 137 n.†, "One measure of the depths of opposition to World War I is that some 300,000 men evaded the draft during the course of the war," with "Draft-Dodger Memorial to Be Built in B.C.," CBC News, September 8, 2004, http://www.cbc.ca/news/canada/story/2004/09/08/ draft_dogers040908.html, "[A]s many as 125,000 Americans . . . fled to Canada between 1964 and 1977."

80. The Selective Service Act of 1917, Pub. L. 65–12, 40 Stat. 76–83 (May 18, 1917).

81. Executive Order No. 2594 (April 1917) (not listed in CFR or Fed. Reg., available in Nat. Archives), 223.

82. Andrew P. Napolitano, *Theodore and Woodrow: How Two American Presidents Destroyed Constitutional Freedom* (Nashville: Thomas Nelson, 2012), 222; Stone, *Perilous Times*, 153.

83. Michael F. Connors, *Dealing in Hate: The Development of Anti-German Propaganda* (London: Britons Publishing Co., 1966), www.ihr.org/books/ connors/dealinginhate.html.

84. Napolitano, *Theodore and Woodrow*, 221; Sam Greenhill, "Secret of the Lusitania: Arms Find Challenges Allied Claims It Was Solely a Passenger Ship," *Daily Mail* (UK), December 19, 2008, http://www.dailymail.co.uk/news/article-1098904/ Secret-Lusitania-Arms-challenges-Allied-claims-solely-passenger-ship .html#ixzz2YVhrZUQI.

85. "Disaster Bears Out Embassy's Warning," *New York Times*, May 8, 1915, http:// query.nytimes.com/mem/archive-free/pdf?res=F7081FFC385C13738DDDA10894 DD405B858DF1D3.

86. "The Lusitania never was impressed into the Government service . . . and no guns ever were mounted on the emplacements," Special Cable, "Why Lusitania Plans Show Gun Outlines: Made Before Ship Was Built—Merely Indicate Where Rifles Could Be Mounted," *New York Times*, June 19, 1915, http://query.nytimes.com/ mem/archive-free/pdf?res=F50D16FD355E12738DDDA00994DE405B858DF1D3; the emplacements were considered a tourist attraction.

87. "The Lusitania's passengers would, in all human probability, have been saved if the explosion of ammunition on the vessel . . . had not sent her to the bottom

quickly." "Surprise at the Capital," *New York Times*, May 31, 1915; Greenhill, "Secret of the Lusitania," describing that after surveying the wreckage, the Germans, in all human probability, were right.

88. Stone, *Perilous Times*, 136; Greenhill, "Secret of the Lusitania."

89. Thomas Andrew Bailey and Paul B. Ryan, *The Lusitania Disaster: An Episode in Modern Warfare and Diplomacy* (New York: Free Press, 1975), 319.

90. Napolitano, *Theodore and Woodrow*, 221.

91. Thomas G. Paterson, J. Garry Clifford, Shane J. Maddock, Deborah Kisatsky, and Kenneth J. Hagan, *American Foreign Relations: A History Since 1895*, 7th ed., vol. 2 (Boston: Wadsworth Cengage Learning, 2010), 73.

92. Ibid.

93. Ibid.

94. "[T]he truth is, Wilson was never the pacifist he had portrayed himself to be. Rather, his peace platform was a well-devised strategy to get himself elected president. In reality, he had goals on an international scale, which were his top priority, and he was willing to do anything to accomplish them, even if that meant lying about war and then conniving to enter it." Napolitano, *Theodore and Woodrow*, 220.

95. "Sees Mainly Error in Lusitania Note," *New York Times*, June 8, 1915, http://query.nytimes.com/mem/archive-free/pdf?res=F3061FF83E591A7A93CAA9178DD85F418185F9.

96. Stone, *Perilous Times*, 171–72, 137; Harry N. Scheiber, *The Wilson Administration and Civil Liberties, 1917–1921* (Ithaca, NY: Cornell University Press, 1960), 2–3; "Surprise at the Capital," *New York Times*, May 31, 1915.

97. Napolitano, *Theodore and Woodrow*, 221; "Ends Struggle Over Policy," *New York Times*, June 9, 1915, http://query.nytimes.com/mem/archive-free/pdf?res=9C00E7D81E3EE033A2575AC0A9609C946496D6CF.

98. "Wilson Rejects Lusitania Note: Asks Disavowal," *New York Times*, January 26, 1916, http://query.nytimes.com/mem/archive-free/pdf?res=9F05E2D91E38E633A25755C2A9679C946796D6CF.

99. S. Doc. No. 5. (1917), http://historymatters.gmu.edu/d/4943/.

100. Stone, *Perilous Times*, 153.

101. Geoffrey Stone, *War and Liberty: An American Dilemma 1790–Present* (New York: W. W. Norton & Co., 2007), 49–50.

102. Napolitano, *Theodore and Woodrow*, 222; Stone, *Perilous Times*, 154–56.

103. Stone, *Perilous Times*, 155, reprinting the liberty bonds poster; "Propaganda Posters—United States of America," FirstWorldWar.com, http://www.firstworldwar.com/posters/usa.htm.

104. Napolitano, *Theodore and Woodrow*, 222.

105. Ibid., 223.

106. Walter Romig, *Michigan Place Names: The History of the Founding and the Naming of More Than Five Thousand Past and Present Michigan Communities* (Detroit: Wayne State University Press, 1986), 354.

107. "Of Fraud and Force Fast Woven: Domestic Propaganda During the First World War," FirstWorldWar.com, http://www.firstworldwar.com/features/propaganda.htm.

108. *The Kaiser, the Beast of Berlin*, film directed by Rupert Julian, Rupert Julian Productions and Universal Film Manufacturing Co., 1918.

109. Stone, *Perilous Times*, 182, discussing Beethoven bans; "War Hysteria and the Persecution of German-Americans," Authentic History, http://www .authentichistory.com/1914-1920/2-homefront/4-hysteria/index.html, discussing Bach and Mozart ban attempts.

110. Stone, *Perilous Times*, 154.

111. Napolitano, *Theodore and Woodrow*, 221.

112. Stone, *Perilous Times*, 156.

113. Ibid.

114. Ibid., 157.

115. Ibid., 157–58 n*.

116. "Nothing was done to punish this behavior." Napolitano, *Theodore and Woodrow*, 223; "*Il est défendu de tuer; tout meurtrier est puni, à moins qu'il n'ait tué en grande compagnie, et au son des trompettes.*" Voltaire, *Rights* (1771), in *Oeuvres Complètes de Voltaire* (Paris: Garnier Frères, 1878), 425.

117. National Civil Liberties Bureau, *War-Time Prosecutions and Mob Violence: Involving the Rights of Free Speech, Free Press and Peaceable Assemblage* (New York: National Civil Liberties Bureau, 1919), 3–11.

118. Jess Zimmerman, "John Meints & WWI Anti-German Sentiment," *History by Zim* (blog), June 18, 2012, http://www.historybyzim.com/2012/06/ john-meints-wwi-anti-german-sentiment/.

119. Ibid.

120. Ibid.

121. Ibid.

122. Meints v. Huntington, 276 F. 245, 253 (8th Cir. 1921).

123. Zimmerman, "John Meints & WWI Anti-German Sentiment."

124. John Fabian Witt, *Patriots and Cosmopolitans: Hidden Histories of American Law* (Cambridge: Harvard University Press, 2007), 191.

125. National Civil Liberties Bureau, *War-Time Prosecutions*, 4.

126. Stone, *Perilous Times*, 172–73.

127. Ibid., 173.

128. Department of Justice, "Report of the Attorney General of the United States for the Year 1922," 437; Stone, *Perilous Times*, 173n*.

129. Walter Coffey, "Espionage, Sedition and Fascism in World War I," *WalterCoffey .com* (blog), December 6, 2012, http://waltercoffey.wordpress.com/2012/12/06/ espionage-sedition-and-fascism-in-world-war-i/.

130. Jim Robbins, "Silence Broken, Pardons Granted 88 Years After Crimes of Sedition," *New York Times*, May 3, 2006, http://select.nytimes.com/gst/abstract .html?res=F50C17FC355B0C708CDDAC0894DE404482.

131. Stone, *Perilous Times*, 172.

132. Ibid.

133. Ibid., 171–72; see 171–72 n143, providing a detailed discussion of the events.

134. Ibid., 172.

135. "Warn Seditious Pastors," *New York Times*, March 31, 1918, http://query.nytimes .com/mem/archive-free/pdf?res=F50915FA355B11738DDDA80B94DB405B888D F1D3; see Stone, *Perilous Times*, 172 n*.

136. Eugene V. Debs, "Speech in Canton, Ohio", in *Writings and Speeches of Eugene V. Debs*, ed. Arthur M. Schlesinger (New York: Hermitage Press, 1948), 417–18, alterations in original.

137. Burl Noggle, *Into the Twenties: The United States from Armistice to Normalcy* (Champaign, IL: University of Illinois Press, 1974), 113.
138. David Leip, "1912 Presidential General Election Results," USElectionAtlas.org, http://uselectionatlas.org/RESULTS/national.php?year=1912&f=0&off=0&elect=0.
139. David Leip, "1916 Presidential General Election Results," USElectionAtlas.org, http://uselectionatlas.org/RESULTS/national.php?year=1916&f=0&off=0&elect=0.
140. David Leip, "1920 Presidential General Election Results," USElectionAtlas.org, http://uselectionatlas.org/RESULTS/national.php?year=1920&f=0&off=0&elect=0.
141. "Eugene Victor Debs 1855–1926," EugeneVDebs.com, debsfoundation.org/personalhistory.html.
142. Coffey, "Espionage, Sedition and Fascism."
143. Ibid., emphasis added.
144. Ibid.
145. Stone, *Perilous Times*, 180.
146. Witt, *Patriots and Cosmopolitans*, 191.
147. Stone, *Perilous Times*, 184.
148. Ibid., 181n*.
149. David J. Bennett, *He Almost Changed the World: The Life and Times of Thomas Riley Marshall* (Bloomington, IN: AuthorHouse, 2007), 146.
150. Stone, *Perilous Times*, 180–81n†.
151. See *infra*, chapter 5 discussing the federal judiciary.
152. The Alien Act, 40 Stat. 1012 (1918).
153. Ibid.; Stone, *Perilous Times*, 181.
154. Stone, *Perilous Times*, 181.
155. Ibid.
156. Ibid.; Chafee, *Free Speech in the United States*, 207–8.
157. Chafee, *Free Speech in the United States*, 208.
158. Ibid., 207–8.
159. Ibid., 208.
160. Schenck v. United States, 249 U.S. 47 (1919) (per curiam) (Holmes, J.).
161. Frohwerk v. United States, 249 U.S. 204 (1919) (per curiam) (Holmes, J.).
162. Debs v. United States, 249 U.S. 211 (1919) (per curiam) (Holmes, J.).
163. Abrams v. United States, 250 U.S. 616 (1919) (Clarke, J.).
164. Schaefer v. United States, 251 U.S. 466 (1920) (McKenna, J.).
165. Pierce v. United States, 252 U.S. 239 (1920) (Pitney, J.).
166. Schenck v. United States, 249 U.S. 47 (1919).
167. Schenck v. United States, 249 U.S. 47, 51 (1919).
168. U.S. Const. amend. I, emphasis added.
169. Schenck v. United States, 249 U.S. 47, 52–53 (1919).
170. Thomas Healy, *The Great Dissent: How Oliver Wendell Holmes Changed His Mind—and Changed the History of Free Speech in America* (New York: Metropolitan Books, 2013).
171. Frohwerk v. United States, 249 U.S. 204, 208 (1919); Stone, *Perilous Times*, 195.
172. Stone, *Perilous Times*, 195.

173. Frohwerk v. United States, 249 U.S. 204, 205, 208 (1919); Stone, *Perilous Times*, 195.

174. Frohwerk v. United States, 249 U.S. 204, 208 (1919); ibid., at 210 (discussing *Schenck*).

175. Debs v. United States, 249 U.S. 211, 213 (1919).

176. Debs v. United States, 249 U.S. 211, 217 (1919).

177. Abrams v. United States, 250 U.S. 616, 617–18 (1919).

178. Ibid.

179. Abrams v. United States, 250 U.S. 616 (1919).

180. Abrams v. United States, 250 U.S. 616, 628 (1919) (Holmes & Brandeis, JJ., dissenting).

181. Schaefer v. United States, 251 U.S. 466 (1920).

182. Schaefer v. United States 251 U.S. 466, 476–77 (1920) (footnote omitted), emphasis added.

183. Pierce v. United States, 252 U.S. 239 (1920).

184. "Some 4.7 million Americans fought in World War I. Of these, 116,000 died in service and 204,000 were wounded." US Department of Veteran Affairs, "VA History in Brief," 2006, http://www.va.gov/opa/publications/archives/docs/history_in_brief.pdf.

185. Stone, *Perilous Times*, 220; see earlier in this chapter.

186. Ibid., 221; see earlier in this chapter.

187. Ibid.

188. John Milton Cooper, *Woodrow Wilson: A Biography* (New York: Vintage Books, 2009), 535.

189. Ibid., 544, 557–60.

190. Herbert Hoover, *The Ordeal of Woodrow Wilson* (New York: McGraw-Hill, 1958), 271–78.

191. Stone, *Perilous Times*, 221–22.

192. Ibid., 221.

193. Ibid., 222.

194. Ibid.

195. Ibid., 223.

196. Ibid., 223–25.

197. S. Res. 307 (September 19, 1918).

198. "Senators Tell What Bolshevism Means in America," *New York Times*, June 15, 1919, http://query.nytimes.com/mem/archive-free/pdf?res=F50613F6345D147A9 3C7A8178DD85F4D8185F9.

199. Charles H. McCormick, *Seeing Reds: Federal Surveillance of Radicals in the Pittsburgh Mill District, 1917–1921* (Pittsburgh: University of Pittsburgh Press, 2003), 92; "Senators Tell What Bolshevism Means in America."

200. R. G. Brown et al., *To the American People: Report Upon the Illegal Practices of the United States Department of Justice* (Washington, DC: National Popular Government League, 1920), https://archive.org/details/toamericanpeople00natiuoft.

201. Stone, *Perilous Times*, 225.

202. For example, "Union Men Assail Palmer," May 4, 1920, *New York Times*, http://query.nytimes.com/mem/archive-free/pdf?res=F10D13F93555157A93C6A9178E D85F448285F9.

203. Stone, *Perilous Times*, 225.
204. Ibid., 229.
205. Ibid., 231–32.
206. Ibid.
207. Ibid., 230; "American Civil Liberties Union," USLegal.com, http://associations
    .uslegal.com/american-civil-liberties-union/.
208. Meyer v. Nebraska, 262 U.S. 390 (1923).

Chapter 6

1. See chapter 5.
2. 268 U.S. 652 (1925); 274 U.S. 357 (1927).
3. 268 U.S. 652, 654 (1925) (Sanford, J.), emphasis added, (quoting New York Penal
    Law, §§160–161).
4. 268 U.S. 652, 654–55 (1925) (Sanford, J.).
5. 268 U.S. 652, 655–57 (1925) (Sanford, J.).
6. Karl Marx and Friedrich Engels, *The Communist Manifesto* (New York: Signet
    Classic, 1998), 76.
7. 268 U.S. 652, 655–58 (1925) (Sanford, J.).
8. American Civil Liberties Union (ACLU), "The Successes of the American Civil
    Liberties Union," http://www.aclu.org/successes-american-civil-liberties-union.
9. 268 U.S. 652, 672–73 (1925) (Holmes and Brandeis, JJ., dissenting).
10. "For present purposes we may and do assume that freedom of speech and of
    the press—which are protected by the First Amendment from abridgment by
    Congress—are among the fundamental personal rights and 'liberties' protected
    by the due process clause of the Fourteenth Amendment from impairment by
    the States. We do not regard the incidental statement in *Prudential Ins. Co. v.
    Cheek*, . . . , that the Fourteenth Amendment imposes no restrictions on the
    States concerning freedom of speech, as determinative of this question." 268 U.S.
    652, 666 (1925) (Sanford, J.); see ACLU, "The Successes of the American Civil
    Liberties Union" for a list of victories in chronological order.
11. "[Sanford] served seven years [on the Court] and wrote the monumental opinion
    in *Gitlow v. New York*, which first suggested that the Fourteenth Amendment
    incorporated the Bill of Rights." Sam D. Elliott, "A Supremely Strange Mix,"
    Tennessee Bar Journal 47, no. 3(2011): 3.
12. Whitney v. California, 274 U.S. 357, 364–66 (1927).
13. Whitney v. California, 274 U.S. 357, 367 (1927).
14. Whitney v. California, 274 U.S. 357, 369–71 (1927).
15. Whitney v. California, 274 U.S. 357, 372 (1927) (Holmes and Brandeis, JJ.,
    dissenting).
16. Geoffrey R. Stone, *Perilous Times: Free Speech in Wartime, From the Sedition Act
    of 1798 to the War on Terrorism* (New York: W. W. Norton, 2004), 238; 238n11,
    collecting an impressive record of cases invalidating state utterance statutes and
    similar laws.
17. Peter Peel, "The Great Brown Scare: The Amerika Deutscher Bund in the Thirties
    and the Hounding of Fritz Julius Kuhn," *Journal for Historical Review* 7, no. 4
    (1986–87), http://www.ihr.org/jhr/v07/v07p419_Peel.html.

18. ACLU, "Still the Fish Committee Nonsense!: The Answer of the Press to the Fish Committee Proposals to Outlaw Free Speech for Communists" (hereinafter cited as ACLU, "Fish Committee Answers"), 1932, http://debs.indstate.edu/a505s75_1932.pdf.

19. Hamilton Fish III, *Hamilton Fish: Memoir of an American Patriot* (Washington, DC: Regnery Gateway, 1991), 41–42, discussing targeting Communist Party presidential candidate William Foster and the ACLU.

20. William M. Wiecek, "The Legal Foundations of Domestic Anticommunism: The Background of Dennis v. United States," *Supreme Court Review*, 2001, 393.

21. 71 Cong. Rec. 2526 (1931).

22. "More Patrioteering," *Pittsburgh Press*, February 18, 1932, cited in ACLU, "Fish Committee Answers," 4.

23. Wiecek, "The Legal Foundations of Domestic Anticommunism," 393; "Hamilton Fish's 1930 investigative committee wrapped up its work amid derisive laughter when Fish was conned." Ibid., 398.

24. ACLU, "Fish Committee Answers."

25. H. Res. 198, 73 Cong. Rec. 4934, 4949 (1934).

26. 22.87 Special Committee on Un-American Activities, microformed on Guide to the Records of the U.S. House of Representatives at the National Archives, 1789–1989: Chapter 22: Records of the Select Committees of the House of Representatives, Record Group 233 (National Archives, Federal Records), http://www.archives.gov/legislative/guide/house/chapter-22.html.

27. 22.86 Special Committee on Un-American Activities, microformed on Guide to the Records of the U.S. House of Representatives at the National Archives, 1789–1989: Chapter 22: Records of the Select Committees of the House of Representatives, Record Group 233 (National Archives, Federal Records), http://www.archives.gov/legislative/guide/house/chapter-22.html.

28. Remarks of Rep. Lindsay Warren, 81 Cong. Rec. 3287 (1937).

29. 22.87 Special Committee on Un-American Activities.

30. 79 Cong. Rec. 123 (1935), index for "Committee on Investigation of Un-American Activities" and "Committee on Investigation of Nazi Activities in the United States."

31. 79 Cong. Rec. 24, 1405, 2029 (1935); see ibid., 123, index for "Committee on Investigation of Un-American Activities" and "Committee on Investigation of Nazi Activities in the United States."

32. 81 Cong. Rec. 3290 (1937).

33. H. Res. 282, 83 Cong. Rec. 7568–7586 (1938) (introducing, debating and passing); G. L. Tyler, "House Un-American Activities Committee," *Encyclopedia of American Civil Liberties*, vol. 1, ed. Paul Finkelman (New York: Taylor & Francis, 2006), 780.

34. Tyler, "House Un-American Activities Committee," 780. *Guide to Congress*, CQ Press (2012), 322.

35. Remarks of Rep. John E. Rankin (D-MS), 91 Cong. Rec. 10–11 (1945); 14.112 House Un-American Activities Committee, 1945–75: Related Records, microformed on Guide to the Records of the U.S. House of Representatives at the National Archives, 1789–1989: Chapter 14: Records of the Judiciary Committee and Related Committees, Record Group 233 (National Archives, Federal Records), http://www.archives.gov/legislative/guide/house/chapter-14.html.

36. Kent. B. Millikan, "Congressional Investigations: Imbroglio in the Court," *William and Mary Law Review* 8, no. 6 (1967): 406.
37. Stone, *Perilous Times*, 245–46.
38. Ibid., 245.
39. Ibid., 246.
40. Ibid.
41. Ibid.
42. Ibid.
43. 91 Cong. Rec. 10–15 (1945) (debating and passing an amendment to the rules of the House which created the committee permanent); ibid. at 10, Remarks of Rep. John E. Rankin (D-MS) (introducing the amendment); Stone, *Perilous Times*, 246–48.
44. Jose Carlos Palma, "FBI History," *Smart Encyclopedia*, May 20, 2013, http://englishversion.smartencyclopedia.eu/index.php/43-the-fbi/82-fbi-history.
45. Federal Bureau of Investigation, "A Brief History of the FBI," http://www.fbi.gov/about-us/history/brief-history.
46. Ibid.
47. Ibid.
48. Ibid.
49. Ibid.
50. Ibid.; see chapter 5.
51. Federal Bureau of Investigation, "John Edgar Hoover," http://www.fbi.gov/about-us/history/directors/hoover.
52. Ibid.
53. Stone, *Perilous Times*, 249.
54. Ibid.
55. Ibid.
56. Ibid., 249–50.
57. Gary Sheffield, "The Fall of France," BBC, March 30, 2011, http://www.bbc.co.uk/history/worldwars/wwtwo/fall_france_01.shtml.
58. Ibid.
59. Ibid.
60. Ibid.
61. Stone, *Perilous Times*, 251.
62. Franklin Delano Roosevelt, Address to Congress, May 16, 1940, https://www.mtholyoke.edu/acad/intrel/WorldWar2/fdr16.htm; Stone, *Perilous Times*, 251; Remarks of Rep. Clifton A. Woodrum (D-VA), Rep. John Taber (R-NY), and Rep. Robert Rich (R-PA), 86 Cong. Rec. 9019–21 (1940) (discussing approving these so-called emergency defense bills).
63. H.R. 5138, 86 Cong. Rec. 9029–31, 9036 (1940) (codified at 18 U.S.C. § 2385) (introducing and passing the compromise Smith Act).
64. Stone, *Perilous Times*, 251.
65. The Smith Act, 54 Stat. 670, 670–71 (1940), emphases added.
66. The Smith Act, 54 Stat. 670, 671 at title I, §3 (1940) (criminalizing attempts); ibid., §5 (providing for "imprison[ment] of not more than ten years").
67. Walter Coffey, "Espionage, Sedition and Fascism in World War I," *WalterCoffey* .com (blog), December 6, 2012, http://waltercoffey.wordpress.com/2012/12/06/espionage-sedition-and-fascism-in-world-war-i/.

68. John Locke, *Two Treatises of Civil Government*, ed. Thomas Hollis (London: A. Millar et al., 1764), bk. 2, ch. 2, §4; bk. 2, §§149, 155, 168, 207–10, 220–31, 240–43 (1690), discussing rightful rebellion, http://oll.libertyfund.org/?option=com_staticxt&staticfile=show.php%3Ftitle=222.
69. Remarks of Rep. Howard W. Smith, 84 Cong. Rec. 10452 (1939), emphasis added.
70. The Smith Act, 54 Stat. 670, 671–72, at title II, §20.
71. The Smith Act, 54 Stat. 670, 673–75, at title III, §§30–32, 36.
72. "[The Justice Department] arranged for registration to take place at post offices, rather than at FBI or INS offices, thereby easing the sense of foreboding." Stone, *Perilous Times*, 284.
73. Remarks of Rep. Vito Marcantonio (L-NY), 86 Cong. Rec. 9034 (1940).
74. 86 Cong. Rec. 9036 (1940).
75. Remarks of Rep. Hatton Sumners (D-TX), 86 Cong. Rec. 9037 (1940).
76. Stone, *Perilous Times*, 252.
77. "During the present war the Supreme Court up to the date of writing this book had reversed convictions or judgments in five major civil liberties cases . . . entirely on the insufficiency of the evidence, and in no case on a point of law. They know of many appeals in civil liberties cases during this war on points of law which were either lost in the Appellate courts or denied review by the Supreme Court." Maximilian St.-George and Lawrence Dennis, *A Trial on Trial: The Great Sedition Trial of 1944* (Washington, DC: National Civil Rights Committee, 1946), 20.
78. Stone, *Perilous Times*, 252.
79. Ibid., 253.
80. Ibid.
81. Ibid., 253–54.
82. Ibid., 258.
83. Ibid., 258–59.
84. Ibid., 259.
85. Ibid., 263 n*.
86. United States v. Pelley, 132 F.2d 170 (7th Cir. 1942).
87. Ibid.; Stone, *Perilous Times*, 264, discussing Pelley's lawyers.
88. United States v. Pelley, 132 F.2d 170, 177 (7th Cir. 1942).
89. Edward S. Miller, *Bankrupting the Enemy: The U.S. Financial Siege of Japan Before Pearl Harbor* (Annapolis: Naval Institute Press, 2007); Stone, *Perilous Times*, 268–69; "Pelley's accusations about the administration's foreign policy, like his charges about the magnitude of American losses at Pearl Harbor, were *not* 'false' in any objectively verifiable sense." Ibid., 269, 263, n.†; Smedley Butler arguing in 1935 that American naval aggression in waters near Japan would eventually lead to conditions degenerating into war, "War Is a Racket," Archive .org, https://archive.org/details/WarIsARacket.
90. Milkovich v. Lorain Journal Co., 497 U.S. 1, 2 (1990) (citing cases).
91. Ibid.
92. John Stuart Mill, *On Liberty*, 2nd ed. (Boston: Ticknor and Fields, 1863), 36.
93. Stone, *Perilous Times*, 266 n*.
94. 318 U.S. 801 (1943); Stone, *Perilous Times*, 266.
95. Stone, *Perilous Times*, 266.

96. St.-George and Dennis, *A Trial on Trial*, 16.

97. Stone, *Perilous Times*, 273.

98. St.-George and Dennis, *A Trial on Trial*, 92–93.

99. Ibid., 16, 114–21.

100. Frederick R. Barkley, "Sedition Trial Holds Drama," *New York Times*, July 23, 1944.

101. Frederick R. Barkley, "Sedition Trial Even Now Is 'Only' in Its First Stage," *New York Times*, October 29, 1944.

102. St.-George and Dennis, *A Trial on Trial*, 35–44.

103. Ibid., 34–45.

104. Stone, *Perilous Times*, 274.

105. St.-George and Dennis, *A Trial on Trial*, 16.

106. Ibid.; "Sedition Case Ends on Mistrial Order," *New York Times*, December 8, 1944.

107. Frederick R. Barkley, "Sedition Trial's Wrangles Come to an Abrupt Close," *New York Times*, December 10, 1944.

108. "Mass Trial," *Washington Post*, July 16, 1944; "Courtroom Farce," *Washington Post*, July 28, 1944; St.-George and Dennis, *A Trial on Trial*, 431–34; Richard W. Steele, *Free Speech in the Good War* (New York: St. Martin's Press, 1999), 224.

109. St.-George and Dennis, *A Trial on Trial*, 433.

110. Ibid., 403.

111. 18 U.S.C. §2385 (2012), codifying the Smith Act, 54 Stat. 670, as amended.

112. US Civilian Production Administration, *Industrial Mobilization for War: History of the War Production Board and Predecessor Agencies 1940–1945*, vol. 1 (New York: Greenwood, 1969), 453 (hereinafter cited as US CPA); David Novick, Melvin Anshen, and William Charles Truppner, *Wartime Production Controls* (New York: Columbia University Press, 1949), 163–69.

113. Lochner v. New York, 198 U.S. 45 (1905) (Peckham, J.).

114. Lochner v. New York, 198 U.S. 45, 52 (1905) (Peckham, J.).

115. Lochner v. New York, 198 U.S. 45, 52–53 (1905) (Peckham, J.) (citation omitted).

116. Lochner v. New York, 198 U.S. 45, 75 (1905) (Holmes, J., dissenting) (citation omitted).

117. Ibid.

118. U.S. Const. art. 1, §10, cl. 1.

119. U.S. Const. amend. XIII.

120. Geoffrey R. Stone, Louis M. Seidman, Cass R. Sunstein, Pamela S. Karlan, and Mark V. Tushnet, *Constitutional Law*, 6th ed. (New York: Aspen Publishers, 2009), 754.

121. Rosemary D. Marcuss and Richard E. Kane, "U.S. National Income and Product Statistics," Bureau of Economic Analysis, February 2007, 34.

122. Murray N. Rothbard, *America's Great Depression*, 5th ed., (Auburn, AL: Mires Institute, 2000), 262.

123. Geoffrey R. Stone, Louis M. Seidman, Cass R. Sunstein, Pamela S. Karlan, and Mark V. Tushnet, *Constitutional Law*, 6th ed. (New York: Aspen Publishers, 2009), 753–754.

124. Gregory A. Caldeira, "Public Opinion and the U.S. Supreme Court: FDR's Court-Packing Plan," *American Political Science Review* 81 (1987): 1139, 1140–41.

125. H. Doc. No. 142, 81 Cong. Rec. 877, 893–896 (1937) (reporting a letter from FDR to Congress unveiling the plan); ibid., at S. 1378, 883, "to increase the number of justices on the Supreme Court"; ibid., at H. Rept. No. 711, p. 5369 (an "advers[e]" report).

126. Marian C. McKenna, *Franklin Roosevelt and the Great Constitutional War: The Court-Packing Crisis of 1937* (New York: Fordham University Press, 2002), 303–14; Caldeira, "Public Opinion and the U.S. Supreme Court: FDR's Court-Packing Plan," 1139, 1146–47.

127. West Coast Hotel Co. v. Parrish, 300 U.S. 379 (1937) (Hughes, J.).

128. United States v. Carolene Products Company, 304 U.S. 144, 152 & n4 (1938).

129. Pub. L. 328, 55 Stat. 795, 795 (1941) (declaring war on the "Imperial Government of Japan"); Pub. L. 331, 55 Stat. 796, 796 (1941) (declaring war on the "Government of Germany").

130. Ibid.

131. First War Powers Act, 1941, Pub. L. 354, 55 Stat. 838 (1941).

132. First War Powers Act, 1941, Pub. L. 354, 55 Stat. 838, at title I, §1 (1941).

133. First War Powers Act, 1941, Pub. L. 354, 55 Stat. 838–89, at title II, §201 (1941).

134. First War Powers Act, 1941, Pub. L. 354, 55 Stat. 838–39, at title III, §§301–2 (1941).

135. First War Powers Act, 1941, Pub. L. 354, 55 Stat. 839–40, at title III, §§301–3 (1941).

136. First War Powers Act, 1941, Pub. L. 354, 55 Stat. 839–40, at title III, §303 (1941).

137. Second War Powers Act, 1942, Pub. L. 507, 56 Stat. 176 (1942).

138. Second War Powers Act, 1942, Pub. L. 507, 56 Stat. 176–77, at title I, §§101–3 (1942).

139. Second War Powers Act, 1942, Pub. L. 507, 56 Stat. 177, at title II, §201 (1942).

140. Office of Federal Register, "Code of Federal Regulations: The President," 1957, 634-635, support the proposition.

141. Second War Powers Act, 1942, Pub. L. 507, 56 Stat. 178–79, at title III, §301 (1942).

142. Second War Powers Act, 1942, Pub. L. 507, 56 Stat. 179, at title III, §301 (1942).

143. Second War Powers Act, 1942, Pub. L. 507, 56 Stat. 179, at title VI, §601 (1942).

144. Donald M. Nelson, *Arsenal of Democracy: The Story of American War Production* (New York: Harcourt Brace, 1946), 12–13.

145. US CPA, 15.

146. Ibid., 14–15.

147. Ibid., 40.

148. Ibid., 14.

149. Ibid., 201.

150. Nathan Miller, *War at Sea: A Naval History of World War II* (Oxford: Oxford University Press, 1997), 295; Michael Gannon, *Operation Drumbeat* (New York: Harper Perennial, 1991), 296.

151. US CPA, 14.

152. Ibid.

153. Gordon Corrigan, *The Second World War: A Military History* (New York: St. Martin's Press, 2010), 81; US CPA, 14.

154. US CPA, 14.

155. Ibid.
156. Nelson, *Arsenal of Democracy*, 7.
157. US CPA, xiii.
158. Ibid., 6–7, 11.
159. Ibid., 8.
160. Ibid., 9.
161. Ibid., 11.
162. Ibid., 17.
163. Ibid., 18–19.
164. Ibid., 22–23.
165. 54 Stat. 599 (June 26, 1940); 54 Stat. 867 (September 9, 1940); 54 Stat. 964 (October 8, 1940); US CPA, 1 n27.
166. US CPA, 32–33.
167. Ibid., 30, xiii.
168. Exec. Order 8248, 4 Fed. Reg. 3864 (1939); US CPA, 18.
169. US CPA, 89.
170. Exec. Order 8629, 6 Fed. Reg. 191 (1941); US CPA, 94. The final death was in spring 1941 when its budget was reallocated to the Office for Emergency Management (OEM); Ibid., 95.
171. US CPA, 89, xiii.
172. Nelson, *Arsenal of Democracy*, 5.
173. US CPA, 95.
174. Ibid., 96.
175. Ibid., 108, 181–82, 195–97.
176. Exec. Order 8875, 6 Fed. Reg. 4483 (1941); US CPA, 108, 110.
177. US CPA, 102, 177; Special Combined Commission on Nonfood Consumption Levels, *The Impact of the War on Civilian Consumption in the United Kingdom, United States, and Canada* (Washington, DC: Government Printing Office, 1945) (hereinafter cited as Special Combined Commission), 1, 3, 27–28.
178. US CPA, 165.
179. Ibid., 165–66.
180. Ibid., 175.
181. Ibid., iii.
182. Ibid.
183. Ibid., 547.
184. Ibid., xiii–xiv.
185. Robert B. Stinnett, *Day of Deceit: The Truth About FDR and Pearl Harbor* (New York: Freedom Press, 1999); Miller, *Bankrupting the Enemy*.
186. Interview by Douglas Cirignano with Robert B. Stinnett, author of *Day of Deceit: The Truth About FDR and Pearl Harbor*, March 11, 2002, http://www.independent.org/newsroom/article.asp?id=408.
187. Lt. Cmdr. Arthur McCollum, "Memorandum for the Director: Estimate of the Situation in the Pacific and Recommendations for Action by the United States," 1940, *WhatReallyHappened.com* (blog) (hereinafter McCollum Memo), http://whatreallyhappened.com/WRHARTICLES/McCollum/index.html.
188. Interview by Douglas Cirignano with Robert B. Stinnett.

189. Commissioner Dudley Wright Knox, "Comment Attached to McCollum Memorandum," *WhatReallyHappened.com* (blog), 1940, http://whatreallyhappened.com/WRHARTICLES/McCollum/index.html.
190. Interview by Douglas Cirignano with Robert B. Stinnett.
191. McCollum Memo, ¶10.
192. Ibid., ¶9; Miller, *Bankrupting the Enemy*.
193. McCollum Memo, ¶9.
194. McCollum Memo, ¶10.
195. Exec. Order 9024, 7 Fed. Reg. 329 (1942); Exec. Order 9040, 7 Fed. Reg. 527 (1942); US CPA, 207–8.
196. US CPA, xiv; Youngstown Sheet & Tube Co. v. Sawyer, 343 U.S. 579 (1952) (Jackson, J., concurring).
197. "[T]he Chairman of the War Production Board, with the advice and assistance of the members of the Board, shall perform the additional functions and duties, and exercise the additional powers, authority and discretion conferred upon the President of the United States by Title III of the Second War Powers Act 1942." Exec. Order 9125, 7 Fed. Reg. 2719 (1942); Nelson, *Arsenal of Democracy*, xi; compare US CPA, 212.
198. US CPA, 204; ibid., 547.
199. Ibid., 307.
200. Ibid., 309–10.
201. Ibid., 314–15.
202. Special Combined Commission, 12.
203. Ibid., 13–14.
204. Exec. Order 9301, 8 Fed. Reg. 1825 (1943); US CPA, 703–4.
205. US CPA, 557–58.

Chapter 7

1. Proclamation No. 2561, 7 Fed. Reg. 5101 (1942).
2. U.S. Const. art. III, §3.
3. Randal John Meyer, "The Twin Perils of the al-Aulaqi Case: The Treason Clause and the Equal Protection Clause," *Brooklyn Law Review* 79, no. 1 (2013): 287.
4. Eike Frenzel, "Operation Pastorius: Hitler's Unfulfilled Dream of a New York in Flames," *Der Spiegel*, September 16, 2010, http://www.spiegel.de/international/zeitgeist/operation-pastorius-hitler-s-unfulfilled-dream-of-a-new-york-in-flames-a-716753.html; Federal Bureau of Investigation, "George John Dasch and the Nazi Saboteurs" (hereinafter cited as FBI, "George John Dasch"), http://www.fbi.gov/about-us/history/famous-cases/nazi-saboteurs/george-john-dasch-and-the-nazi-saboteurs.
5. Ibid.
6. FBI, "George John Dasch."
7. Ex parte Quirin, 317 U.S. 1, 21 (1942) (Stone, C.J.) (per curiam); Frenzel, "Operation Pastorius"; FBI, "George John Dasch."
8. Ex parte Quirin, 317 U.S. 1, 21 (1942) (Stone, C.J.) (per curiam); Frenzel, "Operation Pastorius"; FBI, "George John Dasch."
9. Frenzel, "Operation Pastorius"; FBI, "George John Dasch."

10. Frenzel, "Operation Pastorius"; FBI, "George John Dasch."
11. Frenzel, "Operation Pastorius"; FBI, "George John Dasch."
12. Ex parte Quirin, 317 U.S. 1, 21 (1942) (Stone, C.J.) (per curiam); FBI, "George John Dasch."
13. Ex parte Quirin, 317 U.S. 1, 21 (1942) (Stone, C.J.) (per curiam); FBI, "George John Dasch."
14. Frenzel, "Operation Pastorius."
15. Ibid.
16. Ibid.
17. Frenzel, "Operation Pastorius"; FBI, "George John Dasch."
18. Frenzel, "Operation Pastorius."
19. Ibid.
20. Frenzel, "Operation Pastorius"; FBI, "George John Dasch."
21. Frenzel, "Operation Pastorius."
22. Ibid.
23. Frenzel, "Operation Pastorius"; FBI, "George John Dasch."
24. Harvey Ardman, "World War II: German Saboteurs Invade America in 1942," *HistoryNet*, June 12, 2006, http://www.historynet.com/world-war-ii-german-saboteurs-invade-america-in-1942.htm.
25. Haupt v. United States, 330 U.S. 631, 633–34 (1947) (Jackson, J.).
26. Cramer v. United States, 325 U.S. 1, 3–5 (1945) (Jackson, J.).
27. Frenzel, "Operation Pastorius"; FBI, "George John Dasch."
28. Frenzel, "Operation Pastorius."
29. FBI, "George John Dasch."
30. Frenzel, "Operation Pastorius."
31. FBI, "George John Dasch."
32. 1–18 Stenographic Transcript of Proceedings before the Military Commission to Try Persons Charged with Offenses Against the Law of War and the Articles of War, Washington DC, July 8 to July 31, 1942 (Samaha et al. eds., 2004), http://www.soc.umn.edu/~samaha/nazi_saboteurs/indexnazi.htm; Proclamation No. 2561, 7 Fed. Reg. 5101 (1942).
33. FBI, "George John Dasch."
34. Ibid.
35. Ex parte Quirin, 47 F. Supp. 431 (D.D.C. 1942), *aff'd* 317 U.S. 1 (1942).
36. Ibid.
37. Ex parte Quirin, 63 S. Ct. 1 (1942).
38. 1 Stenographic Transcript of Proceedings before the Military Commission to Try Persons Charged with Offenses Against the Law of War and the Articles of War, Washington DC, July 8, 1942, (Samaha et al. eds., 2004), 11 http://www.soc.umn.edu/~samaha/nazi_saboteurs/nazi01.htm.
39. 18 Stenographic Transcript of Proceedings before the Military Commission to Try Persons Charged with Offenses Against the Law of War and the Articles of War, Washington DC, August 1, 1942, (Samaha et al. eds., 2004), http://www.soc.umn.edu/~samaha/nazi_saboteurs/nazi018.htm; FBI, "George John Dasch."
40. FBI, "George John Dasch."
41. Ex parte Quirin, 317 U.S. 1, 63 S. Ct. 2 (1942).

42. Haupt v. United States, 330 U.S. 631 (1947) (Jackson, J.); Cramer v. United States, 325 U.S. 1 (1945) (Jackson, J.); Ex parte Quirin, 317 U.S. 1 (1942).

43. Hague Conventions of 1907, ch. II, art. 30.

44. U.S. Const. art. I, §9, cl. 3.

45. Calder v. Bull, 3 (Dall.) U.S. 386, 390 (1798) (Chase, J.).

46. 1 Stenographic Transcript of Proceedings before the Military Commission to Try Persons Charged with Offenses Against the Law of War and the Articles of War, Washington DC, July 8, 1942, (Samaha et al. eds., 2004), 10–11, http://www.soc.umn.edu/~samaha/nazi_saboteurs/nazi01.htm.

47. Fed. R. Evid. 403.

48. Ex parte Quirin, 317 U.S. 1, 20–22 (1942).

49. Meyer, "Twin Perils."

50. Ex parte Quirin, 317 U.S. 1, 37–38 (1942).

51. Ex parte Quirin, 317 U.S. 1, 45 (1942) (quotations and citations omitted) (quoting Ex parte Milligan, 71 U.S. (4 Wall.) 2, 118, 121, 122, 131 (1866)).

52. Ex parte Quirin, 317 U.S. 1, 45 (1942) (quotations and citations omitted).

53. Ex parte Milligan, 71 U.S. (4 Wall.) 2, 118 (1866), emphasis added.

54. Duncan v. Kahanamoku, 327 U.S. 304 (1946) (Black, J.).

55. Duncan v. Kahanamoku, 327 U.S. 304, 307–11 (1946) (Black, J.).

56. Duncan v. Kahanamoku, 327 U.S. 304, 324 (1946) (Black, J.).

57. Duncan v. Kahanamoku, 327 U.S. 304, 313–14 & n8, 322 (1946) (Black, J.).

58. See generally Duncan v. Kahanamoku, 327 U.S. 304 (1946) (Black, J.).

59. Ex parte Milligan, 71 U.S. (4 Wall.) 2, 120–21 (Davis, J.) (1866).

60. Geoffrey R. Stone, *Perilous Times: Free Speech in Wartime, From the Sedition Act of 1798 to the War on Terrorism* (New York: W. W. Norton, 2004), 287, 291.

61. Ibid., 285.

62. Ibid., 286.

63. Ibid.

64. Ibid.

65. Exec. Order 9066, 7 Fed. Reg. 1407 (1942); Stone, *Perilous Times*, 289.

66. Stone, *Perilous Times*, 290–91.

67. Ibid., 291–92.

68. Ibid., 293–94.

69. Ibid., 292.

70. Ibid., 292–93.

71. Ibid., 292.

72. Ibid.

73. Ibid., 294.

74. Exec. Order 9066, 7 Fed. Reg. 1407 (1942).

75. Stone, *Perilous Times*, 295.

76. Hirabayashi v. United States, 320 U.S. 81, 86 (1943) (Stone, C.J.).

77. Public Proclamation No. 1, 7 Fed. Reg. 2320 (1942); Public Proclamation No. 2, 7 Fed. Reg. 2405 (1942); Hirabayashi v. United States, 320 U.S. 81, 86–87 (1943) (Stone, C.J.).

78. Exec. Order 9102, 7 Fed. Reg. 2165 (1942); Hirabayashi v. United States, 320 U.S. 81, 86–87 (1943) (Stone, C.J.).

79. Public Proclamation No. 3, 7 Fed. Reg. 2543 (1942).

80. Civilian Exclusion Order No. 1, 7 Fed. Reg. 3725 (1942).
81. Public Proclamation No. 4, 7 Fed. Reg. 2601 (1942).
82. Hirabayashi v. United States, 320 U.S. 81, 88 (1943) (Stone, C.J.).
83. Civil Liberties Public Education Fund, "Chronology of the Japanese American Internment," http://www.momomedia.com/CLPEF/chrono.html.
84. Leslie T. Hatamiya, *Righting a Wrong: Japanese Americans and the Passage of the Civil Liberties Act of 1988* (Stanford: Stanford University Press, 1993), 25.
85. U.S. National Archives, "Brief Overview of the World War II Enemy Alien Control Program," http://www.archives.gov/research/immigration/enemy-aliens-overview.html; Stone, *Perilous Times*, 285–86.
86. Stone, *Perilous Times*, 287.
87. Hirabayashi v. United States, 320 U.S. 81, 83 (1943) (Stone, C.J.).
88. Hirabayashi v. United States, 320 U.S. 81, 84 (1943) (Stone, C.J.).
89. Hirabayashi v. United States, 320 U.S. 81, 100 (1943) (Stone, C.J.). The case was also decided on anti-delegation grounds.
90. Hirabayashi v. United States, 320 U.S. 81, 101–02 (1943) (Stone, C.J.), emphasis added.
91. Korematsu v. United States, 323 U.S. 214 (1944) (Black, J.).
92. Korematsu v. United States, 323 U.S. 214, 215–16 (1944) (Black, J.).
93. Korematsu v. United States, 323 U.S. 214, 216 (1944) (Black, J.).
94. Korematsu v. United States, 323 U.S. 214, 224 (1944) (Black, J.).
95. Ibid.
96. Korematsu v. United States, 323 U.S. 214, 219–20 (1944) (Black, J.).
97. Eugene V. Rostow, "The Japanese American Cases—A Disaster," *Yale Law Journal* 54, no. 3 (1945): 489–90.
98. Ibid.
99. "42nd Regimental Combat Team," Go for Broke National Education Center, http://goforbroke.org/history/history_historical_veterans_442nd.asp.
100. Ibid.
101. Korematsu v. United States, 323 U.S. 214, 233 (1944) (Murphy, J., dissenting).
102. Korematsu v. United States, 323 U.S. 214, 240 (1944) (Murphy, J., dissenting).
103. War Powers Act (repeal), Pub. L. 89–554, 80 Stat. 651, §8(a) (1966). Some portions relating to troop mail had been repealed earlier.
104. Stone, *Perilous Times*, 302–3.
105. Ex parte Endo, 323 U.S. 283, 218–19 (1944) (Douglas, J.).
106. Japanese American Evacuation Claims Act, Pub. L. No. 80–886, 62 Stat. 1231 (1948).
107. Stone, *Perilous Times*, 303.
108. Civil Liberties Act, Pub. L. 100–383, 102 Stat. 903–16 (1988); ibid., title I, §105(a) (1); ibid., §1(6).
109. Hatamiya, *Righting a Wrong*, xxiii.

Chapter 8

1. National Security Act, Pub. L. 80–253, 61 Stat. 495 (July 26, 1947).
2. National Security Council Intelligence Directive No. 9 (1952), http://www2.gwu.edu/~nsarchiv/NSAEBB/NSAEBB24/nsa02b.pdf; National Security Agency, NSA/CSS Manual 22-1 (Ft. Meade, MD: NSA, 1986), 7.

3. Michael R. Belknap, "Cold War in the Courtroom: The Foley Square Communist Trial," *American Political Trials* (Westport, CT: Greenwood, 1994), 207, 209.

4. Ibid., 209.

5. Ibid., 208–10.

6. Ibid., 209.

7. Ibid.

8. Belknap, "Cold War in the Courtroom," 201.

9. Ibid., 210; J. Edgar Hoover, *Masters of Deceit: The Story of Communism in America and How to Fight It* (New York: Pocket Books, 1958), 5.

10. Exec. Order 9835, 12 Fed. Reg. 1935 (Mar. 21, 1947).

11. Christopher P. Latimer, *Civil Liberties and the State: A Documentary and Reference Guide* (Santa Barbara, CA: Greenwood, 2011), 113.

12. James L. Stokesbury, *A Short History of the Korean War* (New York: Harper Perennial, 1990), 27.

13. Ibid., 14; Kathryn Weathersby, "'Should We Fear This?': Stalin and the Danger of War with America," working paper no. 39, Scholars Cold War International History Project, Woodrow Wilson International Center (Washington, DC, 2002), 9–11, http://www.wilsoncenter.org/sites/default/files/ACFAEF.pdf. Also, Donggil Kim and William Stueck, "Did Stalin Lure the U.S. into the Korean War?," Wilson Center, June 2008, 1.

14. S.C. Res 83, U.N. Doc. S/RES/84 (June 27, 1950).

15. McCarran Internal Security Act, Pub. L. 81–831, 64 Stat. 987 (1950).

16. McCarran Internal Security Act, 64 Stat. 987 at title I, at 987–1019.

17. McCarran Internal Security Act, 64 Stat. 987 at title II, at 1019-1031.

18. McCarran Internal Security Act, 64 Stat. 987 at title I, §5, at 992–93.

19. McCarran Internal Security Act, 64 Stat. 987 at title I, §6, at 993.

20. McCarran Internal Security Act, 64 Stat. 987 at title I, §§7–8, at 993–95.

21. McCarran Internal Security Act, 64 Stat. 987 at title I, §10, at 996.

22. McCarran Internal Security Act, 64 Stat. 987 at title I, §§12–13, at 997–1001.

23. McCarran Internal Security Act, 64 Stat. 987 at title I, §14, at 1001–02.

24. McCarran Internal Security Act, 64 Stat. 987 at title I, §15, at 1002–03.

25. McCarran Internal Security Act, 64 Stat. at title I, §4, at 991–92.

26. McCarran Internal Security Act, 64 Stat. at title II, §102, at 1021.

27. McCarran Internal Security Act, 64 Stat. at title II, §§103–04 at 1021–23; Remarks of Sen. Patrick A. McCarran (D-NV), 96 Cong. Rec. 14577–78.

28. McCarran Internal Security Act, 64 Stat. at title II, §§112, at 1029–30.

29. McCarran Internal Security Act, 64 Stat. at title II, §§ 105–11, at 1023–29.

30. H. Res. 826, 96 Cong. Rec. 13721–70, calling the question; H.R. 9490, 96 Cong. Rec. 13721–70, debating and passing the act. Arguments for the merits were made in debating whether to call the question and on the question itself. It is most convenient to consider the debates on H. Res. 826 and H.R. 9490 consolidated.

31. Remarks of Rep. Clarence J. Brown (R-OH), 96 Cong. Rec. 13724; Remarks of Rep. James W. Wadsworth Jr. (R-NY), 96 Cong. Rec. 13721–22.

32. Remarks of Rep. Clarence J. Brown (R-OH), 96 Cong. Rec. 13724.

33. Remarks of Rep. Emanuel Celler (D-NY), 96 Cong. Rec. 13722.

34. Ibid.

35. Ibid.

36. Ibid.
37. Remarks of Rep. Vito Marcantonio (L-NY), 96 Cong. Rec. 13275.
38. Ibid.
39. Remarks of Rep. Clarence J. Brown (R-OH), 96 Cong. Rec. 13724.
40. Ibid.
41. Remarks of Rep. Emanuel Celler (D-NY), 96 Cong. Rec. 13725.
42. Remarks of Rep. John E. Rankin (D-MS), 96 Cong. Rec. 13725.
43. Remarks of Rep. John E. Rankin (D-MS), 96 Cong. Rec. 13725–27.
44. Remarks of Rep. John E. Rankin (D-MS), 96 Cong. Rec. 13727.
45. Remarks of Rep. Usher L. Burdick (R-ND), 96 Cong. Rec. 13768, 13769.
46. H.R. 9490, 96 Cong. Rec. 13721, 13769–70.
47. S. 4037, 96 Cong. Rec. 14575, 14575–628.
48. See Remarks of Sen. Patrick A. McCarran (D-NV), 96 Cong. Rec. 14575–628; ibid., Remarks of Sen. Scott W. Lucas (R-IL); ibid., Remarks of Sen. Karl E. Mundt (R-SD).
49. Remarks of Sen. Homer S. Ferguson (R-MI), 96 Cong. Rec. 14585–86.
50. S. 4037, H.R. 9490, 96 Cong. Rec. 14575, 14628.
51. Harry S. Truman, Internal Security Act of 1950 Veto Message from the President of the United States (September 22, 1950), in 96 Cong. Rec. 15629–32.
52. Remarks of Rep. John E. Rankin (D-MS), 96 Cong. Rec. 15632.
53. 96 Cong. Rec. 15632–33.
54. H.R. 9490, 96 Cong. Rec. 15668–726.
55. "Let This Be Our Last Mass Trial," *Saturday Evening Post*, January 6, 1945, cited in Maximilian St.-George and Lawrence Dennis, *A Trial on Trial: The Great Sedition Trial of 1944* (Washington, DC: National Civil Rights Committee, 1946), 403.
56. The Smith Act, 54 Stat. 670, 670–71 at title I §§1–3 (1940), which criminalized attempts; ibid., §5, providing for "imprison[ment] of not more than ten years."
57. The Smith Act, 54 Stat. 670, 670–71 at title I §§1–3 (1940); Michael R. Belknap, "Cold War in the Courtroom: The Foley Square Trial," in *American Political Trials* (Westport, CT: Greenwood, 1994), 208–9.
58. Belknap, "Cold War in the Courtroom," 210.
59. Ibid., 210–11.
60. Ibid., 211.
61. Ibid.
62. Ibid.; "Indicted Reds Get Wallace Support: Communists Are Held Victims of Truman-Bipartisan Move to Remain in Power," *New York Times*, July 22, 1948, http://query.nytimes.com/mem/archive/pdf?res=F20615F73F59157A93C0AB178 CD85F4C8485F9.
63. Belknap, "Cold War in the Courtroom," 212.
64. Ibid.
65. "1948 Presidential General Election Data—National," U.S. Election Atlas, 2012, http://uselectionatlas.org/RESULTS/data.php?year=1948&datatype=national&d ef=1&f=0&off=0&elect=0.
66. Belknap, "Cold War in the Courtroom," 207–8, 211–12.
67. Ibid., 212; Jack Alexander, "The Ordeal of Judge Medina," *Saturday Evening Post*, August 12, 1950, 84; Felix Frankfurter to Learned Hand, April 24, 1951, in *Papers of Felix Frankfurter, General Correspondence, 1878–1965* (Washington, DC: Library of Congress, 1998), microformed, reel 39, box 64.

68. Belknap, "Cold War in the Courtroom," 212.
69. Ibid., 220.
70. Ibid., 212.
71. Ibid., 220.
72. Ibid., 214.
73. Ibid., 214–15.
74. Ibid., 214.
75. Fed. R. Evid. 401, 403 (2013).
76. Belknap, "Cold War in the Courtroom," 220.
77. Ibid., 219.
78. Ibid., 220.
79. Ibid.
80. Ibid.
81. Ibid.
82. Ibid., 221.
83. Ibid.
84. Ibid.
85. Ibid.
86. Ibid.; George D. Wilkinson, "Letter to the Editor of the Times: Communist Threat Not Ended," *New York Times*, October 19, 1949, http://query.nytimes .com/mem/archive/pdf?res=FB0815F83F5F177B93CBA8178BD95F4D8485F9.
87. United States v. Dennis (hereinafter cited as Dennis I), 183 F.2d 201, 206–07 (2d Cir. 1950), *aff'd* Dennis v. United States, 341 U.S. 494 (1951).
88. American Communications Ass'n, C.I.O. v. Douds, 339 U.S. 382, §IV, at 394–400 (1950), discussing applications of and giving dicta about the "clear and present danger" test; Dennis I, 183 F.2d at 207–12, discussing applications of and giving dicta about the "clear and present danger" test.
89. Belknap, "Cold War in the Courtroom," 222–23.
90. Dennis I, 183 F.2d at 212–213.
91. Dennis I, 183 F.2d at 234.
92. Dennis I, 183 F.2d at 212.
93. Dennis I, 183 F.2d at 214.
94. Ibid.
95. Ibid.
96. Dennis I, 183 F.2d at 215–16.
97. Ibid.
98. Dennis I, 183 F.2d at 216.
99. Ibid.
100. Belknap, "Cold War in the Courtroom," 223.
101. "'Home by Christmas' Oct. 1950–Jan. 1951," BBC News, http://news.bbc.co.uk/2/ shared/spl/hi/asia_pac/03/the_korean_war/html/home_by_christmas.stm.
102. Dennis v. United States (hereinafter cited as Dennis II), 341 U.S. 494 (1951); "[A] [25] November attack by the Chinese sent the overextended American troops into the longest retreat in U.S. military history." Jesse Greenspan, "8 Things You Should Know About the Korean War," History.com, July 26, 2013, http://www .history.com/news/8-things-you-should-know-about-the-korean-war.
103. Dennis II, 341 U.S. at 498.

104. Dennis II, 341 U.S. at 501.
105. Ibid.
106. Dennis II, 341 U.S. at 502.
107. Dennis II, 341 U.S. at 503.
108. Dennis II, 341 U.S. at 507.
109. Dennis II, 341 U.S. at 510; Belknap, "Cold War in the Courtroom," 223–24.
110. Dennis II, 341 U.S. at 509.
111. Dennis II, 341 U.S. at 511.
112. Ibid.
113. Dennis II, 341 U.S. at 495.
114. Dennis II, 341 U.S. at 579 (Black, J., dissenting).
115. Belknap, "Cold War in the Courtroom," 224–25.
116. Belknap, "Cold War in the Courtroom," 225.
117. Ibid.
118. Yates v. United States (hereinafter cited as Yates), 354 U.S. 298 (1957).
119. Yates, 354 U.S. at 301–302 n1.
120. Belknap, "Cold War in the Courtroom," 226.
121. Yates, 354 U.S. at 320.
122. Ibid.
123. Yates, 354 U.S. 178 (1957).
124. Watkins vs. United States (hereinafter cited as Watkins), 354 U.S. at 182–83.
125. Watkins, 354 U.S. at 181–82, 185.
126. Watkins, 354 U.S. at 208.
127. Watkins, 354 U.S. at 209.
128. Watkins, 354 U.S. at 215.
129. John J. Patrick et al., The Oxford Guide to the United States Government (Oxford: Oxford University Press, 2001), 723.
130. Ibid.
131. "Inquiry Reform Seen Inevitable," New York Times, June 19, 1957.
132. William Shakespeare, Merchant of Venice, New Folger's ed. (New York: Washington Square Press, 1992), act 2, scene 7, line 65.
133. United States v. O'Brien, 391 U.S. 367 (1968); Scales v. United States, 367 U.S. 203 (1961).
134. Youngstown Sheet & Tube Co. v. Sawyer, 343 U.S. at 589 (1952).
135. William H. Harbaugh, "The Steel Seizure Reconsidered," review of Truman and the Steel Seizure Case: The Limits of Presidential Power, Maeva Marcus, Yale Law Journal 87, no. 6 (1978): 1272.
136. Edward S. Corwin, "Comment: The Steel Seizure Case: A Judicial Brick Without Straw," Columbia Law Review 53, no. 1 (1953): 55.
137. Ibid., 53.
138. Ibid., 55.
139. Ibid.
140. Defense Production Act, Pub. L. 81-774 (1950).
141. Labor Management Relations Act, 29 U.S.C. § 401–531.
142. Selective Service Act, 62 Stat. 604 (1948).
143. Corwin, "The Steel Seizure Case," 53.
144. Ibid., 56.

145. Youngstown Sheet & Tube Co. v. Sawyer, 343 U.S. 579, at 589 (1952).

146. Corwin, "The Steel Seizure Case," 57.

147. "The opinions of judges, no less than executives and publicists, often suffer the infirmity of confusing the issue of a power's validity with the cause it is invoked to promote, of confounding the permanent executive office with its temporary occupant. The tendency is strong to emphasize transient results upon policies—such as wages or stabilization—and lose sight of enduring consequences upon the balanced power structure of our Republic." Arthur H. Garrison, "National Security and Presidential Power: Judicial Deference and Establishing Boundaries in World War Two and the Korean War," Cumberland Law Review 39, no. 3 (2009): 672.

148. Youngstown Sheet & Tube Co. v. Sawyer, 343 U.S. 579, 636–39 (1952) (Jackson, J., concurring).

149. Tara L. Branum, "President or King? The Use and Abuse of Executive Orders in Modern-Day America," Journal of Legislation 28 (2002): 71n356.

150. Youngstown Sheet & Tube Co. v. Sawyer, 343 U.S. 579, 589 (1952) (Jackson, J., concurring).

151. Branum, "President or King," 71n356.

152. Ibid., 72.

153. Ibid.

154. Chamber of Commerce v. Reich, 74 F.3d 1322 (1996); Building & Construction Trades Department v. Allbaugh, 295 F.3d 28 (2002).

155. Branum, "President or King," 41, 47.

156. Chamber of Commerce v. Reich, 74 F.3d 1322 (1996).

157. Branum, "President or King," 71 n365; see Chamber of Commerce v. Reich, 74 F.3d 1322 (1996), the "later statute displaces the first only when the statute 'expressly contradict(s) the original act' or if such a construction 'is absolutely necessary . . . in order that (the) words (of a later statute) shall have meaning at all."

158. Building & Construction Trades Department v. Allbaugh, 295 F.3d 28 (2002).

159. Branum, "President or King," 74.

160. Reid v. Covert, 351 U.S. 487 (1956) (plurality opinion).

161. Vincent J. Samar, "The Treaty Power and the Supremacy Clause: Rethinking Reid v. Covert in a Global Context," Ohio Northern University Law Review 36, no. 1 (2010).

162. Jules Lobel, "Separation of Powers, Individual Rights, and the Constitution Abroad," Iowa Law Review 98, no. 4 (2013): 1639.

163. Ibid.

164. Reid v. Covert, 354 U.S. 1, 16.

165. Reid v. Covert, 351 U.S. 487.

166. Reid v. Covert, 351 U.S. 1; "The majority did not find it necessary to pass on the constitutional provision governing the power of Congress to make rules governing the Armed Forces." Roger J. Miner, "The Last Civilian Court-Martial and Its Aftermath," Ohio State Law Journal 67, no. 2 (2006): 414.

167. Reid v. Covert, 351 U.S. 1.

168. Anthony F. Renzo, "Making a Burlesque of the Constitution: Military Trials of

Civilians in the War Against Terrorism," *Vermont Law Review* 31, no. 2 (2009): 460–62; Miner, "The Last Civilian Court-Martial and Its Aftermath," 401.

169. Samar, "The Treaty Power and the Supremacy Clause."

170. Reid v. Covert, 354 U.S. at 5–6 (Black, J.).

Chapter 9

1. Michael R. Belknap, "The Warren Court and the Vietnam War: The Limits of Legal Liberalism," *Georgia Law Review* 33, no. 1 (1998): 72.

2. See ibid., discussing Secretary Dean Acheson's recommendation to President Truman that the United States support France in its struggle against nationalist rebels in Indochina. Acheson considered this necessary to contain the threat of communism.

3. Belknap, "The Warren Court and the Vietnam War," 72.

4. "Lyndon Johnson envisioned a "Great Society [that] entailed social and economic reform at home, and globalism abroad to preserve capitalism and to fight poverty and injustice." Ibid., 72–73.

5. Ibid., 73.

6. Scales, 367 U.S. at 228–29; ibid., 224–30, discussing the First and Fifth Amendment implications.

7. "Clemency for Scales," *New York Times*, December 28, 1962, http://query .nytimes.com/mem/archive/pdf?res=FA0C14FA3C581A7B93CAAB1789D95F46 8685F9.

8. Ibid.

9. "The Court on Communism," *New York Times*, June 7, 1961, http://query .nytimes.com/mem/archive/pdf?res=F60810FE395F147A93C5A9178DD85F4586 85F9.

10. Many sources discussed this episode. See Robert J. Hanyok, "Skunks, Bogies, Silent Hounds, and the Flying Fish: The Gulf of Tonkin Mystery, 2–4 August 1964," *Cryptologic Quarterly* 19-20, 200-01, at 2–3, 16; Elisabeth Bumiller, "Records Show Doubt on '64 Vietnam Crisis," *New York Times*, July 14, 2010, http://www.nytimes.com/2010/07/15/world/asia/15vietnam.html?_r=1&; Scott Shane, "Vietnam War Intelligence 'Deliberately Skewed,' Secret Study Says," *New York Times*, December 2, 2005, http://www.nytimes.com/2005/12/02/ politics/02tonkin.html.

11. "Vietnam War: Allied Troop Levels 1960–73," American War Library, December 6, 2008, http://www.americanwarlibrary.com/vietnam/vwatl.htm.

12. Albertson v. Subversive Activities Control Board, 383 U.S. 70, 77 (1965).

13. United States v. Robel (hereinafter cited as Robel), 389 U.S. 258 (1967).

14. Robel, 389 U.S. at 260.

15. Ibid.

16. Robel, 389 U.S. at 260–61.

17. Robel, 389 U.S. at 259–61. Also, David J. Dionisi, *American Hiroshima* (Trafford Publishing, 2005), 64.

18. Robel, 389 U.S. at 261–62.

19. Ibid.

20. Robel, 389 U.S. at 262.

21. Robel, 389 U.S. at 263–64 (citations omitted), emphasis added.

22. Korematsu v. United States, 323 U.S. 214, 219–20 (1944).

23. United States v. O'Brien, 391 U.S. 367 (1968).

24. James M. McGoldrick Jr., "United States v. O'Brien Revisited: Of Burning Things, Waving Things, and G-Strings," *University of Memphis Law Review* 36, no. 4 (2006): 903–4.

25. 50 U.S.C. §462(b)(6) (1966), knowing violation of any Selective Service regulation constitutes a violation of the Act.

26. Act of Aug. 30, 1965, Pub. L. No. 89–152, *amending* 50 U.S.C. App. §462(b)(3) (1964)(codified at 50 U.S.C. App. §462(b)(3)(Supp. I, 1966)).

27. "The Court assumed that O'Brien's conduct qualified as speech, but said that, when speech was combined with conduct, "a sufficiently important governmental interest in regulating the non-speech element [could] justify incidental limitations on First Amendment freedoms." McGoldrick, "United States v. O'Brien Revisited," 905.

28. United States v. O'Brien, 391 U.S. at 383 (Warren, C.J.).

29. McGoldrick, "United States v. O'Brien Revisited," 904.

30. Brandenburg v. Ohio (hereinafter cited as Brandenburg), 395 U.S. 444 (1969) (per curiam).

31. Brandenburg, 395 U.S. at 447–48.

32. Brandenburg, 395 U.S. at 444–45.

33. Ibid.

34. Brandenburg, 395 U.S. at 446.

35. Brandenburg, 395 U.S. at 447–48, 449.

36. Brandenburg, 395 U.S. at 448.

37. Stone, *Perilous Times*, 459.

38. Ibid., 460.

39. Ibid.

40. Ibid., 461.

41. Ibid., 462.

42. Memorandum from Alexander Butterfield, Deputy Assistant to the President, to Richard Nixon, President of the United States, 1969, "*Game Plan for Post-Speech Activities—Second Post-Speech Up-dating . . . Covers Period Nov. 10–Dec. 31*," in Bruce Oudes, *From: The President: Richard Nixon's Secret Files* (New York: Harper and Row, 1989), 65–69, reprinted.

43. James Madison, *Federalist* No. 51, *Library of Congress*, http://thomas.loc.gov/home/histdox/fed_51.html.

44. Protesters gathered to "convey the message that if the government did not end the war, it would face 'social chaos.'" Stone, *Perilous Times*, 470.

45. "The Biggest Bust," *Newsweek*, May 17, 1971, 24.

46. Garrett M. Graff, *The Threat Matrix: The FBI at War in the Age of Global Terror* (New York: Little, Brown, 2011), 63.

47. "In some instances the FBI's actions were clearly authorized; in others, Hoover disobeyed direct orders to terminate his activities." Stone, *Perilous Times*, 488; see also 487.

48. "[T]he anti-war, free-love student movements that sprang up in the shadow of Vietnam." Graff, *Threat Matrix*, 63.

49. Five were domestic operations, and two focused on foreign intelligence. Graff, *Threat Matrix*, 63.

50. Ibid.

51. David Cunningham, "State versus Social Movement," *States, Parties, and Social Movements*, ed. Jack A. Goldstone (Cambridge: Cambridge University Press, 2003), 48, 56–60; David Cunningham and John Noakes, "The Effects of Covert Forms of Social Control on Social Movements," *Sociology of Crime, Law and Deviance: Surveillance and Governance: Crime Control and Beyond*, ed. Mathieu Deflem, vol. 10 (Bingley, UK: Emerald Group, 2008), 184–85.

52. Final Report of the Select Committee to Study Governmental Operations with Respect to Intelligence Activities, bk. 2, §I.C.7.

53. Five were domestic operations, and two focused on foreign intelligence. Graff, *Threat Matrix*, 63.

54. Stone, *Perilous Times*, 490.

55. "What Is the FBI Up To?" *Washington Post*, March 25, 1971.

56. Stone, *Perilous Times*, 497.

57. Anthony Lewis cited in *Inside the Pentagon Papers*, ed. John Prados and Margaret Pratt Porter (Lawrence: University Press of Kansas, 2004), 2–3.

58. "He later explained that his [the secretary's] objective in ordering the report was to bequeath to scholars the raw material from which they could reexamine the events of the time." Stone, *Perilous Times*, 490.

59. David Halberstam, *The Best and the Brightest* (New York: Random House, 1972), 408–14.

60. Stone, *Perilous Times*, 500.

61. Senator Gravel ed., *The Pentagon Papers: The Defense Department History of United States Decisionmaking on Vietnam* (Boston: Beacon, 1971), xi–xii.

62. Stone, *Perilous Times*, 502.

63. "Were the papers for real? Was it worth the effort to review thousands of pages of material that might have nothing new in them? Was it 'right' for the *Times* to publish material that had been 'stolen' from the government?" Stone, *Perilous Times*, 503.

64. United States v. New York Times Co., 328 F. Supp 324, 325 (SDNY 1971).

65. Louis Henkin, "The Right to Know and the Duty to Withhold: The Case of the Pentagon Papers," *University of Pennsylvania Law Review* 120, no. 2 (1971): 273.

66. Ibid.

67. Louis D. Brandeis, "What Publicity Can Do," *Harper's Weekly*, December 20, 1913, http://3197d6d14b5f19f2f440-5e13d29c4c016cf96cbbfd197c579b45.r81.cf1.rackcdn.com/collection/papers/1910/1913_12_20_What_Publicity_Ca.pdf.

68. Ibid., 10.

69. Daniel Ellsberg, *Secrets: A Memoir of Vietnam and the Pentagon Papers* (New York: Penguin, 2002), 400–401, emphasis added.

70. Stone, *Perilous Times*, 508.

71. New York Times Co. v. United States, 403 U.S. 713 (1971).

72. "The First Amendment protected the press so that it could bare the secrets of government and inform the people." New York Times Co. v. United States, 403 U.S. 713 (1971) (Black, J.).

73. New York Times Co. v. United States, 403 U.S. 713.

74. "Trials: Practicing on Ellsberg," *Time*, May 7, 1973, http://content.time.com/time/magazine/article/0,9171,907160,00.html.

75. Stone, *Perilous Times*, 515n362.

76. "The Watergate Story: Timeline," *Washington Post*, April 24, 2007, www.washingtonpost.com/wp-srv/politics/special/watergate/timeline.html.

77. Ibid.

78. Non-Detention Act, Pub. L. 92–128, 85 Stat. 347 (1971) (codified at 18 U.S.C. §4001(a)).

79. Non-Detention Act, 85 Stat. at 347.

80. U.S. National Archives, "Statistical Information about Fatal Casualties of the Vietnam War, Military Records," http://www.archives.gov/research/military/vietnam-war/casualty-statistics.html.

81. "[W]as the Gulf of Tonkin Resolution, which authorized the use of military force in Southeast Asia, sufficient to constitute a declaration of war for the Vietnam War?" Erwin Chemerinsky, *Constitutional Law: Principles and Policies*, 4th ed. (New York: Aspen Publishers, 2011), 382.

82. War Powers Resolution of 1973, 50 U.S.C. 1541–1548 (2012); "Although it is called 'The War Powers Resolution,' it is a properly adopted federal statute," Chemerinsky, *Constitutional Law*, 291n22, 382.

83. "Comment: Congressional Control of Presidential Warmaking Under the War Powers Act," 1218.

84. War Powers Resolution, 50 U.S.C. §1544(c).

85. Chemerinsky, *Constitutional Law*, 291.

86. War Powers Resolution, 50 U.S.C. §1544(b); Chemerinsky, *Constitutional Law*, 291.

87. War Powers Resolution, 50 U.S.C. §1544(b).

88. Morrison v. Olson 487 U.S. 654 (1988).

89. "The Act, taken as a whole, does not violate the principle of separation of powers by unduly interfering with the Executive Branch's role. This case does not involve an attempt by Congress to increase its own powers at the expense of the Executive Branch." Morrison v. Olson 487 U.S. 654 (1988).

90. Saikrishna Prakash, "Unleashing the Dogs of War: What the Constitution Means by 'Declare War,'" *Cornell Law Review* 93, no. 1 (2007): 51; "Comment: Congressional Control of Presidential Warmaking Under the War Powers Act."

91. U.S. Const. arts. I, II.

92. Bill Moyers, "The Church Committee and FISA," PBS.org, October 26, 2007, http://www.pbs.org/moyers/journal/10262007/profile2.html.

93. Ibid.

94. "Since Franklin Roosevelt, Presidents had asserted their 'inherent authority' to authorize wiretaps and other surveillance for national security purposes." Peter P. Swire, "The System of Foreign Intelligence Surveillance Law," Working Paper no. 18, Public Law and Legal Theory Series, Center for Law, Policy and Social Science (Ohio State University Moritz College of Law, 2007), 3.

95. Foreign Intelligence Surveillance Act of 1978, 50 U.S.C. §§1801–11.

96. Swire, "The System of Foreign Intelligence Surveillance Law," 3.

97. A "United States person" is anyone who is a citizen, a lawfully admitted permanent alien resident, or a corporation incorporated in the United States. Foreign Intelligence Surveillance Act of 1978, 50 U.S.C. §1801(a)(1)-(3).

98. Rick Perlstein, "The NSA Doppleganger," *Nation* (blog), June 7, 2013, http://www.thenation.com/blog/174722/nsa-doppelganger#; see Swire, "The System of Foreign Intelligence Surveillance Law."

99. Foreign Intelligence Surveillance Act of 1978, 50 U.S.C. §1801.

Chapter 10

1. 1920–28, Redline Agreement.

2. Anglo-American Petroleum Agreement of 1944; Daniel Yergin, *The Prize: The Epic Quest for Oil, Money & Power* (2012), 384.

3. Saeed Kamali Dehghan and Richard Norton-Taylor, "CIA Admits Role in 1953 Iranian Coup," *Guardian* (UK), August 19, 2013, http://www.theguardian.com/world/2013/aug/19/cia-admits-role-1953-iranian-coup.

4. Alexander L. George and Richard Smoke, *Deterrence in American Foreign Policy: Theory and Practice* (New York: Columbia University Press, 1974), 313n8.

5. "The Iranian Hostage Crisis," PBS.org, 2002, http://www.pbs.org/wgbh/americanexperience/features/general-article/carter-hostage-crisis/.

6. The Soviets began to send the Soviet Army into Afghanistan in 1979 and pursued occupying the country to install themselves in a key Asian location. "The Soviet Occupation of Afghanistan," PBS.org, October 10, 2006, http://www.pbs.org/newshour/updates/asia/july-dec06/soviet_10-10.html.

7. Michael Moran, "Bin Laden Comes Home to Roost: His CIA Ties Are Only the Beginning of a Woeful Story," NBC News, August 24, 1998, http://www.nbcnews.com/id/3340101/#.UtGFQZTk9cR.

8. Richard Miniter, *Losing Bin Laden: How Bill Clinton's Failures Unleashed Global Terror* (Washington, DC: Regnery, 2003), 9.

9. Ibid., 9–10.

10. Ibid.

11. Andy Newman and Daryl Khan, "Brooklyn Mosque Becomes Terror Icon, but Federal Case Is Unclear," *New York Times*, March 9, 2003, http://www.nytimes.com/2003/03/09/nyregion/brooklyn-mosque-becomes-terror-icon-but-federal-case-is-unclear.html?pagewanted=all&src=pm.

12. David G. Fivecoat, "Leaving the Graveyard: The Soviet Union's Withdrawal from Afghanistan," US Army Strategic Studies Institute, Summer 2012, 46–47, http://strategicstudiesinstitute.army.mil/pubs/parameters/Articles/2012summer/Fivecoat.pdf.

13. "Afghanistan and the Soviet Withdrawal, 1989: 20 Years Later," *George Washington University National Security Archive*, February 15, 2009, http://www2.gwu.edu/~nsarchiv/NSAEBB/NSAEBB272/.

14. Bill Moyers, "Brief History of al Qaeda," PBS.org, July 27, 2007, https://www.pbs.org/moyers/journal/07272007/alqaeda.html.

15. Ibid.

16. U.S. Department of State, Office of the Historian, "The First Gulf War," http://history.state.gov/departmenthistory/short-history/firstgulf.

17. "A Chronology: The House of Saud," PBS Frontline, August 1, 2005, http://www.pbs.org/wgbh/pages/frontline/shows/saud/cron/.

18. "Origins of the Bin Laden Family," PBS Frontline, April 1999, http://www.pbs.org/wgbh/pages/frontline/shows/binladen/who/family.html.

19. U.S. Const. art. II, §1, cl. 8.

20. Miniter, *Losing Bin Laden*, xvi–xviii, 4; Byron York, "The Facts About Clinton and Terrorism," *National Review Online*, September 11, 2006, http://www.nationalreview.com/articles/218683/facts-about-clinton-and-terrorism/byron-york.

21. Dick Morris, *Behind the Oval Office: Winning the Presidency in the Nineties*, 1st ed. (New York: Random House, 1997), 308; ibid., 305–8; York, "The Facts About Clinton and Terrorism."

22. Compare Miniter, *Losing Bin Laden*, xvi–xviii, 4, and York, "The Facts About Clinton and Terrorism," against Richard Sale, *Clinton's Secret Wars: The Evolution of a Commander in Chief* (New York: St. Martin's Press, 2009), 308–9, providing a more lukewarm, albeit still critical view of Clinton's response to terrorism.

23. See generally Osama bin Laden et al., "Al-Qaeda's Second Fatwa," PBS Newshour, 1998, http://www.pbs.org/newshour/updates/military/jan-june98/fatwa_1998.html; Osama Bin Laden, "Declaration of War Against the Americans Occupying the Land of Two Holy Places," 1996 (hereinafter cited as Bin Laden 1996), http://www.pbs.org/newshour/updates/military/july-dec96/fatwa_1996.html.

24. Laurie Mylroie, *Study of Revenge: The First World Trade Center Attack and Saddam Hussein's War Against America* (La Vergne, TN: AEI Press, 2001), 45.

25. Sale, *Clinton's Secret Wars*, 282, 288; Verbatim Transcript of Combatant Status Review Tribunal Hearing for ISN 10024 (2007), 18, http://intelfiles.egoplex.com/ksm-transcript.pdf. A deeper investigation would have revealed strong "ties to al-Qaeda," as a later *New York Times* report would. Craig Pyes et al., "One Man and a Global Web of Violence," *New York Times*, January 14, 2001, http://www.nytimes.com/2001/01/14/world/one-man-and-a-global-web-of-violence.html?pagewanted=all&src=pm; York, "The Facts About Clinton and Terrorism."

26. York, "The Facts About Clinton and Terrorism."

27. United States v. Rahman, 189 F.3d 88, 111 (2d Cir. 1999) (per curiam), *cert. denied*, 528 U.S. 1094 (2000).

28. Sale, *Clinton's Secret Wars*, 282, 288.

29. United States v. Rahman, 189 F.3d 88, 111 (2d Cir. 1999) (per curiam), *cert. denied*, 528 U.S. 1094 (2000); Nosair is an Egyptian-born U.S. citizen, Steven Emerson, "Osama Bin Laden's Special Operations Man," *Journal of Counterterrorism and Security International*, September 1, 1998, http://www.investigativeproject.org/187/osama-bin-ladens-special-operations-man.

30. United States v. Rahman, 189 F.3d 88, 149–161 (2d Cir. 1999) (per curiam), *cert. denied*, 528 U.S. 1094 (2000); *accord* United States v. Augustin, 661 F.3d 1105 (11th Cir. 2011), *cert. denied*, 132 S. Ct. 2444 (2012); United States v. Awadallah, 349 F.3d 42, 59 (2d Cir. 2003), *cert. denied*, Awadallah v. United Stated, 543 U.S. 1056 (2005); United States v. Rodriguez, 803 F.2d 318 (7th Cir. 1986), *cert. denied*, 480 U.S. 908 (1987); Randal John Meyer, "The Twin Perils of the al-Aulaqi Case: The Treason Clause and the Equal Protection Clause," *Brooklyn Law Review* 79, no. 1 (2013): 230 n10, 265–69, discussing the circuit court's conclusions about the treason defense asserted by citizens and collecting cases.

31. United States v. Rahman, 189 F.3d 88, 112 (2d Cir. 1999) (per curiam), *cert. denied*, 528 U.S. 1094 (2000).

32. United States v. Rahman, 189 F.3d 88, 113 (2d Cir. 1999) (per curiam) (citing Ex parte Quirin, 317 U.S. 1, 37–8 (1942)), *cert. denied*, 528 U.S. 1094 (2000).

33. Presidential Decision Directive 39: U.S. Policy on Counterterrorism (20631), at 4, (June 21, 1995), http://www.clintonlibrary.gov/_previous/Documents/2010%20FOIA/Presidential%20Directives/PDD-39.pdf; Sale, *Clinton's Secret Wars*, 288.
34. Sale, *Clinton's Secret Wars*, 288.
35. Compare Bill Roggio, "Former Taliban Defense Minister Dies in Pakistani Custody," *Long War Journal*, February 13, 2012, http://www.longwarjournal.org/archives/2012/02/former_taliban_defen.php; Daniel Eisenberg, "Secrets of Brigade 055," *Time*, October 28, 2001, http://content.time.com/time/magazine/article/0,9171,181591,00.html.
36. Eisenberg, "Secrets of Brigade 055."
37. Roggio, "Former Taliban Defense Minister Dies in Pakistani Custody."
38. Jay S. Bybee, Memorandum for Alberto R. Gonzales . . . and William J. Haynes II . . . Re: Application of Treaties and Laws to al Qaeda and Taliban Detainees (2002), 19.
39. Ibid.
40. Bin Laden 1996.
41. Sale, *Clinton's Secret Wars*, 229.
42. York, "The Facts About Clinton and Terrorism."
43. Ibid.
44. Ibid.; Elsa Walsh, "Louis Freeh's Last Case," *New Yorker*, May 14, 2001, http://www.newyorker.com/archive/2001/05/14/010514fa_fact_walsh?currentPage=all.
45. Sale, *Clinton's Secret Wars*, 233–34; Walsh, "Louis Freeh's Last Case."
46. Sale, *Clinton's Secret Wars*, 233, 236; Walsh, "Louis Freeh's Last Case."
47. Sale, *Clinton's Secret Wars*, 235.
48. York, "The Facts About Clinton and Terrorism."
49. Louis Freeh, *My FBI* (New York: St. Martin's Press, 2005), 31–32; York, "The Facts About Clinton and Terrorism"; Walsh, "Louis Freeh's Last Case."
50. York, "The Facts About Clinton and Terrorism"; Walsh, "Louis Freeh's Last Case."
51. Sale, *Clinton's Secret Wars*, 295; Henry Munson, "Lifting the Veil," *Harvard International Review*, May 6, 2006, http://hir.harvard.edu/religion/lifting-the-veil?page=0,1.
52. York, "The Facts About Clinton and Terrorism."
53. Sale, *Clinton's Secret Wars*, 298–300.
54. York, "The Facts About Clinton and Terrorism"; Miniter, *Losing Bin Laden*, 182.
55. Sale, *Clinton's Secret Wars*, 300, stating that Clinton pressed military action despite "[his] problem."
56. Ibid., 300–302; Miniter, *Losing Bin Laden*, 182–86; York, "The Facts About Clinton and Terrorism."
57. Miniter, *Losing Bin Laden*, 183.
58. Ibid., 183–85.
59. Sale, *Clinton's Secret Wars*, 301; York, "The Facts About Clinton and Terrorism."
60. John F. Harris, "President Freezes Bin Laden's Assets," *Washington Post*, August 23, 1998, http://www.washingtonpost.com/wp-srv/inatl/longterm/eafricabombing/stories/strikes082398.htm.
61. Sale, *Clinton's Secret Wars*, 306.
62. Oriana Zill, "The U.S. Embassy Bombings Trial—A Summary," PBS Frontline, April 1999, http://www.pbs.org/wgbh/pages/frontline/shows/binladen/bombings/bombings.html.

63. In re Terrorist Bombings of U.S. Embassies in East Africa, 552 F.3d 157 (2d Cir. 2008), *aff'g* United States v. Bin Laden, 126 F. Supp. 2d 264 (S.D.N.Y. 2000), *cert denied*, 558 U.S.1137 (2010).

64. Miniter, *Losing Bin Laden*, 216–17; York, "The Facts About Clinton and Terrorism."

65. Miniter, *Losing Bin Laden*, 217–18.

66. Ibid., 221.

67. Cited in York, "The Facts About Clinton and Terrorism."

68. York, "The Facts About Clinton and Terrorism."

69. Miniter, *Losing Bin Laden*, 219–21; York, "The Facts About Clinton and Terrorism."

70. Bob Woodward, *Bush at War* (New York: Simon & Schuster, 2002), 39.

71. Jane Mayer, *The Dark Side: The Inside Story of How the War on Terror Turned into a War on American Ideals* (New York: Anchor Books, 2009), 6.

72. Sidney Blumenthal, "Bush's Brand New Enemy Is the Truth," *Guardian* (UK), March 25, 2004, http://www.theguardian.com/world/2004/mar/25/usa .september11.

73. Charles Perrow, "The Disaster After 9/11: The Department of Homeland Security and the Intelligence Reorganization," *Journal of Homeland Security Affairs* 2, no. 1 (2006), http://www.hsaj.org/?fullarticle=2.1.3.

74. Ralph Lopez, "Bush-Cheney Began Illegal NSA Spying Before 9/11, Says Telcom CEO," *Digital Journal*, June 17, 2013, http://digitaljournal.com/ article/352455#ixzz2b0vepcjB. The former Qwest CEO Joseph Nacchio was indicted and convicted for nineteen counts of securities fraud when he refused to cooperate with the Bush administration. This is discussed later on in this book.

Chapter 11

1. Carolee Walker, "Five-Year 9/11 Remembrance Honors Victims from 90 Countries: Nations United Will Win War on Terror, Officials Say," America.gov, September 11, 2006, http://iipdigital.usembassy.gov/st/english/article/2006/09/2 0060911141954bcreklaw0.9791071.html#axzz32aNJP4At.

2. Jess Bravin, *The Terror Courts: Rough Justice At Guantanamo Bay* (New Haven, CT: Yale University Press, 2013), 218.

3. Jane Mayer, *The Dark Side: The Inside Story of How the War on Terror Turned into a War on American Ideals* (New York: Anchor Books, 2009), 6, 11.

4. See chapter 10, discussing the Clinton administration.

5. Jeremy Scahill, *Dirty Wars: The World Is a Battlefield* (New York: Nation Books, 2013), 15–16.

6. U.S. Department of State, Document 9: Cable, Deputy Secretary Armitage-Mamoud Phone Call—September 18, 2001, 4, 1–42 (hereinafter cited as State Department Document 9), http://www.gwu.edu/~nsarchiv/NSAEBB/ NSAEBB358a/doc09.pdf.

7. For a description of the imperial presidency, see generally Steven G. Calabresi and Christopher S. Yoo, *The Unitary Executive: Presidential Power from Washington to Bush* (New Haven, CT: Yale University, 2008); Arthur M. Schlesinger Jr., *The Imperial Presidency* (New York: Houghton Mifflin, 1973); Steven G. Calabresi and

Christopher S. Yoo, "The Unitary Executive During the First Half-Century," *Case Western Reserve Law Review* 47, no. 4 (1997); John C. Yoo, "The Continuation of Politics by Other Means: The Original Understanding of War Powers," *California Law Review* 84, no. 2 (1996), http://www.bard.edu/civicengagement/usfp/resources/index.php?action=getfile&id=3029367.

8. State Department Document 9.

9. Authorization for Use of Military Force (hereinafter cited as AUMF I), Pub. L. 107–40, 115 Stat. 224–25 (2001).

10. AUMF I, 115 Stat. 224–25.

11. "The Taliban Clerics' Statements on Bin Laden," *Guardian* (UK), September 20, 2001, http://www.theguardian.com/world/2001/sep/20/afghanistan.september115.

12. "President Bush Addresses the Nation," *Washington Post*, September 20, 2001, www.washingtonpost.com/wp-srv/nation/specials/attacked/transcripts/bushaddress_092001.html.

13. John F. Burns, "A Nation Challenged: The Taliban; Clerics Answer 'No, No, No!' and Invoke Fates of Past Foes," *New York Times*, September 22, 2001, http://www.nytimes.com/2001/09/22/world/nation-challenged-taliban-clerics-answer-no-no-no-invoke-fates-past-foes.html.

14. Burns, "A Nation Challenged."

15. "Taliban 'Will Try Bin Laden if US Provides Evidence,'" *Guardian* (UK), October 5, 2001, http://www.theguardian.com/world/2001/oct/05/afghanistan.terrorism.

16. Dudley Althaus, "Pakistan Satisfied with U.S. Evidence Against Bin Laden," *Cape Cod Times*, October 5, 2001, http://www.capecodonline.com/apps/pbcs.dll/article?AID=/20011005/NEWS01/310059920&cid=sitesearch.

17. Mayer, *Dark Side*, 15.

18. Defs. Ex. 941, "Substitution for the Testimony of Khalid Sheikh Mohammed," United States v. Zacarias Moussaoui, No. 01-455-A (E.D. Va., July 31, 2006), *perm. app. denied*, 591 F.3d 263 (4th Cir. 2010).

19. Nic Robertson and Kelly Wallace, "U.S. Rejects Taliban Offer to Try Bin Laden," CNN, October 7, 2001, http://archives.cnn.com/2001/US/10/07/ret.us.taliban/.

20. Ibid.

21. "Bush Rejects Taliban Offer to Hand Bin Laden Over," *Guardian* (UK), October 14, 2001, http://www.theguardian.com/world/2001/oct/14/afghanistan.terrorism5.

22. Ibid.

23. Rory McCarthy, "New Offer on Bin Laden," *Guardian* (UK), October 16, 2001, http://www.theguardian.com/world/2001/oct/17/afghanistan.terrorism11.

24. Ibid.

25. Associated Press, "The War in Afghanistan: A Timeline," CBS News, December 1, 2009, http://www.cbsnews.com/2100-501704_162-5850224.html.

26. "The CIA and Special Forces campaign in Afghanistan was, in the beginning, a rout." Scahill, *Dirty Wars*, 15; Azam Ahmed, "As Afghan Pullout Nears, Civilian Casualties Rise," *New York Times*, July 31, 2013; Associated Press, "The War in Afghanistan."

27. Scahill, *Dirty Wars*, 447–49, 451, describing bin Laden being shot while unarmed and without ammunition.

28. Azam Ahmed and Habib Zahori, "Despite West's Efforts, Afghan Youths Cling to Traditional Ways," *New York Times*, July 31, 2013, http://www.nytimes .com/2013/08/01/world/asia/despite-wests-efforts-afghan-youths-cling-to-traditional-ways.html.

29. Contra, e.g., United States v. Gurrola-Garcia, 547 F.2d 1075, 1079 (9th Cir. 1976) ("the principle that Congress may delegate broad authority to the President in foreign affairs is clearly controlling law today"); Mottola v. Nixon, 464 F.2d 178, 179, 184 (9th Cir. 1972) (directing the district court to dismiss a complaint where the petitioners "allege that the Executive has acted unconstitutionally in committing American combat forces to Cambodia since Congress has not declared war against Cambodia under Article I, Section 8(11) of the United States Constitution."), *rev'g* 318 F. Supp. 538 (N.D. Ca. 1970).

30. Scahill, *Dirty Wars*, 14.

31. Ibid., 14–15.

32. Ibid., 28.

33. Ibid., 28–29.

34. Ibid., 15, 81–84.

35. Ibid., 29.

36. Authorization for Use of Military Force Against Iraq Resolution of 2002, Pub. L. 107–243, 116 Stat. 1498–1502 (October 16, 2002); H. J. Res. 114, 148 Cong. Rec. 18962 (October 2, 2002).

37. H. J. Res. 114, 148 Cong. Rec. 20277, 22490 (October 10–11, 2002).

38. U.N. SCOR, 58th Sess., 4707th mtg., U.N. Doc. S/PV.4707 (Feb 14. 2003); "Hans Blix's Briefing to the Security Council," February 14, 2003, http://www .theguardian.com/world/2003/feb/14/iraq.unitednations1; "President Bush Addresses the Nation," White House.gov, March 19, 2003, http://georgewbush-whitehouse.archives.gov/news/releases/2003/03/20030319-17.html.

39. "Iraq War: 190,000 lives, $2.2 Trillion," *Brown University Watson Inst. for International Studies*, March 14, 2013, http://news.brown.edu/ pressreleases/2013/03/warcosts; David Brown, "Study Claims Iraq's 'Excess' Death Toll Has Reached 655,000," *Washington Post*, October 11, 2006, www .washingtonpost.com/wp-dyn/content/article/2006/10/10/AR2006101001442_2 .html; Associated Press, "Last U.S. Troops Leave Iraq, Ending War," *USA Today*, December 18, 2011, http://usatoday30.usatoday.com/news/world/ story/2011-12-17/iraq-us-troops/52032854/1?csp=ip.

40. Ralph Lopez, "Bush-Cheney Began Illegal NSA Spying Before 9/11, Says Telcom CEO," *Digital Journal*, June 17, 2013, http://digitaljournal.com/ article/352455#ixzz2b0vepcjB; Shane Harris, "NSA Sought Data Before 9/11," *National Journal*, November 2, 2007, http://news.nationaljournal .com/articles/071102nj1.htm; Shane Harris and Tim Naftali, "Tinker, Tailor, Miner, Spy: Why the NSA's Snooping Is Unprecedented in Scale and Scope," *Slate*, January 3, 2006, http://www.slate.com/articles/news_and_politics/ politics/2006/01/tinker_tailor_miner_spy.html.

41. National Security Agency, Office of the Inspector General, "Review of the President's Surveillance Program," March 24, 2009 (hereinafter cited as NSA OIG Report 2009), 3, http://www.theguardian.com/world/interactive/2013/jun/27/ nsa-inspector-general-report-document-data-collection.

42. Ibid., 3.
43. Ibid., 4; Garrett M. Graff, *The Threat Matrix: The FBI at War in the Age of Global Terror* (New York: Little, Brown, 2011), 483.
44. Ibid.
45. Graff, *Threat Matrix*, 483–84.
46. Ibid., 483.
47. Ibid.
48. NSA OIG Report 2009, 7; Graff, *Threat Matrix*, 483.
49. NSA OIG Report 2009, 7; Graff, *Threat Matrix*, 483–84.
50. Graff, *Threat Matrix*, 484.
51. Ibid.
52. NSA OIG Report 2009, 7–8.
53. "Timeline of NSA Domestic Spying," Electronic Frontier Foundation (hereinafter cited as EFF, "Timeline"), https://www.eff.org/nsa-spying/timeline.
54. Harris and Naftali, "Tinker, Tailor, Miner, Spy."
55. NSA OIG Report 2009, 11.
56. EFF, "Timeline."
57. Uniting and Strengthening America by Providing Appropriate Tools Required to Intercept and Obstruct Terrorism Act of 2001, Pub. L. 107–56, 115 Stat. 272 (2001) (codified at scattered sections of 8, 18, 22, 31, 42, 49, and 50 U.S.C.). Including private law sessions, the PATRIOT Act is codified at and touches upon fifteen titles of the U.S.C.A. See P. L.107–56, Table 2, Statutes at Large, U.S.C.A. (2013).
58. "USA Patriot Act," Electronic Privacy Information Center (hereinafter cited as EPIC, "PATRIOT Act"), http://epic.org/privacy/terrorism/usapatriot/.
59. EPIC, "PATRIOT Act."
60. See notes 32 and 33 and accompanying text, discussing the 1937 congressional rejection of an attempt to create a special HUAC and the 1938 creation of one when war hysteria neared; see chapter 8, discussing the 1950 Congress.
61. PATRIOT Act, title VIII, §805, 115 Stat. at 377–78.
62. PATRIOT Act, §201, 115 Stat. at 278.
63. EPIC, "PATRIOT Act."
64. See note 57.
65. PATRIOT Act, §206, 115 Stat. at 282.
66. EPIC, "PATRIOT Act."
67. U.S. Const. amend IV.
68. "The 'generic' roving wiretap orders raise significant constitutional issues, as they do not comport with the Fourth Amendment's requirement that any search warrant 'particularly describe the place to be searched.'" EPIC, "PATRIOT Act."
69. EPIC, "PATRIOT Act."
70. Ibid.
71. PATRIOT Act, §206, 115 Stat. at 282; EPIC, "PATRIOT Act."
72. PATRIOT Act, §210, 115 Stat. at 283; EPIC, "PATRIOT Act."
73. PATRIOT Act, §§204, 209, 115 Stat. at 281, 283; EPIC, "PATRIOT Act."
74. PATRIOT Act, §213, 115 Stat. at 285–86, emphasis added.
75. PATRIOT Act, §213, 115 Stat. at 285–86.
76. PATRIOT Act, §214, 115 Stat. at 286–87; EPIC, "PATRIOT Act."

77. PATRIOT Act, §216, 115 Stat. at 290.
78. EPIC, "PATRIOT Act"; see PATRIOT Act, §215, 115 Stat. at 287–88 (codified at 50 U.S.C. §1861).
79. PATRIOT Act, §218, 115 Stat. at 291.
80. PATRIOT ACT, title. V, §505, 115 Stat. 272, 365 (2001) (codified at 18 U.S.C. § 2709 (2013)); Doe v. Ashcroft, 334 F. Supp. 2d 471, 483 & n40 (S.D.N.Y. 2004), *vacated by* Doe v. Gonzalez, 449 F.3d 415 (2d Cir. 2006).
81. Encyclopedia Britannica Online, s.v. "Writ of Assistance," http://www.britannica.com/EBchecked/topic/39372/writ-of-assistance.
82. PATRIOT Act, title VIII, §805, 115 Stat. at 377–78 (codified at 18 U.S.C. §2339A).
83. PATRIOT Act, 18 U.S.C. §2339A (2012).
84. Ibid.
85. Ibid.
86. PATRIOT Sunsets Extension Act of 2011, Pub. L. 112–14, 126 Stat. 216 (May 26, 2011) (codified at 50 U.S.C. §§1805, 1861, 1862), extending the PATRIOT Act to June 1, 2015.
87. John Markoff, "Pentagon Plans a Computer System That Would Peek at Personal Data of Americans," *New York Times*, November 9, 2002, http://www.nytimes.com/2002/11/09/politics/09COMP.html.
88. William Safire, "You Are a Suspect," *New York Times*, November 14, 2002, http://www.nytimes.com/2002/11/14/opinion/you-are-a-suspect.html.
89. Markoff, "Pentagon Plans a Computer System."
90. Ibid. Many of these speeches are available on the Internet. See, e.g., John Poindexter, Director, Information Awareness Office, Remarks (DARPATech 2002 Conference, Anaheim, CA, August 2, 2002), http://www.fas.org/irp/agency/dod/poindexter.html.
91. Mark Williams, "The Total Information Awareness Project Lives On," *MIT Technology Review*, April 26, 2006, http://www.technologyreview.com/news/405707/the-total-information-awareness-project-lives-on/.
92. Safire, "You Are a Suspect."
93. Williams, "The Total Information Awareness Project Lives On," emphasis in original.
94. Hendrik Hertzberg, "Too Much Information," *New Yorker*, December 9, 2002, http://www.newyorker.com/archive/2002/12/09/021209ta_talk_hertzberg.
95. Graff, *Threat Matrix*, 484.
96. Ibid., 485.
97. Ibid.
98. Ibid., 484. This particular abuse of executive power is discussed further in this chapter.
99. Ibid., 485.
100. Ibid.
101. Ibid., 486.
102. Ibid.
103. Ibid.
104. Ibid., 486–89, 492–93.
105. Ibid., 489.
106. Ibid., 484–88.

107. Ibid., 487–88.
108. Ibid.
109. Ibid., 488.
110. Ibid.
111. Ibid.
112. Ibid., 489.
113. Ibid., 490.
114. Ibid., 489.
115. Ibid., 490.
116. Ibid., 490–92.
117. Ibid., 490, 492–93.
118. Ibid., 492.
119. Ibid.
120. Ibid.
121. Ibid.
122. Ibid.
123. Ibid., 492–93.
124. Ibid., 493.
125. James Risen and Eric Lichtblau, "Bush Secretly Lifted Some Limits on Spying in U.S. After 9/11, Officials Say," *New York Times*, December 15, 2005, http://www.nytimes.com/2005/12/15/politics/15cnd-program.html?pagewanted=1&_r=0&ei=5088&en=46373698e4101aca&ex=1292302800&partner=rssnyt&emc=rss.
126. Scott Shane, "Former Phone Chief Says Spy Agency Sought Surveillance Help Before 9/11," *New York Times*, October 14, 2007, http://www.nytimes.com/2007/10/14/business/14qwest.html?pagewanted=print&_r=0.
127. Section 5 CIPA Submission on Behalf of Defendant (Redacted), United States v. Nacchio, No. 05-CR-00545, 2006 WL 3292818, at *8 (D. Colo. November 13, 2006).
128. Section 5 CIPA Submission on Behalf of Defendant (Redacted), United States v. Nacchio, No. 05-CR-00545, 2006 WL 3292818, at *8–9 (D. Colo. November 13, 2006).
129. Section 5 CIPA Submission on Behalf of Defendant (Redacted), United States v. Nacchio, No. 05-CR-00545, 2006 WL 3292818, at *1–2, 8–9 (D. Colo. November 13, 2006).
130. Katherine Thompson, "Ex-Qwest CEO Claims Spy Effort Began Before 9/11," Newser, October 13, 2007, http://www.newser.com/story/9419/ex-qwest-ceo-claims-spy-effort-began-before-911.html; Shane, "Former Phone Chief Says Spy Agency Sought Surveillance Help Before 9/11."
131. "Nacchio was convicted of illegal insider trading in 2007 for selling $52 million in Qwest stock in 2001 on the basis of nonpublic information about the Denver company's deteriorating finances. He has contended that he had a bright outlook on the company at the time of the stock sales." Andy Vuong, "Former Qwest CEO Joe Nacchio Completes His Prison Sentence," *Denver Post*, September 21, 2013, http://blogs.denverpost.com/techknowbytes/2013/09/21/former-qwest-ceo-joe-nacchio-completes-his-prison-sentence/11484/.
132. Ibid.
133. Ibid.

134. American Academy of Religion v. Chertoff (hereinafter cited as American Academy of Religion I), 463 F. Supp. 2d 400 (S.D.N.Y. 2006) (Crotty, J.), ordering the government to issue a final ruling on Tariq Ramadan's visa; Susan Herman, *Taking Liberties: The War on Terror and the Erosion of American Democracy* (Oxford: Oxford University Press, 2011), 9.

135. American Academy of Religion I, 463 F. Supp. 2d 404; *accord* American Academy of Religion (hereinafter cited as American Academy of Religion II), No. 06 CV 588, 2007 WL 4527504, at *1 (S.D.N.Y. December 20, 2007) (Crotty, J.).

136. American Academy of Religion I, 463 F. Supp. 2d 404.

137. American Academy of Religion I, 463 F. Supp. 2d 404–05.

138. American Academy of Religion I, 463 F. Supp. 2d 406.

139. American Academy of Religion I, 463 F. Supp. 2d 406 & n10.

140. American Academy of Religion I, 463 F. Supp. 2d 406–08.

141. American Academy of Religion I, 463 F. Supp. 2d 408 (quoting Govt's Mem. Opp'n Mot'n Prelim. Inj. 7–8).

142. American Academy of Religion I, 463 F. Supp. 2d 407.

143. American Academy of Religion I, 463 F. Supp. 2d 407 (quoting Decl. of Christopher K. Derrick, Apr. 24, 2006 ¶5.).

144. American Academy of Religion I, 463 F. Supp. 2d 422–23.

145. American Academy of Religion I, 463 F. Supp. 2d 422.

146. American Academy of Religion II, No. 06 CV 588, 2007 WL 4527504 (S.D.N.Y. December 20, 2007) (Crotty, J.)

147. American Academy of Religion II, 2007 WL 4527504, at *1.

148. Ibid.

149. American Academy of Religion II, 2007 WL 4527504, at *15.

150. American Academy of Religion v. Napolitano (hereinafter cited as American Academy of Religion III), 573 F.3d 115, 137–38 (2d Cir. 2009) (Newman, J.).

151. American Academy of Religion III, 573 F.3d at 137–38.

152. Ibid.

153. Herman, *Taking Liberties*, 9.

154. Humanitarian Law Project et al. v. Ashcroft, 309 F. Supp. 2d 1185 (C.D. Cal. 2004), *rev'd* Holder v. Humanitarian Law Project, 561 U.S. 1, 130 S. Ct. 2705 (2010); Sean Moulton, "Court Rules Portion of Patriot Act Illegal," Center for Effective Government, February 9, 2004, http://www.foreffectivegovorg/node/1834.

155. Humanitarian Law Project et al. v. Ashcroft, 309 F. Supp. 2d at 1204.

156. Humanitarian Law Project et al. v. Ashcroft, 309 F. Supp. 2d at 1188 (citing 62 Fed. Reg. 52, 649–51).

157. Humanitarian Law Project et al. v. Ashcroft, 309 F. Supp. 2d at 1188.

158. Ibid.

159. Humanitarian Law Project et al. v. Ashcroft, 309 F. Supp. 2d at 1188–89.

160. Humanitarian Law Project et al. v. Ashcroft, 309 F. Supp. 2d at 1190, 1193.

161. Humanitarian Law Project et al. v. Ashcroft, 309 F. Supp. 2d at 1198–99 (alterations in original) (quotations and citations omitted).

162. Humanitarian Law Project et al. v. Ashcroft, 309 F. Supp. 2d at 1200–01 (alterations in original) (quotations and citations omitted).

163. Doe v. Ashcroft (hereinafter cited as Doe I), 334 F. Supp. 2d 471, 526 (S.D.N.Y. 2004), *vacated by* Doe v. Gonzalez, 449 F.3d 415 (2d Cir. 2006).

164. Doe I, 334 F. Supp. 2d at 499.
165. Doe I, 334 F. Supp. 2d at 522.
166. Doe v. Gonzales (hereinafter cited as Doe II), 386 F. Supp. 2d 66 (D. Conn. 2005).
167. Doe II, 386 F. Supp. 2d at 83.
168. Intelligence Reform and Terrorism Prevention Act of 2004, Pub. L. No. 108–458, 118 Stat. 3638 (December 17, 2004).
169. USA Patriot Improvement and Reauthorization Act of 2005, Pub. L. No. 109-177, 120 Stat. 192 (March 9, 2006).
170. Doe v. Gonzales (hereinafter cited as Doe III), 449 F.3d 415 (2d Cir. 2006), *vacating as moot and remanding Doe I*, 334 F. Supp. 2d 471 (S.D.N.Y. 2004).
171. Doe v. Gonzales (hereinafter cited as Doe IV), 500 F. Supp. 2d 379, 389 (S.D.N.Y. 2007), *reversed in part by* John Doe, Inc. v. Mukasey, 549 F.3d 861 (2d Cir. 2008).
172. Doe IV, 500 F. Supp. 2d at 389, 425.
173. John Doe, Inc. v. Mukasey (hereinafter cited as Doe V), 549 F.3d 861 (2d Cir. 2008).
174. Doe V, 549 F.3d at 885.
175. Mayfield v. United States (hereinafter cited as Mayfield I), 504 F. Supp. 2d 1023 (D. Oregon 2007), *vacated and superseded* 599 F.3d 964 (9th Cir. 2010), *cert. denied* 131 S. Ct. 503.
176. Mayfield I, 504 F. Supp. 2d at 1027.
177. Mayfield I, 504 F. Supp. 2d at 1026–27.
178. Mayfield I, 504 F. Supp. 2d at 1027–28.
179. Mayfield I, 504 F. Supp. 2d at 1028.
180. Ibid.
181. Mayfield I, 504 F. Supp. 2d at 1029.
182. Mayfield I, 504 F. Supp. 2d at 1028 (citation omitted).
183. Mayfield I, 504 F. Supp. 2d at 1029.
184. Ibid.
185. Ibid.
186. Ibid.
187. Ibid.
188. Mayfield I, 504 F. Supp. 2d at 1042–43, concluding that "that 50 U.S.C. §§1804 and 1823, as amended by the Patriot Act, are unconstitutional because they violate the Fourth Amendment of the United States Constitution."
189. Mayfield I, 504 F. Supp. 2d at 1036.
190. See 50 U.S.C. §§1804, 1823 (2012); Mayfield I, 504 F. Supp. at 1042–43.
191. Mayfield I, 504 F. Supp. 2d at 1042.
192. Mayfield v. United States (hereinafter cited as Mayfield II), 599 F.3d 964 (9th Cir. 2010), *vacating and superseding* 588 F.3d 1252 (9th Cir. 2009), *cert. denied* 131 S. Ct. 503 (2010).
193. Mayfield II, 599 F.3d at 966.
194. Exec. Order No. 12,958, 60 C.F.R. 19826 (1995), *revoked by* Exec. Order No. 13,292, 68 Fed. Reg. 15315 (2003).
195. John Podesta, Speech (National Press Club, October 22, 2002), http://web.archive.org/web/20060311232421/http://www.freedomofinfo.org/foi/podesta_transcript.pdf., emphasis in original.
196. Ibid.
197. Ibid.

198. Ibid.

199. Ibid.

200. Stinnett; see Edward S. Miller, *Bankrupting the Enemy* (Annapolis: Naval Institute Press, 2007); Interview by Douglas Cirignano with Robert B. Stinnett, author of *Day of Deceit: The Truth About FDR and Pearl Harbor*, March 11, 2002, http://www.independent.org/newsroom/article.asp?id=408.

201. Interview by Douglas Cirignano.

202. Ibid.

203. Risen and Lichtblau, "Bush Secretly Lifted Some Limits on Spying in U.S. After 9/11, Officials Say."

204. Exec. Order No. 13292, 68 Fed. Reg. 15315 (2003), *revoked by* Exec. Order No. 13526, 75 Fed. Reg. 13526 (2006).

205. General Order No. 38, *Ohio Central History*, http://www.ohiohistorycentral. org/w/General_Order_No._38. But see Kevin R. Kosar, *Security Classification Policy and Procedure: E.O. 12958, as Amended* (Washington, DC: Library of Congress, Congressional Research Service, December 31, 2009), 5. Kosar's report erroneously puts the date at 1869. This is an inconsequential difference in the historical narrative but should be indicated.

206. Exec. Order No. 8381, 5 Fed. Reg. 1147 (1940); Kosar, *Security Classification Policy and Procedure*.

207. Kosar, *Security Classification Policy and Procedure*, 5.

208. Ibid.

209. Ibid., 6.

210. Ibid., 10.

211. See chapter 5.

212. Donald M. Rumsfeld, DoD News Briefing—Secretary Rumsfeld and Gen. Myers at the Pentagon, February 12, 2002, www.defense.gov/transcripts/transcript .aspx?transcriptid=2636.

213. "Q: You ever done it unilaterally? The Vice President: I don't want to get into that. There is an executive order that specifies who has classification authority, and obviously focuses first and foremost on the President, but also includes the Vice President." See "Interview of the Vice President by Brit Hume, Fox News," at the vice president's Ceremonial Office, Eisenhower Executive Office Building, February 15, 2006, http://georgewbush-whitehouse.archives.gov/news/ releases/2006/02/print/20060215-3.html.

214. Great Film Projects Co., "Yellow Journalism," in the series "Crucible of Empire: The Spanish-American War," PBS, 1999, http://www.pbs.org/crucible/frames/_ journalism.html.

215. Risen and Lichtblau, "Bush Secretly Lifted Some Limits on Spying in U.S. After 9/11, Officials Say."

216. Ibid.

217. Graff, *Threat Matrix*, 484–94, 493n.

218. Risen and Lichtblau, "Bush Secretly Lifted Some Limits on Spying in U.S. After 9/11, Officials Say."

219. Ibid.

220. Eric Lichtblau, "The Education of a 9/11 Reporter: The Inside Drama Behind the Times' Warrantless Wiretapping Story," *Slate*, March 26, 2008, http://www.slate .com/articles/news_and_politics/politics/2008/03/the_education_of_a_911_ reporter.html.

221. Most of these cases and events were just discussed, *supra*. The Supreme Court cases are discussed *infra*, chapter 12. For examples of other disadvantageous court decisions, see, e.g., Hepting v. AT&T Corp., No. C-06-672 VRW, 2006 WL 1581965 (N.D. Cal. June 6, 2006), ordering the government to give out documents despite the assertion of the States Secrets privilege; Dan Eggen and Dafna Linzer, "Judge Rules Against Wiretaps," *Washington Post*, August 18, 2006, http://www.washingtonpost.com/wpdyn/content/article/2006/08/17/ AR2006081700650.html; Byron York discussed the Cheney order in "The Little-Noticed Order That Gave Dick Cheney New Power," *National Review*, February 16, 2006, http://www.nationalreview.com/articles/216820/ little-noticed-order-gave-dick-cheney-new-power/byron-york.

222. Benjamin R. Farley, "Drones and Democracy: Missing Out on Accountability?" *South Texas Law Review* 54, no. 2 (2013): 396–401, describing the contours of "political accountability" and the effect of the vote on accountable leaders.

223. Offices of Inspectors General, "Unclassified Report on the President's Surveillance Program," Report No. 2009-0013-AS, V, at 30–31 July 10, 2009 (hereinafter cited as OIGs Unclass Report), www.fas.org/irp/eprint/psp.pdf.

224. OIGs Unclass Report, 30.

225. FISA Amendments Act of 2008, Pub. L. 110–261, 122 Stat. 2436 (2008); Protect America Act of 2007, Pub. L. 110–55, 121 Stat. 552 (2007).

226. Protect America Act of 2007, 121 Stat. at 552–53; "ACLU Fact Sheet on the 'Police America Act,'" ACLU, August 7, 2007, https://www.aclu.org/national-security/ aclu-fact-sheet-%E2%80%9Cpolice-america-act.

227. Protect America Act of 2007, 121 Stat. at 552–53.

228. Protect America Act of 2007, 121 Stat. at 555.

229. FISA Amendments Act of 2008, 122 Stat. at 2437.

230. FISA Amendments Act of 2008, title VII, §702 122 Stat. at 2441.

231. FISA Amendments Act of 2008, 122 Stat. title VII, §702, at 2438–2448.

232. Margot Kaminski, "PRISM's Legal Basis: How We Got Here, and What We Can Do to Get Back," *Atlantic*, June 7, 2013, http://www.theatlantic .com/national/archive/2013/06/prisms-legal-basis-how-we-got-here-and- what-we-can-do-to-get-back/276667/; Timothy B. Lee, "How Congress Unknowingly Legalized PRISM in 2007," *Washington Post WonkBlog* (blog), June 6, 2013, http://www.washingtonpost.com/blogs/wonkblog/wp/2013/06/06/ how-congress-unknowingly-legalized-prism-in-2007/.

233. "The American Civil Liberties Union filed a landmark lawsuit today. . . . The FISA Amendments Act of 2008, passed by Congress on Wednesday and signed by President Bush today, not only legalizes the secret warrantless surveillance program the president approved in late 2001, it gives the government new spying powers, including the power to conduct dragnet surveillance of Americans' international communications." ACLU, "ACLU Sues Over Unconstitutional Dragnet Wiretapping Law," July 10, 2008, https://www.aclu.org/national- security/aclu-sues-over-unconstitutional-dragnet-wiretapping-law, referring to *Clapper v. Amnesty Int'l*.

Chapter 12

1. Richard Sale, *Clinton's Secret Wars: The Evolution of a Commander in Chief* (New York: St. Martin's Press, 2009), 290.
2. Ibid.
3. Presidential Decision Directive 39: U.S. Policy on Counterterrorism (20631), at 4, (June 21, 1995), http://www.clintonlibrary.gov/_previous/Documents/2010%20 FOIA/Presidential%20Directives/PDD-39.pdf; Jeremy Scahill, *Dirty Wars: The World Is a Battlefield* (New York: Nation Books, 2013), 26; Sale, *Clinton's Secret Wars*, 288, 290.
4. Scahill, *Dirty Wars*, 27.
5. Sale, *Clinton's Secret Wars*, 291.
6. Ibid., 292.
7. Scahill, *Dirty Wars*, 26, 28; Jess Bravin, *The Terror Courts: Rough Justice at Guantanamo Bay* (New Haven, CT: Yale University Press, 2013), 409–10n26, compare 230.
8. Foreign Affairs Reform and Restructuring Act of 1998, Pub. L. 105–277, 112 Stat. 2681–822–23, at §2242(a) (1998).
9. 144 Cong. Rec. 27404–05.
10. "It would also bring to surface how little regard the Bush White House had for anything vaguely resembling a law enforcement approach to the perpetrators of 9/11." Scahill, *Dirty Wars*, 27–28, 29.
11. Ibid., 29.
12. Ibid.
13. Ibid.
14. Presidential Decision Directive 39: U.S. Policy on Counterterrorism (20631), at 1, (June 21, 1995), http://www.clintonlibrary.gov/_previous/Documents/2010%20 FOIA/Presidential%20Directives/PDD-39.pdf.
15. Bravin, *Terror Courts*, 22, 25.
16. Marbury v. Madison, 5 U.S. (1 Cranch) 137 (1803) (Marshall, C.J.).
17. Scahill, *Dirty Wars*, 25.
18. Bravin, *Terror Courts*, 161.
19. Standards of Conduct for Interrogation under 18 U.S.C. §§2340–2340A.
20. 18 U.S.C. §§2340–2340A (2012) (the Torture Statute).
21. U.S. Const. amend. VIII.
22. 18 U.S.C. §2340(1) (2012).
23. 18 U.S.C. §2340(2) (2012).
24. Ibid.
25. "Magna Charta in 1215 had in fact outlawed torture, except by royal torture warrant." "§2.9 Humanitarianism," *National CV of Britain*, http://www .thenationalcv.org.uk/humanity.html.
26. Jay S. Bybee, Memorandum for Alberto R. Gonzales, Counsel to the President, Re: Standards of Conduct for Interrogation Under 18 U.S.C. §§2340–2340A (August 1, 2002) (hereinafter cited as Bybee Memo I), 1, emphasis added.
27. Ibid., 2, 31–39.
28. Pub. L. 102–256, 106 Stat. 73–74, (March 12, 1992), codified at 28 U.S.C § 1350); Bybee Memo I, 1, 22–27.

29. Bybee Memo I, 22; Elise Keppler, Shirley Jean, and J. Paxton Marshall, "First Prosecution in the United States for Torture Committed Abroad: The Trial of Charles 'Chuckie' Taylor, Jr.," Human Rights Brief, *Human Rights Watch*, 2008, 18, http://www.hrw.org/sites/default/files/related_material/HRB_Chuckie_Taylor.pdf.
30. Bybee Memo I, 5.
31. Ibid., 5–6.
32. Ibid.
33. Ibid., 7–8.
34. Ibid., 7–8, 10–11.
35. Ibid., 24.
36. Ibid., 27–31.
37. Ibid., 47–50.
38. Ibid., 47–48.
39. William Saletan, "Rape Rooms: A Chronology," *Slate*, May 5, 2004, http://www.slate.com/articles/news_and_politics/ballot_box/2004/05/rape_rooms_a_chronology.html (quoting President Bush).
40. Bybee Memo I, 39–46.
41. Jay S. Bybee, Memorandum for John Rizzo, Acting General Counsel of the Central Intelligence Agency Re: Interrogation of al Qaeda Operative, August 1, 2002 (hereinafter cited as Bybee Memo II), 1, 2.
42. Bybee Memo II, 3.
43. John Yoo to Alberto Gonzales, Attorney General, August 1, 2002, (on file with the Department of Justice), (hereinafter cited as Yoo Letter), http://www.justice.gov/olc/docs/memo-gonzales-aug1.pdf.
44. Ibid.
45. Scahill, *Dirty Wars*, 26.
46. "Mauritania Criminalizes Slavery," CarnegieEndowment.org, September 18, 2007, http://carnegieendowment.org/2008/08/18/mauritania-criminalizes-slavery/6dcj.
47. Scahill, *Dirty Wars*, 58–59.
48. Ibid., 59.
49. Ibid.
50. Ibid., 81–82, 85, 93–101.
51. Ibid., 81–84, 93.
52. Ibid., 28–29, 85.
53. Ibid., 86, 91.
54. Ibid., 86–91; Bravin, *Terror Courts*, 85–87, 316.
55. Scahill, *Dirty Wars*, 86.
56. Ibid.
57. Ibid., 86–91.
58. Ibid., 89.
59. Ibid., 85.
60. Amrit Singh, *Globalizing Torture: CIA Detention and Extraordinary Rendition* New York: Open Society Foundations, 2013, 6, 9, 30–31, http://www.opensocietyfoundations.org/sites/default/files/globalizing-torture-20120205.pdf.
61. Ibid.
62. Scahill, *Dirty Wars*, 89–90; Bravin, *Terror Courts*, 101.

63. Scahill, *Dirty Wars*, 85.

64. Ibid., 90.

65. Ibid.

66. Ibid.

67. Ibid.

68. Ibid.

69. Ibid., 87.

70. Ibid., 85–86, 91, 146.

71. Ibid., 147, 152.

72. Bravin, *Terror Courts*, 101–2.

73. Ibid., 101; Vernon Loeb, "Planned Jan. 2000 Attacks Failed or Were Thwarted; Plot Targeted U.S., Jordan, American Warship, Official Says," *Washington Post*, December 24, 2000, http://www.washingtonpost.com/wp-dyn/content/article/2007/08/02/AR2007080201174.html.

74. Bravin, *Terror Courts*, 102.

75. Ibid., 294–96.

76. Ibid., 101–3; Compare ibid., 101–2, detailing transfer treatment, with Scahill, *Dirty Wars*, 89–90, quoting Int'l Comm. of the Red Cross, "ICRC Report on the Treatment of Fourteen 'High-Value Detainees' in CIA Custody" (2007); see n62 and accompanying text.

77. President George W. Bush, Memorandum: Humane Treatment of Taliban and al Qaeda Detainees para. 2.a, cd, at 12 (2002) (denying rights), http://www.pegc.us/archive/White_House/bush_memo_20020207_ed.pdf; see Bravin, *Terror Courts*, 101–2, detailing FBI treatment.

78. Bravin, *Terror Courts*, 103.

79. Ibid., 104–5.

80. Gartrell v. Ashcroft, 191 F. Supp. 2d 23 (D.D.C. 2002), applying strict scrutiny to sincerely held religious beliefs under the Religious Freedom Restoration Act.

81. Bravin, *Terror Courts*, 257.

82. Ibid.

83. Ibid., 268.

84. Ibid., 268–69.

85. Ibid., 269.

86. Ibid., 155–56.

87. Tim Golden, "In U.S. Report, Brutal Details of 2 Afghan Inmates' Deaths," *New York Times*, May 20, 2005, http://www.nytimes.com/2005/05/20/international/asia/20abuse.html?ex=1274241600&en=4579c146cb14cfd6&ei=5088.

88. Scahill, *Dirty Wars*, 155.

89. For example, Scahill, *Dirty Wars*, 155.

90. Scahill, *Dirty Wars*, 152.

91. Mark Benjamin, "Taguba Denies He's Seen Abuse Photos Suppressed by Obama," *Salon*, May 30, 2009, http://www.salon.com/2009/05/30/taguba_2/; Seymour M. Hersh, "The General's Report," *New Yorker*, June 25, 2007, http://www.newyorker.com/reporting/2007/06/25/070625fa_fact_hersh?printable=true.

92. "The Senate Armed Services Committee report on detainee abuse, made public in December 2008, traces the Abu Ghraib abuse in late 2003 to Rumsfeld's December 2002 authorization and subsequent policies and plans." Alliance for

Justice, "Accountability for Torture: Torture Timeline," www.afj.org/wp-content/uploads/2013/09/torture_timeline.pdf.

93. Bravin, *Terror Courts*, 403n7.

94. Seymour M. Hersh, "Torture at Abu Ghraib," *New Yorker*, May 10, 2004, http://www.newyorker.com/archive/2004/05/10/040510fa_fact?currentPage=all.

95. Jeffrey Rosen, "Conscience of a Conservative," *New York Times*, September 9, 2007, http://www.nytimes.com/2007/09/09/magazine/09rosen.html?_r=0&pagewanted=all.

96. Ibid.

97. Jack Goldsmith, *The Terror Presidency: Law and Judgment Inside the Bush Administration* (New York: W. W. Norton, 2007), 148–51.

98. Rosen, "Conscience of a Conservative."

99. Ibid.

100. Goldsmith, *Terror Presidency*, 161; Rosen, "Conscience of a Conservative."

101. US Department of Justice, "Legal Standards Applicable under 18 U.S.C. §§2340–2340A," December 30, 2004, http://www.justice.gov/olc/18usc23402340a2.htm.

102. See generally Steven Bradbury, Memorandum for John Rizzo: Application of 18 U.S.C. §§2340–2340A to Certain Techniques That May Be Used in the Interrogation of a High Value al Qaeda Detainee (2005), 46, http://media.luxmedia.com/aclu/olc_05102005_bradbury46pg.pdf; ibid., 20; Steven Bradbury, Memorandum for John Rizzo: Application of United States Obligations Under Article 16 of the Convention Against Torture to Certain Techniques That May Be Used in the Interrogation of a High Value al Qaeda Detainee (2005), http://media.luxmedia.com/aclu/olc_05302005_bradbury.pdf.

103. Alliance for Justice, 2.

104. Ibid.; David S. Cloud, "Navy Officer Found Not Guilty in Death of an Iraqi Prisoner," *New York Times*, May 28, 2005, http://www.nytimes.com/2005/05/28/national/28seal.html?pagewanted=print.

105. Detainee Treatment Act of 2005, Pub. L. 109–148, 119 Stat. 2739–44, at div. A, title X, §§1001–06 (2005).

106. Detainee Treatment Act of 2005, Pub. L. 109–148, 119 Stat. 2740–44, at div. A, title X, §1005 (2005).

107. Detainee Treatment Act of 2005, Pub. L. 109–148, 119 Stat. 2739, at div. A, title X, §1003 (2005).

108. Detainee Treatment Act of 2005, Pub. L. 109–148, 119 Stat. 2742, at div. A, title X, §1005(e)(1) (2005).

109. George W. Bush, "President's Statement on Signing of H.R. 2863," the White House, December 30, 2005, emphasis added, http://georgewbush-whitehouse.archives.gov/news/releases/2005/12/print/20051230-8.html.

110. Rasul v. Bush, 542 U.S. 466 (2004) (Stevens, J.).

111. Bravin, *Terror Courts*, 167–69; Jane Mayer, *The Dark Side: The Inside Story of How the War on Terror Turned into a War on American Ideals* (New York: Anchor Books, 2009), 260.

112. Mayer, *Dark Side*, 260.

113. Hamdan v. Rumsfeld, 548 U.S. 557 (2006) (Stevens, J.).

114. Hamdan v. Rumsfeld, 548 U.S. 557, 631–32 (2006) (Stevens, J.).

115. Geneva Convention Relative to the Treatment of Prisoners of War, art. 3, August 12, 1949, 6 U.S.T. 3316, 75 U.N.T.S. 135.

116. Exec. Order 13,440, 72 Fed. Reg. 40707–09, 40707 (July 20, 2007), emphasis added.
117. Exec. Order 13,440, 72 Fed. Reg. 40707, 40708 (July 20, 2007).
118. Steven Bradbury, Memorandum for John Rizzo: Application of the War Crimes Act, the Detainee Treatment Act, and Common Article 3 of the Geneva Conventions to Certain Techniques That May Be Used by the CIA in the Interrogation of High Value al Qaeda Detainees (2007), 48–49 n34.
119. Alliance for Justice, 4.

Chapter 13

1. See Chapter 7, discussing and criticizing the *Quirin* case.
2. Duncan v. Kahanamoku, 327 U.S. 304 (1946); see Chapter 7, discussing how *Duncan* overruled *Quirin*.
3. Jess Bravin, *The Terror Courts: Rough Justice At Guantanamo Bay* (New Haven, CT: Yale University Press, 2013), 168.
4. Ibid., 21–23.
5. Ibid.
6. Department of Justice, Office of Legal Counsel, "Legality of the Use of Military Commissions to Try Terrorists," *Opinions of the Office of Legal Counsel*, vol. 25 (2001): 1, emphasis added, http://www2.gwu.edu/~nsarchiv/torturingdemocracy/documents/20011106.pdf.
7. Ibid., 14.
8. Bravin, *Terror Courts*, 41–42.
9. Federal Bureau of Investigation, "George John Dasch and the Nazi Saboteurs," http://www.fbi.gov/about-us/history/famous-cases/nazi-saboteurs/george-john-dasch-and-the-nazi-saboteurs.
10. Bravin, *Terror Courts*, 35–39.
11. Ibid., 39.
12. Ibid., 38, 50–51.
13. Fed. R. Evid. 403 (2013).
14. Bravin, *Terror Courts*, 38.
15. Ibid., 43.
16. Ibid., 43–44.
17. See generally Military Order of November 13, 2001, *Detention, Treatment, and Trial of Certain Non-Citizens in the War Against Terrorism*, 66 Fed. Reg. 57,833–36 (November 16, 2001). See Military Order of November 13, 2001, *Detention, Treatment, and Trial of Certain Non-Citizens in the War Against Terrorism*, 66 Fed. Reg. 57,833, 57,835, at §4.c(4) (November 16, 2001).
18. Military Order of November 13, 2001, *Detention, Treatment, and Trial of Certain Non-Citizens in the War Against Terrorism*, 66 Fed. Reg. 57,833–36 (Nov. 16, 2001).
19. U.S. Department of Defense, Military Commission Order No. 1: Procedures for Trials by Military Commissions of Certain Non-United States Citizens in the War Against Terrorism (March 21, 2002); ibid., §5.B, at 6; Bravin, *Terror Courts*, 59–60.
20. President George W. Bush, Memorandum: Humane Treatment of Taliban and al Qaeda Detainees para. 2.a, cd, at 12 (2002) (denying rights), http://www.pegc.us/archive/White_House/bush_memo_20020207_ed.pdf.

21. Bravin, *Terror Courts*, 278.

22. Ibid., 65.

23. Patrick F. Philbin and John C. Yoo, Memorandum for William J. Haynes II: Possible Habeas Jurisdiction Over Aliens Held in Guantanamo Bay, Cuba, (December 28, 2001) (hereinafter cited as Philbin and Yoo Memo), http://www .torturingdemocracy.org/documents/20011228.pdf.

24. Philbin and Yoo Memo; Bravin, *Terror Courts*, 75–76.

25. Bravin, *Terror Courts*, 77.

26. Ibid., 79.

27. Ibid., 93–94, 110–11, 156–61.

28. Convention Against Torture, Rochin v. California, 342 U.S. 165 (1952) (Frankfurter, J.).

29. Bravin, *Terror Courts*, 115–16.

30. Ibid., 116, 119–20, 134–35, 156–61.

31. Ibid., 119–20.

32. Ibid., 128.

33. Ibid., 128–130.

34. Hamdan v. Rumsfeld, 548 U.S. 557, 598–613 (2006) (plurality opinion).

35. Bravin, *Terror Courts*, 129–30.

36. Ibid., 116, 119–20, 134–39, 156–61.

37. Associated Press, "Military Denies Rigging Guantanamo Trials," *Washington Post*, August 2, 2005, http://www.washingtonpost.com/wp-dyn/content/ article/2005/08/01/AR2005080101488.html.

38. Bravin, *Terror Courts*, 138.

39. Jackie Northam, "Chief Guantanamo Prosecutor Departs," NPR, April 22, 2004, http://www.npr.org/templates/story/story.php?storyId=1846734.

40. Bravin, *Terror Courts*, 150–52.

41. Ibid., 167.

42. Rumsfeld v. Padilla, 542 U.S. 426 (2004) (Rehnquist, C.J.); Rasul v. Bush, 542 U.S. 466 (2004) (Stevens, J.); Hamdi v. Rumsfeld, 542 U.S. 507 (2004) (Stevens, J.).

43. Bravin, *Terror Courts*, 167–69; Jane Mayer, *The Dark Side: The Inside Story of How the War on Terror Turned into a War on American Ideals* (New York: Anchor Books, 2009), 260.

44. Bravin, *Terror Courts*, 170–71.

45. Rumsfeld v. Padilla, 542 U.S. 426, 430 (2004) (Rehnquist, C.J.).

46. Rumsfeld v. Padilla, 542 U.S. 426, 430–31 (2004) (Rehnquist, C.J.).

47. Ibid.

48. Rumsfeld v. Padilla, 542 U.S. 426, 431 (2004) (Rehnquist, C.J.); Padilla *ex rel.* Newman v. Bush, 233 F. Supp. 2d 564, 571 (S.D.N.Y. 2002), aff'd sub. nom., Padilla *ex rel.* Newman v. Rumsfeld, 243 F. Supp. 2d 42 (S.D.N.Y. 2003).

49. Rumsfeld v. Padilla, 542 U.S. 426, 431 (2004) (Rehnquist, C.J.).

50. Rumsfeld v. Padilla, 542 U.S. 426, 432 (2004) (Rehnquist, C.J.).

51. Rumsfeld v. Padilla, 542 U.S. 426, 431 (2004) (Rehnquist, C.J.).

52. Rumsfeld v. Padilla, 542 U.S. 426, 432 (2004) (Rehnquist, C.J.); Padilla v. Yoo, 678 F.3d 748, 751 (9th Cir. 2012).

53. Padilla v. Yoo, 678 F.3d 748, 766–67 (9th Cir. 2012); see Padilla v. Yoo, 678 F.3d at 767n15, collecting cases and describing various torture cases ongoing.

54. Rumsfeld v. Padilla, 542 U.S. 426 (2004) (Rehnquist, C.J.) (citations omitted).
55. Ibid.
56. Rumsfeld v. Padilla, 542 U.S. 426, 442, 428 (2004) (Rehnquist, C.J.).
57. Rumsfeld v. Padilla, 542 U.S. 426, 430, 433–34 (2004) (Rehnquist, C.J.).
58. "Reaching the merits, the Court of Appeals held that the President lacks authority to detain Padilla militarily. The court concluded that neither the President's Commander in Chief power nor the AUMF authorizes military detentions of American citizens captured on American soil. To the contrary, the Court of Appeals found in both our case law and in the Non-Detention Act, a strong presumption against domestic military detention of citizens absent explicit congressional authorization. Accordingly, the court granted the writ of habeas corpus and directed the Secretary to release Padilla from military custody within 30 days." Rumsfeld v. Padilla, 542 U.S. 426, 434 (2004) (Rehnquist, C.J.)
59. Interview with Shafiq Rasul, Detainee #086, GWU Torturing Democracy Project, October 22, 2007, http://www.gwu.edu/~nsarchiv/torturingdemocracy/interviews/shafiq_rasul.html#interrogations.
60. Rasul v. Bush, 542 U.S. 466 (2004) (Stevens, J.).
61. Rasul v. Bush, 542 U.S. 466, 471–72 (2004) (Stevens, J.).
62. Rasul v. Bush, 542 U.S. 466, 471–72 (2004) (Stevens, J.) (quoting 215 F. Supp. 2d 55, 68 (D.D.C.2002)).
63. Rasul v. Bush, 542 U.S. 466, 473 (2004) (Stevens, J.).
64. Rasul v. Bush, 542 U.S. 466, 484–85 (2004) (Stevens, J.) (citations and parallel citation omitted), emphasis added.
65. Rasul v. Bush, 542 U.S. 466, 485 (2004) (Stevens, J.).
66. Rasul v. Bush, 542 U.S. 466, 489 (2004) (Scalia, Rehnquist & Thomas, C.J., J.J., dissenting).
67. Hamdi v. Rumsfeld, 542 U.S. 507, 508 (2004).
68. Hamdi v. Rumsfeld, 542 U.S. 507, 510, 511 (2004) (O'Connor, J.) (plurality op.).
69. Hamdi v. Rumsfeld, 542 U.S. 507, 510 (2004) (O'Connor, J.) (plurality op.).
70. Ibid.
71. Hamdi v. Rumsfeld, 542 U.S. 507, 511 (2004) (O'Connor, J.) (plurality op.).
72. Ibid.
73. Ibid.
74. Hamdi v. Rumsfeld, 542 U.S. 507, 516–17 (2004) (O'Connor, J.) (plurality op.).
75. Hamdi v. Rumsfeld, 542 U.S. 507, 528–35 (2004) (O'Connor, J.) (plurality op.).
76. Hamdi v. Rumsfeld, 542 U.S. 507, 525–28 (2004) (O'Connor, J.) (plurality op.).
77. Hamdi v. Rumsfeld, 542 U.S. 507, 533 (2004) (O'Connor, J.) (plurality op.).
78. Hamdi v. Rumsfeld, 542 U.S. at 517.
79. Ibid.
80. Hamdi v. Rumsfeld, 542 U.S. at 518.
81. Hamdi v. Rumsfeld, 542 U.S. at 519.
82. Hamdi v. Rumsfeld, 542 U.S. 507, 554 (2004) (Scalia & Stevens, J.J., dissenting).
83. Habeas Corpus Suspension Act, 12 Stat. 755–58 (1863).
84. Bravin, Terror Courts, 170–71.
85. Paul Wolfowitz, Memorandum for the Secretary of the Navy: Order Establishing Combatant Status Review Tribunals, July 7, 2004, http://www.defense.gov/news/Jul2004/d20040707review.pdf.

86. Ibid., 3, emphasis added.
87. Bravin, *Terror Courts*, 185.
88. Ibid., 185–90.
89. Ibid., 201, 205–13, 220.
90. Hamdan v. Rumsfeld, 344 F. Supp. 2d 152 (D.D.C. 2004) (Robertson, J.); Bravin, *Terror Courts*, 219–20.
91. Bravin, *Terror Courts*, 223.
92. 415 F.3d 33 (D.C. Cir. 2005).
93. 546 U.S. 1002 (2005) (granting cert.).
94. Bravin, *Terror Courts*, 276–77.
95. U.S. Const. art. III.
96. Bravin, *Terror Courts*, 276.
97. Detainee Treatment Act of 2005, Pub. L. 109–148, 119 Stat. 2739–44, 2742, at div. A, title X, §1005(e)(1) (2005).
98. Detainee Treatment Act of 2005, Pub. L. 109–148, 119 Stat. 2739–44, 2742, at div. A, title X, §1005(e)(2), (3) (2005).
99. Nat'l Mut. Ins. Co. of Dist. of Col. v. Tidewater Transfer Co., 337 U.S. 582, 655 (1949) (Frankfurter & Reed, J.J., dissenting), emphasis in original.
100. Bravin, *Terror Courts*, 276.
101. Hamdan v. Rumsfeld, 548 U.S. 557, (2006).
102. Associated Press, "Bin Laden's Driver Outmanoeuvres Guantanamo Trials," *Sydney Morning Herald*, November 9, 2004, http://www.smh .com.au/news/Global-Terrorism/Osamas-driver-outmanoeuvres-terror-trials/2004/11/09/1099781361307.html.
103. Bravin, *Terror Courts*, 278.
104. "Triple Suicide at Guantanamo Camp," BBC News, June 11, 2006, http://news .bbc.co.uk/2/hi/americas/5068228.stm; "Guantanamo Suicides a 'PR move'," BBC News, June 11, 2006, http://news.bbc.co.uk/2/hi/americas/5069230.stm.
105. Bravin, *Terror Courts*, 281.
106. Hamdan v. Rumsfeld, 548 U.S. 557 (2006).
107. Hamdan v. Rumsfeld, 548 U.S. 557 (2006).
108. Hamdan v. Rumsfeld, 548 U.S. 557, 560 (2006).
109. Hamdan v. Rumsfeld, 548 U.S. 557, 613–17 (2006) (Stevens, J.).
110. Hamdan v. Rumsfeld, 548 U.S. 557, 620 (2006) (Stevens, J.).
111. Hamdan v. Rumsfeld, 548 U.S. 557, 623–24 (2006) (Stevens, J.).
112. Hamdan v. Rumsfeld, 548 U.S. 557, 631–32 (2006) (Stevens, J.).
113. Bravin, *Terror Courts*, 306.
114. Ibid., 306–8.
115. Ibid., 308.
116. Ibid.
117. Ibid., 310.
118. Military Commissions Act of 2006, Pub. L. 109–366, 120 Stat. 2600–37 (2006).
119. Bravin, *Terror Courts*, 310–11.
120. Bravin, *Terror Courts*, 311.
121. Bravin, *Terror Courts*, 310.
122. Military Commissions Act of 2006, Pub. L. 109–366, 120 Stat. 2600–37, §3, at 2607 (2006).

123. Military Commissions Act of 2006, Pub. L. 109–366, 120 Stat. 2600–37, §3, at 2609 (2006).

124. Military Commissions Act of 2006, Pub. L. 109–366, 120 Stat. 2600–37, §7, at 2635–36 (2006).

125. Bravin, *Terror Courts*, 312.

126. Ibid., 285, 312.

127. Ibid., 312–14; "David Hicks: 'Australian Taleban'," BBC News, May 20, 2007, http://news.bbc.co.uk/2/hi/asia-pacific/3044386.stm.

128. Bravin, *Terror Courts*, 316–17; Michael Melia, "Ex-Gitmo Prosecutor Charges Pentagon Interference," *Star*, April 29, 2008, http://www.thestar.com/news/world/2008/04/29/exgitmo_prosecutor_charges_pentagon_interference.html.

129. Andy Worthington, "Breaking: New Chief Prosecutor Tapped for Military Commissions at Guantanamo," AlterNet.org, May 6, 2009, http://www.alternet.org/story/139842/breaking%3A_new_chief_prosecutor_tapped_for_military_commissions_at_guantanamo.

130. Boumediene v. Bush, 476 F.3d 981 (D.C. Cir. 2007).

131. Boumediene v. Bush, 549 U.S. 1328, *vacated by* 551 U.S. 1160 (2007).

132. Boumediene v. Bush, 551 U.S. 1160 (2007).

133. Boumediene v. Bush, 553 U.S. 723, 723 (2008) (Kennedy, J.), emphasis added.

134. Boumediene v. Bush, 553 U.S. 723, 738–39 (2008) (Kennedy, J.) (citations omitted).

135. Boumediene v. Bush, 553 U.S. 723, 770 (2008) (Kennedy, J.).

136. Boumediene v. Bush, 553 U.S. 723, 771 (2008) (Kennedy, J.).

137. Ibid.

138. Boumediene v. Bush, 553 U.S. 723, 792 (2008) (Kennedy, J.).

139. Bravin, *Terror Courts*, 380.

Chapter 14

1. "U.S. Officials Guilty of War Crimes for Using 9/11 as a False Justification for the Iraq War," *Washington's Blog*, October 24, 2012, http://www.washingtonsblog.com/2012/10/5-hours-after-the-911-attacks-donald-rumsfeld-said-my-interest-is-to-hit-saddam-he-also-said-go-massive-sweep-it-all-up-things-related-and-not-and-at-2.html; Lydia Saad, "Bush Presidency Closes with 34% Approval, 61% Disapproval," Gallup, January 14, 2009, http://www.gallup.com/poll/113770/bush-presidency-closes-34-approval-61-disapproval.aspx.

2. The Who, "Won't Get Fooled Again" (MCA Records, 1971).

3. Jacob Weisberg, *The Bush Tragedy* (New York: Random House, 2008).

4. Jeremy Scahill, *Dirty Wars: The World Is a Battlefield* (New York: Nation Books, 2013), 250.

5. Alison Smale, "Amid New Storm in U.S.-Europe Relationship, a Call for Talks on Spying," *New York Times*, October 25, 2013, http://www.nytimes.com/2013/10/26/world/europe/fallout-over-american-spying-revelations.html?_r=0.

6. Bob Woodward, *Obama's Wars* (New York: Simon & Schuster, 2010).

7. Scahill, *Dirty Wars*, 513–21, "Epilogue: Perpetual War."

8. Scahill, *Dirty Wars*, 118–29, 191–209, 219–29, 270–78, 294–302 393–97, 453, 487–494, discussing the U.S. history in Somalia; 48–60, 75–81, 130–134, 210–15, 230–44, 259–69, 314–24, 375–85, 398–402, 430–34, 460–69, 495–511, discussing the United States in Yemen and al-Aulaqi; 167–79, 215–18, 298–353, 403–29, 444–50, 458–59, discussing the United States in Pakistan; John Barry, "America's Secret Libya War," Daily Beast, August 30, 2011, http://www.thedailybeast.com/articles/2011/08/30/america-s-secret-libya-war-u-s-spent-1-billion-on-covert-ops-helping-nato.html.

9. Scahill, *Dirty Wars*, 124–27.

10. Ibid., 118–19.

11. Ibid., 119.

12. Ibid., 119, 121, 123.

13. Ibid., 120–21.

14. Ibid., 121–22.

15. Ibid., 121.

16. Ibid., 123–24.

17. For example, ibid., 127.

18. For example, ibid., 127–28.

19. Ibid., 128.

20. Ibid.

21. Ibid., 129.

22. Ibid., 121.

23. Ibid., 191.

24. Ibid., 192.

25. Ibid.

26. Ibid., 192–93.

27. Ibid., 193.

28. Ibid., 193–94.

29. Ibid., 193.

30. Ibid., 196.

31. Ibid., 200.

32. Ibid., 201.

33. Ibid., 202.

34. Ibid., 203.

35. Ibid.

36. Ibid., 203–4.

37. Ibid., 202.

38. Ibid., 208–9.

39. Ibid., 206–8.

40. Ibid., 208–9.

41. Ibid., 220.

42. Ibid., 219–21, 223–24.

43. Ibid., 224.

44. Ibid.

45. Ibid., 225.

46. Ibid.

47. Ibid., 225–26.

48. Ibid., 226–27.

49. Ibid., 226–28.

50. Ibid.

51. Ibid., 228.

52. Steven Lee Myers, "Putin's Silence on Syria Suggests His Resignation Over Intervention," *New York Times*, August 28, 2013, quoting Russian Foreign Minister Sergey V. Lavrov, http://www.nytimes.com/2013/08/29/world/middleeast/putin-on-syria.html.

53. Scahill, *Dirty Wars*, 270–73.

54. Ibid., 270–73, 276–77.

55. Ibid., 277.

56. Ibid., 393.

57. Ibid., 395.

58. Ibid., 453.

59. Ibid., 487–91.

60. Ibid., 493.

61. Ibid., 487.

62. Ibid., 493.

63. Ibid.

64. Ibid., 64–65, 210–11.

65. Ibid., 64.

66. Ibid., 65; Charlie Savage, "Secret U.S. Memo Made Legal Case to Kill a Citizen," *New York Times*, October 8, 2011, http://www.nytimes.com/2011/10/09/world/middleeast/ secret-us-memo-made-legal-case-to-kill-a-citizen .html?pagewanted=all&_r=0.

67. Scahill, *Dirty Wars*, 65–66.

68. Ibid., 66, 75–80.

69. Ibid., 130.

70. Ibid., 130–33.

71. Ibid., 132.

72. Ibid., 133.

73. Ibid., 210–14.

74. Ibid., 235–36, 243.

75. Ibid., 237.

76. Ibid., 254–55.

77. Ibid., 255.

78. Ibid., 261.

79. Ibid., 256–263.

80. Ibid., 304–8, 321.

81. Ibid., 306.

82. Ibid., 306–7; see the unpaginated photographic insert in the book.

83. Ibid., 310–11.

84. Ibid., 309–10.

85. Ibid., 311–13.

86. Ibid., 321–23.

87. Ibid., 350.

88. Ibid., 350–51.

89. Ibid., 356–63.
90. Ibid., 386–92.
91. Ibid., 398.
92. Ibid., 431–432, 464.
93. Ibid., 465.
94. Ibid., 466, 499.
95. "Obama: Israel Has 'Every Right' to Defend Itself from Gaza Missile Attacks," NBC News.com, November 18, 2012. The president was then traveling in Asia; he delivered the speech while in Thailand.
96. Scahill, *Dirty Wars*, 168–69, 176–79.
97. Ibid., 168–69, 176–79.
98. Ibid., 168–69, 215–16.
99. Ibid., 168–69, 216.
100. Ibid., 168–169, 217.
101. Ibid., 168–69, 217–218.
102. Ibid., 168–169, 250.
103. Ibid., 251.
104. Ibid., 252.
105. Ibid., 418.
106. Ibid., 418–19.
107. Ibid., 420.
108. Ibid., 403, 406.
109. Ibid., 404.
110. Ibid., 405.
111. Ibid., 406–7.
112. Ibid., 404.
113. Ibid., 418–19.
114. Ibid., 419.
115. Ibid.
116. Ibid.
117. Ibid., 420, 423.
118. Ibid., 421.
119. Ibid.
120. Ibid., 423.
121. Ibid., 424.
122. Ibid., 424–25.
123. Ibid., 425; Declan Walsh and Ewen MacAskill, "American Who Sparked Diplomatic Crisis Over Lahore Shooting Was CIA Spy," *Guardian* (UK), February 20, 2011, http://www.theguardian.com/world/2011/feb/20/us-raymond-davis-lahore-cia.
124. Scahill, *Dirty Wars*, 425; Glenn Greenwald, "The NYT's Journalistic Obedience," *Salon*, February 21, 2011, http://www.salon.com/2011/02/21/nyt_16/.
125. Scahill, *Dirty Wars*, 426.
126. Ibid., 425–27.
127. Ibid., 427.
128. Ibid., 427–28.
129. Ibid., 428.

130. Ibid.
131. Eric. S. Margolis, "The Gaddafi I Knew," *American Conservative*, October 24, 2011, http://www.theamericanconservative.com/the-gaddafi-i-knew/.
132. Ronald Reagan, The President's News Conference, Washington, DC, April 9, 1986, http://www.presidency.ucsb.edu/ws/index .php?pid=37105#axzz2iMbNB7st.
133. "Bush Speaks with Gaddafi in Historic Phone Call," *Washington Post*, November 18, 2008, http://articles.washingtonpost.com/2008-11-18/world/36863733_1_saif-al-islam-gaddafi-libya-s-moammar-gaddafi-human-rights.
134. Mark Ensalaco, "The Great Debate: Our Disturbing Relationship with Gaddafi," Reuters, August 23, 2011, http://blogs.reuters.com/great-debate/2011/08/23/ our-disturbing-relationship-with-gaddafi/.
135. Human Rights Watch, *Delivered into Enemy Hands*, September 6, 2012, 2, http:// www.hrw.org/reports/2012/09/05/delivered-enemy-hands.
136. US Department of State, "U.S. Embassy in Tripoli," http://libya.usembassy.gov/; Scott Macleod, "Why Gaddafi's Now a Good Guy," *Time*, May 16, 2006, http:// content.time.com/time/world/article/0,8599,1194766,00.html.
137. "Bush Speaks with Gaddafi in Historic Phone Call."
138. Manilo Dinucci, "McCain-Hillary in 2009: Libya Is 'An Important Ally in the War on Terrorism,' Gaddafi Is 'a Peacemaker in Africa,'" Center for Research on Globalization, April 25, 2011, http://www.globalresearch.ca/ mccain-hillary-in-2009-libya-is-an-important-ally-in-the-war-on-terrorism-gaddafi-is-a-peacemaker-in-africa.
139. Sec. Con. Res. 1973, U.N. S/RES/1973 (March 17, 2011); Alistair Macdonald, "Cameron Doesn't Rule Out Military Force for Libya," *Wall Street Journal*, March 1, 2011, http://online.wsj.com/article/SB10001424052748704615504576172383796 304482.html.
140. Bruce Ackerman, "Legal Acrobatics, Illegal War," *New York Times*, June 20, 2011, http://www.nytimes.com/2011/06/21/opinion/21Ackerman.html.
141. Ibid.
142. Ibid.
143. Ibid.
144. Ibid.
145. Ibid.
146. "Libya Crisis: Gaddafi Army 'Not at Breaking Point,'" BBC News, March 31, 2011, http://www.bbc.co.uk/news/world-us-canada-12924807.
147. Barry, "America's Secret Libya War."
148. Ibid.
149. Michael S. Schmidt and Eric Schmitt, "U.S. Officials Say Libya Approved Commando Raids," *New York Times*, October 9, 2013, http://www.nytimes .com/2013/10/09/world/africa/us-officials-say-libya-approved-commando-raids.html; Carlotta Gall and David D. Kirkpatrick, "Libya Condemns U.S. for Seizing Terror Suspect," *New York Times*, October 7, 2013, http://www.nytimes .com/2013/10/07/world/africa/american-raids-in-africa.html; Benjamin Weiser and Eric Schmitt, "U.S. Said to Hold Qaeda Suspect on Navy Ship," *New York Times*, October 7, 2013, http://www.nytimes.com/2013/10/07/world/africa/a-terrorism-suspect-long-known-to-prosecutors.html.

150. Paul Cruickshank et al., "Phone Call Links Benghazi Attack to al Qaeda Commander," CNN, March 5, 2013, http://www.cnn.com/2013/03/05/world/africa/benghazi-al-qaeda.

151. Clifford Krauss, "In Libya, Unrest Brings Oil Industry to Standstill," *New York Times*, September 12, 2013, http://www.nytimes.com/2013/09/13/world/africa/in-libya-unrest-brings-oil-industry-to-standstill.html.

152. Ibid.

153. Carl Herman, "US War Crimes: Torture and a Call for Truth and Reconciliation," *Examiner*, August 21, 2009, http://www.examiner.com/article/us-war-crimes-torture-and-a-call-for-truth-and-reconciliation.

154. Exec. Order No. 13491, 74 Fed. Reg. 4893 (January 22, 2009).

155. Exec. Order No. 13491, 74 Fed. Reg. 4893, 4894 (January 22, 2009).

156. Human Rights Watch, "Delivered Into Enemy Hands," 2.

157. Scott Horton, "The Black Hole of Bagram," *Harper's*, December 1, 2009, http://harpers.org/blog/2009/12/the-black-hole-of-bagram/.

158. Ibid.; Joshua Partlow and Julie Tate, "2 Afghans Allege Abuse at U.S. Site," *Washington Post*, November 28, 2009, http://www.washingtonpost.com/wp-dyn/content/article/2009/11/27/AR2009112703438.html.

159. Nat Hentoff, "Torture Under Obama," Cato Institute, February 17, 2010, http://www.cato.org/publications/commentary/torture-under-obama.

160. Sarah Childress, "Six Reasons the 'Dark Side' Still Exists Under Obama," PBS Frontline, April 22, 2013, http://www.pbs.org/wgbh/pages/frontline/criminal-justice/six-reasons-the-dark-side-still-exists-under-obama/; Dan Froomkin, "New Torture Report Blames Obama and the Media for Not Confronting the Truth," *Huffington Post*, April 17, 2013, http://www.huffingtonpost.com/dan-froomkin/torture-report-obama-media_b_3099792.html; Hentoff, "Torture Under Obama."

161. Barack Obama, Speech (Woodrow Wilson International Center, August 1, 2007), http://www.cfr.org/elections/obamas-speech-woodrow-wilson-center/p13974.

162. Bravin, *Terror Courts*, 355, 381.

163. Jason Leopold, "Former Guantanamo Chief Prosecutor: 'A Pair of Testicles Fell Off the President After Election Day,'" Center for the Study of Human Rights in the Americas, November 13, 2011, http://humanrights.ucdavis.edu/projects/the-guantanamo-testimonials-project/testimonies/testimonies-of-prosecution-lawyers/former-guantanamo-chief-prosecutor-a-pair-of-testicles-fell-off-the-president-after-election-day.

164. Exec. Order No. 13,491, 74 Fed. Reg. 4893, 4894 (2009).

165. Exec. Order No. 13,492, 74 Fed. Reg. 4897 (2009).

166. Exec. Order No. 13,493, 74 Fed. Reg. 4901 (2009).

167. Bravin, *Terror Courts*, 355.

168. Ibid.

169. Jason Leopold, "A Campaign Promise Dies: Obama and Military Commissions," Truthout, April 4, 2011, http://www.truth-out.org/news/item/285:a-campaign-promise-dies-obama-and-military-commissions.

170. Barack Obama, Statement on Military Commissions, the White House, May 15, 2009, http://www.whitehouse.gov/the_press_office/Statement-of-President-Barack-Obama-on-Military-Commissions/.

171. "Accused 9/11 Plotter Khalid Sheikh Mohammed Faces New York Trial," CNN, November 13, 2009, http://edition.cnn.com/2009/CRIME/11/13/khalid.sheikh.mohammed/index.html.

172. Military Commissions Act of 2009, 123 Stat. 2574, div. A, title XVIII, §1802, at 2582 (2009); ACLU, "House Passes Changes to Guantánamo Military Commissions," October 8, 2009, http://www.aclu.org/national-security/house-passes-changes-guantanamo-military-commissions.

173. Military Commissions Act of 2009, 123 Stat. 2574, div. A, title XVIII, §1802, at 2587 (2009).

174. ACLU, "House Passes Changes to Guantánamo Military Commissions."

175. Bravin, *Terror Courts*, 363.

176. National Defense Authorization Act for Fiscal Year 2012, Pub. L 112–18, 125 Stat. 1297, div. A, title X, §1021, at 1562 (2009).

177. National Defense Authorization Act for Fiscal Year 2012, Pub. L 112–18, 125 Stat. 1297, div. A, title X, §1022, at 1563–64 (2009).

178. National Defense Authorization Act for Fiscal Year 2012, Pub. L 112–18, 125 Stat. 1297, div. A, title X, §1027, at 1566–67 (2009).

179. Geneve Mantri, "House Passes NDAA & White House Won't Veto Indefinite Detention," Amnesty International, December 15, 2011, http://blog.amnestyusa.org/us/house-passes-ndaa-white-house-wont-veto-indefinite-detention/.

180. Andy Worthington, "US Military Admits Only 2.5 Percent of All Prisoners Ever Held at Guantánamo Will Be Tried," *AndyWorthington.com* (blog), June 18, 2013, http://www.andyworthington.co.uk/2013/06/18/us-military-admits-only-2-5-percent-of-all-prisoners-ever-held-at-guantanamo-will-be-tried/#sthash.xFKv1Quf.dpuf.

181. Jason Ryan, "In Reversal, Obama Orders Guantanamo Military Trial for 9/11 Mastermind Khalid Sheikh Mohammed," ABC News, April 4, 2011, http://abcnews.go.com/Politics/911-mastermind-khalid-sheikh-mohammed-military-commission/story?id=13291750.

Chapter 15

1. Lloyd C. Gardner, *Killing Machine: The American Presidency in the Age of Drone Warfare* (New York, New Press, 2013), xii.

2. Ibid.

3. See ibid., xii, 128–29.

4. Exec. Order No. 12,333, 3 C.F.R. 1981 Comp. at 200, 46 Fed. Reg. 59941 (1981).

5. Gardner, *Killing Machine*, 129; Ian G. R. Shaw, "The Rise of the Predator Empire: Tracing the History of U.S. Drones," *Understanding Empire*, 2013, http://understandingempire.wordpress.com/2-0-a-brief-history-of-u-s-drones/.

6. Gardner, *Killing Machine*, 129.

7. Ibid.

8. Ibid., 128–29.

9. Jeremy Scahill, *Dirty Wars: The World Is a Battlefield* (New York: Nation Books, 2013), 168–69, 251.

10. "Out of Sight, Out of Mind: Victims," Pitch Interactive, July 3, 2013, http://drones.pitchinteractive.com/; Jack Serle and Chris Woods, "Six-Month Update: U.S. Covert Actions in Pakistan, Yemen, and Somalia," Bureau of Investigative

Journalism, July 1, 2013, http://www.thebureauinvestigates.com/2013/07/01/six-month-update-us-covert-actions-in-pakistan-yemen-and-somalia/.

11. Gardner, *Killing Machine*, xii.

12. Chris Woods, "'Drones Causing Mass Trauma Among Civilians,' Major Study Finds," Bureau of Investigative Journalism, September 25, 2012, http://www.thebureauinvestigates.com/blog/2012/09/25 drones-causing-mass-trauma-among-civilians-major-study-finds/.

13. "Drones: Has the United States Committed War Crimes?" *Week*, November 8, 2013, 6.

14. Gardner, *Killing Machine*,132.

15. Ibid., ix.

16. Scahill, *Dirty Wars*, 32.

17. Ibid., 31–33.

18. Randal John Meyer, "The Twin Perils of the al-Aulaqi Case: The Treason Clause and the Equal Protection Clause," *Brooklyn Law Review* 79, no. 1 (2013): 244; Scahill, *Dirty Wars*, 33–36.

19. Scahill, *Dirty Wars*, 41–42, 45.

20. Ibid., 37–38, 40–41; Meyer, "Twin Perils," 244nn94–95.

21. Scahill, *Dirty Wars*, 37–38, 47.

22. Ibid., 67–74; Meyer, "Twin Perils," 244–45.

23. Scahill, *Dirty Wars*, 67, 74; Meyer, "Twin Perils," 244.

24. Designation of ANWAR AL-AULAQI Pursuant to Executive Order 13224 and the Global Terrorism Sanctions Regulations, 31 C.F.R. Part 594, 75 Fed. Reg. 43233-01 (2010).

25. Meyer, "Twin Perils," 246n. 110.

26. Ibid., 246.

27. Mark Mazzetti, Eric Schmitt, and Robert F. Worth, "Two-Year Manhunt Led to Killing of Awlaki in Yemen," *New York Times*, September 30, 2011, http://www.nytimes.com/2011/10/01/world/middleeast/anwar-al-awlaki-is-killed-in-yemen.html?pagewanted=all; see Scahill, *Dirty Wars*, 501–3.

28. Scahill, *Dirty Wars*, 289.

29. Ibid., 290–91, 375–76.

30. Ibid., 377–81.

31. Ibid., 496, 507.

32. Ibid., 496.

33. Ibid., 500.

34. Ibid., 501.

35. Ibid., 507.

36. Ibid.

37. Ibid.

38. Ibid., 507–9.

39. Scott Shane and Eric Schmitt, "One Drone Victim's Trail from Raleigh to Pakistan," *New York Times*, May 22, 2013, http://www.nytimes.com/2013/05/23/us/one-drone-victims-trail-from-raleigh-to-pakistan.html?_r=0.

40. Tara McKelvey, "Inside the Killing Machine," *Newsweek*, February 13, 2011, http://www.thedailybeast.com/newsweek/2011/02/13/inside-the-killing-machine.html.

41. Meyer, "Twin Perils," 280.
42. "Islamist Cleric Anwar al-Awlaki Killed in Yemen," BBC News, September 30, 2011, http://www.bbc.co.uk/news/world-middle-east-15121879.
43. New York Times Co. v. U.S. Dep't of Justice, 915 F. Supp.2d 508 (S.D.N.Y. 2013) (McMahon, J.).
44. New York Times Co., 915 F. Supp.2d at 515–16.
45. New York Times Co., 915 F. Supp.2d at 535.
46. New York Times Co., 915 F. Supp.2d at 535–38.
47. See, e.g., ACLU v. CIA, 710 F.3d 422 (D.C. Cir. 2013) (Garland, C.J.).
48. Al-Aulaqi v. Obama, 727 F. Supp.2d 1, 46-47 (D.D.C. 2010), dismissing for lack of standing and giving dicta on the political question doctrine.
49. Al-Aulaqi, 727 F. Supp.2d at 40.
50. Al-Aulaqi, 727 F. Supp.2d at 52.
51. Ibid.
52. U.S. Const. amend V.
53. "[T]he federal right to jury trial attaches where an offense is punishable by as much as six months' imprisonment. I think this follows both from the breadth of the language of the Sixth Amendment, which provides for a jury in 'all criminal prosecutions,' and the evidence of historical practice." Baldwin v. New York, 399 U.S. 117, 119–20 (1970).
54. Meyer, "Twin Perils," 244–45, discussing Anwar al-Aulaqi's criminal history.
55. Ibid., 288–89, emphasis in original.
56. Eric Holder, Speech (Northwestern University School of Law, Chicago, IL, March 5, 2012), http://www.justice.gov/iso/opa/ag/speeches/2012/ag-speech-1203051.html.
57. FAA Modernization and Reform Act, Pub. L. 112–95, 126 Stat. 11 (2012) (codified at 40 U.S.C).
58. 126 Stat. title III.B, §332(a)(1), at 73.
59. Robert Molko, "The Drones Are Coming: Will the Fourth Amendment Stop Their Threat to Our Privacy?" Brooklyn Law Review 78, no. 4 (2013): 1283.
60. 126 Stat. title III.B, §333–34 at 75–76; Molko, "Drones Are Coming," 1282.
61. Molko, "Drones Are Coming," 1282n21.
62. Ibid., 1285.
63. Ibid.
64. Ibid., 1286.
65. Ibid., 1281.
66. Ibid., 1283; Mark Brunswick, "Spies in the Sky Signal New Age of Surveillance," Star Tribune, July 22, 2012, http://www.startribune.com/local/163304886.html?refer=y).
67. Molko, "Drones Are Coming," 1282.
68. Brunswick, "Spies in the Sky Signal New Age of Surveillance."
69. Alexander Lane, "Obama's Wiretapping Flip-Flop? Yes," PolitiFact, July 14, 2008, http://www.politifact.com/truth-o-meter/article/2008/jul/14/obamas-wiretapping-flip-flop-yes/.
70. PATRIOT Sunsets Extension Act of 2011, Pub. L. 112–14, 126 Stat. 216 (May 26, 2011) (codified at 50 U.S.C. §§1805, 1861, 1862) (extending the PATRIOT Act to June 1, 2015).

71. FISA Amendments Act Reauthorization Act of 2012, Pub. L. 112–238, 126 Stat. 1631 (2012).

72. James Risen and Laura Poitras, "N.S.A. Gathers Data on Social Connections of U.S. Citizens," *New York Times*, September 28, 2013, http://www.nytimes.com/2013/09/29/us/nsa-examines-social-networks-of-us-citizens.html.

73. Michael Barone, "More Than All Past Presidents, Obama Uses 1917 Espionage Act to Go After Reporters," *Washington Examiner*, May 25, 2013, http://washingtonexaminer.com/michael-barone-more-than-all-past-presidents-obama-uses-1917-espionage-act-to-go-after-reporters/article/2530340.

74. Kevin Gosztola, "Snowden Becomes Eighth Person to Be Charged with Violating the Espionage Act Under Obama," *FireDogLake.com* (blog), June 21, 2013, http://dissenter.firedoglake.com/2013/06/21/snowden-becomes-eighth-person-to-be-indicted-for-espionage-by-the-obama-justice-department/.

75. Ryan Lizza, "How Prosecutors Fought to Keep Rosen's Warrant Secret," *New Yorker*, May 24, 2013, http://www.newyorker.com/online/blogs/newsdesk/2013/05/how-justice-fought-to-keep-rosens-warrant-secret.html.

76. Ann E. Marimow, "A Rare Peek into a Justice Department Leak Probe," *Washington Post*, May 19, 2013, http://www.washingtonpost.com/local/a-rare-peek-into-a-justice-department-leak-probe/2013/05/19/0bc473de-be5e-11e2-97d4-a479289a31f9_story.html.

77. Ibid.

78. Michael Calderone, "AP CEO Says DOJ Seized Records for 'Thousands and Thousands' of Phone Calls: Staffer," *Huffington Post*, May 29, 2013, http://www.huffingtonpost.com/2013/05/29/ap-doj-records-phone-calls_n_3353978.html.

79. Dana Priest and William M. Arkin, "Top Secret America: A Hidden World, Growing Beyond Control," *Washington Post*, 2010, http://projects.washingtonpost.com/top-secret-america/articles/a-hidden-world-growing-beyond-control/1/; Tom Gjelten, "The Effects of the Snowden Leaks Aren't What He Intended," NPR, September 20, 2013, http://www.npr.org/2013/09/20/224423159/the-effects-of-the-snowden-leaks-arent-what-he-intended.

80. Ewen MacAskill, "Edward Snowden: How the Spy Story of the Age Leaked Out," *Guardian* (UK) June 11, 2013, http://www.theguardian.com/world/2013/jun/11/edward-snowden-nsa-whistleblower-profile.

81. Andrew P. Napolitano, "Obama White House Spying on Half of America," Fox News, June 6, 2013, http://www.foxnews.com/opinion/2013/06/06/why-is-our-government-spying-on-half-america/.

82. Timothy B. Lee, "Here's Everything We Know About PRISM to Date," *Washington Post*, June 12, 2013, http://www.washingtonpost.com/blogs/wonkblog/wp/2013/06/12/heres-everything-we-know-about-prism-to-date/.

83. Glenn Greenwald and Spencer Ackerman, "NSA Collected US Email Records in Bulk for More Than Two Years Under Obama," *Guardian* (UK), June 27, 2013, http://www.theguardian.com/world/2013/jun/27/nsa-data-mining-authorised-obama.

84. James Risen and Eric Lichtblau, "Bush Lets U.S. Spy on Callers Without Courts," *New York Times*, December 16, 2005, http://www.nytimes.com/2005/12/16/politics/16program.html?pagewanted=all.

85. For example, Hepting v. AT&T Corp., No. C-06-672 VRW, 2006 WL 1581965 (N.D. Cal. June 6, 2006), ordering the government to give out documents despite their assertion of the States Secrets privilege; Dan Eggen and Dafna Linzer, "Judge Rules Against Wiretaps," *Washington Post*, August 18, 2006, http://www.washingtonpost.com/wp-dyn/content/article/2006/08/17/AR2006081700650.html.
86. Associated Press, "Timeline: Edward Snowden's Journey," Yahoo! News, August 1, 2013, http://news.yahoo.com/timeline-edward-snowdens-journey-150444823.html.
87. Ibid.
88. Lee, "Here's Everything We Know About PRISM to Date."
89. Ibid.
90. United States v. Snowden, Case No. 1:13 CR 265 (CMH) (E.D. Va. May 2013), http://apps.washingtonpost.com/g/documents/world/us-vs-edward-j-snowden-criminal-complaint/496/.
91. Holder v. Humanitarian Law Project, 561 U.S. ___, 130 S. Ct. 2705, 2719–22 (2010).
92. In re Nat'l Sec. Letter, C 11-02173 SI, 2013 WL 1095417, at *2 (N.D. Cal. Mar. 14, 2013).
93. Ibid.
94. Trevor Timm, "Hundreds of Pages of NSA Spying Documents to Be Released as Result of EFF Lawsuit," Electronic Frontier Foundation, September 5, 2013, https://www.eff.org/deeplinks/2013/09/hundreds-pages-nsa-spying-documents-be-released-result-eff-lawsuit.
95. Ibid.
96. Paul Elias, "Feds Plan to Release Details of Secret Spy Court," Yahoo! News, September 10, 2013, http://news.yahoo.com/feds-plan-release-details-secret-spy-court-144030488.html.
97. Ibid.
98. Order, In re Application of the Federal Bureau of Investigation for an Order Requiring the Production of Tangible Things from [Redacted] (In re FBI Application for Production of Tangible Things from [Redacted] I), No. BR 06-05, at *2 (FISA Ct. May 24, 2006) (Howard, J.), https://www.eff.org/sites/default/files/filenode/docket_06-05_1dec201_redacted.ex_-_ocr_0.pdf.
99. Ibid.
100. Supplemental Opinion, In re Production of Tangible Things from [Redacted], No. BR 08-13, at *1 (FISA Ct. Dec. 12, 2008) (Walton, J.), https://www.eff.org/sites/default/files/filenode/4_february_2011_production_br10-82_final_redacted.ex_-_ocr_1.pdf.
101. In re Production of Tangible Things from [Redacted], No. BR 08-13 (FISA Ct. January 28, 2009) (order regarding preliminary notice of compliance incident dated January 15, 2009) (Walton, J.), https://www.eff.org/sites/default/files/filenode/br_08-13_alert_list_order_1-28-09_final_redacted1.ex_-_ocr_0.pdf; Order, *In re* Production of Tangible Things from [Redacted], No. BR 08-13 (FISA Ct. March 2, 2009) (Walton, J.), https://www.eff.org/sites/default/files/filenode/br_08-13_order_3-2-09_final_redacted.ex_-_ocr_1.pdf; Order, *In re* Application of the Federal Bureau of Investigation for an Order Requiring the Production of Tangible Things from [Redacted] (*In re* FBI Application for Production of Tangible Things from [Redacted] II), No. BR 09-06 (FISA Ct. June 22, 2009)

(Walton, J.), https://www.eff.org/sites/default/files/filenode/br_09-06_order_
and_supplemental_order_6-22-09_final_redacted.ex_-_ocr_0.pdf.

102. In re [CNR], at *16 n.14 (FISA Ct. Oct. 3, 2011) (Bates, J.), http://epic.org/privacy/
terrorism/fisa/fisc.html#legal.

103. Andrew P. Napolitano, "Domestic Spying Is Dangerous to Freedom," Fox
News, August 8, 2013, http://www.foxnews.com/opinion/2013/08/08/
domestic-spying-is-dangerous-to-freedom/.

104. Andrew P. Napolitano, "Liberty in Shambles," Fox News, June 13, 2013, http://
www.foxnews.com/opinion/2013/06/13/liberty-in-shambles/.

105. Andrew P. Napolitano, "The Truth Shall Keep Us Free—Edward Snowden
Has Awakened a Giant," Fox News, June 27, 2013, http://www.foxnews.com/
opinion/2013/06/27/truth-shall-keep-us-free/.

106. Andrew P. Napolitano, "Spying and Lying," Fox News, September 19, 2013,
http://www.foxnews.com/opinion/2013/09/19/spying-and-lying/.

107. Andrew P. Napolitano, "Is the FISA Court Constitutional?" Fox News,
September 26, 2013, http://www.foxnews.com/opinion/2013/09/26/
is-fisa-court-constitutional/.

108. Ibid.

109. Ibid.

110. Alison Smale, "Amid New Storm in U.S.-Europe Relationship, a Call for
Talks on Spying," New York Times, October 25, 2013, http://www.nytimes
.com/2013/10/26/world/europe/fallout-over-american-spying-revelations
.html?_r=0.

Index

About the Author

Andrew P. Napolitano was born on June 6th 1950 in Newark, New Jersey. He is a graduate of Princeton University and the University of Notre Dame Law School. He sat on the Superior Court of New Jersey from 1987 to 1995, when he presided over more than 150 jury trials and thousands of motions, sentencings, and hearings.

Judge Napolitano taught constitutional law and jurisprudence at Delaware law School for two years and at Seton Hall Law School for eleven years. He was often chosen by his students as their most outstanding professor. He returned to private law practice in 1995 and began television work in the same year.

As the Senior Judicial Analyst for Fox News since 1998, Judge Napolitano broadcasts nationwide daily on the Fox News Channel and the Fox Business Network. He is nationally known for watching and reporting on the government as it interferes with personal liberty, private property, and economic opportunity.

Judge Napolitano lectures nationally on the U.S. Constitution, the rule of law, civil liberties in wartime, and governmental assaults on human freedom. He has been published in the *New York Times*, the *Wall Street Journal*, the *Los Angeles Times*, and numerous other publications.

His weekly newspaper column is hosted by the *Washington Times*, foxnews.com, and numerous print and Internet venues and is seen by millions every week. The Judge is also Distinguished Visiting Professor of Law at Brooklyn Law School, where he teaches basic and advanced courses on the Constitution, and Distinguished Scholar in Law and Jurisprudence at the Mises Institute in Auburn, Alabama, where he teaches constitutional law to future economists.

Judge Napolitano is a nationally recognized champion of personal freedom. The present book is his ninth book on the U.S. Constitution.